Mark Twain

and Human Nature

Mark Twain and His Circle Series

Mark Twain
and Human Nature

———— Tom Quirk ————

University of Missouri Press   Columbia and London

Library of Congress Cataloging-in-Publication Data

Quirk, Tom, 1946–
    Mark Twain and human nature / Tom Quirk.
        p.   cm.
    Summary: "Explores Mark Twain's works—including *The Innocents Abroad,*
Following the Equator, The Adventures of Tom Sawyer, Adventures of Huckleberry Finn,
Puddn'head Wilson, and *What Is Man?*—in terms of his interest in the subject of
human nature, examining how his outlook on the human condition changed over
the years"—Provided by publisher.
    Includes bibliographical references and index.
    ISBN 978-0-8262-1758-5 (alk. paper)
    1. Twain, Mark, 1835–1910—Criticism and interpretation.   2. Humorous stories,
American—History and criticism.   I. Title.
    PS1338.Q575 2007
    818'.409—dc22

                                                                        2007020863

Designer: Jennifer Cropp
Typesetter: The Composing Room of Michigan, Inc.
Printer and binder: The Maple-Vail Book Manufacturing Group
Typefaces: Palatino and Adobe Garamond

Contents

Acknowledgments

Portions of this book have been published before, though they have been revised to fit the theme and purposes of this work. Specifically, my discussion of "Facts Concerning the Recent Carnival of Crime in Connecticut" and "Extract from Captain Stormfield's Visit to Heaven" borrow from earlier analysis in *Mark Twain: A Study of the Short Fiction* (Twayne Publishers, 1997). Much of my discussion of *The Innocents Abroad* derives from my "Introduction" to an edition of that text (Penguin Classics, 2002). Parts of Chapter Six draw upon an earlier essay—"Mark Twain in Large and Small: The Infinite and the Infinitesimal in Twain's Late Writing" in *Constructing Mark Twain: New Directions in Scholarship*, ed. Laura Skandera-Trombley and Michael Kiskis (University of Missouri Press, 2001). These borrowings indicate to me that, without really knowing it, I had been contemplating the subject of Mark Twain and human nature for some time before committing myself to a larger inquiry. Another essay, however, was written after this project was well under way and drew upon passages from the book in progress. That essay is "Mark Twain and Human Nature" in *A Companion to Mark Twain*, ed. Peter Messent and Louis J. Budd (Blackwell Publishing, 2005).

Anyone in this line of work piles up a lot of debts. The characteristic generosity of Twain scholars makes the load heavier still. I am tempted to recycle the maneuver of Flip Wilson in one of his stand-up routines. Midway through he abruptly changes the subject: "Now, I am going to talk about ugly people!" Then looking thoughtfully at the audience, he adds: "I am not going to point you out. You know who you are." Not a single one of the people I am thinking of is ugly, not a single one. Decency requires, however, that I supply at least a first-name census of those who, either through encouragement or example, make this sort of endeavor worthwhile. There are a couple of Bobs, two Vics, a Sue, a Laura or two, a Linda, an Ann, and a Catherine. There is a James, a Jeff, and a Jim, a Howard, a Henry, a Fred, a David, a Gretchen, a Tom, a Gary, a Michael, an Alan, and two Joes. There is a Larry and, believe it or not, a Mo. There is no Curly that I remember. There is a Ron, a Pete and another Pete, a Horst and a Holger, and many, many others. Once there were two Leons, a George, and a Ham, but no longer. Louis Budd read the entire manuscript and at least tried to steer me clear of the grosser stupidities. There is and always will be only one Lou.

A Note on the Texts

I have attempted to cite authoritative texts throughout. In most instances that means texts prepared by the Mark Twain Project and published by the University of California Press. In some instances (with *No. 44, The Mysterious Stranger,* for example) I have referenced the paperback edition, also published by the University of California Press, on the assumption that readers would appreciate general availability of a given work when there was no compromise in the reliability of the text. In the absence of texts approved by the Modern Language Association's Committee on Scholarly Editions, I have usually referenced the first American edition, and those may be found in the facsimile editions published as The Oxford Mark Twain, edited by Shelley Fisher Fishkin. Again, there are some exceptions. The Penguin editions of *The Innocents Abroad, The Gilded Age,* and *Life on the Mississippi* are an improvement over the first American editions, and those are the texts cited here. Likewise, the edition of *Pudd'nhead Wilson and Those Extraordinary Twins* published by W. W. Norton is superior to the first American edition.

Abbreviations

AMT   *The Autobiography of Mark Twain.* Ed. Charles Neider. New York: Harper and Row, 1959.

BMT   *The Bible According to Mark Twain.* Ed. Howard G. Baetzhold and Joseph B. McCullough. New York: Touchstone, 1996.

CTSS1   *Mark Twain: Collected Tales, Sketches, Speeches, and Essays, 1852–1890.* Vol. 1. Ed. Louis J. Budd. New York: Library of America, 1992.

CTSS2   *Mark Twain: Collected Tales, Sketches, Speeches, and Essays, 1890–1910.* Vol. 2. Ed. Louis J. Budd. New York: Library of America, 1992.

CY   *A Connecticut Yankee in King Arthur's Court.* Ed. Bernard L. Stein. Berkeley: University of California Press, 1979.

Fables   *Mark Twain's Fables of Man.* Ed. John S. Tuckey. Berkeley: University of California Press, 1972.

FE   *Following the Equator: A Journey around the World.* 1897. New York: Oxford University Press, 1996.

GA   *The Gilded Age* by Mark Twain and Charles Dudley War-
             ner. Ed. Louis J. Budd. New York: Penguin Books, 2001.

HF   *Adventures of Huckleberry Finn.* Ed. Walter Blair and Victor
             Fischer. Berkeley: University of California Press, 2001.

IA   *The Innocents Abroad.* Ed. Tom Quirk. New York: Penguin
             Books, 2002.

Interviews   *Mark Twain: The Complete Interviews.* Ed. Gary Scharn-
             horst. Tuscaloosa: University of Alabama Press, 2006.

JA   *Personal Recollections of Joan of Arc.* New York: Oxford Uni-
             versity Press, 1996.

L1   *Mark Twain's Letters, Volume 1: 1853–1866.* Ed. Edgar Mar-
             quess Branch, Michael B. Frank, and Kenneth M. Sander-
             son. Berkeley: University of California Press, 1988.

L2   *Mark Twain's Letters, Volume 2: 1867–1868.* Ed. Harriet Eli-
             nor Smith and Richard Bucci. Berkeley: University of Cal-
             ifornia Press, 1990.

L3   *Mark Twain's Letters, Volume 3: 1869.* Ed. Victor Fischer and
             Michael B. Frank. Berkeley: University of California Press,
             1992.

L4   *Mark Twain's Letters, Volume 4: 1870–1871.* Ed. Victor Fi-
             scher and Michael B. Frank. Berkeley: University of Cali-
             fornia Press, 1995.

Letters   *Mark Twain's Letters.* 2 vols. Ed. Albert Bigelow Paine.
             New York: Harper and Brothers, 1917.

LH   *Mark Twain's Letters from Hawaii.* Ed. A. Grove Day. Hon-
             olulu: University Press of Hawaii, 1975.

LLMT   *The Love Letters of Mark Twain.* Ed. Dixon Wecter. New
             York: Harper and Brothers, 1949.

LOM   *Life on the Mississippi.* Ed. James M. Cox. New York: Penguin, 1984.

MMT   William Dean Howells. *My Mark Twain: Reminiscences and Criticism.* New York: Harper and Brothers, 1910.

MS   *No. 44, The Mysterious Stranger.* Foreword and notes by John Tuckey. Berkeley: University of California Press, 1982.

MTB   Albert Bigelow Paine. *Mark Twain: A Biography.* 4 vols. in 2. New York: Harper and Brothers, 1912.

MTHL   *Mark Twain-Howells Letters.* 2 vols. Ed. Henry Nash Smith and William M. Gibson. Cambridge: Harvard University Press, 1960.

MTLP   *Mark Twain's Letters to His Publishers.* Ed. Hamlin Hill. Berkeley: University of California Press, 1967.

MTMS   *Mark Twain's Mysterious Stranger Manuscripts.* Ed. William M. Gibson. Berkeley: University of California Press, 1969.

N&J1   *Mark Twain's Notebooks and Journals, Volume 1 (1855–1873).* Ed. Frederick Anderson, Michael B. Frank, and Kenneth M. Sanderson. Berkeley: University of California Press, 1975.

N&J2   *Mark Twain's Notebooks and Journals, Volume 2 (1877–1883).* Ed. Frederick Anderson, Lin Salamo, and Bernard L. Stein. Berkeley: University of California Press, 1975.

N&J3   *Mark Twain's Notebooks and Journals, Volume 3 (1883–1891).* Ed. Robert Pack Browning, Michael B. Frank, and Lin Salamo. Berkeley: University of California Press, 1979.

P&P   *The Prince and the Pauper.* Ed. Victor Fischer and Lin Salamo. Berkeley: University of California Press, 1979.

PWET   *Pudd'nhead Wilson and Those Extraordinary Twins.* Ed. Sidney E. Berger. New York: Norton, 1980.

Reviews   *Mark Twain: The Contemporary Reviews.* Ed. Louis J. Budd. Cambridge: Cambridge University Press, 1999.

RI   *Roughing It.* Ed. Harriet Elinor Smith and Edgar Marquess Branch. Berkeley: University of California Press, 1993.

TA   *A Tramp Abroad.* New York: Oxford U Press, 1996.

TS   *The Adventures of Tom Sawyer.* Foreword and notes by John Gerber. Berkeley: University of California Press, 1980.

TSA   *The Adventures of Tom Sawyer, Tom Sawyer Abroad, Tom Sawyer, Detective.* Ed. John C. Gerber, Paul Baender, and Terry Firkins. Berkeley: University of California Press, 1980.

Weapons   *Mark Twain's Weapons of Satire: Anti-Imperialist Writings on The Philippine War.* Ed. Jim Zwick. Syracuse: Syracuse Univ. Press, 1992.

WIM   *What Is Man? And Other Philosophical Writings.* Ed. Paul Baender. Berkeley: University of California Press, 1973.

WWD   *Mark Twain's Which Was the Dream? and Other Symbolic Writings of the Later Years.* Ed. John S. Tuckey. Berkeley: University of California Press, 1967.

Mark Twain

and Human Nature

Introduction

I

I begin with an unsubstantiated anecdote: "Mr. Twain," an interviewer is supposed to have asked sometime around 1900, "do you believe in infant baptism?" The question had comic opportunity written all over it, and Twain did not hesitate: "Believe it? Hell! I've seen it done."

I have not been able to verify that Twain actually said this. The jest feels and smells like Mark Twain, but, for my purposes, it is better not to know the authenticity of the remark because one can inspect it that much more minutely without inviting the entirely legitimate complaint that Twain's living humor is too often killed by the solvent of analysis. In any event, the witticism possesses the signature qualities of Twainian humor. The adroit maneuvering of his persona; the tacit collaboration of the unnamed interviewer and Clemens in the service of some yet to be disclosed joke; the succinct conflation of two incongruous frames of reference (the realms of religious belief and sense experience); and the compressed but still masterful manipulation of ambiguities: all these supply at least circumstantial evidence that Twain is the likely author of the remark.

Having been on both sides of the reporter's notepad, Clemens understood thoroughly the near absurd drama of the genre of the interview, and he made comic hay out of it in his "An Encounter with an Interviewer" (1874). The interview is a formulaic performance. A reporter seeks information from an authority or a celebrity; the subject (who in a real sense is at once the resource for information about a given topic and the subject matter itself) complies; the information is dutifully recorded and published (as fact or opinion); and in the end the published interview underwrites the authority of the person interviewed to speak in the first place. In his wild and audacious violation of these unstated rules, Twain plays with these conventions in his sketch:

Q. Who do you consider the most remarkable man you ever met?
A. Aaron Burr.
Q. But you never could have met Aaron Burr, if you are only nineteen years—
A. Now, if you know more about me than I do, what do you ask me for?
Q. Well, it was only a suggestion; nothing more. (*CTSS1*, 584)

In the last decades of his life, Twain was badgered by reporters who knew no self-respecting newspaper could be put to bed at night without an effort to extract from him some story or quotable comment. Neither the question nor the answer mattered very much, probably, so long as the result was funny or memorable or both. Clemens's daughter Clara marveled at her father's (or at least his comic persona's) seemingly inexhaustible fund of opinions: "It always puzzled me how Mark Twain could manage to have an opinion on every incident, accident, invention, or disease in the world."[1] He expressed opinions aplenty—on religion and superstition, the conduct of children and congressmen, on typewriters and typhoid, fanaticism and fashion, on clams, turnips, and turkeys, on electricity, sunspots, and osteopathy. A complete inventory of Mark Twain's diverse opinions could not possibly add up to a steady and coherent point of view, and he must have manufactured many of them on the spot to fit the occasion or to sponsor his comedy.

That seems to be the case with his supposed stance toward infant baptism. It is unlikely that any of his contemporaries could have cared much about Mark Twain's belief or nonbelief in this sacrament, any more than we care whether Dick Cheney believes snowboarding should be an Olympic event or how Barbra Streisand feels about oil depletion allowances. Celebrity does not confer authority, and the abuse of the privileges of fame may serve only to damage one's reputation. This was a fact Twain seems to have grasped instinctively, and he was more likely to endorse prevailing opinion, with some comic flourishes thrown in, than oth-

---

1. *My Father Mark Twain* (New York: Harper and Brothers, 1931), 217.

erwise.[2] Or, as in this instance, he might avoid answering the question at all by feigning ignorance or simplicity. In any event, the religious practice of infant baptism might have retained an urgent interest for some, even in the latter half of the nineteenth century, but those Protestant sects that disputed the scriptural authority for the baptism of infants were no longer harassed and persecuted as they had been four hundred years earlier. In this sense, the interviewer's question is really a nonquestion. Even if it had been asked in good faith and Twain had answered in earnest, no real consequences, by way of either belief or conduct, would have resulted. Instead, for the savvy reporter the question is mere bait used in a fishing expedition to see what the master of the comic quip might do with it. And Twain rises to it as delicious opportunity.

The persona he adopts is that of the muggins—self-assured and confident, authoritative, even dogmatic, but wholly lacking in judgment. And, of course, in his supposed understanding of the question, he is fundamentally wrong. A question of faith (a conviction about the transcendent rightness or wrongness of infant baptism), and the consequent religious ritual to demonstrate that faith, in no way depends upon eyewitness testimony that the practice has in fact occurred. But the Twain persona turns the question on its head, pretending to understand that the reporter is asking whether infant baptism has, as a matter of historical record, ever happened. As an unspoken corollary to the question as Twain has taken it, the interviewer seems also to be asking whether the reports of actual instances of infant baptism are mere hearsay and therefore widely held superstition or verifiable events. The comic assumption here is not simply that the Twain figure is stupidly literal-minded, but also that the interviewer is not soliciting a declaration of opinion or belief but is stupidly posing a matter-of-fact question that can be resolved by observation and testimony. If we can imagine the reporter inwardly commenting, "What a simpleton to so misunderstand my question!" we can also imagine Twain thinking, "What a cub not to know this sort of thing happens all the time!"

As to Samuel Clemens's own inherited views on the matter of infant baptism, we can guess at them. He was probably baptized himself, though no record of it survives. At least he claimed he was in "Reflections on the Sabbath" (1866): "I was sprinkled in infancy, and look upon that as conferring the rank of Brevet Presbyterian." Thus he is entitled to "the sub-

2. See Leland Krauth's *Proper Mark Twain* (Athens: University of Georgia Press, 1999) on this point.

stantial Presbyterian punishment of fire and brimstone instead of this heterodox hell of remorse of conscience of these blamed wildcat religions" (*CTSS1*, 208). Clemens's children, including his son Langdon, who died at the age of eighteen months, were baptized as well. His father was something of a freethinker, but his mother, by turns, attended the Presbyterian and Methodist churches in Hannibal, Missouri, and dragged the children along. Samuel Clemens and his wife, Olivia, were members of The Park Church in Elmira, New York, but regularly attended the Asylum Hill Congregational Church in Hartford, Connecticut. Congregationalists, along with Presbyterians and Methodists, upheld the principle of infant baptism, and, at least by affiliation, we could say Clemens did as well. To the extent that Presbyterians and Methodists derived their teachings in some measure from Calvinist doctrine, they shared Calvin's belief in the universal dominion of God and that the church should not be restricted, as Baptists maintained, to a community of knowing believers who entered into the church of their own volition. Somewhat paradoxically for Calvinists, though God's extent was immeasurable, he nevertheless kept a pretty short dance card with the names of the elect who were to join him in the hereafter. That said, however, and despite the fact that Twain wrote a great deal about biblical figures and subjects throughout his life, Clemens probably took no serious interest in this sort of debate. He might have warmed to the comic (and schismatic) nuances of sprinkling, dunking, or splashing, and he would have been aggravated, if not infuriated, by the implied vile assumptions about the human condition that lay behind the dispute. In "Is Shakespeare Dead?" (1909), Twain was sardonic about such matters: "it has taken several centuries to remove perdition from the Protestant Church's program of postmortem entertainments; it has taken a weary long time to persuade American Presbyterians to give up infant damnation and try to bear it the best they can."[3] And given the fact that he had himself lost two children by this time, one of them virtually an infant, the comment may have had more contempt behind it than we can know.

In light of this comment on perdition, we can say that Twain's rather gratuitous insertion of "Hell!" into his quip is a touch of pure genius. On the one hand, the expletive exposes his persona's hearty cocksureness and fortifies our sense of his self-satisfied ignorance. On the other hand, the word serves as a reminder that hell remained in some minds the inevitable

3. *1601 and Is Shakespeare Dead*, ed. Shelley Fisher Fishkin (New York: Oxford University Press, 1996), 130.

and eternal consequence and condition of the unbaptized infant. The baptized child might be handed over to God's mercy and, for the believing parent, its destiny be dissolved in the mysteries of faith, but woe unto him who had not been so anointed. These sorts of speculations about an apocryphal interview exceed anything that might possibly have occurred either to the interviewer or to Twain. If the event ever happened at all, the reporter was surely looking for copy and not much more, and Twain, almost by nature, couldn't resist a comic opportunity if the right words came to him. At best, the exchange provided a moment's amusement. Nevertheless, my laborious and tendentious explication of what was, essentially, a throwaway line is not quite complete. I risk two final observations.

Twain's riposte ("Believe it? Hell! I've seen it done") is hardly menacing; given the imagined situation, it is rather genial. Twain has supplied the reporter with what he wants most, something he can take to his editor. For his part, Twain has indulged in a bit of comic sport. The exchange implicates the two men in a cooperative social project—the instant creation of humor fit for public consumption—but the laugh could not be had without both participants. At the same time they are notable for their apparent differences. The question emanates from a realm and temperament fashioned by certain regnant features—principled solemnity, Christian belief, otherworldly hope, and otherworldly fear. The answer presupposes a hardheaded realism, a supremely secular confidence in fact and experience, and, quite literally, a "seeing is believing" attitude. As such, the two men are emissaries from competing views of human nature. And the hypothetical infant itself is poised between these two worlds— one essentially Calvinist, in which the gulf between the Creator and his human creatures is immeasurable, and innate depravity is an existential given; the other Lockean, in which the child enters the world a tabula rasa, an epistemological and ontological innocent but pre-enrolled in the school of hard knocks, nonetheless.

Or, to change the terms of this conflict and to better align it with the mentality of the age, one might say with William James that the opposition is between the "tender-minded" and the "tough-minded"—the first essentially "rationalistic (going by 'principles')," "idealistic," "religious," and "dogmatical"; the second "empiricist (going by 'facts')," "materialistic," "irreligious," and "sceptical." This, said James, was the "present dilemma in philosophy," but it was also the dilemma for the man and woman in the street, for whom pure philosophical inquiry was arcane and remote and logical rigor irrelevant to the practical uses of everyday life.

In fact, James observed, ordinary people have "a hankering for the good things on both sides of the line. Facts are good, of course—give us lots of facts. Principles are good—give us plenty of principles. The world is indubitably one if you look at it in one way, but as indubitably is it many, if you look at in another. . . . And so forth—your ordinary philosophic layman never being a radical, never straightening out his system, but living vaguely in one plausible compartment of it or another to suit the temptations of successive hours."[4]

James's *Pragmatism* (1907) was at once a call to his fellow philosophers to take into account the requirements of everyday experience as it affected those whose business it was to live the good life, not merely to contemplate it. It was as well a proffered answer to the dilemma he described by supplying "a method of settling metaphysical disputes that otherwise might be interminable." That such a resolution was needed was beyond question. In the latter half of the nineteenth century, the average American was afflicted with a certain bifocal vision, in which abstract absolutes, on the one hand, and a congeries of discrete facts, on the other, vied for one's attention and commitment. And there seemed no way to reconcile the opposing claims that each system had upon the individual sensibility. James named his method "pragmatism," a "melioristic" position whereby one might dismiss such ponderous questions if the answer to them would make no concrete difference either in one's understanding of the phenomenon in question or in one's actual conduct in the world. As such, pragmatism was conceived as a method for negotiating disputes, a form of shuttle diplomacy that, in the pursuit of harmonizing conflicting interests and encouraging the common good, meant to laugh out of court troubling irrelevancies or tedious pseudo-questions. By analogy (but only by analogy) much of Mark Twain's humor serves an equivalent function. This is a subject we will at length explore.[5] For the moment, it is enough to say that, at the level of physiological reaction, laughter was a means to relieve or transcend the terms of incessant intellectual debate or paralyzing social tension by dramatizing absurdities or implicitly offering friendly alternatives to ugly situations. Mere contemplation of incongruities can

4. *Pragmatism and Four Essays from The Meaning of Truth* (New York: Meridian Books, 1970), 22–23.

5. My comparison of Twain to William James is not wholly adventitious. As Merle Curti remarks in *Human Nature in American Thought: A History* (Madison: University of Wisconsin Press, 1980), 210–15, though James never paused to define the phrase or explicitly address it as a philosophical question, his central subject was "human nature."

cause one to laugh, but the formula for laughter is not necessarily a binomial one.

Take, by way of contrast, Robert Frost's familiar poem "Fire and Ice":

> Some say the world will end in fire,
> Some say in ice.
> From what I've tasted of desire
> I hold with those that favor fire.
> But if it had to perish twice,
> I think I know enough of hate
> To say that for destruction ice
> Is also great
> And would suffice.

There is nothing funny in the poem. It is tidy and efficient, and the terms of opposition in this futile dispute are unmistakable. Either desire or hate is sufficient to bring about the end of the world. If that were all there is to the poem, it would be not much more than a cautionary jingle, I think. But, at the level of tone, Frost has slyly smuggled in a third position. The speaker is self-satisfied and jaundiced, evidently more interested in his own attitude as a swing voter in the fateful contest than in its dreadful consequence. The obnoxious concluding line, in particular, testifies to his indifference. The clear implication is that a tepid apathy may well be as sinister a force in the destruction of the world as is desire or hate, but Frost nowhere says this. It is the invisible third term in an apparent dichotomy.

The same may be said for Twain's innumerable encounters between two or more "types," characters who either represent competing points of view about human nature or carry with them a fund of assumptions about the human condition. Unlike the alienated and alienating dramatic monologue of "Fire and Ice," the third term for Twain is (to borrow a phrase from Kenneth Burke) a "comic corrective,"[6] some form of social adjust-

---

6. Comic correctives tend to translate or synthesize oppositions by installing "the *charitable* attitude toward people that is required for purposes of persuasion and cooperation." In this sense, the comic is, for Burke, a dialectical third term that helps preserve an ecological balance between antithetical positions, recognizing that "a well balanced ecology requires the symbiosis of the two." "In sum," he continues, "the comic frame should enable people *to be observers of themselves, while acting.* Its ultimate would not be *passiveness,* but *maximum consciousness.* One would 'transcend' himself by noting his own foibles. He would provide a rationale for locating the irrational and the non-rational" (*Attitudes toward History* [1937; rpt. Boston: Beacon Press, 1961], 166, 167, 171).

ment that, if it does not transcend the apparent conflict, at least agreeably arrives at some unexpected place. More than most writers, Twain, early and late, was fond of the dramatic encounter between two characters whose backgrounds, stocks of assumptions, or temperaments are dramatically opposed and who are, presumably, socially incompatible. From "The Dandy and the Squatter" to Scotty Briggs and the parson in *Roughing It* (1872); from Huck's surprise meeting of Jim on Jackson's Island to David Wilson's unfortunate introduction of himself to the citizens of Dawson's Landing in a way that gets him the label *pudd'nhead;* from a perplexed Hank Morgan waking up in King Arthur's England to Captain Eli Stormfield's entrance into a heaven where one-legged blue people serve as gatekeepers, these, and a hundred other instances like them, thrive on social transactions between two antithetical points of view and the comic or satiric consequences that can never quite be anticipated.

The anonymous interviewer who interrogated Twain on infant baptism presumably expected a typical question-and-answer exchange. According to protocol, the reporter was to be the mere recorder of things said and opinions expressed. Instead, he became an unwitting participant in a brief and empty encounter in which (to all intents and purposes) no information was conveyed, no opinion extracted, no position taken. He became as well a straight man in a piece of dramatic fun where no egos were bruised, no humiliation inflicted, no insults delivered. For all the absences and silliness in the anecdote, however, it remains substantive: two contending views of human nature are quickly paraded by, the absurdity of the question (along with the absurdity of the response) is brought into focus, and the auditor or the reader is, through the auspices of humor, encouraged to redirect his or her attention to the practical business of life.

II

This is an inquiry into a central feature of Mark Twain's art and thinking—his long-standing fascination with human nature. So blunt a statement of purpose requires some qualification, however. This is not a book about the existence or nonexistence of human nature per se. I have not the slightest interest here in deciding whether human beings (as a biological species or as a collection of individuals) are socially constructed, culturally conditioned, genetically programmed, divinely sanctioned, or satanically hatched. In one sense, the "truth" of the concept of human nature lies entirely outside the scope of this study. In another sense, however, in a Jamesean pragmatic sense, the truth of the matter is precisely my concern. If, as William James said, "Truth is what happens to an idea," one can say that Mark Twain profoundly "happened" to the idea of human nature. And he happened to it so variously, even recklessly, so antically and, at times, so irreverently, that it is more than a bit surprising he should have come to be regarded as its great interpreter. Throughout his career, he spoke confidently and it appears persuasively of human nature, here and abroad, in his own day and, in wholly imaginative terms, in the days of prelapsarian Eden, or King's Arthur's Camelot, or the imagined future kingdom of Mary Baker Eddy. He inflicted his insights indifferently upon animate and inanimate nature, upon the heavens and the microbe, upon angels and devils, and nearly always with a comic flair that limbered up any rigid conception of the human.

The phrase *human nature* itself is impossibly vague and full of contradictions; in our own day it is immediately suspect. Broadly speaking, human nature is that impulse, condition, or mechanism that somehow explains physical and mental activity, moral or immoral inclination, godlike aspirations or pitiful mortal shortcomings. It is grounded in the assumption that there is a fundamental disposition of character that permits one to speak meaningfully of humanity, or humanness, as an intelligible and universal possession. As such, any notion of human nature is a theory of the human. Merle Curti has identified four fundamental theories of human nature. They are:

1. human nature is innately constituted apart from experience (Aristotle and Aquinas)
2. human nature has alleged psychological powers or faculties—perception, memory, judgment, desire (Calvin)
3. human nature is essentially empty or formless (Locke)
4. human nature can be identified only through its institutions or products—language, religions, and so forth (Hegel)[7]

Due in large part to scientific advances in genetics, biology, physiology, and psychology, these categories have been considerably refined or modified in the twentieth and twenty-first centuries. However, for our purposes Curti's description is sufficient, and I would add to his list only the concrete yet indefinite theory of the human that I will persist in calling "vernacular." This is the arena of commonsense realism, and it tends to

7. *Human Nature in American Thought*, 4–7.

avoid system and often to express itself in anecdote, parable, maxim, or familiar observation ("Kids will be kids"; "Isn't that just like a man, always afraid to ask for directions"; "Mad dogs and Englishmen go out in the noonday sun"). Isolated and insulated comments on the familiar oddities of human conduct are convincing to the degree that they conform to observation and repeated experience. Mark Twain pondered in imaginative terms the other four theories of human nature, but he had a special genius for expressing or dramatizing the vernacular point of view, as in his maxim, "Few of us can stand prosperity. Another man's I mean." In general, the adage may seek to reform human behavior, on the one hand, yet recognize the perversity of human nature on the other. "People who live in glass houses shouldn't throw stones" is one sort of admonitory maxim, and so is the African proverb "People with wooden noses should not sniff around axes." The advice is sound, but it presupposes a certain constant in flawed human nature. If your neighbor builds a glass house, you can bank on him dragging a peach basket full of rocks into the living room and letting fly; and if you want to find someone with a wooden nose, bait your trap with a couple of sharp axes and see what happens. These comments on human nature (direct or oblique) do not, and probably cannot, add up to a theory as such.

Samuel Clemens was an inquisitive, intelligent, and remarkably well read man, but despite his forays into intellectual system building (in *What Is Man?* and elsewhere) he was not really a philosopher. He was an intellectual, after a fashion, and a public moralist. He was an amateur political theorist, an amateur historian, and an amateur ethnographer, but he was a professional humorist. In his later years, Twain took some pains to formulate his own deterministic theory of human nature. And when he did, he was in some measure merely giving shape to his ever-accumulating sense of how people behaved and why. Sometime in the early 1880s Twain's thinking on human nature began to collect around certain convictions (man is a machine, training is everything, for example) and to organize itself into a system that he would eventually call his "gospel." I wish to take Twain's philosophizing seriously, as seriously as one can take an inveterate humorist. In any event, I am not inclined to believe that Twain's embrace of a determinism was in any way a compensatory gesture, an attempt to absolve himself of guilt (real or imagined) by shoving the blame off on an unfeeling and perhaps incompetent God. As Ron Powers has said, Mark Twain was a great "noticer." Over the years, and assisted by his travels throughout the world and his reading (mostly in history and science), Twain's discrete observations collected into a patterned way of thinking and paved the way for a theory of human nature. Insofar as this "gospel" constitutes a system of thought, it is a species of social psychology, and it expresses in a coherent if not always a rigorously systematic way what he had concluded about his fellow creatures from repeated and alert observation over a number of years and in many countries.

This book, at any rate, is necessarily as concerned with Twain's humor as it is with an inspection of Clemens's intellectual attitudes, for he had an ingrained comic "temperament"—another important element in his view of human nature. In a preliminary way, we may say this much about the subject of Mark Twain and human nature. First, he considered humor an indispensable part of a healthy human nature. To be more exact, humor fosters the sort of "healthy-mindedness" William James detected in Walt Whitman (the resistance to all "contractile" elements in this life, the expansiveness of one's worldview, the imaginative multiplication rather than restriction of possibilities, the elation felt in excess and exuberance). Second, humor was a basic part of Mark Twain's nature (and perhaps Clemens's also). In an 1865 letter to his brother Orion, he declared his decision to become a professional humorist, but he recognized his own limitations: "Though the Almighty did His part by me—for the talent [of making people laugh] is a mighty engine when supplied with the steam of education—which I have not got, & so its pistons & cylinders & shafts move feebly & for a holiday show & and are useless for any good purpose" (*L1*, 323). Later, he would engage in a lifelong effort to repair the deficiencies in his education, but he had at that point in his career resisted his natural calling in favor of other ambitions. This was to be expected because, he continued, "it is human nature to yearn to be what we were never intended for." Finally, Twain's humor is what makes his own, more general thinking on human nature memorable and important. It was not the *what* but the *how* of his estimates of human creatures that gives his thinking permanent interest. That said, it is important to remember that Twain, the humorist, also wanted to be taken seriously as a moralist. I have tried to take him on his own terms while at the same time remembering that he was, above all, very, very funny.

Twain published *What Is Man?* (1906) anonymously, supposing his private philosophy was scandalous and would damage his public image, and he probably overestimated the incendiary qualities of the work. Still, the world at large had long taken him to be something of a moralist and had come to expect from him summary, amusing, and often damning commentary on human nature. In his early western years, Twain was alternately known as "The Wild Humorist of the Pacific Slope" and "The Moralist of the Main." William Dean Howells, after long acquaintance with the man, observed that Clemens was "always reading some vital book. It might be some out-of-the-way book, but it had the root of the human matter in it" (*MMT*, 15). Clemens's own knock-about life had acquainted him with all manner of individuals, but his curiosity about his kind was ongoing and apparently insatiable, and any story (historical, autobiographical, and the like) that gave him "life at first-hand" interested him. Howells had witnessed the reversals of fortune in Twain's life—his bankruptcy, the death of his daughter Susy and, later, his wife Olivia—and had noted his resiliency and fortitude as well. Twain's abiding fascination with human nature often served as tonic relief from personal grief and humiliation. In *My Mark Twain* (1910) Howells felt competent to identify one of the mainsprings of Twain's character, a deep and abiding interest in "the world and the human race" (*MMT*, 91).

As Twain's popular reputation grew over the years, so did the perception of him as a companionable commentator on the human condition. In the end he was reckoned an acute observer of mankind, though one essentially given to a sympathetic interest in his fellows and a shared feeling for their plight. After Mark Twain died on April 21, 1910, newspapers and magazines throughout the country printed obituaries the next day that attempted to sum up the man and the significance of his writings. "He was a humanist," and his writings were illuminated by "the keenest insight into human nature" (*Kansas City Star*). "How keen he was in his knowledge of human nature" (*Hartford Courant*). He had "a deep knowledge of human nature, which made every character that he described live and breathe. He knew men, through and through" (*[Richmond] Times Dispatch*). His writings "go to the very heart of human nature and sound the depths of its aspirations, aims, and hopes" (*Los Angeles Times*). I could multiply instances of this sort of encomium, but what is interesting here is not so much the notes of appreciation articulated along similar lines as the fact that, in 1910, "human nature" was a vexed concept, as it had been for a hundred years.

III

In the early decades of nineteenth century, America was heir to an Enlightenment notion of human nature, though by 1835, the year of Samuel Clemens's birth, the inheritance of the eighteenth century was being reshaped by the giddy, and sometimes shrewd, enthusiasms of men as different from one another as Ralph Waldo Emerson and Andrew Jackson. For the man or woman of the Enlightenment, knowledge and conduct were ultimately referable to right reason; for the Romantic, to subjective intuition. Both notions are detectable in Twain's writings. Furthermore, whatever understanding of human nature the young Sam Clemens may have had, it would almost certainly have been affected in some measure by those surviving ingredients of Calvinism in his own religious training. Van Wyck Brooks overstated the case when he argued that Twain was repressed and permanently damaged by a Puritanical mother, however. At length, Twain was to make his own departure from the religious orthodoxy of his upbringing, but all his life he suffered from an overly tender conscience he would have happily throttled could he but get his hands on it.

He was probably helped along in his thinking by a thorough and impressionable reading of Thomas Paine's *The Age of Reason* while he was a riverboat pilot, and perhaps he fancied himself something of a deist. That book, writes Sherwood Cummings, assisted greatly in cultivating in Clemens a fundamentally secular outlook and it gave "shape and sanction" to his increasing religious skepticism. Cummings may well be right in arguing that it "is nearly impossible to exaggerate the impact of *The Age of Reason*" on Samuel Clemens.[8] Still, one needs to be cautious in assigning too much influence to a single book or point of view. Even before he read Paine, while in New York, young Sam Clemens read in the printer's free library on Sundays instead of going to church, and apparently without a twinge of conscience. Nevertheless, Clemens might well have sat up and taken notice when he read in Paine's "Credo," "My mind is my own church. All national institutions of churches—whether Jewish, Christian, or Turkish—appear to me no other than human inventions set up to terrify and enslave mankind and monopolize power and profit."[9]

Clemens might assent to such a proposition, and it may have liberated his own thinking, but it did not necessarily revise habitual attitudes. In his early years, he freely confessed, in private correspondence and in print, to anti-Catholic and anti-Jewish sentiments, and he frequently demonstrated little understanding or sympathy for people of color. In his "Letters from the Sandwich Islands" Twain could describe the native Hawaiians and their customs with genuine liking. And he characterized

8. *Mark Twain and Science: Adventures of a Mind* (Baton Rouge: Louisiana State University Press, 1988), 20.

9. *Literature of the Early Republic,* ed. Edwin H. Cady (New York: Holt, Rinehart and Winston, 1969), 58.

Protestant missionaries as having many good qualities but also as being "bigoted; puritanical; slow; ignorant of all white human nature and natural ways of men, except the remnant of these things that are left in their own class or profession; old fogy—fifty years behind the age; uncharitable toward the weaknesses of the flesh; considering all shortcomings, faults, and failings in the light of crimes, and having no mercy and no forgiveness for such" (LH, 129). He could say all these things and still wind up concluding, in light of the earlier native license and feudalism, that "the missionaries have made a better people of this race than they formerly were" (LH, 131). Tom Paine may have inspired Mark Twain to think more freely, but Paine did not prevent him from thinking some pretty dumb things at times. Of greater interest is how Mark Twain, sometimes defiantly and sometimes timidly, outgrew certain ingrained attitudes and ideas.

There were, of course, many other influences upon Twain's thinking. As is typical with all sorts of influence, however, the ground had been fortuitously prepared beforehand in order for Twain to be receptive to new or uncustomary ways of regarding any given subject. Gregg Camfield has traced another eighteenth-century influence upon the writer in the theory of moral sentiments of the Scottish Common Sense philosophers, and Leland Krauth has convincingly shown just how much Twain wanted to be, and was, a card-carrying member of his own Victorian culture. Jason Horn has explored the friendship and the affinities Twain had with William James and with pragmatism. Others have detected more general formative influences in region, and as such characterize Twain as a quintessentially southern, western, or midwestern writer. Finally, any conception of human nature in the nineteenth century was informed and tested by the revolutionary science of the time, a subject Sherwood Cummings has thoroughly explored. Twain read (and met) Darwin and Herbert Spencer, and he read in the intellectual magazines that dealt with scientific subjects. He seems to have accepted with relative calm the Darwinian revolution that so disturbed many of his contemporaries.

In short, several competing or contradictory explanations of human nature (what the human creature is and how it came to be that way) coexisted, somewhat uneasily, in the nineteenth-century mind. If Twain's thinking on the matter eventually became more deliberate and acute than that of his contemporaries, it was no less stratified. Understood as political and social animals, human beings, Twain came to believe, were shaped by training and motivated by the desire for self-approval. From a strictly scientific point of view, human nature was a collection of ancient impulses and chemical properties. As the "damned" creation of an all-powerful God, human beings were plagued with a painful moral sense but without the wherewithal to lead the sort of life that would appease it. From the vernacular perspective, human beings had always shared certain foibles, yielded to common temptations, and demonstrated common sympathies. It was this last sense of the term that permitted Twain to observe in *The Innocents Abroad* (1869), "Human nature is *very* much the same all over the world" (*IA*, 165). However, as a humorist, Twain was ever alert to alternate frames of reference he could bring into comic conjunction. Such is the case, for example, with this maxim that pits the deep time of a vast geological history against a temporary human fussiness: "There was once a man who, not being able to find any fault with his coal, complained that there were too many prehistoric toads in it" (*PWET*, 44).

Twain was aware that human nature (whatever it might in substance be) was modified and shaped by all manner of things—race, gender, class, health, climate, superstition, geography, creed, history, economics, opportunity, accident, and the like. He was equally aware that real differences existed between and among individuals; differences in intelligence, ability, ambition, temperament, and inclination. Nevertheless, as variable as human creatures are, there was for him some something that was pretty much the same in all of us. That fact is not necessarily heartening. In response to the news of President McKinley's assassination, Clemens wrote Joseph Twichell in 1901:

> Evidently the Human Race is the same old Human Race. . . . Under the unsettling effects of powerful emotion the talkers are saying wild things, crazy things—they are out of themselves, and do not know it; they are temporarily insane, yet with one voice they declare the assassin *sane*—a man who has been entertaining fiery and reason-debauching maggots in his head for weeks and months. Why, no one is sane, straight along, year in and year out, and we all know it. . . . an immense upheaval of feeling can at any time topple us distinctly over the sanity-line for a little while; and then if our form happens to be of the murderous kind we must look out—and so must the spectator. (*Letters*, 2:713).

Every person is subject to a certain mental and emotional weather that may well bring out murderous feelings. But there was something else in humankind, something precious and distinctive, something decent and forbearing, at times something heroic. That common something might be past knowing or beyond retrieval, but without it the democratic vision that was so obviously a part of Clemens's own nature was not much more than a curious astigmatism. In "Extract from Captain Stormfield's Visit to Heaven" (1909), Twain imagined a truly equitable hereafter, where a man or woman was rewarded not according to good deeds, firm belief, or noble conduct, but according to some innate quality that might have come to fruition if the conditions had been right. This is not to say that Clemens believed in this sort of heaven or any other kind; it is to say, however, that this was the only sort of heaven that might compel his belief. The only discernible article of faith on display in this late piece of fantasy is the conviction that there is some quality or force that makes us human and implicates us, for good or ill, in a common destiny. Even so, there are no final statements or pat answers about Twain's view of human nature. His humor was so habitual and expansive that it tends to nullify or confound plain statement or philosophical system. Around the same time Twain wrote "Captain Stormfield's Visit to Heaven" he also wrote a bit of unfinished future-history called "The Secret History of Eddypus." In this satirical dystopia, where Christian Science has taken over the world, Twain consigns himself to the lowly rank of the "Bishop of New Jersey."

However, even in clear-cut instances of intellectual transformation, one must be careful. In 1902, his close friend and minister, Joseph Twichell, loaned Twain a copy of Jonathan Edwards's *Freedom of the Will*. At a time in his life when theology, particularly of the Calvinist sort, had ceased to disturb him, he showed an excitable anger toward Edwards. The book left him with a "strange and haunting sensation of having been on a three days' tear with a drunken lunatic. It is years since I have known these sensations" (*Letters*, 2:719). Clemens was as down on Edwards as Jim had been on King Solomon in *Huckleberry Finn*. Similarly, in 1908, Clemens recalled to his biographer Albert Bigelow Paine that he had read *The Age of Reason* as a cub pilot, "marveling at its fearlessness and wonderful power. I read it again a year or two ago, for some reason, and was amazed to see how tame it had become" (*MTB*, 1445). The following pages attempt to chart in chronological fashion Twain's evolutionary path through a multitude of views about human nature. But the way was not straight, and it sometimes doubled back on itself. This is probably true for most people, but in a man with powerful imaginative resources of memory, at times capable of vividly displacing impinging present realities, the situation may be extremely complex. We have no reason to doubt that the remembered "sensations" Edwards awakened in him were real enough, at any rate.

In *Mark Twain and Science,* Sherwood Cummings describes four stages of intellectual "strata" in Clemens's life. His youth until around the age of seventeen was markedly Calvinistic. Inspired in part by his reading in Thomas Paine when he was an apprentice riverboat pilot, Clemens became something of a deist. From 1868 to 1870 (the period, not so coincidentally, when he was courting Olivia Langdon) Clemens was a believing Christian. It was not the Christianity of his youth, but the muscular, liberal kind expressed by Horace Bushnell, Henry Ward Beecher, and others. The final stratum began shortly after reading Darwin's *Descent of Man* in 1871. During the 1880s Clemens was content to reaffirm, in a quasi-scientific way, his earlier deism and to assume that God, if there is one, has a rational plan for human beings and that justice and mercy are part of that plan. After 1891 and until his death in 1910, however, there is no trace of belief in a teleological plan for the universe. One can accept Cummings's schematized description without hesitation, so long as we understand that, as he says, these strata "cohabited" in Twain's mind throughout his life. Despite his scientific readings, in his late years he still tended to imagine the genesis of the universe in essentially biblical terms. Occasionally, eruptions or evocations of earlier sensations break through the strata of settled conviction—sometimes in volcanic seizures (as in his reaction to Jonathan Edwards); as often in bubbling reminiscences of youth.

We should recognize, too, that Clemens never quite straightened his own system out, but, as William James said most people do, lived in one compartment of it or another to suit his own needs or desires. By way of illustration, it is interesting to note that Mark Twain, in his last years, was the founder of two clubs—"The Human Race Luncheon Club" and the "Juggernaut Club." The first was limited to four members, who never quite managed to get together at one time; it was to be devoted to elaborating the nature of the "damned human race" and doubtless would have recapitulated Twain's jaundiced thinking about the selfishness, vanity, and cruelty of the species. The second had a more expansive membership—ideally, one member from each country, characterized by "intellect and the spirit of good will; other distinctions, hereditary or acquired, do not count" (*Letters*, 2:718). The members were in fact Twain's "angelfish," school-age girls with whom he corresponded. Twain himself was designated the "Chief Servant," a "Member at Large for the Human Race." No point needs to be made about the fact that Twain created these two clubs (one decidedly tough-minded, the other tender-minded) at approximately the same time in his life other than that, like most of us, he wanted the good things on both sides of the line—angry, spirited, profane, adult debate about the meanness of one's species on the one hand and grandfatherly, good-willed, innocent, even utopian contemplation of human possibility on the other.

The variegated thought and feeling of Samuel Clemens on this, as on other subjects, over the course of his seventy-four years, spreads out in space easily enough, but it moves forward in time by fits and starts. This quality in the man is not to be regretted; instead, Twain's spontaneity and unpredictability make him perpetually interesting. And always his constitutional temptation to be humorous tends to undercut any clear demarcation of his intellectual and philosophical development. Twain took on board new ways of thinking, and jettisoned old ones, at least for a time. His days of prosperity and his days of the other kind certainly affected his outlook. His peripatetic readings (particularly in history) and global travels broadened his vision of human nature. Still, he insisted in his notebook, "Human nature cannot be studied in cities except at a disadvantage—a village is the place. There you can know your man inside & out—in a city you but know his crust; & his crust is usually a lie" (N&J2, 503). But the village was by no means a fixed, laboratory environment. Twain's renderings of the village of his youth, Hannibal, Missouri (the St. Petersburg of *Tom Sawyer* and *Huckleberry Finn,* and Dawson's Landing in *Pudd'nhead Wilson,* not to mention his other villages and towns, such as Hadleyburg or Eseldorf), are different enough from one another to signal real changes in attitude in the author.

It would be misleading to assign watershed "moments" in Twain's thought (his sudden celebrity, his marriage, his bankruptcy, his reading of Thomas Carlyle or W. E. H. Lecky, and so forth) as a way of organizing and composing the picture I want to present on the subject of Twain and human nature. Instead, I have chosen to move through Clemens's life more or less decade by decade. That is, after a chapter on his early years (his apprenticeship period as typesetter, pilot, miner, and journalist), there are chapters on the 1870s, 1880s (two of them), 1890s, and finally on the last decade of his life. Each of these periods is sufficiently rich and diverse to sketch a picture of the man, his thought, and his craft at various stages in his life. I don't pretend that they are any more than sketches. Twain was too prolific a writer for me to offer anything close to an exhaustive and continuous account of him as thinker or artist. Besides, he was too fidgety to sit for a series of portraits. Sketches will have to do. Moreover, because all his life the humorous element (sometimes unbidden) entered into and colored his many moods, these sketches may at times approach caricature, even cartoon. That is the risk one runs with such a figure as Mark Twain. I trust the result will prove detailed and concrete enough to provide a recognizable semblance of the man.

Only the foolhardy would try to put words in the mouth of Mark Twain. He was a man of extraordinary verbal facility. (George Bernard Shaw reckoned him one of the great masters of the English language.) Nonetheless, there are many critics and scholars who have attempted to put sentiments in Mark Twain's heart and ideas in his head that, so far as I can tell, simply were not there. The reader may decide I have done the same thing. For by way of clarification of some of his statements and attitudes I will from time to time take up the thinking of some figures who, while they figured prominently in the intellectual climate of the nineteenth century, are probably unfamiliar and obscure to most readers. My purpose is to somehow account for how Mark Twain might have reasonably believed the things he said he believed. In short, this is an unembarrassed intentionalist argument at the same time that it is unavoidably a speculative one. I try to hold fast to Twain's intentions both about his purposes in his fiction but also about his often ad hoc remarks regarding the human condition. Sometimes those intentions are stated; sometimes they are inferable from textual or extratextual contexts and cultural or intellectual circumstances. I am rather more certain in my own mind, at any rate, that human nature was one of the central preoccupations of Mark Twain's life, and, as such, his thinking on the subject deserved as open and charitable a hearing as I felt capable of giving it.

Chapter One

1852–1869

In 1865, Samuel Clemens wrote his brother Orion: "I *have* had a 'call' to literature, of a low order—i.e., humorous. It is nothing to be proud of, but it is my strongest suit, & if I were to listen to that maxim of stern *duty* which says that to do right you **must** multiply the one or the two or the three talents which the Almighty entrusts to your keeping, I would long ago have ceased to meddle with the things for which I was by nature unfitted & turned my attention to seriously scribbling to excite the **laughter** of God's creatures. Poor, pitiful business!" (*L1* 322–23).

The timing of this announcement is interesting. It occurs only a month before the publication of his jumping frog story in the *Saturday Press*, which vaulted Clemens into literary celebrity and made the "Mark Twain" signature a familiar commodity. And it was not much more than a signature. Clemens adopted the pen name *Mark Twain* in 1863 with the publication of the first of his three "Letters" from Carson City. He had adopted other aliases before that, but this one stuck, even though it was at the time far from the firmly established literary persona it would become. With the widespread circulation of the jumping frog tale, his literary reputation grew and was cemented with the publication and instant success of *The Innocents Abroad* (1869). At the time, however, Mark Twain was an obscure presence in the literary scene, at least as far as the lucrative and necessary eastern literary market was concerned, and we have no reason to think he was responding to an unexpected opportunity instead of to the "maxim of stern duty."

In fact, the language of his declaration argues otherwise. In 1848, at the age of thirteen, he became a printer's apprentice, the first of a string of apprenticeships that preceded his rather flat-footed decision to become a scribbler and a humorist. Clemens had been instructed in the employable arts of typesetting, riverboat piloting, and journalism, and by all accounts (except perhaps his own, set down in "Old Times on the Mississippi" and elsewhere) he was an able pupil. These were forms of occupational training and derived from nineteenth-century notions of putting one's oar in the water and, through application and shrewd opportunism, making one's way in the world. But his decision to become a literary person was framed by a Christian sense of using what God has entrusted to him. After all, Matthew's parable had instructed that the man who had hidden his lord's money was cast into "outer darkness" where there shall be "weeping and the gnashing of teeth"; this was not a place for one equipped with a humorist's temperament.

By announcing his submission to an ordained and divinely approved "calling" to do the Lord's work as he has appointed all his servants in their various ways to perform it, Clemens was returning to the fold, though perhaps on his own terms. One always needs to be somewhat careful in assessing Clemens's statements of purpose. St. Paul had named the "diversities" of gifts that in mysterious ways contribute to the expression of a single Spirit—gifts of healing, wisdom, prophecy, miracles, and the like (1 Corinthians 12)—but he nowhere identified merrymaking as one of them.[1] Still, Clemens seemed to believe that making God's creatures laugh was part of his own "nature," in the sense both that humor was instinctual with him and that the social utility of his work in the world might be a "poor" and "pitiful" business but was sanctioned nonetheless.

On the other hand, Clemens may simply have been bearding his brother Orion, one of his favorite pastimes. Orion was considering entering the ministry in those years, and Sam promised to read all of his sermons when that time came, though as "unsympathetically as a man of stone." "I have a religion," he added, "but you will call it blasphemy. It is that there is a God for the rich man but none for the poor." In the same letter, Clemens identified the two "powerful ambitions" in his life—to be a riverboat pilot and to be a preacher of the gospel. He succeeded at the first, but the Civil War effectively put a stop to this career. As for the other, Clemens confessed to utter failure because "I could not supply myself with the nec-

1. Some "primitive" religious cultures include a clown figure in their most solemn rituals—the Hopis and the Navajos, for example—a custom Twain might well have approved.

essary stock in trade—i.e. religion." Many years later, Clemens would describe himself as "God's fool"; for the moment, he was content to be God's jester, even if he privately granted the Lord no special authority, and may in fact have thought him a mere pretender to the throne. On the other hand, as opposed to his own stated ambitions, the call to literature was his compromised destiny. To be a humorist, it seemed, was part of his natural constitution; to make a living at that game required a bit more calculation.

I

Hannibal, Missouri was, and is, a small town. But during Sam Clemens's childhood it must have been a hive of activity. In 1830, the township could claim only thirty inhabitants; by 1840 the population had grown thirtyfold. Hannibal had become an important river port and a jumping-off place for goods being shipped to St. Joseph and on to the Far West. It also had become, in Dixon Wecter's word, a "porkopolis," with two pork-houses that annually processed around ten thousand head of swine. It had, as well, a whiskey distillery, a tobacco manufactory, sawmills and planing mills, and a hemp factory. There were four general stores, two hotels, two schools, two churches, and four saloons—probably the right proportion for any self-respecting community. Part of the relative prosperity and security of the place surely had to do with the geographical fact that it was on the way to somewhere else. Human traffic passed through the town from east to west, north to south.

The corpse Sam Clemens discovered in his father's office in 1844, at the age of nine, was that of a man bound for California. He was one of many abroad in the land who meant to improve his fortunes out west. In the gold rush of 1849, waves of emigrants passed through Hannibal, and around eighty local residents joined them in the pursuit of instant riches. Young Sam Clemens, by contrast, first sought his opportunities in the opposite direction, traveling to New York and Philadelphia in 1853. But the more familiar movement was north and south along the Mississippi River, and river traffic was more apt to give the young Clemens a palpable sense of the variety of the human species. Mark Twain, in "Old Times on the Mississippi," renders exquisitely the awakening of a "white town drowsing" when a steamboat arrives in town, but Herman Melville, perhaps, gives a more provocative sense of the human spectacle on a riverboat in *The Confidence-Man* (1857):

As among Chaucer's Canterbury pilgrims, or those oriental ones crossing the Red Sea towards Mecca in the festival month, there was no lack of variety. Natives of all sorts, and foreigners; men of business and men of pleasure; parlor men and backwoodsmen; farm-hunters and fame-hunters; heiress-hunters, gold-hunters, buffalo-hunters, bee-hunters, happiness-hunters, truth-hunters, and still keener hunters after all these hunters. Fine ladies in slippers, and moccasined squaws; Northern speculators and Eastern philosophers; English, Irish, German, Scotch, Danes; . . . jesters and mourners, teetotalers and convivialists, deacons and blacklegs; hard-shell Baptists and clay-eaters; grinning negroes, and Sioux chiefs solemn as high-priests. In short, a piebald parliament, an Anacharsis Cloots congress of all kinds of the multiform pilgrim species, man.[2]

Melville's description derives from his recollection of his own trip down the Mississippi in September 1840 as far as Cairo, Illinois. If by chance the riverboat Melville traveled on stopped at Hannibal, the twenty-one-year-old New Yorker, without occupation and destined to set sail on the whaler *Acushnet* in only a few months, might have spotted a five-year-old Sam Clemens in the crowd. Even so early in his life Sam Clemens was probably inured to the spectacle, for he would have taken visitors and newcomers as an ordinary part of village life, just as slavery, sickness, and violence were accustomed facts of his experience. But Melville was alert to the "varieties of mortals" who "blended their varieties of visage and garb" along the river: "Here reigned the dashing and all-fusing spirit of the West, whose type is the Mississippi itself, which, uniting the streams of the most distant and opposite zones, pours them along, helter-skelter, in one cosmopolitan and confident tide." The Mississippi was an appropriate setting for Melville's meditations in the novel on the mysteries of human nature, which, as he was to say, in view of its contrasts and inconsistencies, was much like divine nature, "past finding out." Nevertheless, Melville was as convinced as Clemens would come to be that "The grand points of human nature are the same to-day as they were a thousand years ago. The only variability in them is in expression, not in feature."[3] For Melville, the question of human nature was a metaphysical puzzle; for Clemens, it was largely a social condition. This may be simply another way of saying that Melville was a romantic and Clemens was a realist.

2. *The Confidence-Man: His Masquerade,* ed. Harrison Hayford et al. (Evanston and Chicago: Northwestern University Press and the Newberry Library, 1984), 9.
   3. Ibid., 71.

Melville rejected out of hand those "sallies of ingenuity, having for their end the revelation of human nature on fixed principles"; the best judges have "excluded with contempt from the ranks of the sciences" doubtful systems of reading character—palmistry, physiognomy, phrenology, psychology.[4] By 1855, the year Clemens rather casually turned his lesson book for learning French into his first journal, the young man from Hannibal had seen for himself a bit of that pilgrim species, man—in St. Louis, New York, Philadelphia, Washington, and many towns and villages. Among the earliest entries in that notebook, if one can call them that, were passages copied almost verbatim from George Sumner Weaver's *Lectures on Mental Science According to the Philosophy of Phrenology* (1852).[5] Clemens copied passages on the four "temperaments"—the bilious, the sanguine, the lymphatic, and the nervous—identifying himself as sanguine and his brother Orion as nervous. Unlike Melville, apparently Clemens did not dispute the authority of this taxonomy of human character, but neither did he regard it as a sacred and unassailable classification, for he did not hesitate to slightly revise the wording in order to make a more perfect fit between his own self-estimation and the type defined by Weaver.

Phrenology was one available method to scrutinize oneself and others, and to that extent was both introspective and outwardly observant. By assuming that certain faculties were located in definite portions of the brain and that the conformation of the skull disclosed the size and therefore the development of those faculties, the phrenologists purported to be able to read individual character and prescribe a recipe for self-improvement. A phrenological "reading" supplied an inventory of the development of mental faculties, forty-two in all, ranging from "amativeness" (the desire to love and be loved), to "firmness" (a tendency toward obstinacy and tenaciousness), to "tune" (a propensity for making or appreciating music). Through a disciplined attempt to "cultivate" or "restrain" certain faculties, one might achieve a harmony of temperament and know what trade or profession to follow, what mate to choose, and how to educate one's children.[6] The desire to know how to "read" the faces of others par-

4. Ibid.

5. Alan Gribben has discussed Clemens's long-standing interest in phrenology in "Mark Twain, Phrenology, and the 'Temperaments': A Study of Pseudoscientific Influence," *American Quarterly* 24 (March 1972): 45–68. Later, Twain would make phrenology the object of his satire; at this stage in his life, however, he seems to have regarded the system with at least a sense of serviceable belief.

6. Since there are no identified faculties for "restraint" and "cultivation" in the phrenological scheme of things, it is not entirely clear how (that is, by what mental means) the individual was to achieve that sort of discipline. One book I have inspected recommends calling upon a higher power for help. However, one should never

ticipated in what David R. Shi terms a "spectatorial vision."[7] Particularly in large cities, commingling crowds, a diverse ethnic population, and constantly shifting social contexts meant, among many other things, that men and women were watching one another intently. They looked for clues about proper behavior, for a means to interpret obscure purposes and motivations, and for a reason to trust or distrust the strangers one encountered every day.

It is unclear how much or little faith Clemens placed in this pseudo-science. As late as 1885, he evidently got a phrenological reading from a Professor Beall in Cincinnati that disclosed Clemens's temperament to be "favorable to hard sense, logic, general intelligence and insight into human nature." Beall also discovered some indication of Wit and Mirth in him and a deficiency in Self-Esteem and Music.[8] But Twain also made great good fun of the practice years later in *The American Claimant* and "The Secret History of Eddypus." The humor in the man was perpetually bubbling up to the surface, sometimes unbidden, as in his notebook entry in 1865, where the processes of mining for silver and mining for moral sentiments are conflated: "An expert can tell no more about what kind of rock is underneath by the croppings on the surface here than he can tell the quality of a man's brain by the style & material of the hat he wears." As a consequence, the expert concludes the mining company has "got the world by the ass, since it is manifest that no other organ of the earth's frame could have possibly produced such a dysentery of disorganized & half-digested slumgullion as is here presented" (*N&J1*, 88–89). The real point to be made here, however, is that Clemens at this time was at least to some degree interested in acquiring a system and a method for reading human character. Phrenology may well have been one of those early enthusiasms and untested convictions he disavowed in a letter he wrote to J. H. Burrough in 1876:

> You think I have grown some; upon my word there was room for it. You have described a callow fool, a self-sufficient ass, a mere tumble-bug, stern in air, heaving at his bit of dung & imagining he is re-modeling the world & is entirely capable of doing it right. Ignorance, intolerance, egotism, self-assertion,

---

condescend to history; in our own day, it has been repeatedly recommended that we should "Get in touch with our feelings," without ever specifying what sort of non-feeling organ would allow us to "touch" them. Still, phrenologists were, as a rule, insistent that their "science" was neither materialist nor deterministic.

7. *Facing Facts: Realism in American Thought and Culture* (New York: Oxford University Press, 1995), 85–86.

8. Quoted in Alan Gribben, *Mark Twain's Library: A Reconstruction*, 2 vols. (Boston: G. K. Hall, 1980), 2:751.

opaque perception, dense and pitiful chuckle-headedness—& an almost pathetic unconsciousness of it all. That is what I was at 19–20. (*N&J1*, 15)

Though phrenologists might, at times, have been acute in assessing the character of a client, that reflected more on the astuteness of the practitioner than on the "science" he practiced. Besides, a phrenological reading tended to be flattering anyway. Edgar Allan Poe, Walt Whitman, and Ulysses S. Grant received positive readings, and, judging from the few evaluations I have inspected, it is perhaps safe to say, as Garrison Keillor says of the children in Lake Woebegon, that virtually everyone who paid for a reading was bound to come out "above average." As a system, it was impossibly vague and tended to shore up prevailing attitudes. As a form of career counseling, it kept its options open;[9] but as a form of social control, it was very much of its time. A woman's skull generally indicated strong parental feelings and development in the regions of "Inhabitiveness," "Adhesiveness," "Benevolence," and "Veneration"; ergo, this angel in the house belongs at home. An aboriginal American's skull generally reveals a deficiency in "Ideality" and propensities for "Secretiveness," "Cautiousness," and "Pride"; a Negro's skull shows that "animal feelings predominate over both the intellect and the moral sentiments."[10]

As practical explanation, phrenology was not much more than a tautological con game. "Phrenology hardly does more than restate the problem," observed William James in his *Principles of Psychology* (1890). "To answer the question, 'Why do I like children?' by saying, 'Because you have a large organ of philoprogenitiveness,' but renames the phenomenon to be explained."[11] As a scientific theory, it was a logical muddle that presented each organ or faculty as though it were a fully formed person located in a specific region of the brain. As one German psychologist complained, "We have a parliament of little men together, each one of whom, as happens also in a real parliament, possesses but a single idea which he ceaselessly strives to make prevail. . . . Phrenology takes a start to get beyond the point of view of the ghost-like soul entity, but she ends by populating the whole skull with ghosts of the same order."[12] Though Twain's

9. One reading I have shows that the client would make a good architect, college professor, or postmaster.

10. Samuel R. Wells, *How to Read Character: A New Illustrated Hand-Book of Phrenology and Physiognomy* (New York: Fowler and Wells, 1896), vii–viii.

11. *Principles of Psychology,* 2 vols. (1890; rpt. New York: Dover Publications, 1950), 1:28.

12. Quoted in ibid., 1:29.

reasoning on the nature of conscience in his tale "The Facts Concerning the Recent Carnival of Crime in Connecticut" (1876) borrows little, if anything, from the logic of phrenology, the story does portray conscience as something of a little person (a homunculus) that has mysteriously escaped from the narrator's cranium in order to taunt him. The only ingredient in Twain's later thinking on human nature that may owe something to his youthful interest in phrenology is the notion of temperament, but that is a subject to be held in abeyance for a while. For now it is enough to suggest that when Clemens separated himself from the familiar environment of Hannibal and began to travel among strangers, he left what Kenneth Burke has called a "pre-forensic" environment, an "inner circle" of "familiar meanings with which one has grown up." As a consequence, he welcomed any clues that helped him map the terrain of the unfamiliar.[13]

This pre-forensic environment, argues Burke, is "intimate" and authoritative by virtue of unsuspicious familiarity. "The inner circle is essentially the childhood level of experience. Such a thought makes one realize the special appeal that 'regionalism' may have for the poetic mind. For regionalism tends simply to *extend* the perspective of intimacy and immediacy that one gets in childhood. In childhood one does not think by concepts. 'Authority,' for instance, is not an idea—it has some personal embodiment in father, family doctor, teacher, whom the child accepts or rejects as a person. If he had a domineering maiden aunt with a wart on her nose, 'authority' might become the wart on his maiden aunt's nose." Sooner or later, however, an outer circle intrudes on even the most parochial of minds, "new material accumulates. This new material is not adequately handled by the smaller circle of meanings. . . . People then must strive to draw a wider circle that will encompass this new matter, left inadequately charted or located by the smaller circle." The writer, or anyone else for that matter, may reject the incursions of the new and unfamiliar and "freeze" emotionally and intellectually, but he or she may also bridge the gap between these two circles by means of concepts that in their turn may be humanized and made familiar by means of assimilation and integration of childlike and adult experience.[14]

13. The term *pre-forensic circle* is used in *Attitudes toward History* (Boston: Beacon Press, 1959) and elsewhere. The "inner circle" of experience amounts to the same thing and is defined in "Literature and Science," in *The Writer in a Changing World*, ed. Henry Hart (New York: Equinox Cooperative Press, 1937), 158–71.

14. Twain's ongoing interest in integrating and assimilating new material can be demonstrated by his devoting several hours and many pages to calculating the length

I introduce these Burkean notions not to "explain" Samuel Clemens's maturation, or at least not solely for that reason. After all, from our privileged position, the wart on a maiden aunt's nose does not seem a much more primitive form of understanding of human nature than an unusually large protuberance on the skull where the "Sublimity" faculty is supposed to lie. But when one's pre-forensic circle is violated—when strangers come to town, when family fortunes change for the worse, when one leaves the house or leaves the state—some sort of conceptual chart is needed in order to navigate murky waters. That Sam Clemens painstakingly copied into his first notebook a picture of the phrenologist's head, a "chart" for comprehending human nature if ever there was one, seems no accident.[15] More important, though, is the apparent fact that Twain eventually came to understand the intellectual and psychological distance he had traveled since his childhood.

In Chapter 54 of *Life on the Mississippi* ("Past and Present") he describes revisiting the home-place in 1882, after a long absence: "I presently recognized the house of the father of Lem Hackett (fictitious name). It carried me back more than a generation in a moment, and landed me in the midst of a time when the happenings of life were not the natural and logical results of general laws, but of special orders, and were freighted with very precise and distinct purposes—partly punitive in intent, partly admonitory, and usually local in application" (*LOM*, 375). This Wordsworthian "spot of time" is accompanied by the recollection that Lem Hackett had drowned. That was to be expected, of course: "Being loaded with sin he went to the bottom like an anvil"; it was a clear case of "special judgment." However, young Sam Clemens privately cursed Lem Hackett for bringing all of this heavenly attention to the village, for he and his friends, just as sinful as Lem, had thus far escaped notice. The sleepless boy directs his thoughts to God and decides to turn state's evidence against all the other boys in town as a way of diverting blame and punishment from

---

in miles of a light year, his figure of a coat of paint on the top of the Eiffel Tower as representing (in comparison with the height of the tower itself) the human being's brief time in the scheme of things, or his invention of a history game concerning British monarchs to give "children a realizing sense of the length or brevity of a reign." To make palpable and comprehensible and therefore familiar certain sorts of experience or material that lie beyond the realm of childhood is not the same thing as being "nostalgic." In this sense, *The Adventures of Tom Sawyer* and *Adventures of Huckleberry Finn* are anything but evidence of nostalgia; each in its own way banks on an adult perspective returned to but not sentimentally identified with childhood.

15. That Clemens copied the phrenological head in reverse may say more about his training as a typesetter than it does about his skill as a draftsman.

himself, and he resolves to read nothing but tracts and to do no end of good deeds. But when, a few weeks later, the "exasperatingly good" boy Dutchy also drowns, Clemens doesn't know quite what to think. At length, "succeeding days of cheerfulness and sunshine" (*LOM*, 379) solve what the conscience cannot fathom, and the boys forget all about their peril.

Whatever interest Clemens took in phrenology in 1855, sincere or casual, practical or philosophical, it may have helped to wean him of a Calvinistic view of the human condition. All the "faculties" described in phrenology were in themselves "good," though in order to achieve a harmonious mental state a certain amount of instructed tweaking, by way of cultivation or restraint, was required. Following the transcription from Weaver's book of the "bilious" temperament, Clemens made brief reference to "Hopson's notion of hell" and "Manford's reply" (*N&J1*, 25). As the editors of the *Journals* explain, Winthrop Hartly Hopson was a St. Louis physician and evangelist who espoused "a fundamentalist doctrine of eternal damnation and inexorable suffering." Erasmus Manford, a St. Louis Universalist minister, disputed Hopson's fire-and-brimstone preachments and promoted the idea of eventual universal salvation. Hopson had lectured and debated in Hannibal in the 1850s, and Clemens, as well as his uncle, John Quarles (who apparently became a Universalist himself), may have heard him. There is also the possibility that, when he made this entry in his notebook, Clemens had been reading in *The Golden Era*, a magazine published by Manford, with the assistance of George Sumner Weaver, whose book on "mental science" had inspired him to copy descriptions of the four temperaments.

The significance of Clemens's early interest in phrenology does not ultimately have much to do with his belief or nonbelief in a system for reading human nature at a glance. As his lifelong search for various cures and systems of healing attests, Twain could (at least in prospect) muster up the will to believe in the therapeutic powers of most any unconventional treatment, but only for a time. If he felt he had been imposed upon or he was not in the mood to be receptive to the proffered, overneat solution or miracle cure, he could be damning. In 1869, Clemens read the phrenologist Samuel R. Wells's *Wedlock; or the Right Relation of the Sexes* (1869) and dismissed it as "a mass of threadbare old platitudes & maudlin advice shoveled together without rhyme or reason" (*LLMT*, 104–5). Nevertheless, his understanding of the set of assumptions that lay behind phrenology was perhaps quietly preparing the ground for his wholehearted acceptance of the deism of Thomas Paine two years later.

More important for our purposes is the way phrenology might serve a young man who meant to fend for himself in the world. Outside one's "pre-forensic circle," to retrieve that Burkean term for a moment, one necessarily had to be on the lookout and know how to size up a situation. The ability to "read" character in the human face was a prudent art, if nothing more. From his earliest known publication ("The Dandy Frightening the Squatter," 1852) to many of the manuscripts he left incomplete at the time of his death (including the "Mysterious Stranger" manuscripts) Clemens's fiction reveals an apparently insatiable fascination with "encounters" between and among people whose language, background, and sets of assumptions about themselves and others make for a comedy of misapprehension. Sometimes these characters are outsiders, of uncertain origin and inscrutable purpose, the "mysterious strangers" and con men who so frequently populate Twain's fiction; sometimes they are from another time or place (a Connecticut Yankee in Camelot, for example, or any of those curious, exotic "others" Twain meets in his travel books); and sometimes they are an uninitiated apprentice or a swaggering tenderfoot ripe for a hoax or comeuppance. Twain's ongoing interest in social psychology and how people move in and out of diverse and sometimes mutually incomprehensible communities contrasts with the sort of depth psychology one encounters in, say, Nathaniel Hawthorne or Henry James.

In his provocative sketch "Wakefield" (1837), about a London husband who, initially as something of a domestic prank, leaves his wife and moves to a nearby apartment only to return after twenty years, Hawthorne finds occasion to describe a moral parable. "It was Wakefield's unprecedented fate," he writes, "to retain his original share of human sympathies and to be still involved in human interests, while he had lost his reciprocal influence on them." The "moral" Wakefield supplies is this: "Amid the seeming confusion of our mysterious world, individuals are so nicely adjusted to a system, and systems to one another and to a whole, that, by stepping aside for a moment, a man exposes himself to a fearful risk of losing his place for ever. Like Wakefield, he may become, as it were, the Outcast of the Universe."[16] Similarly, Henry James, that "restless analyst" of humanity, in *The American Scene* (1907) often casts himself as a "spectator" who indulges in "his awful modern privilege of this detached yet concentrated stare" at others. James admits there is something perverse, even sinister, in taking in the scene from a safe distance: "It was a monstrous thing,

16. *Nathaniel Hawthorne's Tales*, ed. James McIntosh (New York: W. W. Norton 1987), 81–82.

doubtless, to sit there in a cushioned and kitchened Pullman and deny to so many groups of one's fellow-creatures any claim to a 'personality'; but this was in truth what one was perpetually doing."[17] By contrast, Clemens, or at least Mark Twain, is perpetually doing the opposite—entering, sometimes barging, into the throng, joining in the fun or the confusion, often to his chagrin but most always with an acute awareness of a social world crowded with individual personalities.

According to Daniel J. Boorstin, one of the most conspicuous facts about American character at this time was that "*homo Americanus*" was "more easily identified by his mobility than his habitat." "Of the new space-free man there were two types," Boorstin continues, "the Transients (or Joiners) and the Upstarts (or Boosters). Transient communities bred Joiners by their pace and problems of movement. Upstart communities bred Boosters by their speed of growth."[18] Mark Twain played both parts to the teeth during his lifetime, but when he left his familiar environment of Hannibal, he became, for a time, a gregarious transient who soon discovered that a glad hand and a fund of humor were more powerful and effective possessions than iron nerve and a loaded revolver.[19] Here is a source for what we might call a vernacular vision of human nature—a sense of how human beings are apt to behave under given circumstances, an awareness that competing frames of reference are as potentially comic as they are dangerous, the perhaps unwarranted belief that most people really want to get along, and the conviction that humor and amiability transcend prejudice and relax customary suspiciousness.

His sympathies for individuals did not necessarily translate into an expansive social vision, however. As Louis J. Budd remarks, "One of Twain's finest qualities was his unpretentious, open-hearted way of mixing with all sorts of people he happened to meet. This quality, apparent from the first, grew stronger in the restless melting pot of Nevada and even earlier, to our eternal profit, made him start to savor the vernacular tradition." But when responsible government, civilizing progress, or informed legislation was at stake, "like the antebellum humorists of the Southwest, he

17. *The American Scene* (Bloomington: Indiana University Press, 1968), 397–98.
18. *The Americans: The National Experience* (New York: Vintage, 1965), 49.
19. One of the rare instances in which W. D. Howells seems demonstrably wrong about his friend has to do with his statement that Twain "disliked clubs; I don't know whether he belonged to any in New York, but I never met him in one" (*MMT*, 97). In point of fact, Twain was a natural joiner, from the Cadets of Temperance of his youth, to the Pilots Benevolence Association during his piloting years, to the Lotos Club, Players Club (founding member), Monday Evening Club, Temple Club, Whitefriar's Club, and so on.

could still betray more contempt than warmth in his portraits of common folk."[20] In his early days, Twain's geniality was an effective and prudent way to get on in the world, and it was something of a knack with him, but it had not yet developed into a personal creed with clear-cut social implications.

II

Edgar M. Branch observes that Sam Clemens's "The Dandy Frightening the Squatter" (1852), so far as we know his first published story, is rather the best humorous tale of the writer's apprenticeship work prior to the publication of the jumping frog story in 1865. Both tales draw upon native themes, and both are rooted in the tall-tale tradition of the Old Southwest. The chief difference between them, Branch notes, is a matter of achieved craft. Indeed, the second brings to completion what the first only promised: "In reality of character, in humorous appeal, and in techniques of structure and dramatization, Simon Wheeler's yarn surpasses anything Mark Twain had written earlier."[21] But in its own fashion "The Dandy Frightening the Squatter" predicts that success.

The appeal of "The Dandy Frightening the Squatter" resides, in part, in simplicity of conception. A riverboat approaches Hannibal, Missouri, and the "dandy," spying the "squatter" on the banks, perceives a "fine opportunity to bring himself into notice" and win the favor of the young ladies aboard. Equipped with two pistols and a large bowie knife in his belt, he announces his intention to frighten "into fits" the rustic woodsman: "Say your prayers!" he brags, drawing the pistols, "you'll make a capital barn door, and I shall drill the key-hole myself" (*CTSS1*, 1). The squatter calmly surveyed the man up and down and then "planted his huge fist directly between the eyes of the astonished antagonist, who in a moment, was floundering in the turbid waters of the Mississippi." The would-be hero is "crest-fallen," the ladies award the knife and pistols to the woodsman, and the squatter bids a cheerful adieu to his would-be assailant.

The comedy consists in the dramatized reversal of expectations. The dandy's motives are ordinary and instantly transparent—he will make

---

20. *Mark Twain: Social Philosopher* (Columbia: University of Missouri Press, 2001), 18–19.

21. *The Literary Apprenticeship of Mark Twain* (Urbana: University of Illinois Press, 1950), 121.

himself heroic in the eyes of the young women aboard. The flamboyant and prettified traveler with a "killing moustache" instead becomes a muddied laughingstock. The ladies, whom we are at first supposed to understand are vain enough to be flattered by the dandy's demonstration, show a fine sense of irony in awarding the spoils of this manufactured contest to the rustic victor. For his part, the squatter reveals a casual lack of regard for the aggressor. His parting remark, though couched in an unexceptional, even clumsy dialect, is slyly ambiguous: "I say, yeou, next time yeou come around drillin' key-holes, don't forget yer old acquaintances!" (CTSS1, 2). The statement has a homey and hospitable "you all come back now" flavor to it, but at the same time it serves as a cautionary reminder to the dandy of his misjudgment of the western man. By contrast, the dandy's feeble attempts to play the ring-tailed roarer in uttering his threats give him away as supremely ignorant—for when, in the history of barn doors, has one ever had or needed a key or a keyhole?

Such humor as "The Dandy Frightening the Squatter" possesses comes out of the author's submission to the dramatic situation itself; it owes little to the invention or improvisation of Sam Clemens. For the most part, the realistic and dramatic qualities so visible here are absent or neglected in much that Clemens wrote during his literary apprenticeship. He was content to be a comic journalist (along with many other occupations), and this meant, in part, fashioning sketches, letters, and tales that put on display the audacity and variety of his wit and talent. Branch's *The Literary Apprenticeship of Mark Twain* (1950) remains the most thoughtful and incisive treatment of Clemens's early literary development. Branch charts a literary career in its infancy, showing a young man's broadening of experience (complemented by his omnivorous reading), the cultivation of more refined literary tastes, and a receptiveness to the influences of other writers, particularly the example of the Sagebrush Bohemians in Virginia City, Nevada. Branch describes Clemens's experiments in burlesque, parody, hoaxes, and satire, and shows him to be motivated more by a sense of fun than by firm moral purpose. And he describes the writer's limitations—Clemens's literary self-consciousness, a fondness for the farcical, and, as a consequence, a certain triviality of purpose and a near total neglect of form.

Especially during his Virginia City years, a "theory of formal anarchy defined his practice." Clemens's embrace of literary chaos encouraged unbridled imaginative freedom, but it also tempted him toward meaningless digressions, mere flippancy, and comic self-indulgence. Similarly, a few years earlier, during his time on the river, Clemens's attempts at satire reflected more personal grievance than moral outrage. "Personal satire was nevertheless one mode of his humor," writes Branch, "and personal satire began to take on familiar patterns during his river days. He exposed follies and pretensions in himself and others. . . . His satiric insights of this kind foretell his greatest humorous work, for Mark Twain's lasting portraits imply a satirical comment upon human nature, if only by virtue of their truthful, free delineation. Yet even at this level of his writing, satire is toned down with a sure instinct. The understanding and acceptance implicit in humor are the more basic qualities."[22] In brief, Twain's satire expressed his exasperation with human failings; his humor expressed his sympathy for the human condition.

In much of the early work, we see a comic journalist going for the laugh, exposing sham and absurdity at every opportunity, but with no particular interest in the correction of the faults or the establishment of a surer basis for understanding. Much of his humor is in fact dehumanizingly funny. In "The Great Prize Fight" (1863) between California governor Leland Stanford and governor elect F. F. Low, for example, we get this exchange: Low's fist went "crashing through his opponent's ribs and in among his vitals, and instantly afterward he hauled out poor Stanford's left lung and smacked him in the face with it." Stanford retaliates by tearing off Low's head, but the headless adversary is not to be outdone. He pulled one of Stanford's legs out "by the roots, and dealt him a smashing paster over the eye with the end of it" (*CTSS1*, 53–54). The fight, of course, turns out to be a hoax, and Twain curses himself as a "consummate ass" for believing it. Similarly, in "Whereas" (1864) one Aurelia Maria writes Twain for some advice. She is engaged to a man named Carruthers, but the wedding day keeps being postponed due to one mishap after another. Carruthers gets the smallpox and his face becomes pitted like a "waffle-mould," then he loses a leg; he gives one arm to a Fourth of July cannon and the other to a carding-machine. And so it goes; poor Aurelia sees her lover "passing from her piecemeal" (*CTSS1*, 94). The Twain persona is not exempt from the same sort of disassembly. In "How to Cure a Cold" (1863), he follows every proffered remedy, including drinking a quart of warm salt water: "The result was surprising; I must have vomited three-quarters of an hour; I believe I threw up my immortal soul" (*CTSS1*, 38).

It is not that these specimens of Twain's early humor are not funny; they are. But they are rather cheaply funny. Twain follows in superficial ways one of Henri Bergson's general laws for the comic: "*Any incident is comic*

---

22. Ibid., 58.

that calls our attention to the physical in the person, when it is the moral side that is concerned."[23] When political leaders, ardent lovers, and ailing patients are shown to be made up of so many detachable parts (including a soul that is wretched and retched at the same time), the instinctual reaction is laughter. Likewise, according to Bergson, anything artificially encrusted on a living being and thereby giving "*a person the impression of being a thing*" provokes laughter.[24] When Twain recommends that sick children should be soaked overnight in vinegar or in extreme cases parboiled, the result is surefire. His descriptions of the fashionable ladies in "The Lick House Ball" (1863) is another instance: "Miss B. wore an elegant goffered flounce, trimmed with a grenadine of *bouillonnee*, with a crinoline waist-coat to match; pardessus open behind, embroidered with paramattas of passementerie, and further ornamented at the shoulders with epaulettes of wheat-ears and string-beans; tule hat, embellished with blue-bells, hare-bells, hash-bells, etc., with a frontispiece formed of a single magnificent cauliflower imbedded in mashed potatoes. Thus attired Miss B. looked good enough to eat" (*CTSS1*, 47).

I don't mean to depreciate this aspect of Twain's art. In fact, the extravagance of his humor was his genius, and to some extent that humor was always unruly. Twain himself was often exhilarated and sometimes mystified by his comic imagination. On the other hand, when his humorous writing became too much a performance or was antiseptically detached from the human circumstances it addressed or described, the author had deprived himself of a needed commodity—the social. "You would hardly appreciate the comic if you felt yourself isolated from others," writes Bergson. "Laughter appears to stand in need of an echo. . . . Our laughter is always the laughter of a group."[25] The genre of comic journalism encouraged the epistolary over the dramatized encounter and as a result limited notions of social community. Clemens, at any rate, was adept at addressing his reading public and imagining the most fantastic reports, while at the same time attributing the origins of them to some third party. A brief listing of comic evasions is suggestive:

"A young friend gives me the following yarn as fact, and if it turns out to be a double joke, . . . on his own head be the blame." (*CTSS1*, 3)

23. *Comedy: "Laughter" by Henri Bergson and "An Essay on Comedy" by George Mere-dith* (Garden City, N.Y.: Doubleday, 1956), 93.
24. Ibid., 97.
25. Ibid., 64.

"A youngster gives me the following account of a circumstance." (*CTSS1*, 7)

"Our friend Sergeant Fathom . . . sends us a rather bad account." (*CTSS1*, 11)

"I shall not attempt, by any word of my own, to secure the reader's belief in it, but I will merely relate the simple facts in the case as they fell from the lips of a dying man." (*CTSS1*, 14)

"I found the following letter, or Valentine, or whatever it is." (*CTSS1*, 25)

Is it any wonder that Twain should have liked to play billiards? Bank-shots, carom-shots, massé-shots, two- and three-ball combinations: these are analogues to his versatile management of point of view or dramatic occasion. But evasiveness (of responsibility or judgment) is not the same thing as nonintrusiveness. In a piece written from New York for the San Francisco *Alta California,* entitled simply "The Broadway Bridge," Twain describes the newly erected bridge over Broadway and Fulton streets and the interest it has caused:

> Curiosity runs high here. I saw a washerwoman coming along with three or four hundred pounds on her back to-day, and eyeing the bridge with great interest, and I said, principally to myself, I wonder if that old scalawag really meditates lugging that clothing-store up that tiresome stairway now, when the street below is comparatively free from vehicles? And she not only meditated it, but did it! She tugged, and sweated, and climbed, till she reached the top, cast a critical eye up Broadway, went down on the other side, toiled up again, crossed over to her original point of departure, and went off about her business. There is a great deal of human nature in people.

> I have not been by that bridge for a month without yearning to cross it. I have abused the tardy workmen in my heart for keeping this pleasure from me. I have fairly ached to cross it, and have thought I would give anything in reason or out of reason for the privilege, but the entrances were pitilessly closed, and I had to move on and sigh and suffer in silence. But to-day all obstructions were gone and no soul was there to forbid me. I was free to cross as often as I wanted to. But I didn't want to. As soon as the obstructions were gone the desire went also. Verily, there is a large amount of human nature in people.[26]

26. San Francisco *Alta California,* June 23, 1867, reprinted in *Mark Twain's Travels with Mr. Brown,* ed. Franklin Walker and G. Ezra Dane (New York: Alfred A. Knopf, 1940), 185–86.

In the first instance, the woman, through a sort of impractical interest and superhuman effort, satisfies her curiosity and goes her way; in the second, the Twain persona illustrates the wisdom of Pudd'nhead Wilson's maxim, "Adam was but human—this explains it all. He did not want the apple for the apple's sake, he wanted it only because it was forbidden. The mistake was in not forbidding the serpent; then he would have eaten the serpent" (*PWET,* 6). The washerwoman is comic because she acts in an absentminded way, but she is also heroic in her exertions. Twain is comic because he is indolent and clever; his self-awareness spares him the trouble of climbing the stairway. This brief sketch looks both ways. It is both outwardly observant and introspective, and the two specimens of human nature share the site but not the occasion of self-disclosure. The jumping frog story works otherwise and to better ends.

One need not rehearse the literary qualities of this story.[27] It is enough to point out that from the experience of having heard the tale told by Ben Coon at Angel's Camp and jotting down a telegraphic note about it, Twain fashioned a story of lasting interest. He did so by finding a way to blend three distinct realms of experience and social contexts in a continuous and more or less believable dramatic situation. The tale begins with a letter to Artemus Ward, who resides in New York, announcing that Twain followed Ward's suggestion of looking up one Rev. Leonidas W. Smiley but instead came in contact with Simon Wheeler, who knew and remembered a Jim Smiley and was anxious to talk about him. The prefatory letter contains as well Twain's declaration of his dawning suspicion that Ward has set him up all along. Thus, the western comedian establishes a link with an eastern readership, and this would have been particularly appropriate had the story arrived in time to be included in a collection of tales Ward was assembling. Instead, it came too late and the story was forwarded to the *Saturday Press,* where it was first published before being reprinted throughout the country.

After a few remarks about the manner of Wheeler's storytelling, Twain fades into the background and, despite his obvious annoyance, never interrupts his interlocutor. Wheeler tells with believing simplicity the familiar tale of Jim Smiley and a mysterious stranger who bests him. His halting delivery, modulated by his self-evident admiration of the heroes of his recollected narrative as "men of transcendent genius in finesse," gives his narrative a double immediacy. The story of the jumping frog

27. I have discussed this tale at some length in *Mark Twain: A Study of the Short Fiction* (New York: Twayne Publishers, 1997), 23–28.

(fantastic, even surreal on the face of it) participates in the tall-tale tradition at the same time that it sustains a mounting interest in the outcome of the contest of wits. Simon Wheeler's delivery, too—the authenticity of his talk combined with an earnestness almost to the point of being unaware he is doing anything more than recalling events he had not thought of in a very long time—is realistic after its own fashion. And Twain's access to the tale and the teller issues from another sort of hoodwinking, that of the absent Artemus Ward, who evidently knows the fastidious Mark Twain as a man intent on seeking out improving company, the innocent and garrulous Simon Wheeler as someone whose tongue will be set in motion once the proper cue is given, and the widely familiar even legendary encounter between Jim Smiley and the stranger.

The reader can see from a long way off that Smiley, who keeps his frog in a lattice box and takes him downtown to "lay for a bet," is destined to have his comeuppance. But the mastery of the tale lies in the subtle ways Twain elides other narrative difficulties. Twain cannot be accused of slumming, merely looking up Simon Wheeler in order to absorb something of the local color of the town of Boomerang, for his ambitions run in the other direction, to seek out a genteel companion. The stiff opening of the story ("Mr. A. Ward, Dear Sir:—") establishes in an instant the formality and preciousness of the persona, but it also disguises the winking joke between two friends. In another reversal of convention, Ward, the Yankee literary comedian, concocts this joke on the "Wild Humorist of the Pacific Slope" in order to deprive Twain of some of his buttoned-up proprieties. One consequence of this maneuver is that the eastern reader, if not altogether disallowed, is discouraged from condescending to western characters and tall-tale humor. Simon Wheeler can't be accused of being a squatter who sees in Twain a dandy and sizes him up for a duping, because the comedy itself floats upon the surfaces of Wheeler's sincere admiration for Jim Smiley. By so artfully and quietly sidestepping the customary barriers that separate rich and poor, educated and ignorant, urbane and rustic, east and west, wily and gullible, Twain likewise creates a story that is rooted in region but is also a fundamentally human comedy. Gone is pure burlesque, though the humorous excess remains; gone is the simple hoax, though tricks abound; and gone is the personal grievance, for the satire here is broad enough to be considered universal, not personal.[28]

28. On this score, it is interesting to note that years later Twain was inadvertently tricked into believing the true origins of the jumping frog story were to be located in

The wide circulation of the jumping frog story gave Twain instant celebrity. Though he initially deprecated the achievement, writing to his mother that the story was a "villainous backwoods sketch," a mere "squib," he soon enough acceded to popular opinion. With or without the fortuitous success of this story, however, Clemens had reason to be confident about his future, for he wrote in the same letter that he was "generally placed at the head of my breed of scribblers in this part of the country" (*L1*, 327–38). A few years later, with the publication of *The Innocents Abroad,* his publishers would tout him as the "People's Author." How he moved from the exceptional western writer to a writer with a national appeal involved, among many other things, finding ways to represent characters who were marked by their oddities and shaped by customs and institutions, who were very much of their place and moment, but who were also actuated by common and commonly understood motives and desires. "Nothing can please many, and please long, but just representations of general nature," Doctor Johnson observed in his Preface to Shakespeare. "Particular manners can be known to few, and therefore few can judge how nearly they are copied . . . but the pleasures of sudden wonder are soon exhausted, and the mind can only repose on the stability of truth."[29] How Mark Twain fused the curious oddities of particular individuals and pleasing representations of a general human nature is one of the mysteries of his genius; it is also the means whereby he traveled the distance between being a "Wild Humorist" out West and the "People's Author."

In 1866, Twain boarded the ship *Ajax* bound for the Sandwich (now Hawaiian) Islands. It was the first, but by no means the last, time he would describe his adventures among peoples whose culture was wholly alien to him. He was acting as the traveling correspondent for the Sacramento *Union* and had the commercial interests of San Francisco businessmen firmly in mind when he wrote many of the published letters. Twain the itinerant Transient and Joiner transformed himself into an Upstart and Booster easily enough. He commented on the whaling industry, the du-

---

Boetia some two thousand years ago. Arthur Sidgwick had translated Twain's story for inclusion in his *An Introduction to Greek Composition,* but Twain thought the story was in fact a product of ancient Greece and said so in "Private History of the 'Jumping Frog'" (1894). He was more than ready to disallow his own originality in favor of a universal narrative that, because it is too good to "perish," is reinvented throughout the generations.

29. Samuel Johnson, *Johnson on Shakespeare,* vol. 1, ed. Arthur Sherbo (New Haven: Yale University Press, 1968), 61–62.

ties paid on goods imported from the East, and most of all on the profitable potential for the manufacture and export of sugar. He had no objections, apparently, to commercial monopolies or to wage-slavery, enforceable through binding contracts. He predicted (evidently without flinching) that California, like the sugar plantations, would embrace coolie labor soon: "You will not always go on paying $80 and $100 a month for labor which you can hire for $5" (*LH*, 271). He further advertised the islands by reassuring capitalists that the people, their agriculture and commerce, and their government happily reflected the "American" point of view: "the whole people are saturated with the spirit of democratic Puritanism, and they are—republicans" (*LH*, 173). He gave facts and figures, made economic comparisons, and offered cheery predictions for the financial prosperity of those who moved there. He demonstrated some fellow feeling for the natives and insinuated that Captain Cook got what was coming to him. Twain had some strong feelings about the missionaries—describing them as "puritanical; slow; ignorant of all white human nature and natural ways of men, except the remnant of these things left in their own class or profession" (*LH*, 129)—but he did not lament the passing of what he considered barbarous feudal customs.[30] In sum, Mark Twain's reporting satisfied the obvious interests of his publisher and the perceived interests of his readers.

The crassness of this sort of reporting cannot be offset by lavish and appreciative descriptions of the islands themselves, but his portraits of the place do disclose Twain's lifelong affection for Hawaii. And it is true that one can learn a great deal about the Islands and the Islanders—the history, climate, and landscape of the place; the mores, folkways, and ingrained hospitality of the people—as well as pick up a few Hawaiian phrases and acquire a working vocabulary in whaling slang and argot. Nor did Twain disappoint his readers who had come to expect flashes of humor from him. The wholly imagined figure of his traveling companion Mr. Brown allowed Twain to siphon off some of the cruder jokes and reserve a more respectable, though still antic, persona for himself. Brown served as the object of his fun (Twain has him do most of the dirty work, climb in caves, toss stones at coconuts, run into town to fill his whiskey jug, and the like), but the compassionate Twain also tended to his companion's seasickness by administering a dose of poetry as emetic. Twain could satirize in him-

---

30. Some of his experience and thinking about feudalism versus republicanism would enter into the themes of *A Connecticut Yankee in King Arthur's Court* many years later. See Fred W. Lorch, "Hawaiian Feudalism and Mark Twain's *A Connecticut Yankee in King Arthur's Court*," *American Literature* 30 (March 1958): 50–66.

self a common irritability, as in his complaint about the flute player across the way who keeps skipping the first note of the second bar: "Human nature cannot stand this sort of torture. I wish his funeral was to come off at half past eleven o'clock tomorrow and I had nothing to do. I would attend it" (*LH*, 113). However, Mr. Brown could add a dose of realism as a counterpoint to Twain's fastidiousness when needed. Brown would serve the same function in the letters Twain wrote from Europe and the Holy Land for the *Alta California* about a year later, but the figure remained more of a gimmick than a full-fledged character.

The most important episode in Twain's travels was unplanned. In May 1866, the clipper ship *Hornet* caught fire near the equator. The crew divided into two lifeboats, and forty-three days later one of those boats carrying fifteen emaciated men landed in Hawaii. Twain was bedridden at the time, but a friend, Anson Burlingame, made him aware of the event and helped him get a record of the ordeal. The resulting piece was published on July 19 in the Sacramento *Union* and reprinted widely. After gathering more information, Twain expanded the piece and submitted "Forty-three Days in an Open Boat" to *Harper's Monthly*; it was published there in December. The story is a fine piece of writing, and Twain knew enough to avoid joking about so serious a matter. But he must have also known that one crew's misfortune can be another man's opportunity.

As he recalled many years later in "My Début as Literary Person" (1899), in 1866 the twin ambitions of extending his fame eastward and becoming a "Literary Person" were strong in him, and the "scoop" of the story of the survivors from the *Hornet* seemed to be his ticket out of the newspaper game altogether. He did become a literary person, but the increased fame of his pen name was a disappointment—*Harper's* identified the author as "Mark Swain." In "The Turning Point of My Life" (1910) Twain obscurely refers to the publication of the piece as an "extraneous matter," extraneous, that is, to his assignment of writing about the sugar trade in the Sandwich Islands. But he acknowledges that the event was an important "link" in the "chain of circumstances" that made up his life, as important to Mark Twain as crossing the Rubicon was to Caesar, he says. It did help admit him to the "literary guild," and the ensuing notoriety gave him the opportunity to lecture, yet another avenue to advertise himself. The subject of his lecture, which he took around Nevada and northern California with great success, was "Our Fellow Savages of the Sandwich Islands."

It is easy to see why, at the end of his relatively long life, Twain would recall these early years as an assembly of circumstances that somehow determined his fate. But that should not blind us to the fact that much of his success was the result of an energy, purpose, and will that are remarkable—after all, he wrote up the ordeal of the crew of the *Hornet* while he himself was bedridden. Nor should we forget that his career was also the result of ambition and shrewdness—when he perceived the narrative opportunities in the story, he was on it like a duck on a june bug. Not long after his return to California, Twain became the New York correspondent for the *Alta California*. It was in the East that he became aware of a planned "pleasure excursion" to Europe and the Holy Land. Twain was acting on his own initiative as well as in the interests of his employers when he convinced the paper to pay his passage in exchange for the letters he would write from abroad. Eventually, that trip became one more circumstance in the chain and resulted in the publication of his first important book, *The Innocents Abroad* (1869), but that he was aboard the ship at all says more about calculated self-interest than about destiny. In any event, it is prudent to remember that whatever attitudes or notions Twain had (about human nature and many other things) were nearly always modified by the personal and the practical business of becoming a literary person.

III

When Mark Twain disembarked the steam-driven side-wheeler *Quaker City* in New York on November 19, 1867, he was relieved, exasperated, and furious. He had been on a five-month cruise of Europe, the Near East, and the Holy Land as a correspondent, one of many correspondents it so happened who had booked passage on this widely advertised trip. The pilgrimage was sponsored in part by Rev. Henry Ward Beecher's Plymouth Church in Brooklyn. Beecher and Gen. William Tecumseh Sherman were expected to travel with the passengers for the duration of the voyage, but eventually both of them found better things to do. As it turned out Twain himself was the only passenger who possessed something of the celebrity about him, and he inherited Sherman's stateroom by default.

In retrospect, Twain might have wondered whether Beecher and Sherman knew at the time what he had learned only by degrees—that most of the travelers (he would soon take to calling them "pilgrims") were elderly and generally prosperous, decidedly eastern in their bearing and apparent lack of humor, and supremely self-satisfied, confidently outfitted with the sort of unbending piety typically accorded the religious hypocrite. The trip he had embarked on the previous June had been glorious with expectancy; it was to be a "royal holiday," he reported in *The Inno-*

cents Abroad. To be sure, he had made friends on the trip, but by and large the Christian "fellowship" expected of him, as opposed to a frolicking comradeship, was a bit more than he could bear. Now in port, he was glad the journey was over, and he elbowed his way through customs ahead of the rest. He had decided months before and now was at liberty to say that the pleasure party was anything but exhilarating; it more resembled "a funeral excursion without the corpse," he thought.

That was the sardonic phrase he used that same November evening when he wrote an article for the New York *Herald* summarizing his experience. The letter was deliberately intended to make the *Quaker City* pilgrims "howl," but it was probably meant to be notorious as well. The *Herald* piece was probably inspired rather than calculated, however; for that evening Twain was on his way to have dinner with Mrs. Mary Mason Fairbanks, Charles Langdon, and a few other *Quaker City* passengers he had warmed to on the voyage, when an editor for the *Herald* caught up with him and asked for an article on the excursion.

Evidently, Twain's desire for retribution outweighed his feelings of social obligation or his particular fondness for Mrs. Fairbanks, whom he had taken to calling "Mother" because she had been so solicitous of his appearance, demeanor, and well-being on the trip. He followed the man back to the *Herald* offices without complaint and wrote the piece. The outpouring of spleen that night was probably delicious to him, but it only whetted his appetite; he followed it the next evening with an even more scathing letter to the San Francisco newspaper the *Alta California*. Twain's decision to stand up Mrs. Fairbanks and Charley Langdon is something of an epitome of the crossroads of his life and career at that time. Whether through the accident of circumstance or the result of conscious ambition, Twain's life was about take a turn toward the national literary prominence he would enjoy, and sometimes object to, for the remainder of his life.

The narrating persona of *The Innocents Abroad* often gives the impression of being personally betrayed by events, as though the advertisements for a trip sponsored by the Plymouth Church, a humorless captain and the pharisaical passengers, the reverent and self-important guidebooks, even the Old World itself had conspired to hoodwink and disappoint him. In point of fact, however, Twain approached the venture as a career opportunity, and his participation in the voyage was hardly accidental. To the contrary, when Twain became the traveling correspondent for the *Alta California,* he had removed to New York with an eye to enlarging his audience and securing his reputation as a writer. In a word, Mark Twain had come east to improve his prospects, but he found advancement tougher than he had supposed.

The advertisement for the *Quaker City* excursion combined with his paper's willingness to pay the substantial fare (including side trips, approximately $2,000) spelled yet another opportunity. Twain was obliged to write some fifty letters for the *Alta* on whatever subjects struck his fancy and in the style and mood that had made him popular with his western audience. Western readers, he knew, had expectations and preferences distinctly different from those on the other side of the Rocky Mountains. They had a heartier appetite for slang, were more amused than put off by raciness and coarseness, and did not automatically cringe at descriptions (sometimes jocular, sometimes sardonic) of the grotesque, irreverent, or violent. This passage might have puzzled or disturbed eastern readers, but it is unlikely western readers would have misunderstood the intent:

> Moorish guns are not good and neither are Moorish marksmen. In this instance they set up the poor criminals at long range, like so many targets, and practiced on them—kept them hopping about and dodging bullets for half an hour before they managed to drive the centre. (*IA*, 56)

Twain is in no way condoning this grotesque form of execution, but he is condemning it in a way that is by turns antic, superior, and fiercely indignant. Through comic misdirection, by seeming to criticize Moorish arms and Moorish marksmen instead of the brutality of the act itself, he makes his point, but he does so in a way that another sort of readership might altogether misapprehend or at least find curiously indecent.

He removed from the manuscript this description of the nude bathers at Odessa: "At least a hundred times, in the seven hours I stayed there, I would just have got up and gone away from there disgusted, if I had had any place to go to. . . . Incensed as I was, I was compelled to look, most of the time, during this barbarous exhibition, because it forced them to make a show of modesty, at least." Twain's mixture of self-righteousness and prurience is comically deflated by his companion Mr. Brown:

> I said to Brown: "It makes my heart bleed to look upon this unhallowed scene."
>
> "We better go, then," he said. "If you stay here seven more hours you might bleed to death."[31]

What one gets in this vein in *The Innocents Abroad*, by contrast, is pretty tame, indeed. When in Paris, Twain goes to see the infamous cancan. He

---

31. *Traveling with the Innocents Abroad*, ed. Daniel Morley McKeithan (Norman: University of Oklahoma Press, 1958), 139–40.

covers his eyes for shame at the exposure of female limbs, but he peeks through his fingers. Even so, the published book was advertised as the "most original and spicy volume in existence."

At some point it became clear to Twain that there was something bookable in his *Alta California* letters. That recognition may have occurred even before the voyage began; he thought his letters from Hawaii might make a book at any rate, and he had taken preliminary steps for making a book about the Mississippi. At the very least, he was prepared in advance to ring some changes on conventional travel narratives and guidebook literature and to cast a jaundiced eye upon whatever Europe or the Holy Land might have to offer. The popularity of Twain's letters from abroad prompted Elisha Bliss of the American Publishing Company of Hartford, Connecticut, to write Twain and get him interested in writing such a book. Bliss proposed to publish by subscription a travel book the author would soon be referring to as "The New Pilgrim's Progress." Twain may or may not have had several publishing offers, as he boasted to Mrs. Fairbanks, but after giving the matter some thought he did sign a contract with the American Publishing Company.

To publish with a subscription house meant several things. The subscription book was actively promoted, not through advertisements, reviews, and bookstores, but through the efforts of an army of canvassing agents who worked on commission and roamed the country aggressively selling "subscriptions" to the book before it was ever published. Agents were easy to come by after the Civil War. Many of them were widows, and many were men who had been maimed in the conflict. Customers were generally not interested in the evaluations of reviewers, and this suited subscription houses, since they seldom sent out review copies anyway. On that score, however, a disregard for reviewers was wholly unnecessary; *The Innocents Abroad,* as it turned out, was extensively and favorably reviewed throughout the country. Subscription books tended to be expensive and therefore hefty because the typical customer measured value as much by the pound as by the prose. Often sales figures were astonishingly high. Little wonder that the trade publishers and literary reviewers often thought of subscription publishers and the books they peddled as merely "popular" and thereby distinctly subliterary. Little wonder, too, given the lucrative success of *The Innocents Abroad,* that Twain should afterward be devoted to this method of publication.[32]

Bliss's proposal for subscription publication encouraged in Twain qual-

32. Hamlin Hill offers an instructive chapter on subscription publishing in *Mark Twain and Elisha Bliss* (Columbia: University of Missouri Press, 1964), 1–20.

ities that he already possessed: a discursive imagination that could improvise and digress at will and a supposed affinity with a common readership that was not inclined to form its tastes according to the dictates of the literary establishment. The first quality meant that Twain could, though by no means as easily as he at first thought, meet Bliss's requirement to provide a book that would run six hundred or more printed pages (including illustrations) in a timely fashion. Anyone who can prolong the ascent of Mount Vesuvius indefinitely and still sustain interest, who can deliver a hilarious treatise on oyster shells, recount the love story of Petrarch and Laura and put in a good word for "Mr. Laura," or weep in mock distress at the Tomb of Adam is not lacking invention. The second quality meant that he instinctively understood his potential readers. These were men and women who made their literary judgments by their own lights and therefore might be especially open to what was truly original about his travel book, and from the beginning Twain cultivates a certain genial familiarity with his readers.

Elisha Bliss advertised the author of *The Innocents Abroad* as one who gives his readers "a new and entirely original view of persons, places and things abroad, describing them as they appeared to him." Twain, more modestly but more shrewdly too, identified his view with that of the average American. His purpose in writing the book, he said in the preface, was "to suggest to the reader how he would likely see Europe and the East if he looked at them with his own eyes instead of the eyes of those who traveled in those countries before him."

Subscription publishing provided Twain an opportunity to bypass literary authority and, somewhat ironically, through high-pressure salesmen and saleswomen, to make a direct appeal to what he took to be his true audience. In revising his *Alta California* letters into a book he would acquire the talents necessary to become a full-fledged "literary person." Clemens would also begin to reshape his literary identity as "Mark Twain" in ways that made the persona at once more respectable and more popular. At the time, the bargain Twain struck with Bliss may have seemed appealing, even something of a coup. When he sat down to consider the work that had to be done to transform the letters into a publishable book, however, the reality of his situation bore down on him. Together, the *Alta* letters, even allowing for the space taken up with illustrations, would print out to around 250 pages; he would have to write 350 additional pages in only six months. Twain would use the letters he had written for the New York *Herald* and the New York *Tribune* to help bulk up the book, and he would have to mine his notebooks and his memory for new material. As it turned out he also would have to read the dispatches of other correspondents (including Mrs. Fairbanks) for inspiration.

It also became clear that all of the previously printed letters would have to be "weeded" of various kinds of verbal impurities, and substantial portions would have to be jettisoned altogether. Then, in March 1868, he learned that the *Alta California* denied that the literary material he was transforming into *The Innocents Abroad* was his property and in fact was planning to publish its own book of his letters. This meant Twain had to suspend his work in progress, leave Washington, and travel to San Francisco and raise a ruckus (successfully, it turned out) in order to prevent the publication of what he now thought of as those "wretched, slangy letters unrevised" and the "ruin" that sort of book would bring both to his improving literary image and to the sales of *The Innocents Abroad*. After he had finished a draft of the manuscript in San Francisco, he asked Bret Harte to read it. Harte made suggestions according to his own developing sense of the desires of an eastern readership, and the moralistic tone of the new material may owe something to Harte's recommendations. Harte also urged substantial cuts, including eliminating some chapters entirely, and thus another round of revision was called for. Finally, Bliss would ask for still other changes before the book went to press.

Through heroic, perhaps obsessive, effort, Twain met his deadline, though in point of fact there was no pressure from Bliss, who was at the time busily promoting a biography of Ulysses S. Grant. Nevertheless, Twain apparently had resolved to keep to his self-imposed schedule whatever the cost. As one New York journalist who visited him in Washington while he was working on the manuscript recalled, Twain's room was a chaotic mess of dirty linen, cigar ashes, and manuscript pages. If the story is true, Twain apparently forfeited hygiene, comfort, and domestic order for the sake of expediency. At the same time that he was ridiculing the degradation and filth of alien nations and cleansing his own book of its crudities, he was living amid self-created squalor, an irony that seems to have been lost on him. At last the job was done, however, and at a breakneck pace; in May and June alone he wrote some two hundred thousand words, a testament to his discipline and perhaps to his own ambition to establish himself as a writer with a national appeal.

IV

But what, precisely, had he done in those six months? As Leon Dickinson, Hamlin Hill, John Lauber, Jeffrey Steinbrink, and others have pointed out in rather different fashion, Samuel Clemens's persona was not yet fully formed at this time. "Mark Twain" was getting to be famous, and to a degree Sam Clemens was being tugged in his wake.[33] At the time, however, it was not at all clear that his pen name might serve as anything more than a journalistic byline or an impersonation fit for the stage, perhaps, but not as the putative author of books. When he revised the *Alta* letters and adapted them to a larger audience, Clemens was also, perhaps unknowingly, beginning to alter his literary identity in ways that, ultimately, Samuel Clemens would have to answer for.

Twain revised the manuscript with an eye toward clarity, variety, and propriety. Though he retained his western persona, Twain removed many of those references and comparisons to the West Coast that were likely to be obscure to an eastern audience, but he couldn't resist including an occasional tall tale or his wonderful comparison of Lake Como and Lake Tahoe. He also reordered words, phrases, even passages for the sake of general intelligibility, replacing the journalistic angle of on-the-spot reporting with a more literary point of view. The necessity of interpolating new material into his narrative naturally contributed to the variety of the book, and *The Innocents Abroad* ultimately became an olio of adventure, burlesque, satire, straight description, and humorous anecdote. Despite, or perhaps because of, the necessity of padding his narrative, Twain produced a book that, pound for pound, is probably the funniest of his longer works.

Some of the new material (such as the purchase of the kid gloves) was worked up from notebook entries he kept; other episodes were retrieved from memory (the Fourth of July celebration is an instance); some were comic retellings of the familiar (as in the Abelard and Héloïse story); and some (the visit to the Marseilles zoo, for example) appear to be pure fabrications. Particularly in the latter half of the book, the humorous material Twain added tends to come at the beginning of the chapter, giving an antic flavor to the straight description that follows. At the same time, however, frequently in consultation with Mrs. Fairbanks or others, Twain sought to chasten his comedy. He removed coarse and vulgar passages, as well as statements that he thought might be considered blasphemous. He tended to avoid colloquialisms, and when he used slang expressions

---

33. See Dickinson, "Mark Twain's Revisions in Writing *The Innocents Abroad*," *American Literature* (May 1947): 139–57; Hill, *Mark Twain and Elisha Bliss;* Lauber, *The Making of Mark Twain: A Biography* (New York: Farrar, Straus, and Giroux, 1985); and Steinbrink, *Getting to Be Mark Twain* (Berkeley: University of California Press, 1991).

he put them in quotation marks, sometimes slyly attributing the remark to one or another of the staid pilgrims.

Perhaps the most significant change Twain made was to remove from the manuscript his fictional traveling companion, "Mr. Brown." Brown had played the role of the coarse and often impertinent skeptic, thoroughly unsentimental and unromantic. Twain typically played his antipodal opposite, the erudite, fastidious, somewhat sententious gentleman. The opposition made for the kind of comedy that Twain and his western readers knew well, but it also tended to be repetitive and to present a world more polarized than variegated. Clearly, in a book that meant to sample a wide spectrum of peoples and cultures, this sort of opposition was not the note to sound. Brown's qualities were not entirely eliminated, however. Twain distributed, unequally and in an anecdotal fashion, portions of Brown's personality to other characters. The fictitious passenger Blucher acquired most of Brown's traits, and Twain absorbed some of them into himself. This change was necessary because a book as opposed to a series of journalistic reports required some pervading narrative consciousness to give coherence to otherwise disconnected episodes. The change also permitted him to add discursive materials almost at will.

At times, "Mark Twain" so presides over the events to be rendered that the reactions of the narrator eclipse the interest of any particular holy site or dramatic incident. Still, that persona remained a grab bag of comic, and sometimes not so comic, postures to be used at will but not yet with the self-conscious artistic firmness we have come to associate with the name. Clemens made full use of his developing persona, and in the course of revision "Mark Twain" came to resemble more and more a fictional character and less and less a comic device. That character was not fully realized by any means. "Mark Twain" was Samuel Clemens's most impressive creation, and it would take him several years and many subsequent revisions to bring him to a satisfactory roundness. So compelling was this living character that, later in his life, Clemens would object to the common misapprehension that he was "Mark Twain," and nothing more. But the humorist himself was largely responsible for that identification. In *The Innocents Abroad*, at any rate, the process of becoming Mark Twain is well begun, and Clemens seems to have attempted to consolidate the multiform reactions and comments of his narrator into a recognizable presence. One result was that the Mark Twain of *The Innocents Abroad* became not the reader's guide in this tour of the Old World but the reader's companion, whose travels seemed to be enacted on his or her behalf and whose attitudes and perceptions were, at least in prospect, representative of the reader's own, however unique the expression of them might be.

The net effect of Twain's revisions was to create a different kind of travel book, different not only from other books in that genre but significantly different from his original letters as well. The form remained essentially the same—the ordering of episodes followed the itinerary of the *Quaker City* and the experience of the travelers—but the tone was different in several ways. When he removed local California references and western manners of speech and sought to appeal to a broader national audience, the persona became more amorphously American as well. Perhaps this contributed in some measure to the chauvinistic quality the narrative acquires at times. Some British and American reviewers identified Mark Twain as the quintessential "Yankee" in his outlook, even though an advertisement for the book featured an illustration of Twain in buckskins with a carpetbag in one hand and a tomahawk in the other.

Twain still played the role of the westerner, not only a stranger in strange lands but a stranger among his fellow passengers as well, but he also became a representative of the new America—practical, temperamental but generally good-natured, forward-looking, adventurous, and skeptical. As a matter of principle, this new American was in favor of discovery, innovation, and progress over and above revered institutions and sacred places. Straight and well-paved roads, soap, a sound economy, and efficient railroads impress him; artifacts, museums, holy sites, and antique churches bore him. What is substituted for the grand tour, in Twain's hands, is the new American abroad, whose genius for hard work and progress—in a word, his Protestant self-sufficiency and Anglo-American biases—precondition the way he will see and judge the Old World.

Inferable in the pose Twain adopts toward his subject is the fact that the author is sponsoring an American point of view in much the same way he had done in his letters from the Sandwich Islands. In both instances, there is the prevailing assumption that human nature is a malleable commodity that can be shaped and improved by external influences, in this instance the influences of a rather vague Christian ethos, precise (down to the last decimal point) capitalist inducements, and a scientific efficiency. Twain speaks in the confident voice of a man whose time has come. If the popes have "long been the patrons and preservers of art" our "practical Republic is the encourager and upholder of mechanics" (*IA,* 223). Historically, the chief repository for the first has been the Vatican, he says; the United States Patent Office answers the current need. But Twain is never unmistakably clear in his allegiances. In the same chapter, he analyzes scientifically the emotion of sorrow:

> Fancy a surgeon, with his nippers lifting tendons, muscles and such things into view, out of the complex machinery of a corpse, and observing, "Now this little nerve quivers—the vibration is imparted to this muscle—from here it is passed to this fibrous substance; here its ingredients are separated by the chemical action of the blood—one part goes to the heart and thrills it with what is popularly termed emotion, another part follows this nerve to the brain and communicates intelligence of a startling character—the third part glides along this passage and touches the spring connected with the fluid receptacles that lie in the rear of the eye. Thus by this simple and beautiful process, the party is informed that his mother is dead, and he weeps." Horrible! (*IA*, 220)

Twain is revolted by the mechanical explanation of human grief, and only a few pages later he approvingly quotes an inscription he has seen at the Church of St. John Lateran: "'Glory to God in the highest, peace on earth TO MEN OF GOOD WILL!' It is not good scripture," he adds, "but it is sound Catholic and human nature" (*IA*, 224). Throughout the book, Twain corrects, and sometimes overcorrects, his judgments in ways that express his ambivalence but never quite undermine his authority to speak. Interestingly, what today we may deem a cultural blindness in Twain was at the time regarded in quite a different way. It is true, as Leland Krauth remarks, that Twain "judges" his way through Europe and the Holy Land, measuring other cultures and nations against Anglo-American standards of morality and progress. What is more, Twain only intermittently seems to recognize that he, not the native, is the visiting foreigner, "the other."[34]

However, the book itself was promoted on the merits of its unprejudicial character. The advice to canvassing agents was to point out that the author "relates things as they occurred, without bias or favor, and describes places and things as they really are without prejudice or bias. . . . No one will rise from its reading without having a better and clearer knowledge of the countries it describes than ever before, and more ability to judge between truth and fiction in what he may read respecting them in the future." *The Innocents Abroad* is in fact unbiased in its insistent resistance to artificial sentiment and to paying reverent homage to the authority of history, custom, and tradition. It dramatizes the suspiciousness

34. *Proper Mark Twain* (Athens: University of Georgia Press, 1999), 55.

of the average American who does not want to be taken for a ride, and Twain, who had himself concocted the hoax of a "petrified man" in the Nevada Territory, was probably more alert than most to the gullibility of human beings. At the same time, it displays outrage at those who don't and don't want to speak English, who do not bow down to the altar of progress, whose culture is deemed ignorant and backward, and whose dress, customs, and complexions are unappealingly un-American.

It is well to remember, however, as Bret Harte pointed out in his review of *The Innocents Abroad*, that "Mark Twain" is the "very eccentric creation of Mr. Clemens" and that the "mock assumption" of Twain's righteous indignation gives the prose and humor its energy (*Reviews*, 75). The Twain figure is, as Harte remarks, a thoroughgoing materialist: "Like all materialists, he is an honest hater of cant—except, of course, the cant of materialism—which, it is presumed, is perfectly right and proper" (*Reviews*, 76). A materialist on a spiritual exodus is bound to come into comic collision with events. Still, nothing Twain ever wrote is absolutely and monolithically plain or unequivocal, and this book is no exception, for it is equally true that Twain is capable of damning criticism of his own country and countrymen as well as of revealing self-parody.

As some of the reviewers acknowledged, *The Innocents Abroad* might serve, at least negatively, as a conduct book for those planning to go abroad. For Twain supplies an inventory of ugly Americans as he goes along—the boasters, who brag they always drink wine with dinner; the vandals ("Heaven protect the Sepulchre when this tribe invades Jerusalem!" [*IA*, 351]); the sentimentalists, who, when presented with a desert of stumps, exclaim, "Oh, my soul, my beating heart, what a noble forest is here!" (*IA*, 136); the world-weary "Old Travelers" with their "supernatural ability to bore" (*IA*, 76); the cosmopolitans who can't help calling their friend Herbert "Erbare" and have mastered the French salutation—"two flips of the hand in front of the face" (*IA*, 167). Compared to these transgressions, Twain and his fellow sinners commit forgivable crimes. For them, every exotic foreign guide becomes "Ferguson," every unpronounceable village "Jonesborough" or "Baldwinsville"; this comic maneuver only underscores their provinciality. Their recurrent joke—"Is he dead?"—is not effrontery but a preemptive strike against being imposed upon. Sometimes, Twain's defensiveness takes the form of a vaunted boast.

At the beginning of chapter 26, Twain delivers a paean to democracy in the person of an imagined traveler recently returned from the United States to the Roman Campagna. The traveler tells of the wonders he has seen: the scarcity of soldiers and priests in the streets; common farmers who own their own land; public schools and widespread literacy among men, women, and children; low taxes in a participatory government; eyeglasses, false teeth, newspapers, steam-driven tractors, vast mountains and mighty rivers, fire engines and fire insurance. In this country, he says, "Jews . . . are treated just like human beings, instead of dogs" (*IA*, 194). However, sprinkled throughout this litany of advantages enjoyed by Americans are criticisms too. In the United States, the rich man may not buy his salvation, but he can buy public office. Women's fashions change regularly, but their dress and hairstyles remain absurd. Men wear white shirts that show the dirt and don't change them for a month. More to the point, Americans are a complaining people who do not know when they are well off.

Twain giveth, and Twain taketh away. If Jews are treated like human beings in the United States, we have already learned a few chapters earlier that their guide in Venice was the son of Carolina slaves. He is fluent in four languages, polite, well dressed, cultivated, and knowledgeable. "Negroes are deemed as good as white people in Venice," says Twain, "and so this man feels no desire to go back to his native land. His judgment is correct" (*IA*, 172). Elsewhere, Twain complains that among Muhammadans "morals and whiskey are scarce." His "cheeks burn with shame" to know that Turkey permits its Sultan to have eight hundred wives. "We do not mind it so much in Salt Lake, however," he adds, almost absentmindedly (*IA*, 269). These observations may be simple drollery or stinging rebuke, or they may reflect Clemens's efforts to make Mark Twain a moral as well as a comic presence in the narrative. In any event, the reader is continually asked to distinguish between simple humor and serious satire. What is called into satiric question here, it seems to me, is not the marriage customs of Turks or Mormons but a certain cultural and moral obtuseness in Twain himself. Thus it is that through his persona Clemens can blunder his way into serious social commentary at the same time that he shrewdly sustains his antic comedy. These sorts of contrasts are everywhere in the book.

If, as we are told in chapter 26, the thrill of "discovery" and "invention" makes all "other ecstasies cheap and trivial"; if the inventors of the telegraph, steam engine, and sewing machine are the "men who have really lived" (*IA*, 191); what, then, are we to make of Twain's remarks on Egypt in chapter 58:

> We were glad to have seen that land which had glass three thousand years before England had it . . . ; that land which knew three thousand years ago, well-

nigh all of medicine and surgery which science has *discovered* lately; which had all those curious surgical instruments which science has *invented* recently; which had in high excellence a thousand luxuries and necessities of an advanced civilization which we have gradually contrived and accumulated in modern times and claimed as things that were new under the sun; . . . that walked in the broad highway of civilization in the gray dawn of creation, ages and ages before we were born. (*IA*, 482)

(The italics in this passage are Twain's, as though he meant to call attention to the discrepancy.) And if the Sphinx is the eternal reminder of Egypt's greatness, how are we to take his praise of the gray lizard who darts in and out of the remains of a Roman road?

His coat is the color of ashes: and ashes are the symbol of hopes that have perished, or aspirations that came to naught, of loves that are buried. If he could speak, he would say, Build temples: I will lord it in their ruins; build palaces: I will inhabit them; erect empires: I will inherit them; bury your beautiful: I will watch the worms at their work; and you, who stand there and moralize over me: I will crawl over *your* corpse at the last. (*IA*, 365–66)

Twain giveth and Twain taketh away. It is not so easy to know, precisely, where Twain (much less Samuel Clemens) stands on the variety of subjects he takes up. In fact, it is sometimes easier to know what he is getting at when he is being extravagant than when he is not. We know, more or less, what Twain means when, after his disastrous experiences with the Turkish bath, smoking the Turkish narghile, and drinking Turkish coffee, he says, "I wish Europe would let Russia annihilate Turkey a little—; not much, but enough to make it difficult to find the place again without a divining-rod or a diving-bell" (*IA*, 328). But what does he mean when he says, after praising the rise to power of Napoleon III and his utter transformation of France into a prosperous and secure country, that the French have "a tolerably free land—for people who will not attempt to go too far in meddling with government affairs" (*IA*, 89)? We are happy to take the first statement at a considerable discount; however, the second appears to be troubling to the degree that it may be plainspoken.

The Innocents Abroad is rife with these sorts of inconsistencies. Twain ridicules the American vandals who chip away at holy monuments for keepsakes to take home, but when he meets the Czar of Russia he wants to steal his coat. ("When I meet a man like that, I want something to remember him by" [*IA*, 292]). The sultan of Turkey looks no more imposing than a butcher, but Twain is all aflutter to see Napoleon III. Twain writes an address delivered to the Russian ruler that is so pandering the crew aboard the *Quaker City* are heard making fun of it. Yet the narrator claims he deplores the poverty of several native peoples and their obsequiousness that keeps them in a semi-barbaric state. He curses the "sons of Italy" for their indolence; "why don't you rob your church," he asks (*IA,* 186). He curses Old World lack of energy and enterprise, but he also commends Europe for its sense of comfort and wishes he could export some of it "to our restless, driving, vitality-consuming marts at home" (*IA,* 131). He freely admits that "I have been educated to enmity toward everything that is Catholic" (*IA,* 457), but he stands ready to toast the true Christian charity of the Fathers of Palestine. Twain says the holy cities are too crowded and noisy for proper contemplation, but aboard ship the quiet routine is mind-numbing: morning, noon, and night—dominoes, dominoes, dominoes, relieved only by an evening lecture from Dr. C. Dominoes.

In part the contradictions and inconsistencies may be accounted for by virtue of the fact that parts of the book were composed at different times and for different occasions. But the voice in *The Innocents Abroad* has a certain realistic solidity about it, for all its changeable qualities. The vexations accompanying any weary traveler lend some credibility to Twain's alternating irascibility and sympathy. And the narrator does extenuate himself on these grounds at times. In chapter 7 he breaks out: "'Don't—now don't inflict that most in-FERNAL old legend on me anymore today!' There—; I had used strong language after promising I would never do so again; but the provocation was more than human nature could bear. If you had been bored so, . . . you might have even burst into stronger language than I did" (*IA,* 43).

Time and again, Twain recurs to his confident sense of human nature as the basis of his judgment, the warrant of his excessive indignation, and the forgivable excuse for his social transgressions. In a review of *The Innocents Abroad* (1869), William Dean Howells (before he met Sam Clemens, even before he knew how to spell his name) discerned a quality that set him apart from other humorists: "There is an amount of pure human nature in the book that rarely gets into literature; the depths of our poor unregeneracy—dubious even of the blissfulness of bliss—are sounded by such a simple confession as Mr. Clements [*sic*] makes in telling of his visit to the Emperor of Russia: 'I would as soon have thought of being cheerful in Abraham's bosom as in the palace of an Emperor'" (*Reviews,* 73). For whatever reasons, Twain, and Clemens too, believed in a common human nature, and from time to time he announces that confident belief: "Human nature is very much the same all over the world," he says in chapter 23. The Israelites "were not always virtuous enough to withstand the seductions of a golden calf," he observes in chapter 46, but then, "Human nature has not changed much since then" (*IA*, 358). Elsewhere, he notes that guides took a special pleasure in showing admiring travelers strange sights: "It is human nature to take delight in exciting admiration. It is what prompts children to . . . 'show off' when company is present" (*IA*, 211). And the Samaritans are proud that Jesus sat by their well so many years ago: "Samaritan nature is human nature, and human nature remembers contact with the illustrious always" (*IA*, 418). Human nature is an explanatory principle for Twain—it accounts for human vanity and cowardice and pettiness and irritability; it excuses the narrator's occasional outbursts of profanity and his more than occasional lapses in decorum and judgment. The operant notion of a shared humanity is the basis for the reader's identification with the Twain persona. He is not a condescending guide on this pilgrimage but a companionable presence whose peculiar way of seeing the world combines with a sense of humor that never seems forced or artificial.

Ralph Waldo Emerson and Walt Whitman had attempted to speak to and for the American people before Mark Twain, to encourage their hopes and bolster their confidence. But Twain the western humorist did not indulge in orphic declamations or grand and prophetic sentiments. Or if he did, for at bottom Twain was as sentimental as the next person, he was apt to undercut the excess:

> Toward nightfall the next evening, we steamed into the great artificial harbor of this noble city of Marseilles, and saw the dying sunlight gild its clustering spires and ramparts, and flood its leagues of environing verdure with a mellow radiance that touched with an added charm the white villas that flecked the landscape far and near. [Copyright secured according to law.] (*IA*, 62)

The fact that he does not always deflate his high-flown rhetoric suggests an occasional authenticity of feeling in the author, when comedy and rancor are held in abeyance, that much more profound for being rare. However, there are those who find even his solemn and awed description of the Sphinx one more verbal flourish and not to be believed. Such is the price the perpetual funny man must pay for his tricks.

In any event, the mostly middle-class readers who responded approvingly to Twain's deprecating descriptions of the Azores or Palestine or Constantinople got a double satisfaction, but not necessarily because the author was giving an account of what they would have seen had they too been there. After all, Twain's manner of seeing things was tied to an inimitable comic manner and to a seemingly effortless talent for self-expression that could not be easily replicated. But he seemed to be uttering sentiments that were theirs nonetheless. Howells observed that Twain's "personal books" (his travel narratives and reminiscences) have this advantage over his fictions: "they are of an immediate and most informal hospitality which admits you at once to the author's confidence, and makes you frankly welcome not only to his thought but to his way of thinking. He takes no trouble in the matter, and he asks you to take none. All that he requires is that you will have common sense, and be able to tell a joke when you see it" (*MMT*, 181).

The immense popularity of *The Innocents Abroad* indicates that a great many readers were able to take him on these terms. Twain's account of his travels in Europe and the East was apt to make his readers feel an easy comfort in his presence at the same time they were made to feel a mixture of pity and superiority for those unfortunate peoples who lived in poverty and squalor, amid desolate landscapes, shackled by centuries of tradition, despotism, and habit. But they may also feel superior to those relatively prosperous Americans on the *Quaker City* who had ready cash for such a pricey voyage and were likely to mistake their mementos for genuine experience and parroted sentiments for true reverence.

Twain speaks as knowingly as the authors of the guidebooks he ridicules, but in a rather different way. Of the mosque of St. Sophia in Constantinople he says: "Everywhere was dirt and dust and dinginess and gloom; everywhere were signs of hoary antiquity, but with nothing touching or beautiful about it . . . nowhere was there anything to win one's love or challenge his admiration" (*IA*, 265). "The people who go into ecstasies over St. Sophia must surely get them out of the guide book," he continues. "Or else they are those old connoisseurs from the wilds of New Jersey who laboriously learn the difference between a fresco and a fireplug and from that day forward feel privileged to void their critical bathos on painting, sculpture, and architecture forevermore" (*IA*, 266). There is in his forlorn picture of St. Sophia and his comic dismissal of New Jersey dilettantes a special appeal to those who aren't going, and can't afford to go, to Constantinople (or Naples or Tangiers or Paris) anyway. Those same readers may, in certain moods, find in Twain a defense against the patronizing impositions of their fellow countrymen who would instruct them in the sublimity of the Old Masters. Or, in different moods, they may sympathetically laugh at the narrating persona who embarrasses himself before an American woman he takes for a Parisian beauty or who angrily complains about the weakness of the ship's coffee until he finds out he has been drinking tea. The man who so engagingly confides his embarrassments is bound to make friends easily.

On board the *Quaker City* Twain threw his lot in with that minority of "sinners" whom he found agreeable, but in staking out his reading audience he knew he was in a decided majority. The Twain of *The Innocents Abroad* is an iconoclast without a creed, smashing in gesture and comment all manner of idols, but his cantankerousness and skepticism are temporary. He seems to be able to renew innocent expectation after every disillusionment. If a Paris shave is a form of butchery, perhaps Turkish coffee will live up to its reputation. If the coffee is bitter, the waters of the River Jordan must be sweet. And so on. If the Sea of Galilee is a mournful and barren place, the waters by starlight are beautiful, and if the pilgrimage has been a series of real disappointments and annoyances, there will be recollected pleasures. In the concluding chapter Twain confesses that, day by day, disagreeable incidents vanish from his mind but pleasant memories (more imagined than recollected, perhaps) linger with him. In the aftermath of this pleasure cruise that turned into a funeral procession along the way, memory and time have served him well. He claims that he would do it all over again, even with the same "party of Methuselahs" bound for the same round of aggravations and disappointments. By concluding his book in this way Twain does not quite attain to the sort of triumph of hope over experience that Dr. Johnson expressed, since his anticipations oddly point backward toward a certain nostalgia that only the passage of time can provide. On the other hand, he does adopt the role of someone who is simultaneously innocent and experienced. He will play this role again, at once tenderfoot and veteran, in his next important book, *Roughing It*.

Chapter Two

—————————— 1870–1879 ——————————

I

Given his own circumstances at the time he was writing it, *Roughing It* (1872) is an oddly ironic title for Twain's next important book. Throughout, the author recalls his travels in the West, often far from creature comforts, improving company, and domestic security. Yet at the time he contracted with Elisha Bliss to write this book, Clemens was one-third owner of the Buffalo *Express*, recently married to Olivia Langdon, and living in a furnished house his father-in-law had given the couple as a wedding present. Samuel Clemens had apparently "settled down," but he wrote in *Roughing It* that camping out in desert solitudes "seemed the very summit and culmination of earthly luxury": "It is the kind of life that has a potent charm for all men, whether city or country-bred. We are descended from desert-lounging Arabs, and countless ages of growth toward perfect civilization have failed to root out of us the nomadic instinct" (*RI*, 218). This passage is basically a restatement of a claim he made in *The Innocents Abroad*, but with interesting differences: "The nomadic instinct is a human instinct; it was born with Adam and transmitted through the patriarchs, and after thirty centuries of steady effort, civilization has not educated it entirely out of us yet" (*IA*, 446).

The genealogy of wanderlust in *Roughing It* has its origins in Semitic tribes and has persisted "countless ages"; in *The Innocents Abroad* the same impulse has been inherited from Adam, and civilizing influences are a mere three thousand years old. In either instance, the remark probably says more about Sam Clemens than it does about the human condition. His travels in the Middle East and the Holy Land had acquainted him with nomadic peoples, of course, but far more frequent were his encounters with families, sects, or tribes that had occupied the same few acres of ground for two thousand years. Itinerancy is not necessarily a universal instinct, but it may have been a fundamental part of Samuel Clemens's makeup. He wrote to a friend in December 1867, for example, "I wish I were in the [Sandwich] Islands now—or in California. . . . I am in a fidget to move. It isn't a novel sensation, though—I never was any other way" (*L2*, 138). He sometimes claimed that his conscience began to pinch him when he stayed in any one place too long.

Domestic bliss would not curb that impulse in him, though he assured his bride-to-be otherwise. It might almost be expected that Clemens's courtship of Olivia Langdon would be conducted on the run and largely through correspondence; he was lecturing in several states and writing her continually from one town or another. In one letter he confessed to the "*strong conviction* that, married to you, I would never desire to roam again while I lived." But he quickly added a disclaimer: "If I roamed more, it must be in pursuit of my regular calling & to further my advancement in my legitimate profession," and insisted, "Wandering is *not* my habit, nor my proclivity" (*L3*, 74–75). It is perhaps worth noting that, in the early 1870s, Clemens made two ill-fated and somewhat ludicrous attempts to advance his literary reputation as a travel writer without subjecting himself to that most necessary requirement of the genre—travel.[1] At any rate, despite his efforts and convictions, he managed to travel a great deal after his marriage. In the 1870s alone, when one lumps together the time spent in separate excursions abroad, we find Clemens lived nearly three full years out of the country—pitching his several tents in Germany, France, Bermuda, Switzerland, Ireland, the Netherlands, Italy, Belgium, and, most often, England. It became almost routine for the family to spend the summer months in Elmira, New York, and he frequently embarked on lecture tours in the United States. As often as not, there were practical pro-

1. He decided to do his traveling by proxy, first proposing to write up the around-the-world jaunt of his future brother-in-law and a college professor named Ford as if it were his own experience; and second by sending an agent to report on the diamond mines in South Africa whose reports he would transform into a narrative.

fessional reasons for his travels—to secure British copyright for his books, to make money lecturing, to acquire literary material, to advertise his most recent book, to sustain his popularity—and he often complained about the aggravation of the lecture circuit. But the fact remains that if, as he implied in his remark in *Roughing It*, the perfecting influences of civilization counseled stasis, not movement, then Mark Twain was far from civilized.

It is within this context that we might consider one of the more unusual courtship letters he wrote to Olivia, dated January 8, 1870:

> I have been reading some new arguments to prove that the world is very old, & that the six days of creation were six immensely long periods.[2] For instance, according to Genesis, the *stars* were made when the world was, yet this writer mentions the significant fact that there are stars within reach of our telescopes whose light requires 50,000 years to traverse the wastes of space & come to our earth. And so, if we made a tour through space ourselves, might we not, in some remote era of the future, meet & greet the first lagging rays of stars that started on their weary visit to us a million years ago?—rays that are outcast & homeless, now, their parent stars crumbled to nothingness & swept from the firmament five hundred thousand years after these journeying rays departed. . . .
>
> How insignificant we are, with our pigmy little world!—an atom glinting with uncounted myriads of other atom worlds in a broad shaft of light streaming from God's countenance—& yet prating complacently of our speck as the Great World, & regarding the other specks as pretty trifles. . . .
>
> I do not see how astronomers can help feeling exquisitely insignificant, for every new page of the Book of the Heavens they open reveals to them more & more that the world we are so proud of is to the universe of careering globes as is one mosquito to the winged & hoofed flocks . . . of all the earth. . . .
>
> One of these astronomers has been taking photographs of tongues of flame 17,000 miles high that shoot aloft from the surface of the sun, & waver, & sink, & rise again—all in two or three minutes,—& sometimes in *one* minute swinging a banner of flame from left to right a distance of 5,000 miles—an inconceivable velocity! (*L4*, 12–13)

This letter is interesting for several reasons. First, it reflects Clemens's current reading and interest in science, about which we will have more to say in a moment. Second, Clemens simultaneously endorses and chal-

2. His readings were from "The Early History of Man" and "Solar Wonders," two anonymous articles in *Eclectic Magazine*, January 1870, pp. 1–16, 112–14.

lenges Olivia's religious sensibility. In other letters, Clemens assured Olivia that he was making headway toward becoming an upright Christian and that he would eventually become worthy of her love. In this one, however, he walks a ragged line. On the one hand, he opposes scripture, or at least the book of Genesis, to the "Book of the Heavens," but on the other, he suggests that the findings of science seem not to have sufficiently impressed upon scientists themselves the essentially Christian moral lesson of humility. This may have been a way of announcing that he still clung to the sort of deism he had found so attractive when he read Thomas Paine.

Finally, while it may well be an example of the sort of didactic letter Clemens often wrote to his fiancée as her self-appointed mentor, one may still ask in what fashion this qualifies as a "love letter." The universe Clemens represents to Olivia's imagination is unfixed from its moorings—the earth a mere mosquito among the herds of planets—and he supposes them a pair of star travelers who encounter the light from stars long ago defunct. In this sense, the earth itself is an insignificant nomad. At the same time, he implicitly suggests that in the face of such immensity, their love and impending union is sufficient solace and a world apart from such vast chaos. He is tacitly reaffirming the words of Genesis 2:24: "Therefore shall a man leave his father and his mother, and shall cleave unto his wife: and they shall be of one flesh." This 1870 letter prefigures the depictions of Adam and Eve as thinly veiled (or rather, starkly naked) versions of Clemens and his wife that Twain would write in later years. As such, it belongs in the company of many other texts that, in the words of Howard Baetzhold and Joseph McCullough, attempt to "synthesize [Clemens's] views of human nature and man's relationship to God and the universe" (*BMT*, xvi).

No perfect synthesis was possible, of course, though Twain often brought these frames of reference into comic conjunction. According to Hamlin Hill and Sherwood Cummings, Mark Twain's reaction to science, in the late 1860s and throughout the 1870s, was deep ambivalence. "Its revelations," according to Cummings, "could inspire his expansive acceptance or suspicious recoil."[3] "Brace of Brief Lectures on Science" (1871) and "Some Learned Fables for Good Old Boys and Girls" (1875) are satires of the vaunted claims of scientists. The first is a parody of the overly confident leaps of reasoning paleontologists make on the basis of scanty or

3. *Mark Twain and Science: Adventures of a Mind* (Baton Rouge: Louisiana State University Press, 1988), 14.

ambiguous evidence, and Twain occasionally quotes from an anonymous review of Louis Figuier's *Primitive Man* entitled "Our Earliest Ancestors" and published in *Chamber's Journal of Popular Literature, Science, and Arts* (1870). The second is a three-part beast fable about a scientific expedition charged to go beyond the confines of the forest and to verify things already believed or to make scientific "discoveries." The expedition returns to great fanfare and armed with fantastic conclusions about the world beyond, but the true hero of the fable is the lowly Tumble-Bug who concludes that all he has learned in his travels is "that science only needed a spoonful of supposition to build a mountain of demonstrated fact out of" (*CTSS1*, 631). The object of satire in both these instances is not science so much as it is the hubris of scientists. At any rate, his comic pictures of the scientific mind-set were not entirely new. In his letters from the Sandwich Islands, for example, Twain and Mr. Brown explore a cavernous tunnel and make a discovery that "may be of high interest to men of science": "We discovered that the darkness in there was singularly like the darkness observable in other particularly dark places—exactly like it, I thought" (*LH*, 255). In *The Innocents Abroad*, Twain advances several theories about how three veins of oyster shells in the side of a mountain five hundred feet above the sea came to be there. At length, he concludes that they must have climbed up there of their own accord in order to "look at the scenery" (*LH*, 307). What was new, however, was that, more and more, scientific theory entered into Clemens's thinking about human nature.

Sometime in 1871 he read at least the first volume of Charles Darwin's *The Descent of Man*. From the beginning, Clemens seems to have had a high regard for the naturalist and his writings. Certainly Darwin's diligent accumulation of facts and observations, the patient development of his argument, and the carefully reasoned conclusions he drew were qualities Clemens might appreciate, even admire. What is more, Darwin had a sense of proportion about the importance of his own theory that his disciples did not always share. "Important as the struggle for existence has been and even still is," he wrote in *The Descent of Man*, "yet as far as the highest part of man's nature is concerned there are other agencies more important. For the moral qualities are advanced, either directly or indirectly, much more through the effects of habit, the reasoning powers, instruction, religion, &c., than through natural selection; though to this latter agency may be safely attributed the social instincts, which afforded the basis for the development of the moral sense." What is more, Clemens, particularly in this period of his life, would likely have nodded in assent when he read this passage:

He who has seen a savage in his native land will not feel much shame, if forced to acknowledge that the blood of some more humble creature flows in his veins. For my own part I would as soon be descended from ... that old baboon, who descending from the mountain, carried away in triumph his young comrade from a crowd of astonished dogs—as from a savage who delights to torture his enemies, offers up bloody sacrifices, practises infanticide without remorse, treats his wives like slaves, knows no decency, and is haunted by the grossest superstitions.[4]

Sherwood Cummings is no doubt right to say that Clemens's involvement with Darwinian ideas during these years was an "anguished" one; he is right, too, to observe that his complete and somewhat "resigned" acceptance of evolutionary theory did not take effect until twenty years later. Nevertheless, the scientific point of view afforded him new and often comic ways to think about himself and others. Something of that point of view got into *Roughing It,* and though its significance may be incidental, it is nevertheless pervasive.

II

For reasons that are not altogether clear, Twain thought the Reverend J. G. Wood's *The Uncivilized Races; or Natural History of Man* (1870) necessary to his progress in composing *Roughing It,* for he wrote his publisher Elisha Bliss twice asking for a copy. He does mention the book in chapter 19: "I have been obliged to look the bulky volumes of Wood's 'Uncivilized Races of Man' clear through in order to find a savage tribe degraded enough to take rank with the Goshoots" (*RI,* 166). Clemens's bigoted and embarrassing attitude toward Native Americans is well known, and he certainly did not need any help from Rev. Wood to fulminate in that direction. Perhaps his reading of the *Uncivilized Races* participated in a broader concern with the advances of civilization in eradicating what were considered degraded ancient customs and habits; perhaps his interest was more personal than that. Before and after his marriage to Olivia, he had been making his own efforts to rid himself of certain primitive habits—smoking, drinking, cursing, and other crimes—and his progress had been, at best, uneven. He had read a review of Louis Figuier's *Prim-*

4. *Darwin: A Norton Critical Edition,* ed. Philip Appleman (New York: W. W. Norton and Co., 1970), 275, 276.

itive Man and later the book itself. On the half-title page he had written his name in such a way that it read, "Saml. L. Clemens, The [*Primitive Man*]." This jocular self-identification may say something about his losing battle against his own stubborn vices, as well as about the role of the incorrigible but forgivable backslider he was content to play for a wife who, though ten years younger, called him "Youth."[5]

Perhaps he earnestly believed in his ability to "cast off so many slavish habits" and to make good on his promise to Livy "to be *everything* you would have me be" (*L3*, 75). Perhaps he thought he had outgrown his earlier reputation as the "Wild Humorist on the Pacific Slope," as well as the mischief-making impulses that gave him that reputation. The "Mark Twain" moniker that eventually coalesced into the identifiable and usable persona we are familiar with today was, as Jeffrey Steinbrink has convincingly shown, acquired by degrees, and mostly in his wrestling with the manuscript of what would become *Roughing It*.[6] Specifically, the narrative voice is, at once, one that renders the tenderfoot experiences of a younger Twain and yet smiles on them in recollection from the point of view of a man who has put away childish things.

Part of the problem with writing this new book was that Twain was dealing with recollections several years old, and in some instances with events, such as his overland travels with his brother Orion, that he barely recalled at all. Though, along with many other resolutions, he had decided to be done with journalism altogether and to be a writer of books, his customary practice had been to write out of the stimulus of quite recent impressions, and he found writing this other sort of book difficult. Added to this difficulty was the self-imposed problem of promising Bliss, the *Galaxy* magazine, and others sketches, lectures, collections, and whole books in ways that extenuated his lack of progress on the California book. He proposed a lecture entitled "The Curiosities of California"; he did not write it. He met his obligations to write a column for the *Galaxy*, but the work diverted him from other pressing obligations. He had been working on his "Noah's Ark book" for some time and proposed a "Pre-duluge [*sic*] article," presumably from that manuscript, emphasizing "curious beasts & great contrasts" (*L4*, 296); it did not come to pass. As already noted, he proposed to write two travel works by "proxy." The first would be

5. In *Mark and Livy: The Love Story of Mark Twain and the Woman Who Almost Tamed Him* (New York: Atheneum, 1992), Resa Willis has described in some detail the Tom Sawyeresque qualities Clemens exhibited and his full confidence that his transgressions would be forgiven or overlooked in favor of his basic good nature.

6. See *Getting to Be Mark Twain* (Berkeley: University of California Press, 1991).

his account of Charles Langdon and Darius Ford's experiences in a round-the-world trip as they were reported to him. His "Around the World" letters did not get very far, but the occasion did spur some recollections of his days in Nevada and California. The second was the scheme to send John Henry Riley to South Africa and have him post reports of diamond mining there; Twain proposed to rewrite the reports as his own experience, embellishing wherever he saw fit. The project got nowhere.

Though Twain promised to write day and night, he could not possibly complete all the work he proposed. These were largely gestures that succeeded in making him feel guilty or beleaguered and, if nothing else, seem to prove he was capable of self-delusion in the marketplace as well as on the road to salvation. He had excuses that were real enough, however. He signed a contract to produce a book on the West in July 1870; a few weeks later his father-in-law died. A month later, Emma Nye, a friend of Olivia's, died of typhoid in their house in Buffalo. Their first child, Langdon, was born prematurely on November 7, 1870. He was sickly, and the parents worried whether he would survive; he would die of diphtheria at the age of eighteen months. Olivia, too, became dangerously ill with typhoid in February 1871. Meanwhile, progress on the promised book on the West lagged. All of these factors contributed, both tonally and thematically, to the book he would eventually write.

Certainly, the residue of whatever he had in mind for a lecture on the "Curiosities of California" is observable in *Roughing It*. His worry that perhaps too many books had been written on the West already urged him toward the unusual, even freakish aspects of the West. He merely touched on or avoided altogether familiar topics—Yosemite and the Great Salt Lake are barely mentioned—favoring instead unfamiliar, alien, and exotic subjects. Twain insists that a generosity of spirit has prevented him from inflicting threadbare topics on his audience: "I could give the reader a vivid description of the Big Trees and the marvels of Yo Semite—but what has this reader done to me that I should persecute him? I will deliver him into the hands of less conscientious tourists and take his blessing" (*RI*, 441). On the other hand, Twain wants that same reader to see him as the intrepid reporter of the out-of-the-way: Lake Mono is "sometimes called the 'Dead Sea of California.' It is one of the strangest freaks of Nature to be found in any land, but it is hardly ever mentioned in print and very seldom visited" (*RI*, 273). Its waters are undrinkable and uninhabitable, except for a "white feathery sort of worm" (actually the larvae of brine shrimp) that seems a survival from another geologic era, and undrownable flies that feed on the worms washed ashore. If Walden Pond struck

Thoreau as the "laboratory of the Artist who made the world and me," Twain likewise regards Lake Mono as disclosing "Nature's wisdom," though his conclusions are more antic and a good deal less exhilarating: "Providence leaves nothing to go by chance. All things have their uses and their part and proper place in Nature's economy: the ducks eat the flies— the flies eat the worms—the Indians eat all three—the wild cats eat the Indians—the white folks eat the wild cats—and thus all things are love-ly" (*RI*, 276). This jocular specimen of Nature's wisdom may or may not satirize the Darwinian struggle for existence, but here, as elsewhere, the wisdom of divine Providence is certainly called into question.

Throughout *Roughing It* there are references to the unfamiliar bounty of Nature. Fruits: chirimoyas ("deliciousness itself") and tamarinds ("They pursed up my lips, till they resembled the stem end of a tomato" [*RI*, 455]) and a fanciful turnip vine. Flowers, shrubs, and trees: the *Espiritu Santo*— "In its cup is the daintiest little fac-simile of a dove, as pure as snow" (*RI*, 410); sagebrush, bunchgrass, and greasewood; a perfectly symmetrical pine tree watered continually by steam. Geological and climatic oddities: "alkali" deserts, "a vast, waveless ocean stricken dead and turned to ash-es" (*RI*, 163); snow on the Fourth of July; relentless "zephyr" winds; an earthquake with a sense of humor that perversely enjoys exposing human hypocrisy; an avalanche, a flash flood, and an ice cave; a volcano, "the idea of eternity made tangible" (*RI*, 530); a landslide that, through a "visitation of God," relocates a ranch in a place "more advantageous for its owner" (*RI*, 256); and a "petrified Niagara," a fifty-foot static torrent of lava, "all seamed, and frothed and rippled" (*RI*, 526). Then there are inexplicable "peculiarities": "turret-looking masses and clusters of a whitish, coarse-grained rock that resembles inferior mortar dried hard; and if one breaks off fragments of this rock he will find perfectly shaped and thoroughly petrified gulls' eggs deeply imbedded in the mass. How did they get there? I simply state the fact—for it is a fact—and leave the geological reader to crack the nut at his leisure and solve the problem after his own fashion" (*RI*, 282–83).

Twain supplies the reader with a virtual bestiary as well. If the pro-posed Noah's Ark book was to include many strange creatures that of-fered a "gorgeous chance for the artist's fancy & ingenuity" (*L4*, 296), per-haps something of the same quality got into his description of his travels out West. In any event the bugs and beasts of *Roughing It* qualify as cu-riosities. The timid "jackass rabbit" and the forlorn coyote, "a living, breathing allegory of Want" (*RI*, 76). A Genuine Mexican Plug and, ac-cording to the inveterate liar Bemis, a tree-climbing buffalo. In Hawaii, there is no end of cats: "Tom-cats, Mary Ann cats, long-tailed cats, bob-tailed cats, blind cats, one-eyed cats, wall-eyed cats, cross-eyed cats, gray cats, black cats, white cats, yellow cats, striped cats, regimens of cats, armies of cats, multitudes of cats" (*RI,* 452). In Nevada is Eckert's cocoanut-eating cat; in California, Dick Baker's remarkable cat Tom Quartz, that knew everything there is to know about mining, except for the compromising effects of blasting powder. There is also Jim Blaine's redoubtable ram, about which we learn nothing at all. Twain sees mules that will eat virtually anything, from pine knots to brass filings, and he remembers a manuscript-eating camel he encountered in Syria. He endures a rooster "with a voice like Balaam's ass, and the same disposition to use it" (*RI,* 496). He encounters annoying mosquitoes, venomous scorpions, and hairy tarantulas, "the wickedest-looking desperadoes the animal world can furnish" (*RI,* 183). At night, he is pestered by fleas, rats, centipedes, and cockroaches "as large as peach leaves" (*RI,* 497).

The working title for Twain's western book was "The Innocents at Home," but the author had gone out of his way to make his adventures in his native land seem as exotic and curious as he could. The task he faced in *The Innocents Abroad* had been all the other way round. He discounted the extraordinary and improbable (such as the several hundred board feet of pieces of the true cross that were strewn throughout the Holy Land and available at a price to be negotiated), and he tried to present scenes from Europe and the East in ways his readers could identify with. In *Roughing It,* however, Twain often plays the role of a homespun naturalist cataloging the wonders west of the Rockies and freely mingling tall-tale humor and amusing endorsements of the ways of Providence with documentary fact. It is too much to say that Twain meant to play his own version of Darwin beyond the Great Divide. He was content to dismiss the Goshoot Indians on those grounds, however: "The Bushmen and our Goshoots are manifestly descended from the self-same gorilla, or kangaroo, or Norway rat, whichever animal-Adam the Darwinians trace them to" (*RI,* 167). On the other hand, something more interesting (and personal) than his predictable rant about the Noble Red Man may have been at work in the book as well.

In the margin of his copy of *The Descent of Man,* where Darwin discusses the intellectual faculties of animals, Clemens wrote, "War horses learn the bugle notes. Fire horses rush at the fire alarm."[7] Similarly, in chapter 76 of *Roughing It,* Twain interpolates an apparently invented recollection

7. Quoted in Cummings, *Mark Twain and Science,* 33.

of hiring a horse recently retired from pulling a milk wagon in order to take a young lady for a drive. To impress her, he pretended that he owned the horse, but the ingrained behavior of the animal gave him away; it "delivered imaginary milk at a hundred and sixty-two different domiciles . . . and finally brought up at a dairy depot and refused to budge" (*RI*, 539). Twain also describes horses that have been raised above the range of running water and satisfied their thirst by eating dewy leaves and grasses. When they were removed to lower elevations and presented with a pail of water, they tried to "take a *bite* out of the fluid, as if it were a solid" (*RI*, 540). Such is the force of habit, and of course mechanical behavior deprived of the environment or occasion that gave birth to it is the very stuff of humor. But here and elsewhere, Twain seems more interested in examining habitual impulses as a fundamental part of human and animal nature than in simply seizing a comic opportunity.

It was habit (or perhaps instinct) that permitted the three miners' horses to discover shelter in a snowstorm, while Twain, Ballou, and Ollendorff, sensing the "battle of life was done," tearfully forgive one another, rededicate what remains of their sad lives to reforming their characters, and swear off their bad habits. Ollendorff throws his bottle of whiskey into the snow; likewise Ballou his pack of cards and Twain his beloved pipe. In perfect sympathy with the "spiritual saturnalia necessary to entire and obsolete reform," as Ballou quaintly puts it, the men hunker down in the snow and await their fate. They awake the next morning to discover they are not fifteen steps from a stage station but now saddled with their resolve to lead better lives. Within a couple of hours each man has guiltily resumed his wicked ways, and together they forge a new resolution, "to say no more about 'reform' and 'examples to the rising generation'" (*RI*, 250). Given Clemens's own desire to please his wife and his recent struggles to cast off bad habits and seek redemption, surely there is special pleading in this episode.

But Twain was not so preoccupied with extenuating his own behavior (both past and present) that he was blind to larger cultural matters. To the contrary, throughout the book he plays the role of a droll and peripatetic cultural anthropologist with saddle sores. In Utah he discovers a patriarchal, polygamous society in the Mormons; in Hawaii there are remnants of a matrilineal, polyandrous society among the Kanakas. The Mormons are guided by the ungrammatical and infelicitous but otherwise essentially Christian teachings of the *Book of Mormon*; the Kanakas, prior to the sometimes benignant, sometimes doubtful influences of Christianity, are ruled by superstition and a feudal aristocracy. Brigham Young has his

"Destroying Angels" to enforce a vigilante-style order on society; the Kanakas have the equally potent "tabu."

The Chinese are ancestor worshippers and for that reason resist progress, but they are also efficient, industrious, literate, kind, and well-meaning. No American gentleman or lady ever abuses the Chinese. Those who do are "scum," and their hired proxies, the police and politicians, are the "dust-licking pimps and slaves of the scum" (*RI*, 397). In Virginia City and on the Pacific Coast, the Chinese are scapegoats for the "worst class of white men"—suffering fines, imprisonment, and even death for the white man's sins and crimes. "Any white man can swear a Chinaman's life away in the courts," Twain sardonically remarks, "but no Chinaman can testify against a white man. Ours is the 'land of the free'—nobody denies that—nobody challenges it. [Maybe it is because we won't let other people testify.]" (*RI*, 391). But the Native American, and particularly the Goshoot tribe, is Twain's own scapegoat. He describes the nature of Mormons, Hawaiians, and the Chinese as shaped by creed and custom, but not so the Goshoots. They are innately timid beggars "who produce nothing at all, and have no villages, and no gatherings together into strictly defined tribal communities" (*RI*, 167). He goes further: "how quickly the evidences accumulated that wherever one finds an Indian tribe he has only found Goshoots more or less modified by circumstances and surroundings—but Goshoots after all" (*RI*, 169). Twain backs away from his judgment, but only slightly. It is true the employees of the Baltimore and Washington Railroad Company resemble the Goshoots, he comically remarks, but it is a mistake to confuse the two tribes. Finally, in an about-face that is not quite to be believed, he insists that Christian sympathy for those benighted creatures who scrape out a living in remote and inhospitable deserts commands our pity not our scorn.

The established racial or cultural types of human nature to be found beyond the Great Divide are not Twain's principal interest in *Roughing It*, however. Instead, he focuses on those roughs and rowdies that had so suddenly come upon the scene, and just as suddenly disappeared, leaving an occasional defaced mountain ridge or ghost town as lonely evidence of their existence:

> It was a driving, vigorous, restless population in those days. It was a *curious* population. It was the *only* population of the kind that the world has ever seen gathered together, and it is not likely that the world will ever see its like again. For observe, it was an assemblage of two hundred thousand *young* men—not simpering, dainty, kid-gloved weaklings, but stalwart, muscular, dauntless

young braves, brimful of push and energy, and royally endowed with every attribute that goes to make up a peerless and magnificent manhood—the very
pick and choice of the world's glorious ones. No women, no children, no gray
and stooping veterans,—none but erect, bright-eyed, quick-moving, strong-
handed young giants—the strangest population, the finest population, the most
gallant host that ever trooped down the startled solitudes of an unpeopled land.
(*RI*, 414)

And where are they now? Scattered throughout the world, dead or disappointed, "victims devoted upon the altar of the golden calf—the noblest holocaust that ever wafted its sacrificial incense heavenward. It is
pitiful to think upon." For its brief moment, however, it was a full-fledged
society, a "wild, free, disorderly, grotesque society! *Men*—only swarming
hosts of stalwart *men*—nothing juvenile, nothing feminine visible anywhere!" (*RI*, 415).

Twain is speaking here of the California Forty-niners, but he adopted
much the same attitude toward the Nevada silver miners. He is also implicitly speaking about his bachelor days, unimproved by female influences, and the sort of life he lived before he fell in love with and married
Olivia Langdon. In *Roughing It*, Clemens was learning to write about past
instead of recent experiences, and he would continue to delve deeper into
that past through the decade—summoning up in "Old Times on the Mississippi" (1875) his memory of his apprenticeship days on the river, for example, or in *The Adventures of Tom Sawyer* (1876) his mischievous childhood in Hannibal. He typically enjoyed these nostalgic indulgences, but
what gave his prose emotional color and energy and his episodic narratives thematic coherence often had more to do with his present circumstance than it did with pure recollection. This was also the case with
Roughing It.

III

Twain's contract to write a book about the six years he spent in the Far
West meant imaginatively conjuring up a time when he had sown his wild
oats, but for the last couple of years he had been trying to live down his
misadventures, not revive them. Almost from the beginning of his acquaintance with Olivia, he had been inspected with some suspicion by the
Langdon family and by family friends. In November 1868, Clemens gave
Jervis Langdon the names of half a dozen men who could testify as to the

uprightness of his character. The results were disconcerting. Clemens objected to the "insinuation" and "innuendoes" of some of his references. Included in their "black testimony" that he "would fill a drunkard's grave" (as he would describe the event many years later) was the damning charge made by one not on Clemens's list of names: "I would rather bury a daughter of mine than have her marry such a fellow." This is perpendicular accusation, not oblique insinuation. Evidently, in characterizing the contents of this letter Olivia had softened the complaint considerably. Another letter of reference was more forgiving: "Oh, Mark is rather erratic, but I consider him harmless" (*L3*, 57 n. 6).

In addition to trying to reform his bad habits, Clemens had to answer for his past, and he sometimes must have felt that he was on trial. He insisted to Olivia, à propos of little at all, that he judged her not by her "*acts*" but by her "*intent*," probably as a way of asking for a similar hearing, governed by similar rules of evidence (*L3*, 54). This was not the first time Clemens had had the infuriating experience of being misunderstood (which is the common complaint of almost any humorist), but now it was combined with an obligation to "explain oneself" or to disavow an earlier life or to certify that what one has said is true or, at least, uttered in earnest. The humiliating feeling of having to defend one's moral character must have been exasperating for him. In any event, his current emotional state may have helped shape and define his recollections of the time spent in Nevada and California.

One does not have to look too far to discern that the feeling of being unjustly accused was a concern, perhaps an obsession, with Mark Twain at this time. In the fanciful sketch "Running for Governor" (1870), accusers he has never met from places he has never been come out of the woodwork to testify against him and to undermine Twain's nomination for the governor of New York by making false charges. He signs the piece, "*Once a decent man, but now Mark Twain, I. P., M. T., B. S., D. T., F. C., and L. E.*" (*CTSS1*, 494). These letters of distinction stand for: Infamous Perjurer, Montana Thief, Body Snatcher, Delirium Tremens, Filthy Corruptionist, and Loathsome Embracer. There is more anger than humor in this sketch. In a similar vein, Twain would rail against trial by jury in *Roughing It:* "The jury system puts a ban upon intelligence and honesty, and a premium upon ignorance, stupidity, and perjury." The trustworthy and informed man of social position is dismissed from jury duty in favor of an ignoramus who puts his faith in "street talk and newspaper reports based upon mere hearsay" (*RI*, 349). In a country populated by desperadoes, where not two men out of a hundred murderers suffered the death penalty, more direct systems of jurisprudence proved useful. The uniform opinion of miners, not a jury, decides the fate of the infamous killer Slade, and Captain Ned Blakely "inflicted" justice upon Bill Noakes in a way that was "simplicity and primitiveness itself" (*RI*, 365). Justice and unerring judgment are occasionally to be found in *Roughing It*, but typically outside the courtroom. The fearsome "Arkansas" is overmatched by the tongue-lashing he receives from the landlord's wife in chapter 31, and, as funny as it is, the Hyde vs. Morgan landslide case remains a burlesque of "official" society. The appended chapter on the Mountain Meadows massacre and the inability of the court to exact justice for provable slaughter is in deadly earnest, however, and is meant to convey the author's moral outrage.

Two other thematic elements are related to Twain's preoccupation with the failure of the justice system and his attendant feelings of being misjudged. The first has to do with the scarcity of reliable information and the near impossibility of trustworthy communication out West. The second has to do with Twain's apparently heartfelt contempt for the plea of innocence on the basis of temporary insanity.

Duplicity, deception, and misunderstanding are atmospheric in *Roughing It*. Twain confesses to inventing stories for the newspaper, but that is a single entry in this encyclopedia of deceit and miscommunication. Conrad Wiegend's journalistic assaults are more pernicious. Twain remarks of this timid man, "When a journalist maligns a citizen, or attacks his good name on hearsay evidence, he deserves to be thrashed for it, even if he *is* a 'non-combatant' weakling" (*RI*, 590). The familiar comedy of misunderstanding between Scotty Briggs and the parson is symptomatic of diverse efforts to communicate that simply misfire. The slang and argot of the territories are nearly as undecipherable to the uninitiated as are the Chinese characters printed on Twain's laundry bill. Horace Greeley's handwriting is famously illegible and is the basis for the riotous comedy in chapter 70. Mr. Ballou's fondness for big words and the disposition to use them rather arbitrarily render his statements amusingly incomprehensible. Then there are the liars: The Admiral's "invented histories," enlisted on behalf of those he took to be underdogs and uttered with daunting ferocity, compel silence if not belief. Markiss's suicide note is dismissed by the jury because they know he was incapable of telling the truth. (They later change the verdict to "suicide induced by mental aberration" because he would never tell the truth if he was in his right mind [*RI*, 550]). Bemis's "proofs" about his experience with the buffalo consist entirely of absences—of his horse, his lariat, and the buffalo itself. And the Englishman Eckert, who is famous for his falsehoods, defeats Bascom's and

Twain's expectations by telling an unlikely truth about a cocoa-nut-eating cat and then proving it.

In addition to the mental and moral fog created by lies, legends, tall tales, rumors, disguises, superstitions, and the like, there are several hoaxes or deceptions in the book—salted mines, inflated stock, misleading ore assays, and dishonest assayers. Shrewd telegraph operators buy and sell publicly traded stock but capitalize on "secret" and "private" telegrams in order to strike it rich. And there are many failed attempts to communicate through the mails. The coach taking Twain westward carries some twenty-seven hundred pounds of mail, but most of it will be unloaded in the desert. On the Continental Divide, the author "freighted a leaf with a mental message" to his friends back home and dropped it in a stream that would eventually empty into the Mississippi River. It never arrived and apparently got held up for lack of postage. These are not particularly serious instances, at least so far as Twain is concerned. However, on two occasions Twain thinks he has made his million at last, and in both instances he is defeated by misfired messages. After they stake a claim worth millions, both Higbie and Twain are called away and leave notes telling the other to work the mine in order to secure their rights. Neither one reads the other's note until it is too late. Later, in San Francisco, Twain stays away from the office one day and as a result does not discover a note left for him. He was to sail to New York in order to conclude the sale of a silver mine and to share in the profits. He rushes to the wharf, but the ship is already under way and he has once again missed his opportunity to get rich quick.

Instances of misunderstanding and failed communication abound in *Roughing It*, and in this context Twain's "Prefatory" is curious: "Yes, take it all around, there is quite a good deal of information in the book. I regret this very much; but really it could not be helped: information appears to stew out of me naturally, like the precious ottar of roses out of the otter. Sometimes it has seemed to me that I would give worlds if I could retain my facts; but it cannot be. The more I calk up the sources, and the tighter I get, the more I leak wisdom." In point of fact, however, in the act of writing *Roughing It*, Clemens had imaginatively refashioned his literary persona and made him a man of fun but also of sterling character. This was not merely a feat of rhetoric. Somehow, he conveyed to his reader that "Mark Twain" belonged in the company of those unappreciated "stalwarts" he praised in the book—Buck Fanshaw, Scotty Briggs, Jim Baker, Ned Blakely, and others. Scotty Briggs, he would have us understand, "had it in him to espouse the quarrel of the weak out of inborn nobility of spirit," and this "was no mean timber whereof to construct a Christian"

(*RI*, 345). Clemens would have liked to be understood in much the same way. Likewise Twain made a parable out of his mining experience that applies to a true assessment of a man's character: "So I learned then, once for all, that gold in its native state is but dull unornamental stuff, and that only low-born metals excite the admiration of the ignorant with an ostentatious glitter. However, like the rest of the world, I still go on underrating men of gold and glorifying men of mica. Commonplace human nature cannot rise about that" (*RI*, 224).

If it is human nature to overvalue glitter and show, Twain was nevertheless intent on having his readers know that he was, at bottom, the real article, trustworthy and reliable. And he largely succeeded. In his review of *Roughing It*, Clemens's friend Charles Dudley Warner speculated, "we can imagine the despair with which the less intuitive reader will struggle to separate the nonsense from the sense, the fact from the fiction, the portraiture from the exaggerations in these pages" (*Reviews*, 104), but that was a minority view. And, after all, Warner's concern was restricted to the nonintuitive reader, someone who would likely have fallen for Twain's Petrified Man hoax as well. B. B. Toby, in his review for the *San Francisco Call*, noted, "One peculiarity in Twain is, that the reader is never deceived; there is not the least effort required to discover when [Twain] is in earnest and when joking" (*Reviews*, 104). Another reviewer observed that the author is a man of "sturdy honesty and rugged sense" and suggested further that Twain's prefatory was scarcely needed, for though the book contains "a vast amount of information, it is served up in such a style that the reader absorbs it without effort, and becomes unconsciously instructed while dreaming only of entertainment" (*Reviews*, 107).

During this same period, Twain made sure that on at least one issue his moral earnestness was not in doubt. A recent court case that admitted temporary insanity as a defense strategy and resulted in acquittal excited angry satire in Twain. In 1870, he published three sketches ("The New Crime," "Our Precious Lunatic," and "Unburlesqueable Things") damning the insanity plea, and he made casual reference to it elsewhere. Shortly after he completed writing chapter 48 of *Roughing It*, in which he lambasted the whole idea of trial by jury as a mockery of justice and a model example of imbecility, Twain wrote his publisher with an idea for the dedication for the book:

To the Late Cain

This Book is Dedicated:

Not on account of respect for his memory, for it merits little respect; not on account of sympathy with him, for his bloody deed placed him without the pale of sympathy, strictly speaking: but out of a mere humane commiseration for him in that it was his misfortune to live in a dark age that knew not the beneficent Insanity Plea. (*RI*, 854)

The editors of the California edition of *Roughing It* have surmised that Twain must have been somewhat "giddy" when he proposed this dedication, and Louis J. Budd has rather generously described the idea as "uninspired." However, in an odd way the dedication is revealing.

In concluding a discussion of *Roughing It* by rehearsing Twain's attitudes toward temporary insanity as legal defense, I may appear to be trivializing one of Twain's better and certainly more important books. But in an odd and roundabout way, the issue reaches to the very heart of the book and sheds some light on Clemens's life at this time as well as on the solidity his persona, "Mark Twain," had acquired. It also points to an irony that may have been wholly lost on Clemens himself. The author would have his readers believe that the "wayward" life Sam Clemens had led circa 1860–1867 was in part induced by temporary insanity. "By and by I was smitten with the silver fever," he wrote in chapter 26. Everyone was getting rich, or so it seemed, and Twain got caught up in the excitement: "I would have been more or less than human if I had not gone mad like the rest. Cart-loads of solid silver bricks, as large as pigs of lead, were arriving from the mills every day, and such sights as that gave substance to the wild talk about me. I succumbed and grew as frenzied as the craziest" (*RI*, 211).

What is more, Twain expects the reader to identify with his situation and thereby forgive him his excesses, for "the reader may see what moved me and what would as surely have moved him had he been there" (*RI*, 211). It is clear from comments he later made in "What Paul Bourget Thinks of Us" (1895) that Twain came to believe this form of madness is universally human: "The world seems to think that the love of money is 'American'; and that the mad desire to get suddenly rich is 'American.' I believe that both of these things are merely and broadly human, not American monopolies at all. The love of money is natural to all nations, for money is a good and strong friend" (*CTSS2*, 173). Then he recurs to his western years as evidence: "In the flush times in the silver regions, a cook or any other humble worker stood a very good chance to get rich out of a trifle of money risked in a stock deal; and that person promptly took that risk, no matter what his or her nationality might be. I was there, and saw it" (*CTSS2*, 174).

To the degree that *Roughing It* is an imaginative effort at self-extenuation (a public accounting for the follies of his salad years very much like his private efforts to convince the Langdon family that he was worthy of Olivia) Twain's defense is that he contracted a momentary madness due to a peculiar set of external circumstances. His concluding moral of the book is cautionary because it is not wise to subject frail human nature to such temptations: "If you are of any account, stay at home and make your way by faithful diligence; but if you are 'no account,' go away from home, and then you will *have* to work, whether you want to or not. Thus you become a blessing to your friends by ceasing to be a nuisance to them" (*RI*, 562). The author has earned his right to speak in this way because he has transcended his tenderfoot years and has attained to moral and social respectability. The voice of Mark Twain here and elsewhere in the book is the voice of an older and wiser man. He is now of some account and therefore someone who should be forgiven the follies of an earlier day. Perhaps Samuel Clemens should have listened to Mark Twain in this instance. Clemens, at any rate, was foolish to believe that he was rid of the desire to become suddenly rich. The subsequent record of his inventions, investments, and harebrained schemes to make a bundle throughout his life indicates that he had not outgrown those feverish desires. And Mark Twain, as literary persona, would return to this theme again and again.

IV

In *Roughing It,* Twain had displayed, with comic flair but with a moral earnestness as well, broad democratic sympathies for the stalwart fellows he recalled or invented. Such men (and they were almost exclusively men) were ill-bred, even seedy. They smoked, gambled, fought, cursed, and drank, but they were also loyal, direct, generous, and valiant, even heroic after their own fashion. They possessed a primitive sense of fair play and as a matter of principle stood up for the underdog. The figures of Twain's affection and democratic sympathy at this point were also white, presumably Protestant, and, though rustics themselves, wholly behind American notions of progress. As Louis J. Budd notes, "The ugly truth is that Twain as yet had little respect for any peoples who were outside the pattern of an industrial society."[8] At this time, Samuel Clemens was certainly well positioned within that pattern himself.

During the brief four-year period separating the publication of *Rough-*

8. *Mark Twain: Social Philosopher* (Columbia: University of Missouri Press, 2001), 46.

ing It and that of *The Adventures of Tom Sawyer* (1876), Clemens had done much to secure a reputation as a successful man of his time. He had made money, quite a bit of it. *The Innocents Abroad* had been immensely successful, and *Roughing It* also sold well; so did the novel he wrote with Charles Dudley Warner, *The Gilded Age* (1873). The profits from the play *Colonel Sellers*, derived from the most amusing character in *The Gilded Age*, were substantial, perhaps as much as $100,000 during the thirteen years it was on the stage. Clemens was inclined to judge a country by the straightness of its streets and the efficiency of its railroads and appreciated all manner of "improvements." He had become something of an inventor himself; "Mark Twain's Self-Pasting Scrap-Book" was patented in 1873 and was one of his more lucrative inventions. He was established, and he was famous. The Clemenses built a large house in the fashionable Nook Farm area of Hartford and outfitted it with seven servants. Perhaps as important, in 1874 Twain published his first piece in the *Atlantic Monthly*, and that fact alone conferred a de facto literary respectability on him. Twain was a great favorite in England, and, in addition to lectures, he routinely made after-dinner speeches to delighted audiences. In England, he met such worthies as Herbert Spencer, Wilkie Collins, Anthony Trollope, and Robert Browning.

With these social distinctions came social responsibilities. Twain's early satires were mostly personal grievances, but in the 1870s his comedy became more broadly interested in the state of the republic.[9] At the same time, Twain aimed at enhancing his authority as a morally serious writer. If Twain had not yet become the full-fledged Victorian sage Leland Krauth describes,[10] he nevertheless spoke often as an outraged and indignant citizen, certain of the righteousness of his convictions and of his authority to speak them. Moreover, the present-mindedness required of one who wished to comment on the shortcomings and moral failures of his age was also there, though that impulse urged him in the direction of the journalistic and the topical. Another imaginative impulse drove him back, back to the recollected experiences of his own life. *Roughing It* had traveled this

---

9. An exception is Twain's frequent but basically good-natured satires of Horace Greeley.

10. The sage speaks, says Krauth, "with absolute assurance, with a personal certitude born of—indeed necessitated by—the collapse of traditional authorities, the Sage offers warnings about the evils of the time and wisdom about those things that are timeless. While the Sage may speak on many subjects, ultimately every sage attempts 'to define some crucial aspect of the human'" (*Proper Mark Twain* [Athens: University of Georgia Press, 1999], 192).

latter route and so would "Old Times on the Mississippi" (1875), *Tom Sawyer*, "The Private History of a Campaign That Failed" (1885), and ultimately his rambling, never-to-be-completed "Autobiography." Eventually, he would be tempted toward historical subjects. *1601, Conversation, as It Was by the Social Fireside, in the Time of the Tudors* (1876) was an insubstantial scatological piece, but he was more serious in *The Prince and the Pauper* (1882), *A Connecticut Yankee* (1889), and *Personal Recollections of Joan of Arc* (1896). Neither of these tendencies was pure. Twain's contribution to the plot of *The Gilded Age*, for example, borrowed heavily from his recollections of Clemens family history, particularly the cursed legacy of the Tennessee land his father had purchased in the 1820s, and he bent a personal past to the purposes of social satire; *Life on the Mississippi* (1883) is largely social commentary on the effects of progress since the Civil War, but it is frequently seasoned with personal reminiscence as well.

Twain's social satire during these years was a scattershot affair. Whatever happened to rile him up was liable to his invective. He complained about the charges of the postal service (especially as they pertained to mailing authors' manuscripts); he defended, somewhat tongue-in-cheek, the right of women's temperance groups to protest in saloons and whiskey mills, but condemned the clergyman encouraging criminal trespass by his parishioners to make those protests; he damned the scandalous immigration policies regarding the Chinese; he objected to the execution of an apparently gifted, but not an innocent, man; he petitioned Congress concerning unfair copyright laws; and he lamented the moral degradation of the modern newspaper. His infuriation with the legal defense plea of temporary insanity bordered on monomania. In addition to those sketches mentioned earlier, the insanity defense figures importantly in *The Gilded Age*; and before Tom Sawyer volunteered to testify, Muff Potter's lawyer was prepared to argue that his client acted "under the influence of a blind and irresponsible delirium produced by drink" (*TS*, 166).

In *The Gilded Age*, Twain and Charles Dudley Warner created a satire of the times that many readers found "painful," even "merciless." Some reviewers objected to its ungenerous theme—that the United States has given itself wholly over to graft, corruption, greed, and deception—but few denied its realism. The time was ripe for a reassessment of American society, and the title of the novel gave a name to the era. But the degradation of the national character was not without its causes. "The eight years in America from 1860 to 1868," observes the narrator, "uprooted institutions that were centuries old, changed the politics of a people, transformed the social life of half the country, and wrought so profoundly upon the entire national character that the influence cannot be measured short of two or three generations" (*GA*, 130). The passage was written by Warner, but evidently Twain shared the sentiment. In any event, the attitude Twain would bring to this jointly written novel was made abundantly clear in his sketch "The Revised Catechism" (1871):

First class in Moral Philosophy stand up and recite:

What is the chief end of man?

A. To get rich.

In what way?

A. Dishonestly if we can; honestly if we must.

Who is God, the one only and true?

A. Money is God. Gold and greenbacks and stock—father, son, and the ghost of the same—three persons in one: these are the true and only God, mighty and supreme; and William Tweed is his prophet. (*CTSS1*, 539)

A reviewer for the *Hartford Times* announced that the plot of *The Gilded Age* was a wholly improvised affair in which characters and situations were introduced for a single purpose. "That purpose is to show up human nature and life in the United States" (*Reviews*, 121), life in rural Missouri, Wall Street, Philadelphia, Washington, and elsewhere. The reigning assumption of the book, however, is not so much that human nature is defined by its social and political institutions as that the populace has lost its moral bearings, and that conniving politicians and lobbyists have seized the opportunity to bilk the public coffers. The congressional "Committee on Benevolent Appropriations" plays upon the gullibility and sentimentality of the nation and introduces legislation to aid the nation's dispossessed. But the appropriations never get out to the Indian Territories, and proposed industrial schools for the recently emancipated Negro are mere ruses to fill the pockets of special interest groups.

In the midst of disorienting changes, Warner asks, who can say "that the life of one man is not more than that of a nationality, and that there is not a tribunal where the tragedy of one human soul shall not seem more significant than the overturning of any human institution whatever?" (*GA*, 130). As astute and presumably heartfelt as this question is, however, there are precious few individuated characters in the novel. "The authors portray species, not individuals," as one reviewer put it. "As an exposition of individual human character, therefore, and of the intertangle of passion, motive, and external incident of which life is made up, *The*

Gilded Age is entitled to no rank at all" (*Reviews,* 119), but as a satire of customs and institutions it cannot be too highly praised.

Of the several dozen characters in the book, only Colonel Beriah Sellers has any claim to true originality. The young Quaker physician Ruth Bolton and the murderess Laura Hawkins had possibilities, but they were doomed to rather conventional fates. Colonel Sellers was almost entirely Twain's creation, and he is an epitome of a certain kind of American—visionary, self-deluded, and crass, but also decent, earnest, and charitable. Sellers is continually putting the touch on one or another character, but he earnestly insists on giving out his promissory notes with interest; he proposes one cockamamie money-making plan after another, but he wants to share his imagined good fortune with others. By half, he is a windbag and conniver; by half, a quixotic dreamer and devoted family man. He is as often interested in retaining some scrap of human dignity as he is in get-rich-quick schemes, even those of his own manufacture. Curiously, Sellers escapes the implied condemnation of the title, for finally he is more interested in saving the appearances than in thinly gilded prosperity.

Ruth Bolton, as one reviewer noted, was something of a novelty in fiction—a woman doctor. But she is also self-reliant and insistently distrustful of the role consigned to women. Ruth complains to her sympathetic father, "What a box women are put into, measured for it, and put in young; if we go anywhere it's in a box, veiled and pinioned and shut in by disabilities. Father, I should like to break things and get loose" (*GA,* 105). Likewise, she is dubious of the advantages of marriage. She asks her father, "Would thee have me sit here like a bird on a bough and wait for somebody to put me in a cage?" (*GA,* 189); and she confesses to her mother, "I think I wouldn't say 'always' to any one until I have a profession and am as independent as he is." Her mother quietly smiles at this "newfangled philosophy" (*GA,* 185). Ruth Bolton was Warner's creation, and, though she speaks certain feminist truths, she is actuated by the rather ordinary and conventional desires of Victorian womanhood. In the end her love for Philip Sterling calls her back from the grave and fills her life with the blessings of love.[11] Interestingly, as the narrative passed back and forth between the two writers, Twain scarcely acknowledged Ruth Bolton's existence and had nothing to do with her creation.

11. According to Twain, in a letter to Mary Mason Fairbanks, Olivia and Susan Warner pleaded with Charles Dudley Warner to spare the life of Ruth Bolton, which he did. He added, "I killed my heroine [Laura Hawkins] dead as a mackerel (but Livy don't know it yet)" (*Mark Twain's Letters, Volume 5: 1822–1873,* ed. Lin Salamo and Harriet Elinor Smith (Berkeley: University of California Press, 1997), 339.

Laura Hawkins, on the other hand, was more of a joint production, and when Twain had his innings he assigned her qualities that were broadly human, not much more feminine than masculine. He preferred to make her sarcastic instead of merely witty, as Jane Austen or even Howells might have done. She had been played false by Colonel Shelby, who "married" her and after a few months discarded her to return to his real wife. Victimized though she is, Laura Hawkins is not meant to suffer passively and find true love at last. Twain had other plans for this character. He supplied her with the legend of a mysterious and probably aristocratic father and added other touches of the sentimental novelist, but, by and large, he was not interested in creating a character for readers to pity: "She had more than her rightful share of practical good sense," he wrote, "but still she was human; and to be human is to have one's little modicum of romance secreted away in one's composition. One never ceases to make a hero of one's self, (in private), during life, but only alters the style of his heroism from time to time as the drifting years belittle certain gods of his admiration and raise up others in their stead that seem greater" (GA, 77). She undertakes to educate herself, though it is an even question whether she intends to become more learned or more canny. She is beautiful and vivacious; and she is proud, but not particularly vain. She is coolly indifferent to her many admirers and outsmarts them every time. And though she does die of heartbreak in the end, as one might expect, it is not due to unrequited love. Nor does she even suffer from remorse for shooting Colonel Shelby (twice) at point-blank range. Instead, she dies for reasons Twain himself might well have identified with. After she is found innocent of murder by reason of temporary insanity, Laura refuses to return home to live with her mother; she also refuses six or seven marriage proposals. She decides to go on the lecture circuit instead. Because the lecture hall is virtually empty and those few present insult and assault her, her proud spirit is broken. She returns home, bemoans her fate, and is found dead the next morning. She may have committed suicide, but the inquest discloses the cause of death as heart disease.

These are the traits Twain gives to the independent, intelligent new woman. He may not have been altogether enlightened on the woman question, but neither was he content to follow the well-marked path of sentimentality and convention available to him. On balance, Twain was apt to be reverential toward, even overawed by, the sanctity of womanhood, and he seems never to have doubted that the maternal instinct was a vital part of female human nature. Still, he had outgrown earlier attitudes. In "The Temperance Crusade and Women's Rights" (1873) and

"The Curious Republic of Gondour" (1875) he argued in favor of woman suffrage. He published the sketch "The Curious Republic of Gondour" anonymously so that readers would not suspect some joke lurking in the background. Twain's ideal state was a genuine meritocracy in which power and influence were distributed according to one's education, property, and achievement. (He would later have to relocate his utopia to Heaven, for the mismeasurement of man was inevitable here below.) Not only were women permitted to vote in this republic, they served in parliament and two had been elected "Grand Caliph." On other matters, however, Twain was decidedly unenlightened. He had not yet expunged racial difference from his view of human nature at any rate.

The Irish element in the venality and political corruption of *The Gilded Age* scarcely seems incidental. Twain has Laura sardonically remark of an Irishman she knew who put on airs, "Now you know that when Providence shapes a mouth especially for the accommodation of a potato you can detect that fact at a glance when that mouth is in repose—foreign travel can never remove *that* sign" (*GA*, 241).[12] In a similar vein, in chapter 3 of the novel, Twain is guilty of a crude form of "darky" humor when he has "Uncle Dan'l" mistake an approaching steamboat for the Almighty Himself and fearfully deliver a dialect prayer for deliverance. A Boston reviewer likely had this scene in mind when he complimented the authors on their "delineations of Ethiopian peculiarities" (*Reviews*, 119). And Twain was sufficiently satisfied with that scene to retain it, rather gratuitously, in his play *Colonel Sellers*. In an 1870 letter to Will Bowen, Clemens had boasted, "I am too old & have moved about too much, & rubbed against too many people not to know human beings as well as we used to know 'boils' from 'breaks'" (*L4*, 52).[13] This sort of complacency as it is revealed in *The Gilded Age* and elsewhere and as it relates to Twain's supposed understanding of African American character may have been fortified by his recent reading in Hippolyte Taine's *History of English Literature*.[14] Twain's self-satisfaction about his acquaintance with African American nature was tested at Quarry Farm in the summer of 1874.

12. Evidently, Twain really thought there was something distinctive to the Irish mouth. In 1884, he complained about E. W. Kemble's earliest illustration of Huckleberry Finn, finding the drawings too "Irishy" about the mouth.

13. He is referring to his and Bowen's knowledge of the river. A "boil" is an eddy, and a "break" is a streak on the water that may indicate a snag or some other submerged danger.

14. See, for example, Cathy Boeckmann, *A Question of Character: Scientific Racism and the Genres of American Fiction, 1892–1912* (Tuscaloosa: University of Alabama Press, 2000), 56–59.

Olivia's adopted sister Susan Crane and her husband, Theodore, in the summertime typically welcomed the Clemenses into their home overlooking Elmira, New York, in the Chemung Valley. The two families got along well, but there must have been some uneasiness, too, and there were probably many opportunities for Twain to explain his own point of view to a family whose training and background were so different from his own. One of those differences was sectional. The Langdon family had been active abolitionists; Jervis Langdon had helped found the antislavery church in Elmira and had done important work for the underground railroad in the area. Clemens's family, by contrast, had at one time or another owned slaves, but Sam seemed to believe that close acquaintance with blacks during his childhood spoke in his favor. Specifically, Clemens had more than once claimed that because he had lived among and had known African Americans in Missouri, he was more knowledgeable about their customs and desires. Evidently, Susan Crane was unconvinced by Clemens's authoritative pronouncements on racial matters. In any event, she urged her brother-in-law more than once to have their cook, "Auntie" Mary Ann Cord, tell him her story. More than once, Clemens demurred.

One summer evening in 1874, however, when the Clemenses and Cranes were sitting on the porch of the farmhouse, Samuel Clemens casually asked Auntie Cord about her history and her seemingly inexhaustible good humor. After some hesitation, she agreed to tell her story. The literary result of this exchange was one of Twain's finest sketches, "A True Story, Repeated Word for Word As I Heard It." He sent the piece along to W. D. Howells, not really expecting that his friend would think much of it. Howells liked it exceedingly and published it in the *Atlantic Monthly* the following November. This was Twain's first publication in the country's preeminent literary magazine. A more immediate result of the experience, in Clemens, must have been not only a sudden awareness of his own ignorance of the nature of African Americans, or at least of Mary Cord, but also the recognition that he had been tricked into a new understanding by Susan Crane. In other words, Clemens, like his literary persona in tales he had written before, must have known that he had been set up.

In substance, the sketch he published was indeed a true story. Mary Ann Cord (in the tale she is called Aunt Rachel to give the separation from her children a certain biblical resonance) was in fact born in Maryland and raised in Virginia, and she was separated from her family when she was sold at auction to a man from North Carolina. Her favorite son was named

Henry, he did manage to escape to freedom when he was about thirteen years old, and he did become a barber in Elmira. More important, during the war, Henry did join the Union troops (though perhaps not as a soldier as the sketch indicates), and he kept alive what must have been a desperate hope that he might find his mother somewhere in the South. Finally, against all odds, the two were reunited in rather dramatic fashion.

The story Aunt Rachel tells, then, is autobiographical and therefore personal to her; but it is representative, too. As Philip Foner long ago observed, Twain managed to compress in this brief story much about the humanity of blacks, their liberating role in the Civil War, and their postbellum attempts to find their families, as well as to suggest the barbarity of slavery alongside an unvanquished dignity in the slaves who survived it.[15] Despite the pathos of Aunt Rachel's story, it is not tragic; for every Mary Cord who lived to see at least one of her children again, there were a hundred mothers who did not. That Aunt Rachel knows full well that she is one of the lucky ones only adds to her dignity. Her concluding remarks to "Misto C——" suggest none of the qualities she so obviously possesses—love and forgiveness, defiance and patient suffering, courage, nobility, and pride. Instead, her declaration affirms her prayerful gratitude: "De Lord God ob heaven be praise', I got my own ag'in! Oh, no, Misto C——, I hain't had no trouble. An' no *joy!*" (*CTSS1*, 582).

The story retains its affective power even today, but the critical emphasis upon Aunt Rachel's story and the studied authenticity of her dialect have tended to obscure other, though quite different, affective and artistic qualities in the tale. Twain's subtitle, "Repeated Word for Word As I Heard It," was likely inserted in part to call attention to the vividness of dialect he worked hard to achieve and in part to forewarn readers that the story was not just another comic production. However, the subtitle is misleading in several ways. Although the story Aunt Rachel tells is substantially "true" in most of its details, it has been shaped to achieve a double purpose—first, to dramatize Mary Cord's humanity and, second, to make "Misto C——" not merely foolish but culpable. After hearing Mary Cord's story, Twain told it to John Hay and was encouraged to write it up. As with so many of Twain's oral performances, the story was probably altered with each subsequent retelling; when he came to write the piece, it likely received still other improvements. From a letter he wrote to Howells, we do know that Twain was aware that he was working unfamiliar

15. See *Mark Twain: Social Critic,* 2d ed. (New York: International Publishers, 1966), 265–66.

territory and changed the sequence of the telling: "I enclose also 'A True Story' which has no humor in it. You can pay as lightly as you choose for that, if you want it, for it is rather out of my line. I have not altered the old colored woman's story except to begin it at the beginning, instead of the middle, as she did—& traveled both ways" (*MTHL*, 1:22).

Twain had adopted the mode of the frame tale for this story, but he made the form serve serious purposes. In violation of nearly all the rules he would outline in "How to Tell a Story" (1895), he deliberately avoided the aimlessness that is so amusing in the jumping frog and old ram tales. Moreover, although Aunt Rachel is earnest, she shares very little else with Twain's vernacular narrators. She does not speak in a monotone, she does not ramble, and she is not self-absorbed in the telling—if anything, she is rather sly in the way she involves Misto C—— in the narration. And Clemens's own persona in the story is clearly altered to enhance Rachel's dignity and to emphasize his own unfeeling stupidity. By appearing as "Misto C——" (an only slightly disguised version of Mr. Clemens) instead of Mark Twain, the author has removed the armor of a literary persona in order to absorb more completely the guilt and humiliation that properly belong to him. Moreover, the author does not sponsor the good character of his vernacular narrator, as he had done in the *Roughing It* stories. Instead, he is manifestly wrong about Aunt Rachel, or rather, his appreciation of her is altogether misplaced and self-deceived: "She was a cheerful, hearty soul, and it was no more trouble for her to laugh than it is for a bird to sing. She was under fire, now, as usual when the day is done. That is to say, she was being chaffed without mercy, and was enjoying it" (*CTSS1*, 578). To reread the opening paragraph after having read the story is to see clearly and feel strongly the sting of a basically well-meaning but clearly self-satisfied bigotry. In the end, by giving the last words to Aunt Rachel, the author invites us to imagine more fully the shame that Misto C—— has brought upon himself by the unwanted recognition of the cook's dignity and of his own insufficiency.

Twain's rendering of this "true story" surely exceeded whatever Susan Crane had in mind when she urged him to hear Mary Cord's tale. Perhaps the scales did not fall from Clemens's eyes that evening, but the fact that he published the sketch and thereby willingly subjected himself to public humiliation is significant. The story does more than merely indict Clemens, however. Aunt Rachel's story is both personal to her and severely representative (of both the past and the present), but Misto C—— is representative, too, not merely of the antebellum South but of a continuing and pervasive white guilt. If Clemens was beginning to outgrow certain racial attitudes that had been trained into him since he was a boy, however, his depiction of his boyhood in Missouri in *The Adventures of Tom Sawyer* did not show it.

V

In July 1875, Twain wrote William Dean Howells that he had finished writing *Tom Sawyer:* "I have finished the story & didn't take the chap beyond boyhood. I believe it would be fatal to do it in any shape but autobiographically—like Gil Blas. I perhaps made a mistake in not writing it in the first person. . . . It is *not* a boy's book, at all. It will only be read by adults. It is only written for adults" (*MTHL*, 1:48). He continued: "I wish you would promise to read the MS of Tom Sawyer some time, & see if you don't really decide that I am right in closing with him as a boy" (*MTHL*, 1:49). Howells did read the manuscript and was in agreement with the second point, but took Clemens to task on the first: "It's altogether the best boy's story I've ever read. It will be an immense success. But I think you ought to treat it explicitly as a boy's story. Grown-ups will enjoy it just as much if you do; and if you should put it forth as a study of boy character from the grown-up point of view, you'd give the wrong key to it" (*MTHL*, 1:61). Clemens deferred to Howells's judgment and revised the manuscript according to his friend's suggestions.[16] This was not the first time Twain had altered the tone and conception of the novel, however.

He probably began writing the book in 1873 and returned to it intermittently. But by September 1874 Twain's progress on the novel had stopped dead in its tracks. As he was to recall many years later, it "refused to proceed another step. . . . I could not understand why I was not able to go on with it. The reason was very simple—my tank had run dry; it was empty; the stock of materials in it was exhausted; the story could not go on without materials; it could not be wrought out of nothing."[17] Hamlin Hill's convincing explanation of why Twain's imagination balked is, briefly, that the original plan he had for his title character broke down when, in chapters 14 and 15, he had Tom secretly leave Jackson's Island to give his Aunt a note scratched on a piece of sycamore bark. According

16. Among other things, Twain eliminated the last chapter about Huck's life under the Widow's roof and superintending care, toned down the language, and made less suggestive Becky Thatcher's perusal of the teacher's anatomy book.

17. Bernard DeVoto, ed., *Mark Twain in Eruption* (New York: Harper and Brothers, 1940), 197.

to the original plan, this was to be a crucial moment in the narrative, and
the note, Hill argues, would have been one of dramatic and affectionate
leavestaking, not, as the note later became, simple reassurance that Tom
was not dead but merely playing pirates.[18] Twain's original designs for
the book are indicated by a statement he wrote on the first page of the
manuscript:

> I, Boyhood & youth; 2 y & early manh; 3 the Battle of Life in many lands; 4 (age
> 37 to [40?],) return and meet grown babies & toothless old drivelers who were
> the grandees of his boyhood. The Adored Unknown a [illegible cancellation]
> faded old maid & full of rasping, puritanical vinegar piety. (TS, 8–9)   .

This four-part plan never got beyond the first section, obviously, and
Twain may have abandoned that sort of story quite early. By chapter 6 at
any rate, the "Adored Unknown" has a name, Becky Thatcher. As he portrayed her, Becky hardly seems destined to become a vinegary old maid
or, even in prospect, the object of Tom's pity and Clemens's satire. Had he
stuck to this plan, however, Clemens might have followed, more or less,
his own experiences, both in Hannibal and in his uneven advance in the
battle of life that had taken him as far west as California and the Sandwich
Islands and as far east as Russia and Palestine. The imagined return to lord
it over all those adults who had scolded him or had written him off as no-
account would have been delicious social satire, as well as personally
gratifying revenge. The grown Tom, between thirty-seven and forty years
old, revisiting his childhood home would have been approximately the
same age as Clemens was when he was writing the book. Even without
these correspondences, there were many reasons Clemens might have
identified with his created character, for several of the episodes derived
from spontaneous and often unbidden recollections of his youth.

The distance between Sam Clemens and Tom Sawyer would not have
diminished had he dramatized these several adventures in first person,
however. "By and by," he promised Howells, "I shall take a boy of twelve
& run him on through life (in the first person) but not Tom Sawyer—he
would not be a good character for it" (MTHL, 1:49). Twain would discover soon enough that Huckleberry Finn was a candidate for such a story
and that Huck must tell his own story. Only a third-person narrator could
properly tell Tom Sawyer's tale because the boy's conduct is framed and

18. See "The Composition and Structure of The Adventures of Tom Sawyer," American
Literature 32 (January 1961): 379–92.

to a degree motivated by an adult world that means to scold, plead, and spank him into submission. The narrator's voice emanates from that precinct of grown-up respectability, though mostly in a tone of amused and often delighted sympathy. Henry B. Wonham identifies a "tension" in the novel that he says derives from a certain indecision on the author's part: "Like the novel's author, the narrator of *Tom Sawyer* appears suspended between two attitudes toward his material—one detached and ironic, the other engaged and romantic—and he remains peculiarly undecided about which attitude he prefers."[19] This may be so, but it seems to me that this was exactly the right sort of fix for Twain to be in, for the narrator's voice is simultaneously that of one sort of adult (who has learned from experience and has made his necessary compromises with the world and must perforce approve of the dominant culture) and of another sort (one who happily remembers and therefore sympathizes with a reckless energy and the kind of intelligence that can only find expression in fantasy and mischief).

The narrative voice fuses these positions when it turns from attending to Tom's story and addresses the reader and comments on the significance of the boy's adventures. If the boy had been "a great and wise philosopher, like the writer of this book," Twain observes, Tom's successful conning of the village boys into whitewashing the fence, and forking over their treasures for the privilege, would have disclosed to him "a great law of human action"—"in order to make a man or a boy covet a thing, it is only necessary to make the thing difficult to attain." Tom might have also learned that "Work consists of whatever a body is *obliged* to do, and that Play consists of whatever a body is not obliged to do" (*TS*, 16). Neither of these lessons was what Aunt Polly intended when she decided to punish him for prior offenses, and it is not entirely certain what Tom himself did learn. He "muses" over his good fortune and then trots off to let his aunt see what a fine job he did.

Similarly, the Cadets of Temperance required him to abstain from smoking and cursing. The social intent of the corps was to make a better boy of him, but what the experience actually taught him was "that to promise not to do a thing is the surest way in the world to make a body want to go and do that very thing" (*TS*, 161). Tom's "noble" lie to the schoolmaster spares Becky a dreaded punishment, and the Judge later pronounces it "a generous, a magnanimous lie" that belongs alongside George Washing-

---

19. *Mark Twain and the Art of the Tall Tale* (New York: Oxford University Press, 1993), 125.

ton's "lauded Truth" about cutting down the cherry tree (*TS*, 255). The irony of that remark is self-evident. What is less clear is how much, if anything, Tom has learned from the event. If running around telling "noble" lies would get him the sort of attention and glory he aches for, Tom would do it right away. However, the reader has no secure sense that the boy knows, or ever will know, the difference between a noble and an ignoble lie. In this light, the vexed question of whether Tom "matures" in the course of the novel seems out of place. Discovering that Tom can work when he wants to, as the whitewashing episode has proved to her, Aunt Polly gives Tom an apple along with an "improving lecture" on how much better it will taste when it "came without sin through virtuous effort" (*TS*, 18). While she is lecturing however, he "hooked" a doughnut. He was applauded for the truth he told in the courtroom, and he was applauded for the lie he told at school. And his stint with the Cadets only taught him that "Abstinence makes the heart grow fonder" (of profanity and tobacco, that is). If, as Hank Morgan insists in *A Connecticut Yankee*, "Training is everything," the consequences of training in *Tom Sawyer* seem unpredictable indeed.

Tom continually tests the adult world by one sort of excess or another, usually designed to keep his aunt at her wit's end, the Sunday school superintendent in anxious despair, or his teacher in high dudgeon. His aunt's vexed perplexity with him reassures Tom of the depth of her affection; the community's exasperation adds to his glory. Nevertheless, it is mutually understood, if never stated, that the adult world is one Tom will eventually inherit as well. The exciting prospect of attending his own funeral is irresistible, even if it means his aunt must grieve a bit longer. The grown-up world of St. Petersburg is one that Tom might escape from time to time, but only with the proviso that he can and will return, ideally to great fanfare. Tom casts himself in the role of the Prodigal Son, and his timing is exquisite, for he waits until the preacher's funeral sermon has set everyone into tearful remembrance before marching up the aisle. Amid the weeping and kisses, a time Tom believes to be the proudest moment of his life, he complains, "Aunt Polly, it ain't fair. Somebody's got to be glad to see Huck" (*TS*, 131). Tom's amazement and sense of injustice is sincere, but his reaction is also incredible. Tom obviously envies certain features of Huck's apparently carefree existence, but just as clearly he doesn't have an inkling about his "comrade's" actual life.

Tom's conduct throughout the novel is a repeated pattern of transgression, punishment, and forgiveness; he is nearly always straining at the end of his tether, but for Twain to unleash him upon the world at large would have meant losing him altogether. A boy like Tom can't be induced to get away with anything (whether it is a lump of sugar or playing hooky) if there is no guardian dozing at the gates, and his achievements go for naught unless he is, minimally, rapped on the head with a thimble. Twain must have instinctively known this, and that is why his imagination froze at that moment he was to have his hero leave home for many lands.[20] To see how vividly complicitous Tom is in the social order he provisionally defies, we might look at the first and final chapters.

The novel begins, appropriately enough, with Aunt Polly calling Tom home. She catches him, discovers he has been in the jam again, and the "switch hovered in the air" above the boy. He tricks her and escapes before the switch can fall. Aunt Polly laughs to herself and delivers a self-chastising soliloquy:

> Hang the boy, can't I never learn anything? Ain't he played me tricks enough like that for me to be looking out for him by this time? But old fools is the biggest fools there is. Can't learn an old dog new tricks, as the saying is. But my goodness, he never plays them alike two days, and how is a body to know what's coming? He 'pears to know just how long he can torment me before I get my dander up, and he knows if he can make out to put me off for a minute or make me laugh, it's all down again, and I can't hit him a lick. I ain't doing my duty by that boy, and that's the Lord's truth, goodness knows. Spare the rod and spile the child, as the Good Book says. I'm a-laying up sin and suffering for us both, I know. . . . Every time I let him off my conscience does hurt me so; and every time I hit him my old heart most breaks. Well-a-well, man that is born of woman is of few days and full of trouble, as the Scripture says, and I reckon it's so. . . . I've *got* to do some of my duty by him, or I'll be the ruination of the child. (*TS*, 2–3)

Her speech is a compound of platitudes, freely mixing scripture and folk wisdom, none of which she seems to believe very much. What is more, she, not Tom, is the transgressor, for in her failure to punish the boy more severely than her heart will permit, she has also failed in her Christian duty. Forrest G. Robinson might see in her remarks a specimen of the "bad faith" that he claims is pervasive in St. Petersburg, but neither the boy nor

---

20. Twain ignored or forgot this lesson years later when he sent Tom aloft in a hot air balloon to the Far East in *Tom Sawyer Abroad* (1894) and into the Indian Territory in "Huck Finn and Tom Sawyer among the Indians" (unpublished but written probably in 1884) with rather unsatisfactory results.

his aunt is deceived in the drama of their relations.[21] For Tom and Aunt Polly alike, right conduct is prescribed by books (for Tom the book may be *Robin Hood* and for Aunt Polly it may be the Good Book) and both freely finesse or abandon established precedent or protocol according to their interests or affections.

In the final chapter, Tom, in trying to bring Huck back into the fold, plays a role very much like his aunt's, for he pleads with, bribes, and even threatens to punish Huck, if excommunication from a proposed band of robbers can be construed as punishment. Huck has been impressed into the ranks of St. Petersburg society, and his list of complaints is substantial: "He had to eat with knife and fork; he had to use napkin, cup and plate; he had to learn his book; he had to go to church; he had to talk so properly that his speech was become insipid in his mouth; whithersoever he turned, the bars and shackles of civilization shut him in and bound him hand and foot" (*TS*, 255). After three weeks of this, Huck bolts. The citizens drag the river for him, but Tom knows where to find him—curled up in one of his familiar hogsheads. Tom's answer to Huck's charges against the cruelty of domestication is, from Tom's point of view, irrefutable: "Well, everybody does that way, Huck." And Huck's retort is, for Huck, just as cogent: "Tom, it don't make no difference. I ain't everybody, and I can't *stand* it" (*TS*, 257).

Tom finds his opportunity to rehabilitate Huck in the vagabond's lament, "Blame it all! just as we'd got guns, and a cave, and all just fixed to rob, here this dern foolishness has got to come up and spile it all!" Tom reassures him that the plan to become robbers is on again, but Huck will have to be respectable if he means to belong to Tom Sawyer's Gang, because "a robber is more high-toned than what a pirate is—as a general thing." Huck does not want to be "shut out" from such a tempting enterprise, but Tom, in yet another of his sly maneuvers, falls back on his own obligations to the community. His hands are tied: "Huck, I wouldn't want to, and I *don't* want to, but what would people say! Why they'd say, 'Mph! Tom Sawyer's Gang! pretty low characters in it!' They'd mean you, Huck. You wouldn't like that, and I wouldn't" (*TS*, 258). We are not here principally interested in Huck's nature, but Tom's, and Twain makes it clear that Tom Sawyer is fully implicated in the social order and ever mindful of the sort of self-respect that can only be conferred (or withheld) by others. The boy is shaped by the common, and rather adult, desire to be thought well

---

21. See, for example, *In Bad Faith: The Dynamics of Deception in Mark Twain's Imagination* (Cambridge: Harvard University Press, 1986), 50.

of and in this sense conforms to the analysis of human nature Twain articulated in *What Is Man?* and elsewhere. But Tom and the other boys do have a safety valve that relieves them from the vexatious pressures of being good little boys—a rich fantasy life and the ability to manufacture "adventures" almost at will.

Tom is successful, in a provisional way, in getting Huck to cooperate. Huck vows, if the widow will let up on him just a bit, "I'll smoke private and cuss private, and crowd through or bust."[22] They plan an initiation ceremony for the gang for that very night, an opportunity to "swear to stand by one another, and never tell the Gang's secrets, even if you're chopped all to flinders, and kill anybody and all of his family that hurts one of the gang" (*TS*, 259). The novel concludes on this happy note, but to have the boys resolve to become robbers is a curious ending nonetheless. After all, Tom and Huck have seen firsthand what a nasty line of work that is. They have witnessed Injun Joe murder the doctor, and Huck at least knows that he meant to disfigure the widow Douglas. They know as well what a horrible death Joe died. Ironically, Joe actually enacts the same sort of drama Tom means to play at. He has a secret hideout, he assumes a disguise, he discovers a buried treasure, and he avenges himself not merely on those who have injured him but on their families as well. And Huck and Tom mean to begin their gang in the same hideout, armed with the same guns that once were Joe's. If the minister's droning on and on in church, Aunt Polly's scolding, and the teacher's thrashings do not inspire Tom to mend his ways, the lessons of actual experience are also lost on him.

Tom and Huck both believe Joe to be the consort of Satan himself. On the other hand, evidently those tearful petitioners who would have had the governor pardon him believed that Joe was a poor lost lamb who might at last be reformed. For others, Joe's particular brand of cruelty is attributed to the Indian side of his character. The Welshman says of Joe's plan to slit the widow's nostrils and notch her ears, "white men don't take that sort of revenge. But an Injun! That's a different matter altogether" (*TS*, 214). Even Joe says of his desire for revenge upon Dr. Robinson, "The Injun blood ain't in me for nothing" (*TS*, 75). That Twain would have us believe that there is a distinct, and distinctively perverse, Indian nature is more doubtful. Though Twain was originally content to explain Joe's evil

---

22. During his courtship of and shortly after his marriage to Olivia Langdon, Clemens attempted similar concessions and made similar resolutions. This is perhaps the original basis for his identification with his created character.

character as a product of race, he apparently emphatically rejected that explanation in revision. Most of Joe's motivation for revenge has to do with his sense of wounded pride. Dr. Robinson's father had had Joe jailed for vagrancy. The widow Douglas's husband had also had Joe arrested for vagrancy, but Joe adds, "And that ain't all! It ain't all! It ain't a millionth part of it! He had me *horsewhipped*!—horsewhipped in front of the jail, like a nigger!—with all the town looking on! HORSEWHIPPED!—do you understand?" (*TS*, 208). Twain inserted this passage on the back of page 713 of the manuscript, and the punctuation alone (three dashes, the word *horsewhipped* in italics and all capitals, and seven exclamation points) signals the emphasis he wanted to give it.[23]

At bottom, Injun Joe's pride, his sense of what he owes himself, and the memory of public humiliation motivate him, not his Indian blood. Twain had moved beyond the facile racial bigotry concerning Native Americans he revealed in *Roughing It*. Joe's motives are different in degree but not in kind from Tom Sawyer's own desire to show off or to be the hero of his own life.[24] When he feels that he is not appreciated, Tom wants to make people sorry that they treated him so mean by running away, getting in trouble, or even dying (so long as he can attend the funeral). For all that, the reader is never tempted to believe Tom won't turn out well. After Tom testifies in court, he becomes a hero. Some in town thought Tom might "be President yet, if he escaped hanging" (*TS*, 173). Judge Thatcher comes to admire the boy and hopes to see Tom become a great lawyer or a great soldier some day, and he proposes to help him get there. Despite Aunt Polly's fretting, not for a moment does she actually believe that Tom's immortal soul is in peril or that she has been morally lax in her guardianship. She may assent to notions of innate depravity and eternal damnation

---

23. See *The Adventures of Tom Sawyer, a Facsimile of the Author's Holograph Manuscript*, with an introduction by Paul Baender, 2 vols. (Frederick, Md.: University Publications of America and Washington, D.C.: Georgetown University Library, 1982), ms. page 713. This insertion surely has some bearing on Twain's later treatment of the same subject in "Those Extraordinary Twins" and *Pudd'nhead Wilson*.

Twain had long-standing interests in the effects of shame upon human conduct. In a piece of futuristic science fiction he was contemplating, the author noted that public humiliation is a more effective deterrent to crime than capital punishment: in the future, they "changed hanging to insult, humiliation &c——Sense of ridicule is bitterer than death & more feared. . . . Hanging is not based on knowledge of human nature" (*N&J3*, 346–47).

24. Harry J. Brown, in *Injun Joe's Ghost: The Indian Mixed-Blood in American Writing* (Columbia: University of Missouri Press, 2004), 13–16, finds Injun Joe to be much more representative of the half-breed type found in the dime novels of the era.

when they issue from the pulpit on Sunday, but better instincts prevail in the household.

Aunt Polly announces her true estimate of the boy in chapter 15, when she thinks he is dead: "he warn't *bad*, so to say—only misch*ee*vous. Only just giddy, and harum-scarum, you know. He warn't any more responsible than a colt. *He* never meant any harm, and he was the best-hearted boy that ever was." Tom secretly witnesses the grieving of Aunt Polly and Mary, and he "began to have a nobler opinion of himself than ever before" (*TS*, 116). The reader has already formed these sorts of opinions of Tom because, despite his excesses, the boy's moral nature is recognizably sound. As Howells said in his review of the novel, Tom is "merely and exactly an ordinary boy on the moral side." But on the imaginative side "he is very much more, and though every boy has wild and fantastic dreams, this boy cannot rest till he has somehow realized them." Howells goes on, "The story is a wonderful study of the boy-mind, which inhabits a world quite distinct from that in which he is bodily present with his elders, and in this lies its great charm and its universality, for boy-nature, however human nature varies, is the same everywhere" (*Reviews*, 157–58).

The narrator specifies that Tom Sawyer is not the Model Boy in town; his very ordinariness spares him that affliction. In earlier tales, such as "The Christmas Fireside: The Story of the Bad Little Boy That Bore a Charmed Life" (1865), "The Story of the Good Little Boy Who Did Not Prosper" (1870), or "Poor Little Stephen Girard" (1873), Twain debunked the national myth that Providence rewards the good little boy and punishes the bad one. In *Tom Sawyer*, the title character may be unique in his frisky romanticism, but compared to many other boys in town he is a safe bet. Sid is a tattletale; Arthur Temple is a fop; the model boy, Will Mufferson, is a sycophant; and the poor boy "of German parentage," who once rattled off three thousand verses of scripture without stopping, became an idiot as a consequence. However, Tom's ordinary, which is to say his common, good nature and his harum-scarum ways are not necessarily commendable.

He is in thrall of the town's attention and regard. His preferred manner of courtship is to "show off"; he ostentatiously wears his pewter medal for achievement in reading and spelling and is sad to lose it when the distraction of Becky Thatcher causes him to misspell even "baby words"; and he aches for the red sash of the Cadets of Temperance and, once he has attained it, curses Judge Frazer for not dying in due season and allowing him to wear it at the public funeral. He is not above hoodwinking his friends in order to get out of work and depriving them of their prized possessions at the same time. Tom barters for the requisite number of blue and yellow tickets in order to get his Bible and Judge Thatcher's approval. He suffers from stage fright on Examination Day, but he is pleased with his own eloquence in his courtroom testimony against Injun Joe. Even when he contemplates leaving town and turning to a life of crime, he imagines with satisfaction that the town will one day "hear something" of "Tom Sawyer, the Black Avenger of the Spanish Main." One of his happiest moments is when he and Joe Harper and Huck Finn attend their own funeral, for he can rejoice in Aunt Polly's alternating cuffs and kisses all day long, "and he hardly knew which expressed the most gratefulness to God and affection for himself" (*TS*, 132).

As a case study, then, the character of Tom Sawyer may be representative of boy-nature but is hardly an idealization of youth. To reverse Oscar Wilde's witticism, boy-nature knows the value of everything and the price of nothing. Or rather, only a boy knows the going exchange rate for an apple core or a broken piece of blue glass. Was Tom's front tooth really worth Huck's tick, and the very first one of the season at that? Tom is ignorant of the cash nexus and cannot quite conceive how much, or even what is, the $12,000 and more that he and Huck retrieve from the cave. That does not really prevent Tom from putting on display certain primitive entrepreneurial talents, however. Boy-nature is covetous of the trifling rewards (certificates, medals, and sashes) adults offer up, so long as it is not troubled by the lessons (discipline, good behavior, or hard work) they were meant to teach. Boy-nature is capable of thrilling loves, great jealousies, and profound loneliness, but with a difference; these are not existential conditions but temporary "moods" or "phases." In the first chapter, Tom forgets his troubles "not because they were one whit less heavy and bitter to him than a man's are to a man, but because a new and powerful interest bore them down and drove them out of his mind for a time" (*TS*, 5). That interest is in his newfound ability to whistle. Tom is courageous and noble for taking the whipping that should have been Becky Thatcher's, but for a time at least he was ready to let Muff Potter be hanged for a murder Injun Joe committed.

What keeps Tom in the reader's affections and establishes his good nature is the periodic impingement of his conscience, and conscience, in its turn, reflects the boy's emotional and intellectual involvement in social relations. Unlike Injun Joe, who is proud but essentially antisocial, Tom desires the approbation of the world. The village of St. Petersburg, despite the failure of its institutions (such as school and church) to inculcate right feelings in the boy, has its claims upon him. One may attribute Twain's depiction of Tom's moral intuitions to the legacy of the Scottish Common Sense philosophers, as Gregg Camfield has done in *Sentimental Twain*;[25] one may decide that Tom has the sort of "social instincts" that Darwin thought were the foundation of the moral sense, in animals as well as human beings; or one may conclude that Clemens's remembrance of his own youth and his broad acquaintance with humankind were sufficient warrant for his depiction of Tom. At this point, it is enough to say that Twain's interest in the subject of conscience became deeper and more thoughtful soon after *Tom Sawyer* was published. It is more important, perhaps, to point out that Huckleberry Finn is something of a loner himself and has at best an uneven involvement in the boy-nature of Tom and his comrades; they may often be tormented by guilty feelings that do not affect Huck, who in many ways is "conscience-free" (*TS*, 104). But that is a subject for the next chapter.

VI

In January 1876, Twain wrote "The Facts Concerning the Recent Carnival of Crime in Connecticut," and it was published in the *Atlantic Monthly* the following June. From the beginning, the story was meant to make a serious point. Twain prepared the story for presentation to fellow members of the Monday Evening Club, a group of some twenty notable citizens of Hartford. His previous contributions to this discussion group were relatively proper productions, but with this story Twain meant to examine "an exasperating metaphysical question . . . in the disguise of a literary extravaganza."[26] The question had to do with the nature and function of conscience, and the metaphysical quality of the tale derived in large part from his recent reading in W. E. H. Lecky's *History of European Morals from Augustine to Charlemagne* (1869).

Lecky's book would exert a lifelong, though somewhat contradictory, influence upon Twain, who wrestled with and commented upon the book's argument in the margins of his copy. Lecky had divided the history of morals into two opposing camps—the intuitionists and the utilitarians. He advocated the intuitionist view that one's sense of good and evil is innate and harshly criticized the utilitarian position that denied an in-

25. See *Sentimental Twain: Samuel Clemens in the Maze of Moral Philosophy* (Philadelphia: University of Pennsylvania Press, 1994), 116–21.

26. Quoted in Gladys Bellamy, *Mark Twain as a Literary Artist* (Norman: University of Oklahoma Press, 1950), 135.

tuitive moral sense. He argued instead that one's feelings and actions do not depend on the degree to which they contribute to individual happiness. Twain was deeply ambivalent about Lecky's argument. On the whole, he leaned toward the utilitarian view, increasingly so in his later years, but seemed to agree with Lecky's view of conscience.

Howard Baetzhold observes that "A Carnival of Crime" "parallels Lecky's discussion almost exactly." Baetzhold nicely summarizes the historian's philosophical position:

> Conscience is more often a source of pain than of pleasure, and if happiness is actually the sole end of life, then one should learn to disregard the proddings of conscience. If a man forms an association of ideas that inflicts more pain than it prevents, or prevents more pleasure than it affords, the reasonable course would be to dissolve that association or destroy the habit. . . . Therefore, a man who possessed such a temperament would be happier if he were to "quench that conscientious feeling, which . . . prevents him from pursuing the course that would be most conducive to his tranquility."[27]

Twain's wry and antic story of a man who would kill (or "quench") his conscience was largely founded on Lecky's sardonic extension of the utilitarian argument, and the author's reading of the tale was duly appreciated by the Monday Evening Club. A few years later, Howells paid Twain a greater compliment in the pages of the *Century Magazine*, writing that the story "ought to have won popular recognition of the ethical intelligence underlying his humor. . . . Hawthorne or Bunyan might have been proud to imagine that powerful allegory" (*MMT*, 141).

The story is the work of a keen ethical intelligence, but one ought not overestimate its philosophical heft. When Twain identified the metaphysical question of conscience as "exasperating," he was registering his own annoyance with a nagging sense of guilt that had dogged him all his life—for he was temperamentally disposed to feel remorse and, sometimes, to claim responsibility for events he could not possibly have controlled or prevented. His tender feelings aside, Twain flatly rejected John Milton's Calvinist explanation of the divine benefits of conscience. In *Paradise Lost*, God announces his moral blueprint for humankind:

> And I will place within them as a guide,
> My umpire Conscience; whom if they will hear,

---

27. *Mark Twain and John Bull: The British Connection* (Bloomington: Indiana University Press, 1970), 57–58.

Light after light, well us'd, they shall attain,
And to the end, persisting, safe arrive.

When Twain confessed that the question he meant to address was disguised as a "literary extravaganza," he was reaffirming a humorist's customary allegiance to hyperbole and incongruity, however grotesque a turn the tale might take, not so much to make light of a serious matter as to make its painful gravity endurable.

The story opens with the narrator lighting a cigar, feeling "blithe, almost jocund." Ever since the narrator became immune to his Aunt Mary's nagging, particularly about his smoking, "the one alloy that was able to mar my enjoyment of my aunt's society was gone" and her visits have become a "tranquil satisfaction" (*CTSS1*, 644). In other words, conscience in the form of external influence, symbolized by the aunt, has already been defeated before the story ever begins, but the narrator's lies to tramps and budding authors still trouble him a bit. Unlike Aunt Mary, the mossy and misshapen dwarf appears to be an internal agent whose perverse business is to torture the narrator for no other purpose than the satisfaction of it.

Through a series of cagey maneuvers, the narrator manages to kill this figure, this "dim suggestion of a burlesque upon me, a caricature of me in little" (*CTSS1*, 645). The dwarf is, of course, the narrator's conscience, and his death brings "Bliss, unalloyed bliss" (*CTSS1*, 660), though this contentment is rather different from the earlier tranquil satisfaction. The difference between these two states of happiness has little to do with any profound distinction Twain was trying to make between an intuitionist's or a utilitarian's view of conscience. This brassy dwarf does not appear as a recognizable moral sense in any of the manifold shapes that might take—a Quaker inner light, a Calvinistic reminder of innate depravity, a Poesque imp of the perverse, a Jeffersonian "generous spasm of the heart," or a Kantian categorical imperative. Instead, the dwarf is a nuisance and a trial, and Gregg Camfield has provocatively suggested that Twain may have decided that conscience has little or nothing to do with a moral sense at all.

The conscience, Twain seems to be saying, checks our basest impulses by making us agonize and worry but not by mending our flawed human nature, and the toll it takes is worn on the face and experienced in the vitals. The narrator observes that once he had destroyed his conscience, he was free to indulge in his grotesque and whimsical carnival of crime. Since that day, he has been on a delicious rampage: I have committed "scores of crimes of various kinds," he says, "and have enjoyed my work exceedingly, whereas it would have formerly broken my heart and turned my hair gray" (*CTSS1*, 660). Although the social consequences of loosing a man without a conscience upon the world are both funny and disturbing, Twain betrays little interest in determining the ontological nature of conscience or its spiritual function. The middle part of the story is an interrogation of the repulsive figure, but the little man is obscure and evasive and the narrator's questions remain unanswered. If the story poses a metaphysical question, the answer remains a surly and grotesque mystery. The relation between the narrator and his conscience is identified as one between a slave and a master, and the dwarf's proud mastery is as cryptic, dismissive, and tyrannically cruel as he pleases it to be.

"The Facts Concerning the Recent Carnival of Crime in Connecticut" is not really a metaphysical inquiry at all. And as autobiographical as the story sometimes is, it is not solely expressive of Twain's feelings of restraint and regret. Most of the narrator's concerns in the tale have to do with comparative judgments. He accepts the information from his conscience that Robinson and Smith's consciences are taller and more comely than the hideous dwarf that stands before him, and he is willing to believe that his Aunt Mary's conscience "lives in the open air altogether, because no door is large enough to admit her" (*CTSS1*, 657). But he is gratified to know that Hugh Thompson's conscience is a small, misshapen figure who sleeps in a cigar box, and he is absolutely delighted to learn that the conscience of a publisher who once cheated him was put on exhibit under a powerful microscope, though the curious still could not see him.

In other words, the narrator is primarily motivated by a local sense of self-esteem; he measures himself against his neighbors and relatives. His place within the great chain of consciences is a middling one, with a few below him and several above him. The real tyranny of conscience, however, is that he will forever be equally reminded of past sins alongside courteous lies and forgivable misjudgments, for a conscience seems to have no sense of proportion. "Every sentence was an accusation, and every accusation a truth," he recalls. "Every clause was freighted with sarcasm and derision, every slow-dropping word burned like vitriol" (*CTSS1*, 648). Nothing so disturbs the narrator, however, as the awful prospect that the dwarf will continually remind him of himself. The dwarf's pertinacity makes the narrator indignant because it is an "exaggeration of conduct which I myself had sometimes been guilty of in my intercourse with familiar friends" (*CTSS1*, 645). Here in germ is the basis for Twain's later philosophizing. In "Corn Pone Opinions," for example, he locates the universal impulse to conform in the "inborn requirement of Self-Approval" (*CTSS2*, 508), but the source of one's self-esteem always comes from the outside, from the approval of other people. However, it would be a mistake to view the "Carnival of Crime" as a prolegomenon to the fiction and essays belonging to the period of the author's supposed darker cynicism. The story might more accurately be described as an apologia for the humorist as citizen and moralist.

When he delivered this piece before the Monday Evening Club, Twain deliberately engaged in a form of self-mockery and self-accusation that included a satire of the very drawl that club members were hearing as he read it. He intentionally made himself foolish and vulnerable in this story, but the dwarf wields the same weapons that the humorist keeps in his arsenal—burlesque, satire, exaggeration, and caricature. The dwarf of conscience merely holds up the altered and grotesque but still recognizable image of the man and makes his shortcomings comically obvious. Although the dwarf is invisible to everyone but the narrator, his very being is implicated in the social order. Insofar as the narrator's conscience works in concert with other consciences to harass their victims, and because Twain's conscience has become deformed according to his own diminished conduct in a world of living men and women, this comedy is rooted in social community. As a citizen, Samuel Clemens accepted his part in that community and took a vital, if sometimes haphazard and eccentric, interest in the laws, policies, and attitudes that regulate the national life. As a humorist, however, he was much like the dwarf, a disinterested agent who merely exaggerates existing transgressions and absurdities in order to make us see them more clearly and feel them more completely. Twain had expressed in the coordinated strategies of his humor a willingness to play the fool for virtue's sake and to serve as the compromised accomplice to a nation's transgressions and folly. He freely acknowledged his guilty place in the social order, even though that same society had fixed him as a mere humorist. But he was proud, too, and that pride was most eloquent in his sly insistence that, like Aunt Rachel and despite appearances, he was not simply jolly but serious too, not exceptional but representative. Publicly, Twain was willing to play the part of an ass, but privately he might console himself with the pert observation of a dwarf—"I am not an ass; I am only the saddle of an ass" (*CTSS1*, 654).

Clearly, the issues Twain pondered in this tale have a bearing upon *Adventures of Huckleberry Finn*; or rather, an episode he had already dramatized in the novel may have influenced his thinking in the "Carnival of Crime." He had begun writing "Huckleberry Finn's Autobiography" in the summer of 1876 and had gotten to the middle of chapter 18 before he pigeonholed the manuscript. In 1895, Twain recalled that Huck's first bout with his conscience in chapter 16 represented a contest between a "sound heart" and a "deformed conscience" and that "conscience suffers defeat." This is a subject we will explore more minutely and more carefully later on. For now it is enough to say that Huck Finn, who is relatively "conscience free" in *Tom Sawyer*, is largely exempt from the keener pangs of remorse. If Huck belongs to any community it is to a "community of misfortune" he shares with a runaway slave.[28] Because he is a social pariah, Huck is essentially insulated against the sort of public humiliation that might drive Injun Joe to violent retribution or Laura Hawkins to the grave. Twain had rather bravely subjected himself to public embarrassment in "A True Story," and he had sardonically described the feelings of shame he felt under the gaze of an accusing conscience, but these were self-inflicted instances of chagrin over which he had artistic control. This was not the case with the aftermath to his "Whittier Birthday Speech" delivered on December 17, 1877.

Howells had arranged for Clemens to make an after-dinner speech on the occasion of John Greenleaf Whittier's seventieth birthday, in the presence of Boston's literary elite. This speech about Twain trying out the virtue of his nom de plume on a lonely California miner was an amusing and gracious way of affirming the humorist's pleasure, and his right, to be in the company of New England's literary worthies. The miner recalls to Twain three men who had claimed to be Emerson, Longfellow, and Oliver Wendell Holmes. These ruffians ate the miner's food, drank his whiskey, and, in the end, stole his boots. The comedy of this exquisite little speech, as Twain and Howells somewhat inaccurately remembered it, was largely lost on the dinner guests, who remained quizzically and courteously silent.[29] Howells thought the speech a "hideous mistake," a "fatality," an offense that might eventually be repaired but carrying with it a shame that could not be outlived. Critical newspaper notices seemed to confirm Howells's perception. Twain was humiliated and wrote notes of apology to Longfellow, Emerson, and Holmes, protesting the innocence of his intent and at the same time describing himself as a heedless "savage." On December 23, Twain wrote Howells, "My sense of disgrace does not abate. It grows. I see that it is going to add itself to my list of perma-

28. Quoted in Walter Blair, *Mark Twain and Huck Finn* (Berkeley: University of California Press, 1960), 143.

29. For a discussion of this speech and its cultural significance for Twain, Howells, and others, see Harold K. Bush Jr., "The Mythic Struggle between East and West: Mark Twain's Speech at Whittier's 70th Birthday Celebration and W. D. Howells's *A Chance Acquaintance*," *American Literary Realism* 27, no. 2 (Winter 1995): 53–73.

nencies—a list of humiliations that extends back to when I was seven years old, & which keep on persecuting me regardless of my repentancies" (*MTHL*, 1:212). Twain concluded that it "will be best that I retire from before the public at present." In fact Twain did retire from the scene. Though he had planned the trip beforehand, when he took the family to Germany the next April, the journey had the quality of guilty escape. This was an inauspicious beginning to the 1880s, a period that would see the publication of some of his finest work—*Life on the Mississippi, Adventures of Huckleberry Finn,* and *A Connecticut Yankee in King Arthur's Court.*

Chapter Three

I

The first explicit mention of *Huckleberry Finn* occurs in a letter to W. D. Howells dated August 9, 1876:

> I . . . began another boys' book—more to be at work than anything else. I have written 400 pages on it—therefore it is very nearly half done. It is Huck Finn's Autobiography. I like it only tolerably well, as far as I have got, & may possibly pigeonhole or burn the MS when it is done. (*MTHL*, 1:144)[1]

Not long after this date, Twain stopped writing Huck's "Autobiography," and at a curious point in the narrative. The manuscript discloses that on the manuscript page 446, or halfway into chapter 18, Twain stopped at that point in the novel where Huck asks Buck Grangerford:

1. In two separate letters previous to the one sent to Howells—one to Moncure Conway dated August 1, 1876, and the other to Mary Mason Fairbanks dated August 4, 1876—Twain mentioned his progress on a "new book," and this was almost certainly *Huckleberry Finn*.

"What's a feud?"

"Why where was you raised? Don't you know what a feud is?"

"Never heard of it before—tell me about it." (*HF*, 146)

Twain's decision to quit writing at this point is perplexing because the author knew perfectly well what a feud is. His hesitation probably derived in part from the vagueness of his memory of the Darnell-Watson feud he had heard about when he was on the river,[2] and it may have had something to do with a certain unsureness about how he meant to satirize this primitive and barbarous tradition. Huck's dismay about the feud is consistent with his character and his upbringing, since notions of revenge, honor, and aristocracy (misguided or otherwise) are essentially foreign to his experience. But Huck's confusion about the folkways of the well-to-do could provide the author with an entering wedge for a satiric means to condemn the practice, as it already had in his satire of Emmeline Grangerford's "crayons" and poetry. Huck of course is ignorant of feuds and feuders, but Twain may have also felt that he himself did not yet fully comprehend the crude and vengeful aristocratic mentality that fostered and perpetuated a violent institution so obviously self-destructive, possibly even insane. What is there in human nature that would permit, even encourage, people to embark on and to sustain such hurtful practices?

Curious, too, in this letter to Howells is Twain's description of his work in progress as something of an idle amusement ("more to be at work than anything else") and the declaration that he might in any event burn or pigeonhole the manuscript when he was done. There is no reason to dispute this claim, however. Because *Adventures of Huckleberry Finn* looms so large in Twain's corpus, there is the tendency and temptation to see those works that precede it as somehow tributary influences to his masterpiece. This is a perfectly legitimate line of inquiry, and one I mean to follow in the next chapter. The novel's genesis, however, suggests that, for the author, in the early going this narrative had neither commercial nor especially artistic possibilities. If he finished it at all, the novel was destined for the file cabinet or the fireplace, but not for the public.

For the moment, it is worthwhile to take Twain at his word that his work on Huck's "Autobiography" filled his time in an agreeable way. His statements to Moncure Conway that he was "booming along" and to Mary Ma-

---

2. The most instructive analysis of the feud chapters is *The Grangerford-Shepherdson Feud* by Edgar Marquess Branch and Robert Hirst (Berkeley: Friends of the Bancroft Library, University of California, 1985).

son Fairbanks that he was "tearing along" in the writing of the book indicate both Twain's happy involvement in the project and that the work
was stimulating to him, but they do not predict his masterpiece or even
indicate a deep commitment to this work in progress.[3] Perhaps a carefree
attitude toward his material, or at least a happy indifference to prevailing
taste and the requirements of publication and marketing, cultivated in the
author certain innovative and experimental talents that might otherwise
have lain dormant. This was the case with William Faulkner when he began *The Sound and the Fury.* That was to be a book, Faulkner assumed, that
would surely be rejected by his publisher; ironically, his very defiance of
literary convention in that novel resulted in a greater mastery of his craft.[4]
Similarly, Emily Dickinson's poetry almost certainly would have been diminished had she written for publication, that "Auction of the Mind" as
the poet would have it. And Twain himself said about Samuel Pepys's *Diary* that it was a "miracle of candor," though he added that "even Pepys
wrote with the consciousness that his contemporaries were looking over
his shoulder."[5] In later years, Twain tried different ways to escape the felt
scrutiny of his own contemporaries—publishing works anonymously,
writing pieces he did not intend to publish or letters he would never send,
or, as in his "Autobiography," launching into a work that could never be
completed and that was addressed to a readership not yet born. In these
several instances, he was attempting to find a way to speak the plain truth
without timidity or restraint, and that same freedom of view may have
entered into the early stages of Huck's autobiography.

In any event, the point of view Twain chose for his novel in progress
was not simply a matter of stylistic innovation but also a position from
which to regard and to unself-consciously assess existing institutions and
cultural influences. Huck's ignorance is often the reader's insight. If Huck
has not been inoculated against each and every one of the contaminating
influences of civilized life, he has kept clear of the more virulent forms of
the viruses that perpetuate themselves from one generation to the next. I
use the word *virus* deliberately. Richard Dawkins speaks of "memes" as
cultural forms of replication that are at least analogous to computer viruses and to DNA reproduction. The spread and replication of scientific ideas
are generally beneficial, he argues, because they are subjected to a certain

3. Quoted in the "Introduction" to *HF,* 678.
4. In that, he was imitating Hemingway, who had written *The Torrents of Spring* with
the intention of finding a way to break with his publisher, Boni and Liveright.
5. Alan Gribben, *Mark Twain's Library: A Reconstruction,* 2 vols. (Boston: G. K Hall,
1980), 2:540.

process of assessment that involves consistency, testability, evidentiary support, independence of cultural milieu, and the like; in other words, they are at once underwritten by an enlightenment notion of right reason and a Darwinian notion of natural selection.[6]

Other kinds of cultural reproduction (religious faith is Dawkins's particular bugbear) spread without reference to any of those standards of scientific or rational inquiry; they spread epidemiologically. In fact "epidemiology is the root cause" for religious faith, he says, because the cultural memes that go into religious dogma (ritual, unquestioned authority, doctrine, and so on) are imposed upon naive young boys and girls and as a consequence not subjected to rational debate, rules of evidence, or even mature understanding. One might say that the blood feud between the Grangerfords and the Sheperdsons has developed in this way; certainly Buck Grangerford has formed rigid opinions about the matter from a very early age, though his explanations do not make sense to Huck or to us as readers. The same epidemiological process applies to the many other forms of stupid self-destruction that Twain examines in literary terms in the books of the 1880s—student duels, obligatory veneration of opera and the "Old Masters," cruel laws and crazy notions of evidence, superstition and legend, unhygienic burial practices, and a host of other tendencies and activities, including mountain climbing, which Twain viewed as a peculiar form of insanity.

But there is yet another reason that adopting Huck's point of view was so stimulating and important to Twain. Huck's mean position in St. Petersburg society and Twain's imaginative grasp of what that might entail for a young boy of his temperament comes close to a fictional form of what Roger Shattuck describes as the "forbidden experiment." In his book about a feral child who came out of the forest in southern France in 1800 and became known as the Wild Boy of Aveyron, Shattuck identifies the cultural significance of a human being who lived apart from superintending cultural influences:

> What I call the forbidden experiment is one that reveals to us what "human nature" really is beneath the overlays of society and culture. Or at least an experiment that could tell us if there is any such thing as human nature apart from culture and individual heredity.
>
> If we believe people are basically selfish, untrustworthy, and aggressive, then we should favor a fairly strict set of constraints and laws to regulate behavior

6. See *The Selfish Gene* (New York: Oxford University Press, 1976).

and protect us from one another. If we believe people are peaceful and cooperative under favorable conditions (as the system of democracy assumes), then we should create for every individual as much freedom as possible from outward constraints. But we have been unable to prove or even accept either position. We remain uneasy in our estimate of ourselves.[7]

The appearance of a child who had somehow grown up outside the constraints or freedoms accorded socialized beings provided the opportunity for naturalists and philosophers to make a study of the boy but also to draw broader conclusions about human nature in general. Indeed, the child was of particular interest to the "Society of Observers of Man" (obviously a French institution), for here was an experimental human subject who was apparently incubated in the laboratory of nature.

Such an experiment is "forbidden" (at least to the modern sensibility) because it would require inhumanly separating an infant from any kind of social communication or interaction in order to discover what linguistic, intellectual, or moral traits, if any, might develop in a state of nature. The prospect is of course barbarous, but, Shattuck tells us, that did not prevent the Egyptian Pharaoh Psamtik, the Holy Roman Emperor Frederick II, or James IV of Scotland from attempting the experiment. None of these men was interested in reforming society on the basis of an improved idea about human nature, of course; they were principally interested in whether such a child would develop speech and what language (presumably also the language of God) the child would speak.[8] But from the Enlightenment on, there were other reasons to be interested in the conclusions one might draw from such an experiment. If one dismisses or discounts the biblical account of human nature as essentially fallen and depraved (as Locke had done when he defined the infant as a tabula rasa whose identity is constructed of accumulating sense impressions and a psychology of association), then the influences of existing political or social institutions, as well as those that might be established, have a particularly important relation to "man in a state of nature." What is more, the question of the moral nature of human beings, so fundamental to any conception of civil authority, might be settled by closely attending to the be-

7. *The Forbidden Experiment: The Story of the Wild Boy of Aveyron* (New York: Washington Square Press, 1981), 41–42.

8. Shattuck notes that Michel de Montaigne contemplated the same issue: "I believe that a child brought up in complete solitude, far from all intercourse . . . , would have some kind of speech to express his ideas, for it is not likely that nature would deprive us of this resource when she has given it to many other animals" (ibid., 44).

havior and intellectual progress of the feral child. This was a question meant exclusively for white Europeans; non-Europeans, it was generally held, had diminished possibilities, and some, such as pygmies, were ruled not human at all.

Huckleberry Finn is not a feral child, of course. He had a mother and has in Pap something that passes for a father; and he had always been exposed to, though also neglected by, the community. Nevertheless, we know from his reading that Twain was interested in the "uncivilized races" and "primitive man." To the extent that he was an advocate of "progress" (political, technological, moral, and other) and a believer in "civilization," he would necessarily be interested in the efficacy of these social forces. There is no concrete evidence that Twain read or even was intrigued by studies of feral children, however. He did know enough of the case of the castaway Alexander Selkirk, who was marooned on the island of Juan Fernandez for four years, to reassure one of his readers that Selkirk did not discover America, and he acquired J. Ross Browne's *Crusoe's Island: A Ramble in the Footsteps of Alexander Selkirk; with Sketches of Adventure in California and Washoe* (1864) shortly after it was published. In later years, Clemens took an eager and affectionate interest in the case of Helen Keller, who in her silent, dark world was as isolated and (before Anne Sullivan tamed her) as wild as any feral child. In 1896, Clemens wrote the wife of Standard Oil executive Henry H. Rogers, proposing a fund that would permit Keller to attend college and to continue her studies. He assured Mrs. Rogers, "If she [Keller] can go on with them she will make a fame that will endure in history for centuries. Along her special lines she is the most extraordinary product of all the ages" (*Letters*, 2:638). It is difficult to imagine what her "special lines" might be, other than as a remarkably successful example of the sort of linguistic, intellectual, and moral growth attempted and hoped for in other children who had been similarly deprived of formative civilizing influences. And how was Clemens to know that she was "extraordinary" without some reference to other cases of her sort?

Several published studies of feral children were available to him. Jean-Marc Itard's account of the wild boy of Aveyron was published as *De l'éducation d'un homme sauvage* (1801) and appeared in an 1802 English translation as *An Historical Account of the Discovery and Education of a Savage Man, or of the First Developments, Physical and Moral, of the Young Savage Caught in the Woods Near Aveyron, in the Year 1798*. An equally famous case of a fourteen-year-old feral child was that of Peter of Hanover. Discovered in a German forest in 1723, the boy was christened Peter and taken to England, under the protection of George I, and became there something of curiosity and a celebrity. Daniel Defoe wrote of him in "Mere Nature Delineated" (1726); Jonathan Swift went to view the boy and what he saw seems to have influenced his depiction of the Yahoos in *Gulliver's Travels*. Rousseau refers to Peter and several comparable instances in his *Discourse on the Origin and Foundation of Inequality* (1755). Clemens had more immediate access to a succinct account of Peter the Wild Boy in a book he acquired in 1870, Henry Wilson's *Wonderful Characters; Comprising Memoirs and Anecdotes of the Most Remarkable Persons of Every Age and Nation. Collected from the Most Authentic Sources.* (1854).[9] The story of a seventeen-year-old boy who one day in 1828 appeared on the streets of Nuremberg, Germany, with a letter requesting he be put in the cavalry also excited great interest—partly because he could not speak but evidently had some human contact during his childhood and made relatively good progress in his education thereafter. A firsthand account of his case by Anselm von Feuerbach was published in English translation as *Caspar Hauser, or, The power of External Circumstances Exhibited in Forming the Human Character: With Remarks by John Green* (1834).

At best, this list of titles provides circumstantial evidence that Clemens might have been acquainted with one or another case of the discovery and subsequent observation of a young boy in a "natural" state. Rousseau insisted that man in a primitive (or natural) state is not a savage: "On the contrary, nothing is so gentle as man in his primitive state when, placed by nature at equal distances from the stupidity of brutes and the fatal enlightenment of civil man, and limited equally by instinct and reason to protecting himself from the harm that threatens him, he is restrained by natural pity from harming anyone himself, and nothing leads him to do so even after he has received harm. For according to the axiom of the wise Locke, *where there is no property, there is no injury*."[10] This passage may say absolutely nothing about Twain's intention, but it does nicely identify Huck's precarious position—poised, as he is, between the brutality of Pap and the fatal moral "improvements" of the widow and Miss Watson. And it is perhaps worth noting that when Huck sees his father's footprint in the snow, he marches straight to Judge Thatcher's to get rid of his property, immediately recognizing that his six thousand dollars is the sole cause for Pap's return. For his part, Pap, in the mood of wounded indig-

9. See Gribben, *Mark Twain's Library*, 2:777.
10. Jean-Jacques Rousseau, *The First and Second Discourses* (New York: St. Martin's Press, 1964), 150.

nation, inveighs against the "govment" and other forms of authority for depriving him of "his" property.[11] It is also true that Huck hasn't an ounce of vengeance in him; he even feels pity for the duke and dauphin when he sees them tarred and feathered and being ridden out of town on a rail. In a sense, though, none of this really matters. That is to say, I am not making an argument for any of these cases as the source or influence for the creation of Huckleberry Finn.

What does matter is that by choosing to narrate his story from the point of view of a child who had not been extensively shaped by cultural influences, he was also, willy-nilly, choosing a subject that was freighted with significance. Knowingly or unknowingly, Twain outfitted himself with the means to inquire into some portion of human nature. Because Huck was largely exempted from civilizing or brutalizing influences (at least when he was not under the care or subjugation of the widow or his pap), the boy reflected an unaffected portion of human nature. But Twain also gave himself the latitude to examine, through Huck, what the effect of those socializing and coercive influences might be upon others. In short, Twain, as with so many realist writers, conceived of his narrative as something of a pragmatic testing in which the author posited a set of given circumstances and imagined how a person of such and such a temperament might realistically behave under those conditions.[12] Huck's particular situation was at least distinctive. History, etiquette, salvation, other nations and other languages, economics, aristocratic privilege, and many other things were sufficiently mysterious for him to ask fundamental questions or make uninformed but still telling commentary about them.

Huckleberry Finn is not the "restless analyst" Henry James pictured himself to be in *The American Scene,* but he is, almost in spite of himself, a keen observer of manners and mores. To overstate the case, Huck occupies that realm of disinterestedness and commonsense realism where neither the prepossessions nor, ideally, even the presence of the observer interferes with judgments or reports on observed phenomena. One of the reasons this is an overstatement has to do with Huck's own situation. He is not embarked on a fact-finding expedition in the Mississippi River Val-

11. Needless to say, Jim, too, is property—as a runaway slave he is stolen goods and Huck is his abettor. This is an aspect of Huck's so-called moral dilemma that is related to but by no means identical with questions of slavery or racism.

12. Henry James's *The American,* William Dean Howells's *The Rise of Silas Lapham,* Stephen Crane's *The Red Badge of Courage,* and Edith Wharton's *The House of Mirth* follow this pattern. So, in a different way, does Rudyard Kipling's *The Jungle Book,* which may owe something to the example of *Huckleberry Finn.*

ley; he is on the run. In fact, insofar as the novel is a chronicle of Huck's "adventures," most of his exploits have to do with getting out of scrapes and getting shed of people. On the other hand, with some regularity Huck has privileged (which is to say, undetected) access to the customs of people along the river. He peeks through the bushes to watch as the riverboat searches for his body; he hides behind a barrel and reports on the boasts and naughty songs of the raftsmen; he eavesdrops on the villainous threats and pleadings of the scoundrels on board the *Walter Scott*;[13] he is hiding in a tree when he sees Buck Grangerford killed; and he scurries behind the closet curtain to listen to the plans the duke and dauphin have for defrauding the Wilks girls. Even when he is visible, Huck blends into the crowd without noise or notice, as in his "good place at the window," where he watches Boggs breathe his last, or as an inconspicuous part of the audience at the circus. Huck serves as a spectator, then, and given all that he has seen of the criminal stupidity and cruelty along the river, he should not have resolved to go out to the Indian Territory at the end. Instead, he should have been put in the witness protection program.

When Huck is not in hiding, he is incognito, claiming to be George Jackson, Charles William Albright (later corrected to Aleck Hopkins), Sarah Mary Williams (aka George Peters), and of course Tom Sawyer. This maneuver may be the result of simple prudence on Huck's part, but Twain seems to have regarded it as a "method" as well. In chapter 20 of *Life on the Mississippi*, Twain revisits the Mississippi after a twenty-year absence: "As I proposed to make notes, with a view to printing, I took some thought as to methods of procedure. I reflected that if I were recognized on the river, I should not be as free to go and come, talk, inquire, and spy around, as I should be if unknown . . . so I concluded that, from a business point of view, it would be an advantage to disguise our party with fictitious names." But he has trouble remembering what name he has recently adopted: "The idea was certainly good, but it bred infinite bother; for although Smith, Jones, and Johnson are easy names to remember when there is no occasion to remember them, it is next to impossible to recollect them when they are wanted. How do criminals keep an *alias* in mind?" (*LOM*, 167). This is one of many instances in which Twain drew upon the perhaps never to be completed manuscript of *Huckleberry Finn* for inspiration.

13. This episode was written in 1883 and interpolated into that portion of the manuscript composed in 1876; nevertheless it follows a pattern that applies in the first half of the novel.

The gestation of *Huckleberry Finn*, in the words of Henry Nash Smith, reveals a "dialectal interplay" in the author, a process in which "the reach of his imagination imposed a constant strain on his technical resources, and innovations of method in turn opened up new vistas before his imagination."[14] Smith's insight need not be restricted to *Huckleberry Finn*, however; or, rather, the "innovations of method" and the "new vistas" he discovered in writing Huck's story also spilled over into other books he was working on during the same period. Huck's "Autobiography" would eventually be published, but the immediate beneficiaries of Twain's imaginative experiment were the books of the early 1880s: *A Tramp Abroad* (1880), *The Prince and the Pauper* (1881) and *Life on the Mississippi* (1883). A brief (and merely partial) inventory of the resemblances (techniques, episodes, subject matter, attitudes, and so forth), both trivial and substantial, is suggestive of how liberally Twain filched from the completed portions of *Huckleberry Finn*. My purpose in giving such an inventory, to anticipate a later argument, is to assert (without really insisting on the point) that, by looking on life through the lens of Huckleberry Finn, Twain outfitted himself with a fresh way to observe human nature.

Huck is unencumbered, more or less, by the effects of training or the claims of social standing upon him, and, perhaps, he is even free of at least the nastier impingements of conscience. Because Huck has few preconceptions about civilized life (excepting that basic and biased preconception about the natural inferiority of African Americans shared by rich and poor whites alike), his very ignorance often exposes the absurdities of customs and institutions. On the other hand, because Huck has had to fend for himself, he knows how to get out of a bad situation, and he knows how to read character. These are matters to return to when we look at *Huckleberry Finn* directly; for the moment it is enough to say that the manuscript of the uncompleted novel served as a reservoir for scenes and insights that could be put to use in various ways and serve other purposes.

II

The same summer Twain began writing *Huckleberry Finn*, he was reading in English history with an eye toward writing a story of changelings that might also serve as a satire of British aristocracy. After additional reading and intermittent stints of writing, as well as turning his attention

14. *Mark Twain: The Development of a Writer* (New York: Atheneum, 1967), 113.

to other projects (including writing and publishing *A Tramp Abroad*), *The Prince and the Pauper* was published in 1881. In *Mark Twain and Huck Finn*, Walter Blair has itemized most of the parallels between that book and the completed portion of the *Huck Finn* manuscript. Some of them are incidental, such as Huck and Tom Canty's struggling to suppress scratching an itchy nose or a sixteenth-century reveler singing a sanitized version of the song sung by the raftsmen in chapter 16. Other resemblances are more substantive.

In his wanderings, Edward encounters a mad hermit who believes himself to be an archangel. Even so, the hermit is not satisfied and has his complaint against the government, for had it not been for Edward's father, Henry VIII, the hermit believes he would have been pope. Similarly, Pap rails against the "govment" for taking his son away from him and failing to recognize his rights as a white male, but mostly for the six thousand dollars that he believes is rightfully his. And both men resolve to exact a holy vengeance on the boys. In one of Twain's satiric inversions, the men act in the manner of Abraham and mean to kill the boys with a knife in sacrificial fashion.[15] Neither of course is compelled by divine authority; instead they are enraged by a sense of being ill-used by political authority. Surely there was an inside joke involved when Twain created a murderously insane hermit who scourges his body, eats crumbs, and drinks nothing but water and had him re-create the part of Pap, a filthy man clothed in rags, but not for reasons of self-mortification, and who lives for and may well live on forty-rod whiskey. In any event, in dramatic terms, the way up is the way down; the hermit's lunatic piety and Pap's delirium tremens amount to the same thing.

More fundamental are the resemblances of Tom Canty's situation and temperament to Huck Finn's. Both are poverty-stricken and have abusive brutes for fathers; both are made uncomfortable by the constraints of civilized life—the discomfort of doublet or starched collar or the ceremonial fastidiousness at table and toilet contribute to their vexation. Both boys have an innate sympathy that cries out against cruelty and injustice, and this basic goodness of heart often combines with a native shrewdness that derives from making one's way in an indifferent world.

Tom Canty's adventures in opulence may derive something from Huck's experience at the Grangerford plantation. Huck is impressed by

15. In light of Twain's persistent interest in and somewhat vacillating opinions about the insanity defense, it is perhaps of some interest that had either man succeeded in killing a boy, the act would have been defensible as an act of insanity—temporary in the case of Pap, rather more permanent it appears in the case of the hermit.

the chalk fruit and chalk parrots, the brass doorknobs and turkey-wing fans; and he is assigned his personal slave, "who had a monstrous easy time, because I warn't used to having anybody do anything for me" (*HF*, 143). Likewise, Tom marvels at the riches, food, and clothing, as well as the servants who taste his food, take his whippings, dress him, and attend to his every need, whether he needs it or not. But these are merely attitudes toward altered circumstance, and it is the changed environment that, however momentarily, works changes in the boy. Gladys Bellamy probably overstates the case when she says that Tom sinks into a "slothful enjoyment of the splendors that surround him. Finally he sinks into a corrupt resignation."[16] Nevertheless, unlike the adult who is a rigid compound of stultifying habits, Tom possesses the "child's facility in accommodating itself to circumstances" (*P&P*, 181). Before long,

> He came to enjoy being conducted to bed in state, at night, and dressed with intricate and solemn ceremony in the morning. It came to be a proud pleasure to march to dinner attended by a glittering procession of officers of state and Gentlemen-at-Arms. . . . He enjoyed his splendid clothes and ordered more; he found his four hundred servants too few for his proper grandeur, and trebled them. The adulation of salaaming courtiers came to be sweet music to his ears. (*P&P*, 295–96)

At length, Tom concluded that "the one thing worth living for in this world was to be a king, and a nation's idol" (*P&P*, 301). The seduction of public approval contributes its measure to the vilest of Tom's acts, the denial of his own mother, who approaches him in the street during the royal procession. The sting of his conscience instantly "consumed his pride to ashes and withered his stolen royalty" (*P&P*, 305). Tom regains his sympathy for the poor and abused who suffer under unjust laws and gratuitous cruelty and does what he can to ameliorate the severity of those laws.

Edward Tudor learns a different set of lessons. The young and prideful prince, as is to be expected, is not so quick to adjust to his situation as Tom Canty; he has a stubborn attachment to his birth and station that the commoners mistake for lunacy. Still, his exposure to the sinister effects of royal laws softens him, and the protective and affectionate gestures of Miles Hendon acquaint him with a different sort of nobility than that conferred

16. *Mark Twain as a Literary Artist* (Norman: University of Oklahoma Press, 1950), 310.

in the royal court. In an alien natural landscape, immensely indifferent to his royal bearing, the boy "stood solitary, companionless, in the centre of measureless solitude" (*P&P,* 209). In the great scheme of things, a lonely prince has little to brag about and less to amuse him. Alone and friendless, he soon discovers that to sleep cuddled up beside a calf made him as "warm and comfortable as he had ever been in the down couches of the regal palace of Westminster" (*P&P,* 212). Later, in mock coronation of an obviously crazed boy, the band of tramps crowns him with a tin basin and names him "Foo-foo the First, King of the Mooncalves." The jubilant mockery brings tears of "shame and indignation" to the little king's eyes (*P&P,* 219). Likewise, when Miles Hendon insists on taking the stripes meant for the boy, Edward says to himself: "Who saves his prince from wounds and possible death . . . performs high service; but it is little . . . when 'tis weighed against the act of him who saves his prince from SHAME!" (*P&P,* 287). Such pangs of regret as Edward is capable of spring chiefly from a sense of injured merit; nowhere does the boy betray the faintest twinge of conscience.

In a scene reminiscent of Huck's viewing Buck Grangerford's killing, the prince is appalled by the burning of the Baptist women and says, "I shall see it all the days, and dream of it all the nights, till I die. Would God I had been blind!" (*PP,* 283). When he learns of the lawyer's maiming and fines for writing a pamphlet against injustice, Edward concludes, "the world is made wrong; kings should go to school to their own laws, at times, to learn mercy" (*PP,* 284). These remarks indicate the basic soundness of the king's heart and an enlargement of his sympathies, but they do not suggest a felt complicity in the injustices he has witnessed. If he is not the author of unjust laws, as a Tudor he is manifestly responsible for them. Minimally, he should have felt some shame for the sake of his father, Henry VIII, who imposed them. Miles Hendon takes the lashes meant for Edward, but the boy does not feel remorse. He dubs Miles an earl in gratitude, but, so far as we know, Edward makes no connection between that event and the whipping boy back in the palace who has routinely taken the prince's punishment. As Walter Blair and Howard Baetzhold have made clear, Twain took many of his cues from W. E. H. Lecky's *History of European Morals* when he wrote this book. It is true that both the prince and the pauper (like Huckleberry Finn) are in possession of a sound heart and the disposition to correct grosser cruelties, but Twain seems to be making some subtler distinction between the two as well.

In March 1880, Clemens wrote to Howells describing his somewhat altered plan for the novel:

> My idea is to afford a realizing sense of the exceeding severity of the laws of that day by inflicting some of their penalties upon the king himself & allowing him a chance to see the rest of them applied to others—all of which is to account for certain mildnesses which distinguished Edward VI's reign from those that preceded & followed it. (*MTHL*, 1:291–92)

Twain may have inferred the "mildness" of Edward's character from a certain leniency of the king's laws during his brief reign, or he may have assented to David Hume's characterization of the young monarch in his *History of England* as possessing "mildness of disposition, application to study and business, a capacity to learn and judge, and an attachment to equity and justice" (quoted in *P&P*, 21). In either case, however, it is a mystery how Twain could have possibly believed that a fiction about Edward's life would serve to explain certain historical facts. Something that did not happen (the prince's experience as a vagabond and his firsthand exposure to the cruelty of royal justice) simply cannot be asserted as the cause of something that did (a relaxation of irrationally cruel and unjust laws).

This is a much more curious example of the operations of Twain's historical imagination than are certain factual inaccuracies, the importation of manners and customs from one country to another, or occasional anachronisms that appear in the novel. These sorts of liberties can be understood as efforts to improve his fictional narrative. On the other hand, if Twain was principally interested in the moral growth of his prince (or anyone who by virtue of birth, caste, and breeding was inclined to haughtiness and indifference), then he might freely supply events designed to cultivate sympathies that otherwise would have remained latent. If that is the case, then *The Prince and the Pauper* is not so much a historical romance as it is a study in social psychology. This may have been the way Howells took the book when he read it in manuscript. He wrote Clemens, "It is marvelously good. It realizes most vividly the time. All the *picaresque* part—the tramps, outlaws, etc.,—all the infernal clumsiness and cruelties of the law—are incomparable. The whole intention, the allegory, is splendid, and powerfully enforced" (*MTHL*, 1:338). Howells did not specify what he took that allegory to be; perhaps he indicated his thoughts more perfectly in a review of the book he wrote for the New York *Tribune:* "It is only touching the story at one of its many points to speak of it as a satire on monarchy; in this sort it is a manual of republicanism which might fitly be introduced in the schools. It breathes throughout the spirit of humanity and the reason of democracy" (*Reviews*, 210).

Twain's story does indeed have many points to make. Among them is his desire to reaffirm in fictional terms the contention of his Hartford friend J. Hammond Trumbull that the Blue Laws of colonial Connecticut were not nearly so harsh as contemporary English ones. In that, he was once again indulging a patriotic bias, as he had done in *The Innocents Abroad.* Here, though, Twain was insulated by the protective distance of history, which permitted him to satirize English monarchy without risking the disfavor of a nineteenth-century British audience. This was his thinking, at any rate, when he abandoned an earlier plan to place his story in contemporaneous England, and on balance British reviews were more complimentary than he predicted. Twain might also dramatize in his novel, as one reviewer put it alluding to Thomas Carlyle's philosophy of clothes, that the differences in individuals have more to do with one's garments than with one's merits, and that to exchange the former transforms, in the popular mind, an estimation of the latter. For personal and professional reasons, Twain also wanted to establish a reputation as something more than a "mere humorist," someone capable of serious moral respectability and of refined literary purity. In that ambition he succeeded well enough, if one can trust the reviews. Joel Chandler Harris wrote that in *The Prince and the Pauper* we see Twain as the "true literary artist," though also more "strengthened and refined" than his reputation as a wild humorist allowed (*Reviews,* 204). H. H. Boyensen observed that the novel is "ingenious in conception, pure and humane in purpose, artistic in method, and with barely a flaw, refined in execution" (*Reviews,* 201). Other reviewers made similar comments: it is a "book which has other and higher merits than can possibly belong to the most artistic expressions of mere humor" (*Reviews,* 205); the "finer element in Mark Twain's nature," which has till now been lurking in the background, has at last come to the fore (*Reviews,* 208); *The Prince and the Pauper* is "original in conception, and exceedingly felicitous in execution" (*Reviews,* 213); and, finally, the historical romance, "beside being rich in historical facts and teachings, is charged with a generous and ennobling moral" (*Reviews,* 214).

I am not feigning simple-mindedness when I confess that I don't know what that moral might be. Is it suggested by his dedication to his daughters Susy and Clara, "those good-mannered and agreeable children?" Doubtful, since neither Edward nor his sisters nor Tom Canty, as tractable as they may at times be, is distinguished by agreeability. Is it, as suggested by the epigraph from the *Merchant of Venice,* that the quality of mercy is "mightier than the mightiest: it becomes / The thronèd monarch better than his crown?" An impassioned plea for mercy in monarchs is hardly (in fact cannot be) a satire of monarchy itself. If it is a valuable history les-son smuggled in under the guise of an amusing fable "for young people of all ages," as the subtitle insists, then that lesson might be "Thank your lucky stars you live in the nineteenth, and not the sixteenth, century." The preface declares the tale itself "may be history, it may be only a legend, a tradition. It may have happened, it may not have happened: but it *could* have happened." This is more a call to suspend one's historical disbelief than it is to imagine a time other than one's own.

Louis J. Budd is right to say that *The Prince and the Pauper* is "more mixed in performance" than it is in "purpose."[17] That firmness of purpose is not to be detected so much in the conception or the plot of the book as in the prevailing tone in the author. One reviewer thought the tone "healthful" (*Reviews*, 213), and another found the book imbued with "generous" feel-ing (*Reviews*, 214). A reviewer for the *British Quarterly Review* commend-ed Twain's "mingled humour and pathos, his fine perception of human nature, and his nimble fancy" (*Reviews*, 209). Joel Chandler Harris found *The Prince and the Pauper* "a powerful and impressive study of character, wherein the complex relations that bind the highest human being to the lowest are treated with an insight as keen and a touch as faithful and as vivid as any modern writer has employed" (*Reviews*, 205). What these and other comments seem to reveal is that, though one can't put one's finger on the precise moral of the fable, there can be little doubt that there is such a moral.

Because the narrator evidently displays an unwavering focus on his subject, because he dramatizes scenes and records incidents that he obvi-ously finds barbaric and odious with such a knowing equanimity, and be-cause he appears more wise than outraged, more merciful perhaps than Edward VI himself, it is difficult not to assign similar qualities to the text itself. But the novel is rather stark—filled as it is with madness (feigned and real), dire poverty, ignorance and superstition, unnecessary cruelty that includes not only humiliation but also the maiming, hanging, burn-ing, and boiling of innocent people. Were one to look squarely at the un-folding narrative, without the coloring of the author's voice, *The Prince and the Pauper* might well be deemed unsuitable for children, young or old. But the voice is always there invisibly shaping the reader's reactions and sentiments. It is a commonplace to observe Twain's indignation and impatience with sham, pretense, and the like. However, another and equally affecting part of Clemens's persona dramatizes his forbearance,

17. *Mark Twain: Social Philosopher* (Columbia: University of Missouri Press, 2001), 75.

patience, tolerance, and forgiveness. His nineteenth-century readers were more responsive to this quality in the man than modern readers have tended to be. Twain in one way or another continually reveals his own foibles and thereby does not exempt himself from the human lot. He might poke fun at mountain climbing or golf but anyone who could, and did, travel several miles a day around a rectangular table poking a wooden stick at a little white ball could not very well put on airs.

III

If Sam Clemens succeeded in improving his literary image, he may have done so at the expense of Mark Twain. That is, the antic persona, ready to seize any comic opportunity or to satirize with impunity, was held in abeyance to the extent that H. H. Boyensen could remark in a review that the novel is surely by Clemens but it does not seem to be by Mark Twain. For the purposes of satire, however, the Twain figure was unnecessary because, separated from his subject matter by half a millennium and the Atlantic Ocean, it was enough to cast a jaundiced and somewhat condescending historical eye toward the reign of Henry VIII and Edward VI. If, according to their moral nature and native intelligence, a prince and pauper were interchangeable, then this in itself was a strong argument for a republican form of government. The young prince realizes that the "world is made wrong," and we are to believe he took some measures to correct injustices, but in a historical romance his realization does not cry out for redress or political reform. The young reader, safe in the bosom of the nineteenth century, had the comfort of believing that history has somehow "fixed" the problem, such is the redemptive power of "progress." When he came to write another historical romance, *A Connecticut Yankee in King Arthur's Court,* however, Twain would be more aggressively satirical and have Hank Morgan push that article progress with the anxious energy of a real reformer. Only gradually did Morgan, and presumably Twain as well, learn the lesson of that paragon of social progress, Herbert Spencer. Spencer remarked on the "difficulty of understanding that human nature, though indefinitely modifiable, can be modified but very slowly; and all the laws and institutions and appliances which count on getting from it, within a short time, much better results than present ones, will inevitably fail."[18] In the early 1880s, though, Twain

18. *Herbert Spencer on Social Evolution,* ed. J. D. Y. Peel (Chicago: University of Chica-

was equally struck by the obstinacy of habit and custom and the wonderful and wonderfully quick promise of scientific and technological progress.

In *A Tramp Abroad* and *Life on the Mississippi,* Twain narrowed the geographical and chronological gap considerably by reporting on recent jaunts in Europe and the United States, but in both instances he was alternately interested in, nostalgic for, and annoyed by survivals of the past in the present. Twain was present-minded in both these travel books in the sense that he was assessing the mores of his own times and, in the latter, his own country. But he was also inspecting the curious relation between the past and the present. Emblematic of that relation is the documented case in *A Tramp Abroad* of five mountain climbers who in 1820 were swept by an avalanche into the crevasse of a glacier. Forty-one years later, the glacier has descended the mountain and one of the survivors, now wrinkled with age, has the opportunity to grasp the long dead but still youthful hand of his friend: "There is something weirdly pathetic about the picture of that white-haired veteran greeting with his loving hand-shake this friend who had been dead forty years. . . . Time had gone on in the one case; it had stood still in the other" (*TA,* 306). This grisly picture of the dead hand of the past reaching out to the present is worthy of Poe or Hawthorne, but Twain finds a different moral in the instance than they would have. An Englishman, Dr. Hamel, hearing of the slow arrival of the long-lost mountain climbers, sees profit in the matter: "And it will be a great thing for Chamonix, in the matter of attracting tourists. You can get up a museum with those remains that will draw." Twain concedes that that idea is "savage," then adds, "But, after all, the man was sound on human nature" (*TA,* 308), for there is a perverse yet broadly human curiosity about such things. The public officials consider the idea but are eventually dissuaded by friends and relatives of the deceased.

The composition of *A Tramp Abroad,* as Hamlin Hill has convincingly described it, indicates a creative process altogether different from the one

---

go Press, 1972), 110. Spencer also argued that the "alleged constancy of human nature" is mere wishful thinking: "There cannot indeed be a more astounding instance of the tenacity with which men will cling to an opinion in spite of an overwhelming mass of adverse evidence, than is shown in this prevalent belief that human nature is uniform" (6–7). This is an instance of Spencer having his cake and eating it too, a tendency in the man that Josiah Royce, William James, and others found exasperating. That is, if human nature is subject to radical modification, on the one hand, but those modifications occur over so long a time as to make deliberate reform futile, then one is back to square one. So-called progress becomes as much an untestable abstraction as is the constancy of human nature.

Twain employed in *The Innocents Abroad*.[19] In the earlier book, he had the itinerary of the *Quaker City* expedition and the record of his *Alta California* letters to guide him in preparing a subscription book of a definite length. With the initial stages of *A Tramp Abroad*, however, his record of travels and sightseeing in Germany, Switzerland, and Italy was an accumulating hodgepodge of notebook entries, anecdotes, digressive stories, and legends (some of them first-rate, such as the bluejay yarn), with no governing plan or narrative thread to unite them. In the summer of 1878, when his pastor and friend Joseph Twichell arrived to stay with the Clemenses, the two men planned a walking tour of the countryside, and Twain devised a "joke" that would tie the heterogeneous materials together. He wrote Howells from Munich on January 30, 1879, "In my book I allow it to appear,—casually & without stress,—that I am over here to make a tour of Europe *on foot*. I am in pedestrian costume, as a general thing, & *start* on pedestrian tours, but mount the first conveyance that offers, making but slight explanation or excuse, & endeavoring to seem unconscious that this is not legitimate pedestrianizing" (*MTHL*, 1:248–50). The joke was simple enough and actually not very funny, but it served his purpose. And he found a remarkable number of conveyances to carry it off—coaches, canal boats, railway trains, oxcarts, and (borrowing from the pigeonholed manuscript of *Huck Finn*) a raft to float down the Neckar River; he even traveled by glacier and telescope. Twain and Harris (as he named his agent and traveling companion) would embark on a tour of the region and, if there were any heavy lifting to do, Twain would dispatch his agent to do it. If he was in a reverential mood, he'd send Harris to church and report the experience as his own; if he was adventurous, he'd send Harris up the mountain and watch him from below.

In the same letter, Clemens confessed that he was incapable of giving the "sharp satires of European life" that Howells recommended because he was in too foul a mood: "a man can't write successful satire except he be in a calm judicial good-humor—whereas I *hate* travel, & I *hate* hotels, & I *hate* the opera, & I *hate* the Old Masters—in truth I don't ever seem to be in a good enough humor with ANYthing to *satirize* it; no, I want to stand up before it *curse* it, & foam at the mouth,—or take a club and pound it to rags and pulp" (*MTHL*, 1:250). His notebooks written during this period do indicate that he was put out with a good many things—uncomfortable inns, tasteless food, inclement weather, inferior cigars and coffee,

19. See *Mark Twain and His Publishers* (Columbia: University of Missouri Press, 1964), 132–45.

annoying commercial customs, the German and the French languages, and so forth. Even so, by adopting the sort of unself-conscious and self-deluded persona who does not realize he is not tramping through Europe, he had neutralized beforehand any sharp or venomous satire that might occur to him. The Twain of *A Tramp Abroad* is someone who blithely follows the path of least resistance, at least so far as physical effort and cultural improvement are concerned, and is typically more amusing, even quaint, than churlish or afflicted. In that, Twain is at times in the satirical position of a Huck Finn, a person who knows only what he prefers but does not begrudge others their preferences. Both Twain and Huck attempt but fail to appreciate and understand the apparently desirable and esteemed expressions of high culture and revered tradition, whether they be the German student duels and *Lohengrin* or the Grangerford plantation house and Miss Emmeline's drawings and "tributes." The reader understands the blind cruelty and sentimental absurdity involved, but the narrator is not permitted this awareness.

Twain says he visits the German Student's dueling grounds in "the interest of science" and knows that a custom that has continued for two hundred and fifty years must be regarded with a certain reverence, even awe. Still, he cannot help thinking it a barbarous practice, and potentially lethal. Much like Huck's witnessing of Buck Grangerford's death, Twain refuses to describe some of the more violent encounters, and, like him too, his reactions to the fights contrast with those of other spectators, who sometimes laugh and think the contests "farcical affairs." Twain, however, believes the dueling has a "grave side to it" (*TA*, 29). In several ways, he conveys the unnaturalness of this esteemed custom. The wounded students are attended to by a surgeon, but they neither blanch nor wince at the treatment. If a duelist steps back from a descending blow, he is dismissed from the student corps. "It would seem but natural to step from under a descending sword unconsciously, and against one's will and intent," Twain observes, "yet this unconsciousness is not allowed" (*TA*, 30). He also notes that the "usages" of the corps are not laws but have that force nonetheless. For example, when called upon, a sophomore student may decline to duel, but no one ever did decline; "there is no law against declining—except the law of custom, which is confessedly stronger than written law, everywhere" (*TA*, 31).

Twain, who often poses self-importantly as a "scientist" intent on explaining natural and human phenomena, finds that the artifacts of a past have been sustained by habit, custom, and education. These are the mechanisms that foster the high civilization that is Europe itself, and, over time, perhaps they do in fact cultivate certain elevated faculties of appreciation and understanding. But is the price worth the effort? And do habit and training deaden rather than enhance perception? There "is nothing the Germans like so much as an opera. They like it, not in a mild and moderate way, but with their whole hearts. This is a legitimate result of habit and education. Our nation will like the opera, too, by-and-by, no doubt" (*TA*, 48). For the moment however, this American finds the "howlings and wailings and shriekings of the singers, and the ragings and roarings and explosions of the vast orchestra" too much to bear. "I would have cried if I had been alone," he says. His reactions appeared to those sharing his box in the opera house as something that would not have been out of place if he were being skinned alive, but they would have "marveled" at it here. Nevertheless, "there was nothing in the present case which was an advantage over being skinned" (*TA*, 47). His companions reacted differently to the performance—"they sat and looked as rapt and grateful as cats do when one strokes their backs." "This was not comprehensible to me," Twain adds.

When he gets to Venice, Twain benefits from the education in art he has received in Heidelberg. "All that I am today in art I owe to that" (*TA*, 366). Now, he can fathom the deep and beautiful mysteries of the vast canvas, Bassano's "Pope Alexander III, and the Doge Ziani, the Conqueror of the Emperor Frederick Barbarossa":

One cannot see the procession without feeling a curiosity to follow it and learn whither it is going. It leads him to the Pope in the centre of the picture, who is talking with the bonnetless Doge—talking tranquilly, too, although within twelve feet of them a man is beating a drum, and not far from the drummer two persons are blowing horns, and many horsemen are plunging and rioting about—indeed twenty-two feet of this great work is all a deep and happy holiday serenity and Sunday-school procession, and then we come suddenly upon eleven and a half feet of turmoil, and racket, and insubordination. This latter state of things is not an accident, it has its purpose. But for it, one would linger upon the Pope and the Doge, thinking them to be the motive and supreme feature of the picture; whereas one is drawn along, almost unconsciously, to see what the trouble is about. Now at the very *end* of this riot, within four feet of the end of the picture, and full thirty-six feet from the beginning of it, the Hair Trunk bursts with an electrifying suddenness upon the spectator, in all its matchless perfection, and the great master's triumph is sweeping and complete. From that moment no other thing in those forty feet of canvas has any charm. One sees the Hair Trunk and the Hair Trunk only—and to see it is to worship it. (*TA*, 367–68)

Both these satirical maneuvers derive from portions of the *Huckleberry Finn* manuscript Twain had already completed. When Twain returned to the novel in 1880 and dramatized Huck's failure to comprehend the nobility and obscure origins of the feud, he was employing the same satirical technique he had used when his persona tries to grasp the appeal of the "knightly graces" of the student duels. But he had already devised that tactic in early portions of the *Huck Finn* manuscript. Huck's failure to understand why the widow has to "grumble over the victuals; though there warn't really anything the matter with them" (*HF*, 2) or the Grangerford family's adoration of Emmeline's verse and drawings are no less pointed satires for being parochial in character. On the other hand, Huck's admiration may also serve satirical purposes. Huck stands in awe of the magnificence of the Grangerford house:

> I hadn't seen no house out in the country before that was so nice and had so much style. . . . They had big brass dog-irons that could hold up a saw-log. There was a clock on the middle of the mantel piece, with a picture of a town painted on the bottom half of the glass front, and a round place in the middle of it for the sun, and you could see the pendulum swing behind it. It was beautiful to hear that clock tick; and sometimes when one of these pedlers had been along and scoured her up and got her in good shape, she would start in and strike a hundred and fifty, before she got tuckered out. They wouldn't took any money for her. (*HF*, 136)

The essential difference between a failure to understand or even approve certain priceless objects or obviously time-honored customs and an eager willingness to appreciate lavish and garish "style" is the difference between a satire founded on untutored moral or aesthetic perceptions and one founded on an impressionable and class-conscious sensibility. A Wagner opera does no real damage except perhaps to the ears, but becoming inured to violent customs, as the blithe student duelists seem to be, dulls moral perceptions of the unnecessary cruelty in the world at large.

Twain as pedestrian, the self-satisfied simpleton, was not the only role Clemens had his persona play. One of the more conspicuous departures from that role occurs when he appears as the scientist-as-muggins. In part, Twain was merely continuing his satire of the sort of scientist who gets several pounds of theory and speculation out of an ounce of fact. When he activates this persona, the casual tramp through Europe becomes a fact-finding expedition. To insure the accuracy of his instruments, Twain boils his barometer, thermometer, and even his camera. The results are gratifying, for he makes several important discoveries. A reading of his barometer discloses that the party has "attained the extraordinary altitude of 200,000 feet above sea level" (*TA*, 283); another venture and another reading with the boiled thermometer yields this important fact: "This spot, which purported to be 2,000 feet higher than the locality of the hotel turned out to be 9,000 feet *lower*. Thus the fact clearly demonstrated that, *above a certain point, the higher a point seems to be, the lower it actually is.* Our ascent itself was a great achievement, but this contribution to science was an inconceivably greater matter" (*TA*, 291). At another point he announces a truly daring hypothesis: "I had a theory that the gravitation of refraction being subsidiary to atmospheric compensation, the refrangibility of the earth's surface would emphasize this effect in regions where great mountain ranges occur, and possibly so even-handedly impact the odic and idyllic forces together, the one upon the other, as to prevent the moon from rising higher than 12,200 feet above sea level" (*TA*, 329). He considers offering this hypothesis to "Mr. Darwin, whom I understand to be a man without prejudices, but it occurred to me that perhaps he would not be interested in it since it did not concern heraldry" (*TA*, 329–30). He asserts the equally startling observation that the ant only works "when people are looking, and only then when the observer has a green naturalistic look, and seems to be taking notes" (*TA*, 144). Thus, the reputation of the ant as a "moral agent" is destroyed, and it will no longer serve as an example of industry for Sunday school children.

This is pure drollery, of course. At times, though, Twain indulges his patriotic biases with a bit of an edge, as when he observes that a woman in America "will encounter less polish than she would in the old world, but she will run across enough humanity to make up for it" (*TA*, 354). Europe worships the Old Masters, he insists, not because they are masterful but simply because they have acquired the charm of age, something that cannot be attributed to the artist. Occasionally Twain discloses accumulated facts to bear out his judgment. His tabulation of the death rate per thousand in cities throughout the world convinces him that the typical American city is on average twice as healthy as other cities. His inquiry into the history and rules of membership of the Student Corps, on the other hand, results in twelve mutually contradictory discoveries, and Twain properly concludes: "I perceive that each of us, by observing and noting and inquiring diligently and day by day, had managed to lay in a most varied and opulent stock of misinformation" (*TA*, 106). The description of the sheer magnitude of glaciers and the sharp ascent of the Alps, fortified by an array of astonishing facts, has its moral effect on Twain: "These things [information about the dimensions of glaciers] will help the reader to understand why it is that a man who keeps company with glaciers comes to feel tolerably insignificant by and by. The Alps and the glaciers together are able to take every bit of conceit out of a man and reduce his self-importance to zero if he will only remain within the influences of their sublime presence long enough to give it a fair and reasonable chance to do its work" (*TA*, 303–4).

Twain seems never to have abandoned the notion that there were defining national characteristics, though in his later years he became more interested in universal similarities than in regional differences. His notebook entries during this period itemize his attitudes. Of his own patrimony, he was certain: "Take America by & large & it is the most civilized of all nations. Pure-minded women are the rule, in every rank of life of the *native-born*. The men are clean-minded, too, beyond the world's average" (*N&J2*, 324). Of other nations, he was not so sure. Apart from their vexing language, Twain found the Germans a fine people—"The chief German characteristic . . . seems to be kindness, good will to men" (*N&J2*, 100). The Swiss were generally tolerable except for some annoyances—"The hated Cuckoo-clock" (*N&J2*, 140); "Drat this stupid 'yodling'" (*N&J2*, 147). He had his expectations about Italy, "Italy the home of art & swindling; home of religion & moral rottenness" (*N&J2*, 182), but remained undecided: "I was in Venice too brief a time to learn for myself the character of the people—but I got friends to tell me & this way I have got at the absolute truth. . . . Smith—They are divine. Jones—They are devilish" (*N&J2*, 199). His attitudes toward the French were less equivocal: "France has neither winter nor summer nor morals" (*N&J2*, 318); "Scratch an F & you find a gorilla"; "The F is the connecting link between monkey & human being"; "A [*sic*] F's home is where another . . . man's wife is" (*N&J2*, 324). Twain concedes that he may be unfair, though: "You perceive I generalize with intrepidity from single instances. It is the tourist's custom. When I see a man jump from the Vendome column, I say 'They like to do that in France'" (*N&J2*, 318).

On another matter, however, Twain's outlook on human nature was decidedly transnational. From a fairly early stage in his career, he had demonstrated a fascination with the broadly human fear of shame. This was a trait that cut across questions of race, gender, and class. It affected equally (though individual reactions were quite different) Injun Joe, Laura Hawkins, and Prince Edward. Jim, in an already completed portion of the *Huckleberry Finn* manuscript, had also upbraided Huck for his cruel joke when they were separated in the fog—"En all you wuz thinkin' 'bout wuz how you could make a fool uv ole Jim wid a lie. Dat truck dah is *trash;* en trash is what people is dat puts dirt on de head er dey fren's en makes 'em ashamed" (*HF,* 105). Quite apart from the dramatic power of this scolding, and whatever it might have imparted to Huck about Jim's humanity, is the fact that Jim's act is a dangerous one. He cannot afford to alienate Huck at this point in the narrative because they have passed Cairo and are drifting farther south. A black man, without the company of a white person, is in a perilous situation; yet Jim risks whatever measure of safety Huck's presence provides out of an indignant sense of betrayal and shame.

During the 1880s and before, Twain was inching his way toward Hank Morgan's bold pronouncement that "Training is everything." But this conclusion was reached by degrees, and his reasoning was more nuanced than has sometimes been supposed. If, as he was later to say, the chief de-sire of men and women was self-approval, and if self-approval could only be attained through the approval of others, then the human animal was enmeshed in a social order that was in many ways unnatural. I have al-ready noted that, contrary to a natural animal instinct, the German stu-dent duelists do not quail before the imminent blow of a sword, nor do they wince when attended to by the surgeon. These are clear instances of the force of usage and custom that preempt biological instinct. In chapter 23, the "philosopher" Harris recalls that during the Civil War most sol-diers dreaded a tooth-pulling more than amputation and that an "ear-splitting howl of anguish" coming from a tent was a sure sign of an ex-traction. However, when the surgeons instituted "open-air dentistry," the men endured the pain without complaint. "With so big and so derisive an audience as that, a sufferer wouldn't emit a sound though you pulled his head off" (*TA,* 148–49).[20] Capitalizing on the universal dread of being shamed before one's fellows, the surgeons institute a new custom that makes their patients more tractable than any painkiller might. The logic of such a psychological and social order is fairly clear. Custom and usage eventuate in habit. Habit is stronger than instinct, logic, or law. Therefore, neither experience nor reason nor the natural world itself counts for much in understanding human conduct.

The sublimity of the Alps or a glacier should teach one humility; instead expeditions go out to conquer them. Education in music and painting of

20. Clemens's reading in *Uncivilized Races of the World* would have acquainted him with other instances of a similar nature. In Guiana, for example, the men appeared in-sensible to pain, in part because the women in the tribe would scoff at them if they be-trayed any sign of anguish.

the Old Masters should elevate; instead it makes one blind to ugliness and deaf to caterwauling. Twain goes to a public performance of the Fremersberg. Huck-like, he automatically assumes his favorable reaction indicates its deficiencies: "I suppose the Fremersberg is very low-grade music; I know, indeed, that it *must* be low-grade music, because it so delighted me, warmed me, moved me, stirred me" (*TA*, 158). There are two kinds of music, he concludes—one which "feels" and another kind that requires a "higher faculty." If the first sort is gratifying, why should humankind ever want the second? "We want it because the higher and better like it. But we want it without giving it the necessary time and trouble; so we climb into that upper tier, that dress circle, by a lie; we *pretend* we like it" (*TA*, 158). Similarly, Turner's painting *The Slave Ship* used to throw Twain into a rage when he was still "ignorant," that is, before Mr. Ruskin's analysis instructed him on its virtues. The same painting reminded a Boston reporter of a "tortoise-shell cat having a fit in a platter of tomatoes." "In my then uneducated state, that went home to my non-cultivation, and I thought here is a man with an unobstructed eye." Even so, Twain insists most of the picture is a "manifest impossibility,—that is to say, a lie; and only rigid cultivation can enable a man to find truth in a lie" (*TA*, 159).

Predictably, Twain ended *A Tramp Abroad* on a patriotic note. He recommended to his American readers short, not extended, visits to the Old World in order to "keep our pride of country intact." To risk becoming "Europeanised" is to also risk having one's feelings for home "dulled," and that is too high a price to pay, he says. In his review of *A Tramp Abroad*, however, W. D. Howells located the interest of the book in the earnestness of the author and not its nominal subject. There is not the same "frolicsomeness" here as was found in *The Innocents Abroad*, for this is a second visit to European sights seen "through eyes saddened by much experience." Twain "laughs, certainly, at an abuse, at ill manners, at conceit, at cruelty, and you must laugh with him; but if you enter into the very spirit of his humor, you feel that if he could set these things right, there would be very little laughing" (*Reviews*, 187). The somberness Howells detected in the book surely had to do with Twain's own mood, but it also had to do with "being a second time confronted with things he has had time to think over" (*Reviews*, 188).

If the world at large, and not merely Europe, runs on mindless habit and false instruction, as Twain more than once gives his readers to believe, moral earnestness is more likely to be a thorn in one's side than a call to action. In his chapter on "Habit" in *The Principles of Psychology* (1890), William James struck a similar note. After a certain age, one loses the "plasticity" of youth, and the habits acquired early on become fixed and fated: Habit "dooms us all to fight out the battle of life upon the lines of our nurture or our early choice, and to make the best of a pursuit that disagrees, because there is no other for which we are fitted, and it is too late to begin again." What is more, habit, as a part of human nature, is potentially an enemy to democratic reform or social progress; it is certainly a deterrent to revolution. Habit "alone is what keeps us all within the bounds of ordinance, and saves the children of fortune from the envious uprisings of the poor. It alone prevents the hardest and most repulsive walks of life from being deserted by those brought up to tread therein. . . . It keeps different social strata from mixing."[21] By citing James here, I want to convey in a shorthand way that whatever Twain eventually came to think about human nature and the human condition does not mean that he wanted to believe these things. Sad truths were pressing in on Mark Twain, possibly, and he would in time arrive at firm, if unwanted, conclusions. Whether that made a cynic of him is a different kind of question. At any rate, in his next travel narrative, *Life on the Mississippi* (1883), Twain would explore the habits and the habitat of a part of his own country he at one time knew very, very well.

IV

Much of *Life on the Mississippi* is a collage of previously published or at least previously written materials. Chapters 4 through 17 consist of the series of sketches about Clemens's apprenticeship days on the river first published in the *Atlantic* in 1875 as "Old Times on the Mississippi." Karl Ritter's tale of criminal detection and revenge, originally meant for *A Tramp Abroad,* was interpolated as chapters 22 and 23 into this later work. In part to assert his authority over the subject matter, Twain inserted extensive quotations from previous travelers to the Mississippi Valley. And, once again, Twain borrowed from the *Huckleberry Finn* manuscript, most notably by publishing the "raft episode" in chapter 3 of *Life on the Mississippi*[22] and rewriting from his own point of view Huck's description of the Grangerford plantation house as "The House Beautiful" (in chapter 38) and a sunrise on the river (chapter 30), as well as fashioning the irascible

21. *Principles of Psychology,* 2 vols. (1890; rpt. New York: Dover Publications, 1950), 1:121.

22. This episode was not reintroduced into *Huckleberry Finn* when it was published; no edition of the novel published in the author's lifetime included this portion.

pilot Brown's diatribe (chapter 18) after Pap's commentary about Huck's "starchy" ways in chapter 5 of the novel. If we can trust Twain's remarks introducing the raftsmen episode into *Life on the Mississippi*, he continued to have at best a lazy interest in finishing and publishing the novel: "I will throw in, in this place, a chapter from a book which I have been working at, by fits and starts, during the past five or six years, and may possibly finish in the course of five or six more" (*LOM*, 51).

Between March and June 1880, Twain had completed the feud portion of chapter 18 of *Huckleberry Finn* and had written chapters 19 through 21, from the time the duke and dauphin run on board the raft until the shooting of Boggs and the subsequent resolution of the mob to lynch Colonel Sherburn. And, his comments in *Life on the Mississippi* notwithstanding, it would not be another five or six years before he would finish this novel. Instead, perhaps reinvigorated by writing about the places of his youth and the scenes of his riverboat days, Twain would resume the Huck Finn manuscript shortly after seeing his river book through the press; *Life on the Mississippi* was published in May 1883. On the other hand, there is no evidence that Twain was being disingenuous in his projection for completing *Huck Finn* or, conversely, that he was in fact slyly pushing in advance a product in the making. Huck's adventures along the Mississippi River, in any event, contrasted starkly with the information-gathering expedition Clemens, his publisher James R. Osgood, and a shorthand secretary made in 1882. In *Life on the Mississippi*, Twain provides a catalog of reminiscences alongside plentiful evidence of postbellum progress, all the way from New Orleans to St. Paul. Huck, by contrast, is a receptacle for and a fund of all sorts of legends, misinformation, superstition, folklore, and surmise, and he is repeatedly entangled in an antebellum, slaveholding, slothful, and decidedly retrograde social order. The Mark Twain persona, at least in the latter half of *Life on the Mississippi*, is a booster of efficiency and reform, a corrector of mistaken facts and conclusions, a sanguine prophet on future progress, and a commentator on the American character, both north and south, before the war and after.

Edgar M. Branch has argued that "Old Times on the Mississippi" represents and dramatizes a significant portion of Clemens's actual life that would pay dividends in a fiction that seems most remote from the author's lived experience—*A Connecticut Yankee in King Arthur's Court*.[23] Clemens's recollection of the Western Boatman's Benevolent Association,

23. See *Mark Twain and the Starchy Boys* (Elmira, N.Y.: Elmira College Center for Mark Twain Studies, 1992), 62–77.

in particular, described a true meritocracy, where the discipline, intelligence, and loyalty of a select group of common men were effectively combined, and they were able to challenge the greed and false privilege of the established order. His own participation in the WBBA encouraged Clemens to believe that moral and social progress was possible, and many years later he deposited a like hope and ambition in the character of Hank Morgan. But Twain knew that that hope was a fragile one. Even in 1875 he could write the obituary of the piloting profession with tender feelings but little sentimentality:

> As I have remarked, the pilots' association was now the compactest monopoly in the world, perhaps, and seemed simply indestructible. And yet the days of its glory were numbered. First, the new railroad stretching up through Mississippi, Tennessee, and Kentucky, to Northern railway centres, began to divert the passenger travel from the steamers; next the war came and almost entirely annihilated the steamboating industry during several years, leaving most of the pilots idle, and the cost of living advancing all the time; then the treasurer of the St. Louis association put his hand into the till and walked off with every dollar of the ample fund; and finally, the railroads intruding everywhere, there was little for the steamers to do, when the war was over, but carry freights; so straightaway some genius from the Atlantic coast introduced the plan of towing a dozen steamer cargoes down to New Orleans at the tail of a vulgar little tug-boat; and behold, in the twinkling of an eye, as it were, the association and the noble science of piloting were things of the dead and pathetic past! (*LOM*, 137).

Hank Morgan's man factory and his dream of a republic would be eliminated by fiat—the Church imposes an interdict, and virtually overnight medieval order is restored. The agents of change that eliminated the pilots' association were multiple—political and military conflict, petty larceny, improved methods of transportation, entrepreneurial innovation, and so forth—and not so calculated to achieve definite ends. With the exception of the sticky fingers of a corrupt treasurer, these were, truly, outside influences that shaped human lives in the interests of what Twain and others were disposed to call "progress."

Without malediction, and without purpose so far as the pilots' association was concerned, these several forces turned pilots into farmers, once glorious steamboats into unpainted and muddy artifacts of an earlier time, and the river into a relatively easy waterway to navigate. Snag-boats have "pulled the river's teeth"; a system of levees has deepened channels; electric lights have diminished the perils of navigating at nighttime; and his former mentor Horace Bixby and George Ritchie have "charted the crossings and laid out the courses by compass," invented a lamp to go with it, and patented the whole (*LOM*, 204). In the manuscript, Twain had included a summary remark about these improvements: "With these helps, one may run in the fog, now, with considerable security, and with a confidence unknown in the old days of trusting in Providence and guessing one's way along. Trusting in Providence is a very good thing, as far as it goes, but a chart and compass are worth six of it, any time. Statistics have shown this to be true" (*LOM*, 204n). Emily Dickinson had drawn a similar conclusion, though not about steamboating certainly:

"Faith" is a fine invention
When Gentlemen can see—
But *Microscopes* are prudent
In an Emergency.

When Twain came to write of these changes, there was a note of lamentation or regret for a vocation that had passed from the scene. In 1875, he could recall that the pilot was at that time "the only unfettered and entirely independent human being that lived in the earth" (*LOM*, 122). By 1882, however, these "aristocrats of the river" have become so many vassals: "Verily we are being treated like a parcel of mates and engineers. The Government has taken away the romance of our calling; the Company has taken away its state and dignity" (*LOM*, 205). Twain still felt sufficiently tied to the romance of the profession to refer to himself and the other pilots as "we," though he had long before given over the occupation of the riverboat pilot to become a "literary person." But he had also given up grand notions of real independence. In an 1885 speech, "The Character of Man," he spoke of the several lies perpetrated upon the human race, most notably the "sugar-coated" lie that there is any real independence in human thought, opinion, or action. Human beings are caught between those "private" opinions they are too meek to express and the public opinions of the herd which they reluctantly take on, "until habit makes us comfortable in it, and the custom of defending it presently makes us love it, adore it, and forget how pitifully we came by it" (*CTSS1*, 856).

On the other hand, the next year, in "The New Dynasty," Twain expressed if not utopian at least hopeful ambitions for the masses. When working men and women recognize their common plight and consolidate their energies, he wrote, and cease to tie their fortunes too narrowly to the immediate interests of a particular craft or trade, then the irrevocable transfer of power from the few to the many will be complete. This was something of a prelude to the "new deal" Hank Morgan would be intent on giving the serfdom of sixth-century England, but it was also a post-script to some of the thinking he had engaged in while writing *Life on the Mississippi*. After the war, America at large and particularly the South had also been given a new deal, whether they wanted it or not. With so many technological changes all about one and so much transforming power within one's reach, why were the attendant social changes so slow in coming? What was it in human nature that retarded a social advance commensurate with accelerating progress in other ways? This is one of the questions Twain addresses in the latter half of *Life on the Mississippi*.

To say that that book is, in part, a meditation on change is to state the obvious. From the very beginning, Twain makes it clear that this is his theme. The Mississippi River itself is a meandering agent and beneficiary of change and has been so from the beginning of time. The river La Salle descended is nowhere to be found: *"Nearly the whole of that one thousand three hundred miles of old Mississippi River which La Salle floated down in his canoes, two hundred years ago, is good solid dry ground now"* (*LOM*, 41; italics Twain's). Not only can one not step into the same river twice, Twain seems to be saying, but the second time you may not even get your feet wet. But there are distinct differences between the remembrance of his apprentice days and his subsequent visit to the river in 1882. The "Old Times" section, dealing as it does with "learning" the river, is chiefly concerned with eddies, reefs, chutes, bars, crossings, and the like. It is a treatise on how to navigate on the river, how to read, remember, and adapt to the ever-shifting course of the Mississippi. The latter half mostly deals with how one navigates, and likewise adjusts, to living along the river.

Twain observes a strict boundary between life along the upper and lower river before the war and after, but also between the South and the North in post-Reconstruction America. The differences may, at times, be attributable to geography. When Twain and his companions visited the river, floodwaters fed by heavy rains in the North had inundated towns in the South, while northern cities and towns, so often perched upon hills, had shaken off the effects of the deluge and gone about their business. In all these upper-river towns, he says, "one breathes a go-ahead atmosphere which tastes good in the nostrils" (*LOM*, 395). Even in towns of middling size, there are paid fire departments, attractive opera houses, schools, colleges, libraries, and trustworthy newspapers. The people who belong to these towns constitute "an independent race who think for themselves, and who are competent to do it, because they are educated and enlightened; they read, they keep abreast of the best and newest thought," and they fortify their communities with improving institutions (*LOM*, 397). Perhaps most important, this same independent race is disposed to live peaceably under the rule of law.

In the South, however, things are different. During Twain's visit, it was a time of emergency—a flood-time of death and potential disease; of rationing, of rescuing, and of sheltering thousands of people—and he reprints in appendixes descriptions of the devastation and proposed remedies for channeling the river and making it less hostile to the people who live along its shores. Flood-time or no, the aimless but overpowering Mississippi has always had its effects on southern life—changing state boundaries, moving port towns inland or (as in the case of Napoleon, Arkansas) washing whole towns away, and subtracting acreage from one plantation and depositing it on another. But Twain makes it clear that the accidents of geography are not sufficient to explain the differences between upper and lower river life. Much of the hangdog and hang-back ethos of the South is due to what he calls "girly-girly" romance. This retrogressive hankering for romantic mystery and aristocratic privilege survives annually in the ritual of Mardi Gras, a pageant that could not exist in the "practical" North. The morally degrading institution of slavery and the military devastation of the Civil War set the South back a peg or two, but catastrophic change is insufficient to explain a timid attachment to an idealism so contrary to its interests. After all, the French Revolution and Bonaparte's Empire had certain "compensating benefactions"—making a nation of freemen, not slaves; and installing an institutional preference for merit above birth. In light of those progressive measures, he says, the reign of terror and its aftermath may be forgiven other crimes.

By way of partial explanation for southern backwardness, Twain points an accusing finger at Sir Walter Scott: "But for the Sir Walter Scott disease, the character of the Southerner—or Southron, according to Sir Walter's starchier way of phrasing it—would be wholly modern, in place of modern and medieval mixed, and the South would be fully a generation further advanced than it is" (*LOM*, 328). Twain even claims Scott should bear "major responsibility for the war," but he readily admits that this is something of a "wild proposition." The influence of *Ivanhoe*, as opposed to the influence of *Don Quixote*, may go a long way in explaining southern customs—aristocratic titles, clannish pride, even the "whitewashed castle" of a capitol building in Baton Rouge—but there is much that it does not and cannot explain. And Twain knows this. One of the first things he notices when he returns to the river is how freight is loaded by a steam derrick. What once required a crew of several men several hours is now accomplished in a few minutes. The wonder, though, is why this system "was not thought of when the first steamboat was built." This mystery helps him realize what a "dull-witted slug the average human is" (*LOM*, 176). Likewise, he learns from Uncle Mumford that officers will soon be outfitted in uniforms, and passengers won't continue to mistake the cook for the mate, the captain for the barber. The real surprise for Twain is that this improvement was not made fifty years earlier. No technological innovation was required to accomplish so sensible a reform; force of habit barred the way.

In the early years of the nineteenth century, he observes, New York had hogs prowling the streets; garbage heaps blocked the doorways of Cincinnati houses; and chained lunatics, hungry and cold, cried out from cellars in Philadelphia to the curious onlookers up above. In the "old America" these were coarse and dirty towns, but they are up-to-date cities now. New Orleans has lagged behind considerably, but it is has made advances—telephones, electric lights, "flushed" gutters, improved newspapers, and comfortable homes are in abundance. But in other respects it is backward—antique public architecture, cockfights, duels, the annual rite of Mardi Gras, and, most of all, disease-breeding and expensive burial customs are emblematic of social stagnation. Part of the problem, Twain intimates, is a prevailing uniformity of opinion:

> The South is "solid" for a single political party. It is difficult to account for this; that is, in a region which purports to be free. Human beings are so constituted, that, given an intelligent, thinking hundred of them, or a thousand, or million, and convince them that they are free from personal danger or social excommunication for opinion's sake, it is absolutely impossible that they shall tie themselves in a body to any one sect, religious or political. Every thinking person in the South and elsewhere knows this; it is a truism. (*LOM*, 332)

Twain touches lightly upon the cause of an important difference between southerner and northerner—"social excommunication for opinion's sake"—but it is an acute observation that, if we can trust George M. Frederickson, survives into the twenty-first century: Even now, "Southern whites are more likely than whites elsewhere to subordinate their material interests to their desire to maintain the sense of status and the personal satisfaction—'ego enhancement'—that has long been associated with belonging to the white race."[24]

24. See "Is There Hope for the South?" *New York Review of Books*, October 24, 2004, p. 49.

For a book that so much concerns itself with southern life and manners, it is remarkable how little Twain has to say about post-Reconstruction race relations. He does note that the southern planter remains "grouty" (emasculated word, that) toward the former slave and prefers to have some "thrifty Israelite" (presumably a northerner) extend credit to blacks, instead of establishing some mutually beneficial business relationship (*LOM*, 250). As a consequence, both white planter and Negro laborer suffer; the latter, saddled with debt, eventually migrates, while the former is forced to seek other laborers who will repeat the same desperate process. However, Twain is not so much interested in exploring the hurtful consequences of racism as he is in the largely mysterious ways human beings are unthinkingly tied to inherited traditions. He makes this clear when he identifies the differences between the northerner's redeeming aptitude for efficiency and progress and the southerner's docile attachment to public opinion. There is no essential difference between the temperament of the southerner and that of the northerner. Southerners are not a "community of savages," though Twain has suggested that their devotion to Walter Scottism cultivates a certain tribal feeling in them. "Where their prejudices are not in front," they are generally peace-loving, reasonable, and loyal (*LOM*, 332). Despite the legend, they are no more hotheaded that anyone else. The northerner, though, "through training, heredity, and fear of the law" keeps his temper under control; that is the difference (*LOM*, 333). The average man is "timid," but in the North, the interests of average citizens are united in support for the rule of law and, in turn, the law protects them from danger, insult, or "social ostracism." Southerners "do not band themselves together in these high interests, but leave them to look out for themselves unsupported; the results being unpunished murder, against the popular approval, and the decay and destruction of independent thought and action in politics" (*LOM*, 335). Twain's sociological analysis here may be crude, but it is consonant with his developing theory of human nature and, at any rate, refuses to explain things as they are according to legends naively based on the presumption of sectional differences, of hotheaded southerners or go-getting northerners, for example.

Bloc voting and a herd mentality have had serious consequences for southern aspirations, but in a dozen far more trivial and often comic ways Twain demonstrates that the claims of habit have preempted meaningful progress. Consumers in Mississippi and Louisiana buy their fruits and vegetables from upriver because they have concluded that the southerner doesn't know how to grow anything but cotton; blacks pay high prices for big and colorful but worthless drinks and shun a tumbler of first-rate brandy at half the price. Drummers from Cincinnati and New Orleans ply their trade on the basis of artifice and deception. One celebrates the virtues of oleomargarine and proclaims that "Butter's had its *day*—and from this out, butter goes to the wall" (*LOM*, 283). The other pushes a "first-rate imitation" of olive oil made from cotton-seeds and is proud to announce "there ain't anybody that can detect the true from the false" (*LOM*, 284). For both men, the dollar is their "god, how to get it their religion" (*LOM*, 282).

A new kind of carpetbagger has come South—consumer capitalism—and he does a brisk business among the unwary and unschooled. Perhaps no one is so adept at this business as "J. B.——, UNDERTAKER." Evidently chapter 43 of *Life on the Mississippi* was written earlier; it is set in Hartford, Connecticut, or Elmira, New York, and dramatizes the exploitation of Irish immigrants in the North. Twain nevertheless saw fit to interpolate the sketch as appropriate to his examination of southern life.[25] His comic encounter with an undertaker who knows that his is the "dead-surest business in Christendom, and the nobbiest" (*LOM*, 310) exposes the undertaker as something of a con man and the bereaved consumer as something of a dolt. J. B. can bank on even his poorest customers paying top dollar for coffins, hacks and omnibus, ice, embalming, and the like. Simply tell Mrs. O'Flaherty that Mrs. O'Shaughnessy sent her dear departed out in "style," and there is no limit to what she will spend: "they'll take the highest-priced way, every time. It's human nature—human nature in grief" (*LOM*, 311).

For Twain, two factors regulate social life—habit, acquired from the cradle and handed down to future generations, and the desire for self-approval, which ironically can be acquired only through the approval of others. A variety of outside influences may disturb or redirect these human tendencies. The astonishing increase in population in towns all the way from Quincy, Illinois, to Davenport, Iowa, to St. Paul, Minnesota, introduces new ideas and new opportunities and, necessarily, new topics of conversation. Because no more than two out of five people in the North had any direct experience with the war, they are not distracted by memories of it. In the South it is different. In the South "the war is what A.D. is elsewhere: they date from it" (*LOM*, 319). No matter how remote from the subject a conversation begins, it is bound to turn to the war, sooner or

---

25. See Horst Kruse, *Mark Twain and "Life on the Mississippi"* (Amherst: University of Massachusetts Press, 1981), 61–69.

later. The idée fixe that so dominates the hearts and minds of white southerners in their conversation is bound to give "the inexperienced stranger
a better idea of what a vast and comprehensive calamity invasion is than
he can ever get by reading books at the fireside" (*LOM*, 319). The calamity he is speaking of is not economic devastation, massive casualties, or
compromised institutions; it is instead the vivid yet stultifying memory
of a time when "each of us, in his own person, seems to have sampled all
the different varieties of human experience" (*LOM*, 320). Recollection of
shared experience provides a certain social cohesiveness, but in its casual favoritism it shuns variety and discounts future possibilities. In Chicago, on the other hand, "they are always rubbing the lamp and fetching up
the genii, and contriving and achieving new impossibilities. . . . She is always a novelty; for she is never the Chicago you saw when you passed
through the last time" (*LOM*, 416).

These are telling differences, but they do not imply that, correspond-
ingly, there are essential differences between southern and northern temperament. Instead, they point to the sort of conclusions that John Dewey
would draw about custom and habit. Democracy, at least in theory, he argues, stimulates originality and the ability to adjust to new social forces.
But if this is the case, it is largely a fortuitous one. Democracy is a relatively young form of government, and democratic social arrangements do
"multiply occasions for imitation. If progress in spite of this fact is more
rapid than in other social forms, it is by accident, since the diversity of
models conflict with one another and thus give individuality a chance in
the resulting chaos of opinions." Habit, in and of itself, is not regressive.
"In fact only in a society dominated by modes of belief and an admiration
fixed by past custom is habit any more conservative than it is progressive." Habit is not necessarily bad; "what makes a habit bad is enslavement to old ruts."[26]

Twain may have been getting at the same idea when he remarked that
the "horror" of slavery is now gone from the South. "Therefore, half the
South is at last emancipated, half the South is free. But the white half is
apparently as far from emancipation as ever" (*LOM*, 332). At all events,
he appears in *Life on the Mississippi* pretty much as Howells described him
to be—the "most desouthernized Southerner" he ever knew (*MMT*, 35).[27]

26. *Human Nature and Conduct: An Introduction to Social Psychology* (New York:
H. Holt and Co., 1922), 66.
27. In his speech "Plymouth Rock and the Pilgrims," delivered December 22, 1881,
Twain declared, "I am a border-ruffian from the State of Missouri. I am a Connecticut
Yankee by adoption."

Twain betrays little interest in sentimentalizing faded glory or tragic defeat. Instead, he is absorbed by the social psychology of a group of people who have not adapted so readily as they might have to altered circumstance. Howells also remarked that Twain was not content to await the judgment of history about the meaning and motives of the Civil War. "Picturesquely and dramatically he portrayed the imbecility of deferring the inquiry at any point to the distance of future years when inevitably the facts would begin to put on fable" (*MMT*, 35–36). His inquiry in *Life on the Mississippi* was not exactly instant analysis of the South or the North. It was, though, a study of human nature as it was limited by habit and custom and modified by outside influences and conditions that were only coincidentally geographical or cultural. He would take up the same subject when he resumed the writing of *Huckleberry Finn*.

Chapter Four

1885–1889

I

It could not be more than a few hundred yards from the drugstore where Boggs coughed out his last to the picket fence in front of Colonel Sherburn's yard. It took Twain three years to travel that distance. He had pigeonholed the *Huckleberry Finn* manuscript in the late spring of 1880, breaking off at that point where a group of Bricksville citizens, perversely fascinated by the Boggs shooting, coalesce into a lynch mob and start their march toward Sherburn's house, "snatching every clothes line they come to, to do the hanging with" (*HF*, 188).[1] Twain resumed the manuscript in June 1883. Instead of the lynching he had prepared his readers for and despite the indications in his notes that he wanted to dramatize a lynching somewhere in his narrative, Twain was content to have Colonel Sherburn give the mob a tongue-lashing, accompanied perforce with a

---

1. Given his experience with the Western Pilot's Benevolent Association, it should go without saying that Twain distinguished between a mob and a group formed to advance or enact a rational purpose. In "The New Dynasty" speech given to the Hartford Monday Evening Club in 1886, Twain criticized trade unions not for organizing but for being too narrowly interested in their own immediate welfare instead of consolidating their mutual interests and wresting power from the few.

double-barreled shotgun. His powder is dry and his rhetoric is effective; they meekly disperse and go back to business as usual.

The particular interest here is not that Twain defeated his reader's expectations; that is something he does right along throughout the novel.[2] Nor is it that Twain was forced to choose between two equally repellent alternatives—that mob violence should somehow oppose baseless aristocratic pretension and redress the injustice of cold-blooded murder or, conversely, that Sherburn should haughtily expose these publicly outraged citizens for the craven thugs they are. Twain had long-standing objections to both mindless mobs and prideful aristocrats, and preferring to satirize one over the other might have been altogether arbitrary with him. As early as 1869, in an unsigned piece in the *Buffalo Express,* he had found southern gallantry and lynch law perfectly compatible: "Keep ready the halter, therefore, oh chivalry of Memphis! Keep the lash knotted; keep the brand and the faggots in waiting, for prompt work with the next 'nigger' who may be suspected of any damnable crime! Wreak a swift vengeance upon him, for the satisfaction of the noble impulses that animate knightly hearts, and then leave time and accident to discover, if they will, whether he was guilty or no."[3] In *A Tramp Abroad,* he indulged in a similar bit of sarcasm when he observed of Colonel Baker, a well-bred Englishman and known sexual assailant who was confined to a "parlor" for his crimes, "Arkansaw would have certainly hanged Baker. I do not say she would have tried him first, but she would have hanged him, anyway" (*TA,* 354).

Bricksville was apparently modeled after the real town of Napoleon, Arkansas. Twain wrote chapter 21 before he revisited the place Napoleon should have been in 1882; he reveals in *Life on the Mississippi* that, save the remnants of a brick chimney, it washed downriver years earlier. Nevertheless, Twain's recollection of the town was likely an accurate one; it had the reputation of being an exceptionally coarse and violent place, even by regional standards.[4] Bricksville is dirty and unkempt, and populated by a "mighty ornery lot" (*HF,* 181). It is decidedly "southern" in the sense that

2. The most important and obvious instances are Huck's fleeing the abuses of a father who he learns much later is already dead and Jim's flight from slavery, when in fact the widow Douglas's will had freed him some time earlier. There are also minor instances of complications that had done much to advance his plot but that Twain was happy enough to leave as unsolved mysteries, such as the fate of the star-crossed lovers Sophia Grangerford and Harney Shepherdson, the legitimacy of the supposedly English claimants to the Wilks estate, and so forth.

3. *Mark Twain at the "Buffalo Express,"* ed. Joseph B. McCullough and Janis McIntire-Strasburg (DeKalb: Northern Illinois University Press, 1999), 22–23.

4. See Walter Blair, *Mark Twain and Huck Finn* (Berkeley: University of California Press, 1960), 305–6.

the inhabitants are wholly lacking in the "go-ahead" spirit that Twain believed animated northern river towns. Huck observes, "There couldn't
anything wake them up all over, and make them happy all over, like a
dog-fight—unless it might be putting turpentine on a stray dog and setting fire to him, or tying a tin pan to his tail and seeing him run himself to
death" (*HF*, 183). The Bricksville loafers are fine examples of the cruelty of
sloth and boredom; their enthusiasms are unfocused, passive, pointless.
Unlike the host of toughs, stalwarts, and eccentrics that populate the
pages of, say, *Roughing It*, and unlike the proud vengeance in Injun Joe or
the ridiculous but sincere sense of injury in Pap Finn, nothing here serves
to extenuate these Arkansas loafers.

Twain's representation of these sorry specimens of bipeds is stunning,
and chilling too, for the economy with which he transforms the dissolute
men into a frightening mob, full of high purpose and intent on violent retribution for no other reason, perhaps, than to be as amused by a lynching
as they would be by setting a dog on fire. The transformation begins, I
think, when the townsfolk attempt to jostle one another aside to get a good
look at the dead Boggs. One complains, "Say, now, you've looked enough,
you fellows; 'tain't right, and 'tain't fair . . . other folks has their rights, as
well as you" (*HF*, 187). At this point, a fight is evidently brewing over an
individual's rights in a free country; Huck thinks so anyway and moves
away. Next, late-comers are hungry for the news from eyewitnesses about
how the shooting happened, and one lanky man obliges by acting it out
in the street. Those that had witnessed the shooting agree that the re-
enactment was "perfect," and a dozen or so pull out bottles and treat him
to a drink. We must assume that the subsequent conversation is also fu-
eled by whiskey. In any event, almost absentmindedly, Huck recounts,
"Well, by and by somebody said Sherburn ought to be lynched. In about
a minute everybody was saying it; so away they went" (*HF*, 188).

When they set out down the street in 1881, the lynch mob was merely
a representative of . . . what? southwestern violence? backwater southern
sloth? Arkansas character? It doesn't matter. They were at least localized,
as much a product of their environment as the mud and dilapidation that
make Bricksville a "bad" town and its inhabitants an "ornery lot." Three
years later they arrived as emissaries from the human race.

Twain may well have derived many of his notions about mobs from his
reading in Carlyle's *History of the French Revolution*, Dickens's *A Tale of Two
Cities*, or S. Baring-Gould's *In Exitu Israel*, as Walter Blair has argued;[5]
some of it derived from his reading in newspapers. Twain had in *Life on*

5. See ibid., 309–13.

the Mississippi already noted examples of one man standing down a large group. In fact, the substance of Colonel Sherburn's speech is predictable from excised passages in chapter 47 of *Life on the Mississippi:*

> The other day, in Kentucky, a single highwayman, revolver in hand, stopped a stagecoach and robbed the passengers, some of whom were armed—and he got away unharmed. The unaverage Kentuckian, being plucky, is not afraid to attack half a dozen average Kentuckians; and his bold enterprise succeeds— probably because the average Kentuckian is like the average of the human race, not plucky, but timid.
>
> In one thing the average Northerner seems to be a step in advance of the average Southerner, in that he bands himself with his timid fellows to support the law . . . ; whereas the average Southerners do not band themselves together in these high interests, but leave them to look out for themselves unsupported; the results being unpunished murder, against the popular approval, and the decay and destruction of independent thought and action in politics. (*LOM,* 334–35)

There is nothing quite so pitiful, perhaps, as indignant and principled sycophancy. This is a subject worthy of satiric exposure and of critical analysis, but my interest here lies elsewhere—on Twain's repetitive insistence on the "average" man. The same argument he makes in *Life on the Mississippi,* essentially, is put in the mouth of Colonel Sherburn:

> I was born and raised in the south, and I've lived in the north; so I know the average all around. The average man's a coward. In the north he lets anybody walk over him that wants to, and goes home and prays for a humble spirit to bear it. In the south one man, all by himself, has stopped a stage full of men, in the daytime, and robbed the lot. . . .
>
> You didn't want to come. The average man don't like trouble and danger. *You* don't like trouble and danger. But if only *half* a man—like Buck Harkness, there—shouts "Lynch him, lynch him!" you're afraid to back down—afraid you'll be found out to be what you are—*cowards.* . . . The pitifulest thing out is a mob. . . . Now the thing for *you* to do, is to droop your tails and go home and crawl in a hole. If any real lynching's going to be done, it will be done in the dark, southern fashion. (*HF,* 190–91)

Clearly, Mark Twain and Colonel Sherburn have been reading the same Kentucky newspapers. Just as clearly, despite the forcefulness of this rhetoric for the reader, Sherburn's speech to the mob is not very plausible. There are a hundred different and more effective ways he might have faced down his would-be killers—"Don't think I won't pull the trigger. You've already seen me do it once today"; or "Go home. Go back to your families, before someone gets hurt"; or, particularly persuasive given the recent experience of Boggs's sixteen-year-old daughter, "I don't want to make widows of your wives or orphans of your children, but I will. And you know it." Instead, Twain speaks through Sherburn in order to utter angry convictions he had earlier expressed and then suppressed in *Life on the Mississippi*. The point to be made here, though, is that Twain's long-standing desire to inspect and comment on the human race also pushed him toward generalized, which is to say less particularized, dramatic fictions. In later years, his situations, themes, and characters tended to become deracinated conceptions; many of his stories, as we will see in later chapters, became fables, fantasies, science fictions, all describing a wider and wider arc of human experience, but unmoored to plausible human occasions. That generalizing process was already under way when, in 1883, he returned to finish the story of Huck's adventures, a story he had started to tell in 1876.

II

Some reviewers of *Life on the Mississippi* preferred, as later readers have also preferred, the first half of the book to the second half. Filled as it is with facts, figures, and statistics, the latter half seems tedious and contrived, and some have surmised that much of that material was merely padding, introduced to give the book a salable heft. In his study of the composition of the book, however, Horst H. Kruse has established that that was not at all the case.[6] In any event, readers have generally been more attracted to Twain's depictions of characters who live along the Mississippi than to his analysis of the historical and environmental forces that shaped those lives. One reviewer praised Twain's "clever sketching of queer characters" (*Reviews*, 235); another observed that the true "charm" of the book resides not in its history but in the "racy descriptions of real people," of the humorous and distinctive "lives of odd people" (*Reviews*, 241). Twain's own interest and involvement with his material, particularly when he arrived on the upper stretches of the river, more often had to do with "average" people as they are inferable from the population, in-

6. See Kruse, *Mark Twain and "Life on the Mississippi"* (Amherst: University of Massachusetts Press, 1981), esp. chaps. 1 and 5.

stitutions, commercial adventures, or economic security of the towns they live in.

In the earlier portions of the *Huckleberry Finn* manuscript there were many examples of local color and regional behavior—of Pap's railing against the "govment" and insisting on his parental solicitude or the new judge's pie-eyed attempts to reform the drunkard; of Bricksville loafers swapping chaws of tobacco; of ring-tailed roarers and superstitious raftsmen; of Judith Loftis talking about how girls catch and throw; of the slave catchers absolving their "conscience" with forty meager dollars. In other words, Twain was exposing the foibles of his fellow creatures, but the feel of these renderings is decidedly parochial and immediate. These were "snapshots" in the sense that they were grounded in Twain's experience, including his reading, but they do not seem to issue from some thought-out and solidified sense of human nature. Nevertheless, more and more Twain was gravitating toward comprehensive conclusions about his species and lumping them together as characteristic of what he had begun to call the "human race." The last stint of composition frequently revealed this different and broader perspective.[7]

Bernard DeVoto believed that Twain, after his return from his Mississippi trip and the completion of *Life on the Mississippi,* found the "true purpose" of his novel, *Huckleberry Finn*—to dramatize the rich variety of life and customs along the great Mississippi River valley.[8] Southern character, however, was not so individually various as it was shaped by inherited training and habit. At times, it seems that Twain was equally interested in the "averageness" of human behavior and in developing a social psychology that merely happened to be in the South. One factor in shifting his emphasis away from distinctive personalities and more toward a social psychology could be that he had ceased to believe in independence of thought and individuality of personality. Part of the reason he had bolted the Republican Party and turned Mugwump had to do with his conviction that his fellow Republicans had shown themselves to be a bunch of sheep motivated by no higher principle than a desire for mutual admiration. He had reached this sort of conclusion about the human race ear-

7. One consequence of this change was that the author was able to get more out of less. In other words, there are really only two episodes in the second half of the novel (the Wilks funeral and the evasion), and he was able to elaborate them with greater sureness. The feud would have provided as much by way of incident as these two examples above, but it occupies only a few manuscript pages. Of course, some of Twain's motivation was entirely practical, because he now conceived of *Huckleberry Finn* as a marketable commodity.

8. *Mark Twain at Work* (Cambridge: Harvard University Press, 1942), 69.

lier, and he made it abundantly clear in "The Character of Man" (circa 1885): "If we would learn what the human race really *is*, at bottom, we need only observe it in election times" (*CTSS1*, 857). The "so-called individuality" of human beings is in fact "a decayed and rancid mush of inherited instincts and teachings derived, atom by atom, stench by stench," and nothing is quite so obvious as that "the quality of independence was almost wholly left out of the human race" (*CTSS1*, 855).

Still another ingredient in Twain's exasperated opinions about human nature had to do with his extensive travels and his comic but probably sincere attempts to explain the survival of hurtful customs or the peculiarities of national character. When he turned his attention to life along the Mississippi River instead of along the Neckar, familiar acquaintance and intimate memories vied with intellectual abstractions for his imaginative attention. And if he was not entirely objective in his analysis of that life, neither was he content merely to draw unique portraits or to revivify the experiences of an earlier time. Instead, he often meant to make general observations that had a broader application than the sketches that went into "Old Times on the Mississippi." Yet another influence upon Twain may have come from his reading, particularly in history and social science; this is an aspect of his thinking that we will deal with in some detail a bit later. Here, it is enough to say that Twain's shift of interest, as it is detectable in *Huckleberry Finn*, is revealed in several ways.

In the latter half of the narrative, for instance, there are many more people assembled for one reason or another, and their actions are choreographed to demonstrate a point about group behavior. In addition to the Bricksville mob that attempts to lynch Sherburn, there is the mob that tars and feathers the duke and dauphin in chapter 33; there is the group of townsfolk who become a "rattling pow-wow" of a mob as they march to the graveyard and gather round the disinterred coffin in chapter 29, a mob that might well lynch Huck himself; there is the gang of farmers that chases Huck, Tom, and Jim vigilante-style in chapter 40;[9] and there are the men that cuff and curse Jim in chapter 42 and would surely have lynched him if they weren't afraid that they would have to pay for him afterward. There are, as well, other, less menacing but still contemptible assemblies—the third-night audience of the Royal Nonesuch performance, armed with rotten eggs and cabbages; the savvy but somewhat sadistic

9. Perhaps it is worth mentioning that Silas could have contacted the sheriff instead of the fifteen farmers he has on hand to thwart the supposed outlaws' plans to steal Jim. This would not occur to Silas, of course, because he is a typical southerner.

audience at the circus that laughs uproariously at the bareback rider's stunts, while Huck is "all of a tremble" for the man's safety; the gullible yet volatile crowd that buys into the duke and dauphin's impersonation of English brothers and then abruptly begins to doubt them with the appearance of a second pair of claimants. Twain had his chances to dramatize the behavior of crowds in earlier chapters—as for example in the custody hearing brought about by Judge Thatcher and the widow in chapter 5 or several times in the feud episode, though the closest he comes is when the feuding families go to church to hear a sermon on brotherly love. But, by and large, these remained unrealized opportunities.

Dramatized instances of social behavior merely testify to Twain's change of focus in his novel. There are other ways that his emphasis on the "averageness" of human nature actually damaged his narrative. Ernest Hemingway once said that in the last chapters of *Huckleberry Finn* Twain was just "cheating" and that the reader was advised not to read them at all. Hemingway did not explain what sort of cheating Twain was guilty of in the evasion episode; perhaps it was the burlesque elements that came easily to the humorist but did not really come out of the dramatic situation (Jim's captivity) that occasioned it. In any case, Twain, if he did not exactly cheat, at least managed his narrative in other ways that were perhaps expressive of his mood but hurtful to his craft.

Over the years, there have been several well-rehearsed objections to the latter half of *Huckleberry Finn*. The raft drifting ever deeper into the South and away from Jim's avenue to freedom; Miss Watson's mysterious and unlikely change of heart that causes her to free Jim in her will; the implausible reentry of Tom Sawyer into the narrative; the gratuitous burlesque in the evasion episode; Huck's complaining but really timid acquiescence in Tom's romantic adventures; the author's apparent willingness to have Jim play the role of a comic darky figure after having established him as a genuinely sympathetic human being—these are the principal charges leveled against the book. However, there is another sort of criticism one might make of Twain and of this portion of the novel. It has to do with Twain losing hold of Huck's voice and vision and to a degree abandoning his original conception of the figure. Much of the originality and charm of Huck's voice comes out of his untutored perceptions and the unaffected manner in which he delivers them to his readers. Take, for example, a portion of his description of the Grangerford house:

> It was a mighty nice family, and a mighty nice house, too. I hadn't seen no house out in the country before that was so nice and had so much style. It didn't have an iron latch on the front door, nor a wooden one with a buckskin string,

but a brass knob to turn, the same as houses in town. There warn't no bed in the parlor, not a sign of a bed; but heaps of parlors in town has beds in them. . . .

Well, there was a big outlandish parrot on each side of the clock, made out of something like chalk, and painted up gaudy. By one of the parrots was a cat made of crockery and a crockery dog by the other; and when you pressed down on them they squeaked but didn't open their mouths nor look different nor interested. . . . On a table in the middle of the room was a kind of a lovely crockery basket that had apples and oranges and peaches and grapes piled up in it which was much redder and yellower and prettier than real ones is, but they warn't real, because you could see where pieces had got chipped off and showed the white chalk or whatever it was, underneath. (*HF*, 136–37)

Apart from the signature items of Huck's distinctively unliterary manner—his unself-conscious repetition of words and phrases ("bed" or "beds," "crockery," "mighty nice"); nonparallel constructions ("cat made of crockery," "crockery dog"); and of course the exquisite ungrammaticality of it all—the description has a freshness about it because Huck also conveys his unfamiliarity with such houses and such families. Huck has no stock of ready-made assumptions through which to filter his perceptions. He has seen a few country houses before, but never one with so much "style," and of course he uses the word *gaudy* in an entirely complimentary way. He knows firsthand that many houses in town have beds in the parlor, but one suspects that he knows this because he has delivered something to those houses and in any event has never been invited into the house. On the other hand, such experience as he does have fails him in comic ways. He knows enough to get a squeak out of the crockery dog and cat, but he retains expectations that occur outside the parlor, not within—when you press down on a real dog or cat, it is apt to display at least a passing interest in the event. Similarly, Huck knows his chalk, but he is rather uncertain about what that stuff, presumably plaster of paris, is beneath the painted surfaces of the parrots and the fruit. In short, this description has a particularity and vividness that draw some of their energy from Huck's limited acquaintance with artifice. Huck makes no generalizations beyond his limited experience, but that same description is satiric and comic for readers because we do have the broader frame of reference Huck lacks.

Twain wrote the description of the Grangerford house in 1876. In 1883, he wrote the following description of the Wilks house:

So Mary Jane took us up, and she showed them [the king and duke] their rooms, which was plain but nice. She said she'd have her frocks and a lot of other traps took out of her room if they was in uncle Harvey's way, but he said they warn't. The frocks was hung along the wall, and before them was a curtain made out of calico that hung down to the floor. There was an old hair trunk in one corner, and a guitar box in another, and all sorts of little knick-knacks and jimcracks around, like girls brisken up a room with. . . .

That night they had a big supper, and all them men and women was there, and I stood behind the king and the duke's chairs and waited on them, and the niggers waited on the rest. Mary Jane she set at the head of the table, with Susan alongside of her, and said how bad the biscuits was, and how mean the preserves was, and how ornery and tough the fried chickens was,—and all that kind of rot, the way women always do for to force out compliments; and the people all knowed everything was tip-top, and said so—said "How *do* you get biscuits to brown so nice?" and "Where, for the land's sake *did* you get these amaz'n pickles?" and all that kind of humbug talky-talk, just the way people always does at a supper, you know. (*HF,* 220–21)

Of course, *we* know, but how on earth does Huck? It is unlikely that the widow or Miss Watson ever apologized for the cooking to Huck; it is unthinkable that Pap ever did. Is it even conceivable that a boy who usually slept in a hogshead would say about a room, any room, that it was "plain"? Huck's experience with girls' ways and with girls' rooms is, so far as we know, nonexistent. His attendance at sit-down suppers is negligible, though here he appears bored by the all too familiar "talky-talk." The language is Huck's but the voice is Twain's, and it is a weary and impatient voice at that. Twain's interest in representative gestures and habits has infected his narrative at this point, and to have Huck report them is to make the boy act and speak out of character. But this is not an isolated instance, and a brief inventory of other examples drawn from the latter half of the novel may serve to prove the point.

—The king "tried to talk like an Englishman; and he done it pretty well, too, for a slouch" (*HF,* 208), says Huck. Twain had some decided opinions about the differences between English and American speech,[10] but so far as we know Huck has never heard any Englishman speak, outside the mixed-up impersonations of the Royal Nonesuch, until the second pair of claimants arrives in chapter 29. What is more, Huck is out of character when he remarks that "anybody but a lot of prejudiced chuckle-heads

---

10. See "Concerning the American Language," originally intended for *A Tramp Abroad* but published in *The Stolen White Elephant and Other Stories* (1882). Reprinted in *CTSS1,* 830–33.

would a *seen*" that the new claimant is telling the truth and the king is lying. Huck is not apt to be so contemptuous of people he believes are his social superiors.

—When the duke and dauphin masquerade as the bereaved brothers and cry and hug one another, Huck says, "Well, if ever I struck anything like it, I'm a nigger. It was enough to make a body ashamed of the human race" (*HF,* 210). Huck's membership in that race, it should be remembered, is altogether uncertain, and his inclination to speak as its partisan is problematic.

—Huck is struck by how quiet it is at the Wilks funeral, "no other sound but the scraping of the feet on the floor, and blowing noses—because people always blows them more at a funeral than they do at other places except church" (*HF,* 232). What other funeral has Huck attended? He broke in on the one that was meant to commemorate Tom Sawyer and Joe Harper's passing in *The Adventures of Tom Sawyer,* but beyond that he is apparently ignorant of funerals and mourners.

—At times Huck plays the role of the worldly moral philosopher, as when he says about the thoughtful undertaker who lets everyone know the yelping dog in the cellar had a rat, "A little thing like that don't cost nothing, and it's just the little things that makes a man to be looked up to and liked" (*HF,* 233). When he tells a white lie to Mary Jane Wilks, that he won't say she gave the impostors her love, Huck adds, "It was well enough to tell *her* so—no harm in it. It was only a little thing to do, and no trouble; and it's the little things that smoothes people's roads the most, down here below" (*HF,* 243). Whether he is aping the sentiments of the widow or the rationalizations of Pap is unclear, but as an expression of his own point of view the words ring hollow. At other times, Huck is jaded and condescending, as when he describes Pikesville as a "shabby village" (*HF,* 266) or the Phelps farm as just another "one-horse cotton plantation"; "they all look alike" (*HF,* 276).

My point here is not to indulge in faultfinding. Nor, really, is it merely to enumerate defects and inconsistencies in Twain's rendering of Huck's character. Sometimes, Huck serves simply as a satirical device, and in those instances his existence as a fully imagined character tends to flatten out. But this alternating between Huck as an instrument of Twain's satire and Huck as an artfully imagined person occurs throughout the novel. Instead, what I am identifying is a tendency, in Twain, to speak more broadly about his created characters and to contrive situations that dramatize certain aspects of human nature. To approach his material in this way involved a good deal more calculation than had been the case when Twain began to write the book. Sometimes that same tendency, at least in the latter half of the novel, causes the author to have Huck make pronouncements about humankind that are altogether foreign to his experience and contrary to his temperament.

It is something of a commonplace to say that Twain's reintroduction of Tom Sawyer into his narrative is both a moral disappointment and an artistic mistake. Without attempting to extenuate Twain for what generations of readers have found to be a betrayal—a betrayal of Jim and of Huck, of course, but also of the readers' expectations, which the author had evidently cultivated toward other ends, specifically the expectation of a display of Huck's moral heroism—I want to inspect more minutely how the evasion episode bears upon Twain's thinking about human nature. But it is first necessary to look closely at Huck's famous moral decision in chapter 31 to help Jim to freedom and to "go to hell" as a consequence. The significance of that dramatic episode apparently cannot be overstated. Perhaps Norman Podhoretz's fine-tuned exaggeration is sufficiently representative of a host of critics and common readers who find the national identity and a national hope bound up in the lonely deliberations of a fourteen-year-old boy in the middle of practically nowhere. That scene, he says, "is one of the supreme moments in all of literature."[11] "Sooner or later," Podhoretz observed, "it seems, all discussions of 'Huckleberry Finn' turn into discussions of America—and with good reason." The novel "is now read as a key to the very essence of the American imagination, a central document of our most primitive impulses." Those are but preliminary remarks to his own argument for the centrality of the novel to our culture and for the centrality of Huck's decision to the novel:

> The moral, I think, will be obvious to anyone who feels the sharpness of the opposition Mark Twain set up between nature and society. "Huckleberry Finn" is a celebration of the instinctive promptings of the individual against the conditioned self, and a refutation of the heretical idea that reality can be equated with any given set of historical circumstances. This heresy has become even more powerful today than it was seventy-five years ago, and there can be no better protection against the morality of "adjustment" than Mark Twain's uncompromising, hard-headed insistence on the distinction between nature and society.

11. Norman Podhoretz, "The Literary Adventures of Huck Finn," *New York Times,* December 6, 1959.

This is another way of saying Huck was guided by intuitive moral sympathies, not by a utilitarian selfishness that adapts to the environment of circumstance.

A better documented but, in the last analysis, perhaps no less impressionistic assessment of Huck's moral decision appears in Walter Blair's authoritative *Mark Twain and Huck Finn* (1960). Blair places some emphasis upon an 1895 notebook entry Twain made when he was contemplating a "lay sermon on morals and the conduct of life":

> Next, I should exploit the proposition that in a crucial moral emergency a sound heart is a safer guide than an ill-trained conscience. I sh'd support this doctrine with a chapter from a book of mine where a sound heart and a deformed conscience come into collision and conscience suffers defeat. Two persons figure in this chapter: Jim, a middle-aged slave, and Huck Finn, a boy of 14, . . . bosom friends, drawn together by a community of misfortune.[12]

The passages have to do with the scene in chapter 16 where Huck is paddling ashore with the expressed purpose of turning Jim in and then meets the slave-hunters and improvises a story that makes them suspect his supposed family on the raft has smallpox. As Blair points out, this "triumph" of the heart over the conscience resembles a spontaneous decision springing from an innate moral sense, what Thomas Jefferson would characterize as a "generous spasm of the heart." This scene really is a "moral emergency," for now Huck has the ideal opportunity to turn Jim in but does not; instead, he instantly falls back to a clever lie. In a copy of the printed novel he had marked for public reading, also in 1895, Twain had inserted and then marked out this comment: "lie; you always got to do that when you git in a close place. Facts ain't no good when a person is crowded" (*HF*, 639).

Walter Blair goes on to argue that the same sort of moral decision dramatized by Twain in 1876 also occurs in chapter 31, written seven years later: "The representations of Huck and Jim suggest that, for all his talk about believing man 'merely a machine automatically functioning,' Mark had not been completely converted by his own eloquence."[13] In contradiction of his announced opinions about the moral nature of man, Twain had once again allowed an innate moral sense to prevail against the forces of habit, training, and public opinion. "Against all his logic," says Blair,

12. Quoted in *Mark Twain and Huck Finn*, 143.
13. Ibid., 343.

"Mark Twain was fighting for a faith." As much as I appreciate Blair's sentiments here, I find his conclusion doubtful for both textual and extratextual reasons. First, this is not a "moral emergency" of the sort we find in chapter 16. To the contrary, it is a moment of deliberation. No decision is being forced upon Huck due to the exigencies of the moment. Second, his crisis is not really brought on by an immediate concern about Jim's captivity. It is true that Jim's being sold to Silas Phelps for forty dollars is the occasion for his deliberations, but it is not the subject of it. Instead, it has to do with the state of Huck's soul. At first, Huck considers writing Tom Sawyer to pass on the word to Miss Watson that Jim is at the Phelps farm; that way he might spare Jim the misery of being sold downriver. He dismisses this idea for two reasons: first, Miss Watson will be so angry with Jim that she will sell him downriver anyway or, if he remains in St. Petersburg, people will be mean to him for his ingratitude; and second, if Huck ever saw someone from that town again he would be so ashamed that he helped a runaway slave that he would be "ready to get down and lick his boots" (*HF*, 268).

As Huck's conscience begins more and more to "grinding" him, he realizes that an ever-watchful Providence is looking down on him accusingly. He tries to extenuate himself by saying that he was "brung up wicked" (*HF*, 269), but the accusations come from within as well: "something inside me kept saying, 'There was the Sunday School, you could a gone to it; and if you'd a done it they'd a learnt you, there, that people that acts as I'd been acting about that nigger goes to everlasting fire'" (*HF*, 269). The grammar is Huck's, but the sentiments are those of an avowedly Christian slaveholding community. Clearly, this form of conscience is not an internal moral agent but a species of ventriloquism, a social point of view almost but not quite trained into the boy. Huck believes the immorality of helping a runaway slave must be right in the same way Twain pretended to believe that German opera must be sublime—because his social betters believe this. However, since Huck has never really been a part of the social order that maintains these principles, the claims this chastening voice has upon him are wholly artificial. They are as fraudulent as Huck's failed attempts to pray for salvation and forgiveness. The inner voice Huck hears is a carping voice of the sort that also complains "set up straight," "don't gap and stretch like that, Huckleberry—why don't you try to behave?" (*HF*, 3). Thus far in his bout with conscience, as Blair readily concedes, Twain was following a utilitarian course of moral choosing of the sort that W. E. H. Lecky had so clearly attacked but that was consonant with Twain's own professed belief that all ideas, moral and other, are generated from without not within.

The second round in this bout, however, Blair finds more to resemble the intuitionist point of view than otherwise. Huck writes his letter to Miss Watson and suddenly feels cleansed until he begins to recall his experiences with Jim on the river and can't "strike no places to harden me against him" (*HF*, 270). His deliberation reaches a climax: "I'd got to decide, forever, betwixt two things" (*HF*, 270). Huck famously declares, "All right, then, I'll go to hell," tears up the letter, and resolves to "take up wickedness again, which was in my line" (*HF*, 271). There are three points worth making here. First, Podhoretz's claims about the supremacy of this literary moment notwithstanding, Huck's decision to go to hell is rather a bland one. After all, he informs us in the opening chapter that because, as Miss Watson assures him, Tom Sawyer won't be going to heaven and because playing the harp doesn't strike him as a good time, Huck has no ambitions in that direction. Second, it is not at all clear that Huck ever meant to actually mail the letter to Miss Watson. He writes it, he says, in order to see whether the act will permit him to pray and to lead a "better" life. Third, Huck's spontaneous recollections of Jim's kindness toward him are a different but related sort of contemplation. Most of his memories have to do with how he has personally benefited from Jim's kindness, and not with his empathy for Jim's condition or his recognition of Jim's humanity.[14] If I turned Jim in, he seems to be saying, would my conscience then be appeased; would I then feel better; would I be any happier? His decision to go to hell, as he makes explicitly clear, is not to free Jim but to "take up wickedness again" (*HF*, 271). His first evil act, it is true, is to steal Jim out of captivity, but, in Huck's mind, that may merely be a warm-up act for some truly hellish adventure in crime. In any event, Huck's moral crisis is a contest not between right and wrong but between imperfectly absorbed habits of mind in the antebellum South and, for a lack of a better word, a young boy's "druthers."

It may be instructive to inspect this literary "moment" from a rather different angle. I am lingering over this subject not because I am intent on debunking the vaunted claims for Huck's important place in our national identity, but because a clarification of Huck's conduct may help to explain the author's motives in the evasion episode and his subsequent thinking in later writings about human nature as the mechanical adaptation to external influences.

---

14. Though Huck recalls being separated from Jim in the fog, he does not recall the scolding he received from Jim. Nor does he remember Jim's guilt over his mistreatment of his daughter, or Jim's desire to be reunited with his family, nor his desire for freedom. We as readers recognize Jim's humanity; Huck remembers that Jim was nice to him.

John Dewey refined the utilitarian moral argument in ways that better correspond to Twain's point of view than do Lecky's largely unsympathetic redactions of that argument. (Obviously Twain did not read Dewey, and I am merely seeking out clarifying analogies here.) Dewey insists that all thought is invested in a cooperative venture with acquired habits and impulses. Thus when a moral dilemma occurs, it calls for a moral judgment, but not in a matter-of-fact calculation of potential profits and losses, as is sometimes asserted against the utilitarians. Instead, the dilemma is the result of prior habits and newly felt impulses coming into conflict, and that conflict, in its turn, calls forth deliberation:

> [D]eliberation is a dramatic rehearsal (in imagination) of various competing possible lines of action. It starts from the blocking of efficient overt action, due to that conflict or prior habit and newly released impulse to which reference has been made. Then each habit, each impulse involved in the temporary suspense of overt action takes its turn in being tried out. Deliberation is an experiment in finding out what the various lines of possible action are really like....
>
> What then is choice? Simply hitting in imagination upon an object which furnishes an adequate stimulus to the recovery of overt action. Choice is made as soon as some habit, or some combination of elements of habits and impulse, finds a way fully open. Then energy is released. The mind is made up, composed, unified.... All deliberation is a search for a *way* to act, not for a final terminus.[15]

But what of the conscience that figures so prominently and painfully in Huck's deliberation? Here, too, Dewey is instructive: "conscience is said to be a sublime oracle independent of education and social influences. All of these views follow naturally from a failure to recognize that all knowing, judgment, belief represent an acquired result of the workings of natural impulses in connection with environment."[16]

Dewey's observations fit what actually happens during the course of Huck's meditation. Huck searches out, in the imagination, a unified and agreeable course of action first by writing Miss Watson about turning Jim in. Then his imagination turns to the recollected pleasures he has had with Jim in their journey down the river. Had Huck's moral instruction in the self-evident "rightness" of slavery been more perfect and had he a tangi-

---

15. *Human nature and Conduct: An Introduction to Social Psychology* (New York: Henry Holt and Co., 1922), 191–93.
16. Ibid., 187.

ble stake in a society that authorizes the institution, his decision might have been altogether different. After all, Jim displays the same qualities Huck inferentially describes, when he helps the doctor tend to a wounded Tom Sawyer. Jim is helpful, solicitous, loyal, and all the rest, and the doctor speaks a kind word for Jim: "Don't be no rougher on him than you're obleeged to, because he ain't a bad nigger" (*HF,* 352). And he utters the highest praise his own highly socialized conscience permits him: "I tell you, gentlemen, a nigger like that is worth a thousand dollars—and kind treatment, too" (*HF,* 353). More to the point, Huck discovers a way out of his paralyzing dilemma by falling back into his congenial habits of wickedness. Huck feels bad on the one hand because he has had a hand in depriving Miss Watson of her property (Jim) and on the other because he contemplates depriving Jim of his freedom. Here are the fretful effects of conscience, and in both instances it is an interloper in a moral act, advancing no "true" moral position but rather foreclosing on some definite moral act. It is not "good" to steal an old woman's property; it is not "good" to take away a man's liberty. But "being" good in this abstract way only prevents one from "doing" good. That is the riddle Huck solves simply by recognizing that he likes Jim better than he does Miss Watson. He tacitly affirms Jim's humanity because that is the sort of humanity he can understand. But Huck's decision is not an immutable resolution; it can and will be modified by and adapt to a changing environment. That environment does change the moment Tom Sawyer arrives upon the scene, agrees to help Huck, and proposes his "evasion."

III

It goes without saying that much of the evasion episode is mere fluff—burlesque, domestic farce, comic improvisation—and the probable reasons the novel took the turn that it did are several. Twain had invested a good deal of time and energy in the book over a seven-year period, and when he returned to the manuscript in 1883 he no doubt had ceased to think of it primarily as a literary experiment. Here was a potentially profitable commercial product, one that could be published by Twain's new publishing company, Charles E. Webster & Co., but first he needed to resolve to complete a narrative that otherwise might drift along forever. Burlesque came naturally to Twain, and without great effort he could introduce comic episodes that were reminiscent of the escapades in *Tom Sawyer.* This would gratify readers who liked their comedy in broad strokes; besides, by this time Twain had begun to think that his new book would make a nice companion to the earlier novel. It may have seemed to Twain altogether natural to reintroduce Tom if for no other reason than that it would enhance the marketability of the book. His working notes of the period indicate that this was a rather casual decision for him, at any rate.[17]

The evasion episode nevertheless contains some pointed satirical passages. However, the fact remains that all of the imaginative high jinks Tom urges upon Huck and forces upon Jim are childish indulgence. The unfolding of Tom's adventure is guided by, to use Douglas Anderson's nice phrase, his "book-bound loyalties,"[18] but it is also underwritten by a slaveholding mentality. After all, the romanticized obstacles Tom introduces into Jim's path to freedom have been enlisted, we learn at last, to set "a free nigger free." And Tom is unabashed by Aunt Sally's question about the why of it all: "Well that *is* a question, I must say; and *just* like women! Why, I wanted the *adventure* of it" (*HF*, 357). Still, what is simply a summer frolic for Tom Sawyer may have serious satirical implications. As several critics have noted, Twain may have wished to point out the shameful failure of Reconstruction, the subsequent institution of Jim Crow laws and other legal, social, and economic deprivations, as well as the gratuitous violence visited upon an "emancipated" people.[19] The comparisons between a boy's pranks and a nation's (or at least a region's) persecution are pointed and excruciating, for Tom has reveled in his adventure. "He said it was the best fun he ever had in his life, and the most intellectural; and said if he only could see his way to it we would keep it up all the rest of our lives and leave Jim to our children to get out; for he believed Jim would come to like it better and better the more he got used to it" (*HF*, 310). Here is the adolescent high fun of a shameful legacy—freeing the free negro can be deferred indefinitely, if not through the embellishments of witch pies, missing spoons, rope ladders, grindstones, and the like, then through empty promises, political compromise, immoral half-measures, threat, humiliation, and lynching. Whether or not Twain in-

17. In the working notes, Twain had written ^Huck +Tom (*HF*, 506). It is unclear whether his underlining of these names indicates the titles for their respective books or merely the boys' names.

18. "Starting over in *Huckleberry Finn*," *Raritan* 24, no. 2 (Fall 2004): 141–58 (quote on 147).

19. See, for example, Louis J. Budd, *Mark Twain: Social Philosopher* (Columbia: University of Missouri Press, 2001); Victor Doyno, "Afterword" to *Adventures of Huckleberry Finn* (New York: Oxford University Press, 1996), 15–16; and Shelley Fisher Fishkin, *Was Huck Black?* (New York: Oxford University Press, 1993), 70–75.

tended to satirize post-Reconstruction America, the question remains: why would he use Tom Sawyer as such a vile and contemptible vehicle for that satire, and why would Huck Finn put up with it all?

One thing to note is that Huck Finn and Tom Sawyer are not, nor have they ever been, "friends." In *Tom Sawyer,* Joe Harper is repeatedly identified as Tom's friend; Huck never is. Huck does admit at the end of that book that Tom has been "friendly" to him, but he says the same about the widow. In *Huckleberry Finn,* Huck says that he has the opportunity to be Tom's true friend by telling him that a "respectable" and "well brung up" boy such as he is should not "stoop" so low as to help him rescue a runaway slave: "I couldn't understand it no way at all. It was outrageous, and I knowed I ought to just up and tell him so; and so be his true friend, and let him quit the thing right where he was and save himself. And I did start to tell him; but he shut me up" (*HF,* 292–93). The real relation of Huck to Tom is as his "comrade," and that implies, among other things, that Huck may be allowed to join one or another of Tom's gangs, but their fanciful exploits will be determined by Tom's reading in adventurous romances and by Tom's whimsical application of them to yet another contrived adventure. When Tom agrees to "help" Huck free Jim, it is simply understood that Huck will be, at best, an accomplice, for that relation had been trained into him from an earlier time.

Twain's decision to bring Tom back into the novel and make Jim a "prisoner of style" indeed may have been just "cheating," but it was also inspired. After all, what better way to dramatize the "jejune romanticism" (*LOM,* 327) of the South and the affliction of the "Walter Scott disease," as he had characterized it in *Life on the Mississippi,* than to act out those impulses in the imaginative improvisations of a child? Twain had excised from *Life on the Mississippi* much of the more virulent feelings he had expressed about the South's proud attachment to caste, codes of honor, clannish sentiment, and the rest. Tom's "evasion" permitted Twain to vent his spleen and speak his frustrated anger more directly than he was disposed to do in his own person. He could easily disguise his own diatribe by making vivid the unthinking, but still objectionable, pranks of a St. Petersburg boy who constantly tested the patience of his community but never questioned its prevailing assumptions. However, our contemporary disgust at the humiliation Tom inflicts upon Jim should not obscure the fact that Tom, almost by definition, is "innocent," innocent by virtue of not knowing any better. Tom thinks he can, in the end, make it all up to Jim by paying him for his "lost time" and then "waltz him into town with a torchlight procession, and a brass band, and then he [Jim] would be a hero"

(*HF,* 360). That imagined gesture is a measure of the cruel ignorance that has been bred into the boy. And it is not so far-fetched an idea of what Tom, or others, might have taken to be due recompense for a black's humiliating experience. Sad to say, not so many years earlier, Clemens himself had been guilty of a similar sort of misapprehension.[20] In the end, it is not difficult to account for Twain's temptation to bring Tom Sawyer back into Huck's story. Nor is it difficult to understand Huck's behavior when he is recast in the role of comrade.

If for no other reason, Twain's decision to bring Tom Sawyer back into the picture and, indeed, to have him co-opt Huck's purposes served as a means to explore, in Huck, one of the author's steadfast convictions about human nature. Human beings typically want to think well of themselves, but the only way they can achieve the sort of self-approval they desire is by obtaining the approval of others, and more specifically the approval of those perceived to be their betters. Merely by being physically present, Tom Sawyer effectively puts Huck Finn in his place, even though that "place" is not two miles below Pikesville, Arkansas, but several hundred miles north, in St. Petersburg, Missouri. Huck Finn may be a social outcast, but he was cast out of a specific social order. He was ignored or rejected by a town that supposedly knew him by virtue of his condition and his deficiencies. Huckleberry Finn, the only begotten son of a vile drunkard, has not been instructed in the ways of the Lord or the schoolmaster; he does not know how to eat properly or how to pray properly; he occasionally "lifts" a chicken or takes what food the slave Jake offers him because he has to eat; he goes barefoot, curses, and smokes because he can. Huck accepts the town's assessment of him and has grown comfortable in it, much more so than in being called a "poor lost lamb" or being made to wear starched collars.

There is nothing remarkable in Huck's identifying himself by the parochial judgments of his hometown. Clemens himself recalled adult assessments of him and liked the idea of returning to Hannibal and lording it over those now toothless old men and women who once had disparaging opinions about him. Similarly, Willa Cather in *The Song of the Lark*

---

20. In 1877, when John Lewis, a black servant of Theodore and Susan Crane, performed a remarkable feat of heroism by stopping a runaway cart with Olivia's sister-in-law aboard, Clemens's reaction was revealing. He interceded in the family's deliberations about how to reward Lewis by claiming that, since he had grown up among blacks, he therefore knew better than they what blacks would most appreciate. A few trinkets instead of a handsome amount of cash would suit, he claimed. See Arthur G. Pettit, *Mark Twain and the South* (Lexington: University Press of Kentucky, 1974), 96.

wrote that Thea Krönberg, the small-town girl who became an internationally known opera singer, always measured the skyscrapers of New York City against the water tower in her Colorado village of Moonstone. We know, at any rate, that Huck worries about running into people from St. Petersburg who will know he helped a runaway slave and that from time to time he compares his own antics to what he believes Tom Sawyer might have done. But carrying around the idea of Tom Sawyer is not the same thing as actually being in his presence, and Twain knew it. In chapters 12 and 13, which were also written during the last stint of composition, Huck and Jim board the grounded *Walter Scott*. (The irony of the name of the steamboat cannot be accidental.) Jim is reluctant to go aboard, but Huck is insistent: "Do you reckon Tom Sawyer would ever go by this thing? Not for pie, he wouldn't. He'd call it an adventure.... And wouldn't he throw style into it?" (*HF*, 81). What they discover on board, however, is another moral emergency, and what ensues presumably was meant as a deliberate, though ironic, parallel to the evasion episode. Two murderous men are holding Jim Turner captive and the boat is about to break up. Faced with another captive "Jim" and a situation that demands quick action, Huck suspends his admiring dedication to Tom's style and tells Jim this is no time to be "sentimentering." Though his plan ultimately fails (the steamboat sinks and apparently the men aboard drown), Huck acts here with the practical efficiency and dispatch that he tries, unsuccessfully, to urge upon Tom at the Phelps farm.

The implication here is that Twain knew perfectly well that Tom's appearance in the final chapters would dissipate Huck's supposed moral resolve to rescue Jim. That in fact may have been his point. W. D. Howells once observed that Twain was "romantic" (in the sense that he would have preferred fiction to be "stately and handsome and whatever the real world was not") but he was not "romanticistic," for "he was too helplessly an artist not to wish his own work to show life as he had seen it" (*MMT*, 49). Generations of readers and critics have wished that Twain had ended his novel in a different fashion than he did; many would have preferred that the evasion episode had been left out altogether. That wish may testify to a "romanticism" they shared with Twain himself. But to fail to render life as he knew or believed it to be would have subtracted from Twain's keen moral intelligence and have served to palliate the seriousness of the several issues (about slavery, racism, friendship, and many other things) that he had contemplated in the novel. The evasion episode serves to illustrate how friable firm moral purpose may prove to be under given circumstances. Human nature, being what it is, how could it be otherwise? But there remains another sort of moral question that Twain hinted at but left unresolved.

In the same 1895 notebook entry about a proposed "lay sermon on morals and conduct" and the "triumph" of Huck's sound heart over his "deformed" conscience, Twain continued musing upon his subject:

> In those old slave-holding days the whole community was agreed as to one thing—the awful sacredness of slave property. To help steal a horse or a cow was a low crime, but to help a hunted slave . . . or hesitate to promptly betray him to a slave-catcher when opportunity offered was a much baser crime, and carried with it a stain, a moral smirch which nothing could wipe away. That this sentiment should exist among slave-holders is comprehensible—there was good commercial reasons for it—but that it should exist and did exist among the paupers . . . and in a passionate and uncompromising form, is not in our remote day realizable.[21]

Twain made the same observation in *A Connecticut Yankee in King Arthur's Court* (1889), not in the person of a disaffected southerner, but through that epitome of Yankee republicanism and social progress, Hank Morgan. At a crucial point in that novel Hank is reminded "of a time thirteen centuries away, when the 'poor whites' of our South who were always despised and frequently insulted by the slave-lords around them, and who owed their base condition simply to the presence of slavery in their midst, were yet pusillanimously ready to side with the slave-lords in all political moves for the upholding and perpetuating of slavery, and did also finally shoulder their muskets and pour out their lives in an effort to prevent the destruction of that very institution which degraded them" (CY, 297).

It does not matter whether this attitude prevailed in the antebellum South or in King Arthur's England; here was a moral conundrum. The behavior of a large segment of the population that clearly acted against its own self-interest and in its complicity sponsored the degradation of its own members was something of a moral mystery. It could not be explained tidily in terms of a utilitarian moral theory. Huck's willingness to play the role of accomplice is endemic to his St. Petersburg training. But serfs who labor meekly under the rule of Church and State or Georgia sharecroppers who suffer from the "Walter Scott disease" and die on the battlefield in the name of a "code of honor" that is not theirs hint at a pandemic sickness. Ironically perhaps, that same sort of self-sacrificing ges-

---

21. Quoted in Blair, *Mark Twain and Huck Finn*, 143–44.

ture may, in the minds of some, be construed as transcendentally fine and noble. As Twain widened his angle of vision upon social behavior, he became less interested in the depiction of individual personalities—"queer characters" and "odd people." More and more, he was drawn into a broader analysis of "average" human nature as something implicated in existing social arrangements and governed by natural laws beyond its ken. That is the subject we turn to now.

IV

Huck complains at the end of *Adventures of Huckleberry Finn* that if he had known what "trouble" it was to make a book, he would not have tackled the project. However, Twain himself was willing to "tackle" immediately yet another story narrated by the young boy. While *Huckleberry Finn* was in production, he began to write another novel that would make good on Huck's prediction that he and Tom and Jim would "light out" for Indian Territory. Twain did not get very far into "Huck Finn and Tom Sawyer among the Indians" (nine chapters) before he broke off. His immediate purpose in that work was to ridicule romantic notions of the Native American as Tom Sawyer had absorbed them through his readings in Fenimore Cooper, and that was handled easily enough. But as his plot was developing, it was also clear that he was preparing to deal with the abduction and rape of a young woman named Peggy Mills. The editors of the California edition speculate that Twain was constitutionally uneasy about how to treat that subject and abandoned the project altogether.

Circumstantial evidence indicates that Twain had developed a more sympathetic, or at least more paternalistic, understanding of the Indian and would not have returned to the sort of racialist explanations of Native American character found in *Roughing It*.[22] But the manuscript as it stands betrays little of that sympathy. On a different subject, though, "Huck Finn and Tom Sawyer among the Indians" does contain two remarks that show Twain understood that if he were to recuperate Tom Sawyer for future fictions he would also have to rehabilitate him. In chapter 4, Tom resolves to rescue the captured Peggy Mills and Huck willing-

---

22. See Budd, *Mark Twain: Social Philosopher*, 107. Also, it is clear from a notebook entry made a few years later that he saw the impending rape of Peggy Mills as one more example of "absolute power unrestrained by a trained public opinion." The "Droit de Seigneur" "existed in Scotland, there are traces of it in England, you find it lodged in the big medicine man of various savage tribes" (*N&J3*, 414).

ly joins in. "I hoped you would," says Tom, "and I was certain you would; but I didn't want to cramp you or influence you."[23] This is a generous quality notably absent in Tom during the evasion episode. Second, after the abduction of the Mills daughters and the massacre of the remaining Mills family members, Tom, at long last, begins to discern the difference between "book Injuns and real Injuns," as Huck puts it. Had Twain given Tom Sawyer either of these traits in *Huckleberry Finn*, perhaps the evasion episode would not have turned out as it did, or at least not be so offensive to later readers. Evidently, in *Huckleberry Finn* Twain was more intent on disclosing certain facts about human nature as he understood it than he was in dramatizing for his readers moments of redemptive moral awareness. And at this point it is necessary to supply an intellectual context for Twain's turn from his highly particularized studies of boy-nature to his analysis of the "average" man or woman.

One way to do this is to introduce two writers whose works Twain probably read or read about but, even so, who exerted no demonstrable influence on his next important novel, *A Connecticut Yankee in King Arthur's Court.*[24] Nevertheless, by importing a discussion of two significant mid-nineteenth-century thinkers at this point, I hope to clarify the terms of Twain's shift of interest from individual moral nature to a social psychology. The first of those figures is the Belgian scientist and "father of statistics," Adolphe Quetelet; the second is the British historian Henry Buckle. These two names are not arbitrarily linked. In fact one of the essays available to Twain concerning the statistician was written by Edward Burnett Tylor, who was himself an advocate of scientifically based social progress and had done much to advance what he called the "Science of Culture." In his *Primitive Culture* (1874), Tylor admitted that his readers might find it repulsive to acknowledge that human development was subject to certain natural laws, that "our thoughts, wills, and actions accord with laws as definite as those which govern the motions of waves."[25] Given this premise, it is natural that Tylor would endorse the importance of Quetelet and Buckle, who were working the same mother lode but from

---

23. *Huck Finn and Tom Sawyer among the Indians and Other Unfinished Stories,* ed. Dahlia Armon and Walter Blair (Berkeley: University of California Press, 1989), 49.

24. Even though I am not attempting to establish a source for or influence upon Twain's thinking here, prudence and method suggest that one ought to confine this sort of speculation to texts Twain had available to him. Intellectual movements are always somehow "in the air" at any given moment, but I will restrict my considerations to the air Twain might actually have breathed.

25. Quoted in Daniel Boorstin, *The Discoverers* (New York: Vintage, 1985), 647.

different angles. Tylor's review-essay, "Quetelet on the Science of Man,"[26] elaborates the connection between the two men, and in *The History of Civilization in England,* Buckle acknowledges the foundational importance of Quetelet to his own attempt to put history on a solid scientific basis.

Adolphe Quetelet (1796–1874) had begun his professional career as a mathematician then turned his attention to astronomy; in Paris, he had studied probability theory under Joseph Fourier and Pierre Laplace. These endeavors, as it turned out, were fortuitous preparation for his most important work—analysis of documented instances of what he described as the physical, moral, and intellectual qualities of man. Quetelet surveyed statistics of murders and suicides, rates of mortality and disease among men and women of different levels of income and different climates, pulse rates, chest sizes, stillbirths, rheumatic afflictions, marriages, and the like as they had been recorded over several years and in several countries. There was a paucity of data for him to work with; nevertheless, in what today we would call a "longitudinal study," he discovered that there was a startling regularity of occurrences of these events from year to year. The most significant conclusions were published in his *Treatise on Man and the Development of His Faculties* (1835; English translation 1842), and Quetelet continued to refine them in two later volumes—*Social Physics* (1869) and *Anthropometry* (1870). All of these studies were supplied with charts, tables, formulas, and maps of distribution, and the analysis of data was sometimes intricate and complex. For our purposes, Tylor's summary remarks in an essay Twain had on hand are sufficient.

There were two important "generalizations" that Quetelet brought to bear on physical and mental science, according to Tylor. First, that all human actions, even those that seem arbitrary, even whimsical, can be shown to be "subordinate to general laws of human nature." Second, he introduced a conception of the "specific form" of man (in both bodily types and mental faculties) that was susceptible to definite statistical calculation. That form was what Quetelet called the "average man" (*l'homme moyen*).[27] The two concepts worked in concert. From his studies of murders and suicides, Quetelet discovered a striking regularity, more constant and predictable, in fact, than general mortality rates, and he drew the inescapable inference that "*society prepares the crime, and the guilty are only the instruments by which it is executed.* Hence it happens that the unfortunate

---

26. *Popular Science Monthly* 1 (1872): 45–55.
27. Tylor finds the phrase misleading and proposes "mean man" (in the sense of a statistical mean derived from individual instances) as an alternative.

person who loses his head on the scaffold, or who ends his life in prison, is in some manner an expiatory victim for society. His crime is the result of the circumstances in which he is found placed."[28] Social and moral reform, then, takes on a different complexion. Moral exhortations and appeals to one's free will are vain and misguided. "It is curious to see man," writes Quetelet, "proudly entitling himself King of Nature, and fancying himself controlling all things by his free-will, yet submitting, unknown to himself, more rigorously than any other being in creation, to the laws he is under subjection to."[29]

Here was a form of determinism that did not eliminate the role of the moralist in promoting the progress of society; instead it relocated that role in the attention that might be given to influences on human conduct—institutions, habits, and education. For all practical purposes, the most important influences upon human nature come from without; even if there is such a thing as free will it acts within limitations so restricted as not to be "injurious" to the movements of natural law. At all events, free will no longer falls within the exclusive domain of metaphysicians and theologians. Though from time to time there appears a great genius, there are no "great men" in this view of history. Quetelet instances Newton as such a genius, but he insists that "the sciences had arrived at such a point, as to render it necessary that the theory of the motion of the celestial bodies should be reduced to correct principles; and Newton was then the only man who combined the necessary conditions to accomplish this work."[30]

28. *A Treatise on Man, and the Development of His Faculties,* a Facsimile Reproduction of the English Translation of 1842 (Gainesville: Scholars' Facsimiles and Reprints, 1969), 108. A textbook example of this sort of social complicity occurs in chapter 35 of *A Connecticut Yankee,* "A Pitiful Incident," where the government impresses a man into service and leaves his wife and child to starve. The wife steals to save her child's life, and the government hangs the woman. Her accuser, learning that the woman's fate is death, commits suicide. Charge both deaths where they belong, Twain urges—"to the rulers and the bitter laws of Britain" (*CY,* 403).

29. Quoted in Tylor, "Quetelet on the Science of Man," *Popular Science Monthly* 1 (May 1872): 46. Twain may have had Quetelet's studies in mind when in the early 1900s he wrote about the regularity of suicides: "If there was such and such a number in such and such a town last year, that number, substantially, will be repeated this year. That number will keep step, arbitrarily, with the increase of population, year after year. Given the population a century hence, you can determine the crop of suicides that will be harvested in that distant year" (*Fables,* 401).

30. Quetelet, *Treatise on Man,* 101; Henry Buckle reaffirms this principle by noting that Adam Smith's *The Wealth of Nations* (1776) is "probably the most important book that has ever been written," but had it been published in the previous century it would have had no discernible influence on politics at all because the state of civilization was not prepared to receive his doctrines (Buckle, *The History of Civilization in England* [1857; rpt. New York: Appleton and Co., 1929], 1:154).

Progress is made possible by multiplying opportunities, distributing knowledge, and developing technologies. "The more knowledge is diffused," he argued, "so much more do the deviations from the average disappear; and the more, consequently, do we tend to approach that which is beautiful, that which is good."[31] A true study of human nature means studying the "average man" from whom all individuals are measurable departures. Social physics, as Quetelet described it, did not necessarily require a concept of the average man, but the Belgian statistician's natural democratic instincts pushed him toward that conclusion, and he called for a more equitable distribution of knowledge in the interests of social progress. Some found that the statistical method comported well enough with a different sort of social and moral vision,[32] but there were others who appropriated Quetelet's social vision as well as his method.

Even as a young man, Henry Thomas Buckle (1822–1863) had decided it might be worthwhile to create a "science" of history. He had been particularly influenced by Auguste Comte (whose wish to discover the laws governing society and the human mind inspired him) and, even more so, by John Stuart Mill (whose ethics and laissez-faire vision of social progress and human welfare he found convincing). Buckle conceived of a monumental study he entitled *The History of Civilization in England*, but he did not live to complete even that portion of his work he considered an "Introduction." Even so, the two volumes published in 1857 and 1861 run to nearly twelve hundred pages.[33] Buckle thought history lagged woefully behind other disciplines that had better succeeded in discovering the natural laws that lay behind social and mental phenomena. By contrast, history, as he found it, was a miscellany of many interesting collections of facts, anecdotes, and eccentricities that awaited some coordinated method that would connect them. The acts of men and society were not the results of accident or supernatural intervention; they were the consequences of

31. *Treatise on Man*, 108.

32. Francis Galton, for example, adopted Quetelet's premises, but he substituted for an emphasis on the average man an endorsement of the exceptional man and thereby promoted his insidious eugenics. Surprisingly perhaps, Florence Nightingale was also an enthusiast of social statistics and an admirer of Quetelet; however, she found that such studies better equipped her to discern the will of God.

33. Mark Twain apparently had at least read in those volumes. Alan Gribben notes that when Twain planned to include an appendix of the sources for certain incidents in *A Connecticut Yankee*, he cited "Hist Civilization" as the source for the "King's evil" in chapter 26 of his novel (*N&J3*, 506), but the editors of the Notebooks think Lecky was the source for this practice. Twain also referred to Buckle's *History* when he was preparing *Following the Equator*.

antecedent conditions operating according to discoverable laws, laws as constant and regular as those operating in the physical world. He also believed that the progress of civilization had proceeded farther and to greater effect in England than in any other nation because there had been fewer interventionist forces instituted that would inevitably hinder a natural process of development.

"The history of every civilized country," he wrote, "is the history of its intellectual development, which kings, statesmen, and legislators are more likely to retard than to hasten. . . . So far from being able to regulate the movements of the national mind, they themselves form the smallest part of it, and, in a general view of the progress of Man, are only to be regarded as the puppets who strut and fret their hour upon a little stage; while, beyond them, and on every side of them, are forming opinions and principles which they can scarcely perceive, but by which alone the whole course of human affairs is ultimately governed."[34] For Buckle, neither the mental nor the moral capacities of human beings evolve appreciably over the course of history; but the accumulation and distribution of knowledge do increase. The progress of civilization is due inevitably to the changes from without, not within, and it may be fostered or hindered through certain inveterate, national habits of mind. These habits of mind, in combination with three other "physical agents" by which the human race is influenced (Climate, Soil, and Food) account for the conspicuous differences between and among nations. Reference to any sort of "inherent" differences, specifically race, is a factitious evasion of real social and scientific questions concerning progress and civilization.[35] In order to see how and why English civilization outstripped the advancement of other nations, Buckle insisted that a thorough comparison of the histories of other countries was absolutely necessary.

An analysis of those countries where a "protective" spirit of intervention was allowed to curtail the development of individual freedom of thought would thereby shed light on the development of England, where such interference, often due to a weakness of government, was not so intense or so prolonged. Buckle made passing references to the development of civilization in India, Africa, Mexico, and elsewhere, but he gave over several hundred pages to the civilizations of Spain, France, and Scot-

---

34. *History of Civilization in England,* 1:279.

35. Buckle approvingly cites John Stuart Mill on the "supposed differences of race": "of all vulgar modes of escaping from the consideration of the effect of social and moral influences on the human mind, the most vulgar is that of attributing the diversities of conduct and character to inherent natural differences" (ibid., 1:29, n. 1).

land. He compared the development of the French (a "non-superstitious" people but one whose government took too authoritarian an interest in directing the thought of the people) to Spain (where national protectionism took a religious instead of a secular form). He also compared the habits of reasoning of the Scots (essentially deductive in method and thereby restrictive) with those of the English (inquisitive and inductive and therefore progressive). He intended to complete his introduction with a comparative study of a deductive-minded Germany and an inductive-minded United States—in the former, knowledge accumulates and deepens but is restricted to the few; in the latter, knowledge is more scarce but diffused more broadly. However, he died of typhoid at the age of forty-one.

There are four principles that supply the basis for the progress of civilization, he argued. First, human progress depends on the successful investigation of phenomena and the determination of natural laws, as well as upon the general diffusion of that knowledge. Second, before that process can begin, a spirit of "skepticism" must be brought into play. Third, the discoveries of these investigations necessarily increase intellectual truths and at the same time lessen the influence of moral truths, which are, by their nature, fewer and more static. Finally, the perpetual enemy to civilization is the protective spirit, which, in the case of the state, teaches men and women what they are to do and, in the case of the church, instructs them on what they are to believe.[36] There were of course objections to the contentions of both Quetelet and Buckle, among them that attention to a postulated "average man" obscures individual personality, trivializes free moral choice, and dispenses with ideas of originality and genius. In the minds of many people, society was not an aggregate movement but a collection of indecipherable and distinctive individuals. On this point, Herbert Spencer commented on James A. Froude's objection that Henry Buckle "would deliver himself from the eccentricities of this and that individual by a doctrine of averages":

> [Y]et Mr. Froude himself so far believes in the doctrine of averages as to hold that legislative interdicts, with threats of death or imprisonment behind them, will restrain the great majority of men in ways that can be predicted. While he contends that the results of individual will are incalculable, yet, by approving certain laws and condemning others, he tacitly affirms that the results of the aggregate of wills are calculable. . . . If it be held that the desire to avoid punish-

36. Ibid., 2:1.

ment will so act on the average of men as to produce an average foreseen result; then it must also be held that on the average of men, the desire to get the greatest return for labour, the desire to rise into a higher rank of life, the desire to gain applause, and so forth, will each of them produce a certain average result.[37]

As I have already said, I don't mean to establish the works of Adolphe Quetelet or Henry Buckle as sources for or influences upon Twain's thinking or his fiction. My real purpose is to relocate the ground (moral, political, and other) Twain might occupy when he moved beyond the lonely deliberations of a boy in the antebellum South and into questions of what social forces shaped human nature. Some critics and biographers have surmised that Twain embraced a determinist philosophy simply as a way of assuaging his own troubled conscience—after all, a machine cannot be held accountable for its moral shortcomings. However, it seems to me that as a moralist and as an evangelist for democracy and progress, the only responsible position Twain might take was to address questions that might have answers, to propose reforms that might work changes. In our own day, the scores on the reading proficiency tests of third-graders are used by legislators and architects to plan and build the penitentiaries that will be needed to house some number of them fifteen years hence. Between times, learned elders counsel these young charges to make "smart choices," "just say no," or "do the right thing." This is an instance of, at best, pious sentiment and, at worst, a twenty-first-century form of moral barbarism. Twain hoped that we might be doing better by this time. In 1887, the author made notes for a piece of fiction set one hundred years in the future that might complement *A Connecticut Yankee*. In that time, so he imagined, the methods for punishing criminals would have been modified: "changed hanging to insult, humiliation &c. . . . Hanging is not based on knowledge of human nature. When death penalty was instituted . . . revenge was the object, & passionate quick revenge. But now when our object is deterrent, *not* punitive, the death pen[alty] is an anachronism & is irrational & ridiculous. It [capital punishment] is the opposite of a deterrent . . . often" (*N&J3*, 346–47). Though the improvements of the nineteenth century represented an immeasurable advance over medieval feudalism, Twain conceived of progress as movement that did not end with his own day but pushed, little by little, beyond it.

The late 1880s was the high tide of Twain's social optimism, and the sort

37. *On Social Evolution: Selected Writings*, ed. J. D. Y. Peel (Chicago: University of Chicago Press, 1972), 95.

of nineteenth-century "social physics" I have been describing here may or may not have encouraged and influenced that hope. Nevertheless, it does isolate certain features of the author's gospel of progress that would appear, however fleetingly, in *A Connecticut Yankee*. For one thing, this sort of moral and social reform owes nothing to Darwinian evolution; mere "accident" was dismissed, particularly by Buckle, as specious, as were those appeals to supernatural intervention. Real and positive changes would come from the "work of public opinion" when the people themselves take the initiative; or as Hank Morgan might have said, when they assert their "manhood." Idolatry of the past is the source of aristocratic privilege and the hallmark of the aristocratic sensibility, but the people are "growing weary of idle talk about the wisdom of their ancestors, and are fast discarding those trite and sleepy maxims which have hitherto imposed upon them, but by which they will not consent to be much longer troubled."[38] Similarly, the true artist is not someone who, as Twain believed Walter Scott did, creates a yearning for a past that never existed. "A man can have no real influence on masses—he cannot comprehend them and put them in action—except he is infused with the spirit that animates them, and shares their passions, sentiments, and necessities, and finally sympathises completely with them. It is in this manner that he is a great man, a great poet, a great artist. It is because he is the best representative of his age, that he is proclaimed to be the greatest genius."[39]

In contrast to Hank Morgan, who initially intends to work wonders of social progress overnight, Twain instinctively knew that genuine reform takes time, but he also believed that when that moment comes revolutionary changes ensue. In "The Character of Man" (circa 1885) Twain disputed the idea of independent moral choice. "So-called individuality," he argued, is an outright lie; it is a lie to think "that I am I, and you are you; that we are units, individuals, and have natures of our own" (*CTSS1*, 855). We are a "mush of inherited instincts"—sheepish, sullen, reprehensibly patient. "Uncounted millions" take the abuse of railroad companies when reform requires that just one independent man demand his rights. "Statistics and the law of probabilities warrant the assumption that it will take New England forty years to breed this fellow" (*CTSS1*, 856).[40] In "The New Dynasty," a talk he gave to the Hartford Monday Evening Club in

---

38. *History of Civilization in England*, 2:103, 1:362.
39. Quetelet, *Treatise on Man*, 101.
40. Clemens himself played this civic role when he took up the cause of his servant who had been overcharged half a dollar by a cabman. See, for example, "Mark Twain Bests a Grasping Cabman," *New York World*, November 23, 1900, in *Interviews*, 377–81.

1886, however, Twain imagined a foreman for a printing office speaking before Congress not for his shop alone but for five million workers in all manner of trades. When that voice is heard, Twain contended, elected officials will actually become public "servants"—"not masters *called* servants by canting trick of speech" (*CTSS1*, 887).

The worker, Twain continued, "is the most stupendous product of the highest civilization the world has ever seen—and the worthiest and the best; and in no age but this, no land but this, and no lower civilization than this, could he ever have been brought forth. The average of his genuine, practical, valuable knowledge—and knowledge IS the truest right divine to power—is education contrasted with which the education possessed by the kings and nobles who ruled him for a hundred centuries is the untaught twaddle of a nursery, and beneath contempt" (*CTSS1*, 889). The logic and the language here conform to the social vision of progress I have been describing. The new man is suddenly empowered by the "*sum* of his education, as represented, in the ten thousand utterly new and delicate and exact handicrafts, and divisions and subdivisions of handicrafts, exercised by his infinite brain and multitudinous members." Clearly, this is no single man but man (and woman) in the aggregate. Education has liberated the average man who otherwise would have remained a slave, and the time has passed to think of this man as a problem to be solved: "Yes, he is here; and the question is not—as it has been heretofore during a thousand ages—What shall we do with him? For the first time in history we are relieved of the necessity of managing his affairs for him. He is not the broken dam this time—he is the Flood!" (*CTSS1*, 889–90). This enthusiasm (seasoned as it often was with his contempt for nobility, for human venality and cowardice in his own day as well as in a day gone by, and for antique usages that have survived beyond their appointed hour) was a quality he was trying to get into a novel he was working on at the time.

V

In one of his autobiographical dictations made late in his life, Twain insisted that he was first and foremost a serious moralist, and something of a preacher: "I have always preached. That is the reason I have lasted thirty years. If the humor came of its own accord and uninvited I have allowed it a place in my sermon, but I was not writing the sermon for the sake of the humor. I should have written the sermon just the same, whether any humor applied for admission or not" (*AMT*, 273). However, the genesis of his more serious works suggests the process worked the other way round. He started funny and then got serious. *Huckleberry Finn* began as a burlesque elaboration of a young boy's awkward and frustrating routine at the widow Douglas's; *Pudd'nhead Wilson* had its origins in the farcical humor of Siamese twins acting at cross purposes. Certainly the first recorded note for a book about a nineteenth-century Connecticut man in King Arthur's England (made in December 1885) does not predict that this would be a polemical book written with a "pen warmed up in hell" (*MTHL*, 2:613):

> Dream of being a knight errant in armor in the Middle Ages. Have notions and habits of thought of the present day mixed with the necessities of that. No pockets in the armor. No way to manage certain requirements of nature. Can't scratch. Cold in the head—can't blow—can't get at handkerchief, can't use iron sleeve. Iron gets red hot in the sun—leaks in the rain, gets white with frost & freezes me solid in winter. Suffer from lice & fleas. Make disagreeable clatter when I enter church. Can't dress or undress myself. Always getting struck by lightning. Fall down and can't get up. (*N&J3*, 78).

The literary prospects suggested here are pure burlesque. And even after he had written a few chapters of the book, Twain reassured Mary Fairbanks that he would not ridicule Thomas Malory's finely drawn characters in *Morte Darthur* and that his own novel in progress was not "a satire peculiarly" but a book of comic "*contrasts*" between two very different ages.

In fact, his Yankee (at first named Robert Smith, not Hank Morgan) was originally conceived to be an opportunist, not a political redeemer and social revolutionary. "Sir Bob" would prey upon the gullibility of a superstitious people, and he would personally profit more by his ability to tell tall tales about his supposed adventures with ogres and such to believing knights than by his nineteenth-century technological know-how.[41] The Yankee's adventures, then, would be a humorous romp through Camelot, but even at the beginning Twain imagined a sad conclusion to his tale. The

41. The stages of composition of *A Connecticut Yankee* are described by Howard G. Baetzhold in chaps. 6 and 7 of *Mark Twain and John Bull: The British Connection* (Bloomington: Indiana University Press, 1970) and "'Well, My Book Is Written—Let It Go. . . .': The Making of *A Connecticut Yankee in King Arthur's Court*," in *Biographies of Books: The Compositional Histories of Notable American Writings*, ed. James Barbour and Tom Quirk (Columbia: University of Missouri Press, 1996), 41–77.

last chapter would have the Yankee back in the nineteenth century, though in modern England not America; he would grieve over his loss of that earlier time and be found dead in his room the next morning, a suicide (N&J3, 216). Perhaps Twain imagined that by ending on that nostalgic note he might smooth over any feathers of his English readers he might have ruffled along the way. Whatever his early intentions, however, they were to change soon enough. Despite its fanciful burlesque and multiplying implausibilities, when at length the book was published the "last effect," or so it seemed to W. D. Howells, was as a work of moral realism. *A Connecticut Yankee* is a "most matter-of-fact narrative, for it is always true to human nature, the only truth possible, the only truth essential, to fiction" (*Reviews*, 295). It achieved that quality by degrees.

In early 1886, Twain wrote the first three chapters of his novel. In November of the same year, at the Military Service Institute on Governor's Island in the New York Harbor, he read from those chapters and outlined the further adventures of "Sir Robert Smith." He took up the manuscript again when he was at Quarry Farm in the summer of 1887 and wrote from chapter 4 through the opening of chapter 21, except for chapter 10, "The Beginnings of Civilization." By this time, his conception of his title character had changed dramatically. The Yankee was no longer a mere opportunist. Instead, he would seek to eradicate from Arthur's realm all manner of social and political evils and transform the kingdom into a progressive republic. While burlesque elements persisted in the book, Twain was introducing through the Yankee's proposed reforms serious issues and dearly held convictions. When a poor dramatic production of the story was performed in 1890, Clemens complained to his daughter Clara that the dramatist had emphasized the "circus" side of Hank's character and neglected altogether the "good heart & the high intent" of a "natural gentleman" (*LLMT*, 257). On the face of it, the transformation of Robert Smith, sly huckster, into Hank Morgan, humanitarian reformer, would seem to involve abandoning the utilitarian conception of man's moral nature and lapsing into the intuitionist position advanced by Lecky and others. That is, alongside his liberating impulses, the heart of Hank Morgan ought to be swelling with innate moral perceptions and grand sympathies. But this is not the case, and Twain's shift in purpose committed him to a narrative that introduced ambiguities and inconsistencies that could not be resolved.

Twain's comments on Hank Morgan's "good heart" and "high intent" notwithstanding, the author went out of his way to convey the Yankee's fundamental egoism as the motive for reform. Hank recognizes his alto-gether "anomalous" position in the kingdom:

> Here I was, a giant among pigmies, a man among children, a master intelli-gence among intellectual moles: by all rational measurement the one and only actually great man in that whole British world; and yet there and then, just as in the remote England of my birth-time, the sheep-witted earl who could claim long descent from a king's leman, acquired at second-hand from the slums of London, was a better man than I was. . . . There were times when *he* could sit down in the king's presence; but I couldn't. I could have got a title easily enough, and that would have raised me a large step in everybody's eyes. . . . But I didn't ask for it; and I declined it when it was offered. . . . I couldn't have felt really and satisfactorily fine and proud and set-up over any title except one that should come from the nation itself, the only legitimate source; and such an one I hoped to win; and in the course of years of honest and honorable endeavor, I did win it and wear it with a high and clean pride. (*CY*, 67–69)

The nonaristocratic title that assuages his hurt and solves his problem is, of course, "THE BOSS." What this title solves is more than a bit problemat-ic, however. For one thing, even Hank Morgan recognizes his position as a kind of "despot" (*CY*, 66), and he more often sustains his power and au-thority over the people by playing upon their fears and superstitions rather than by enlightening them. He may conclude that when six people out of a thousand hold all the cards it is time for a "new deal," but that does not mean he won't keep a couple of aces up his sleeve, just in case. And though he frequently complains about the moral "baseness" of those aristocrats who condescend to him, Hank several times makes it clear that the mechanics of moral nature in both the sixth century and the nineteenth do not differ very much; both are the result of inherited ideas, habit, and training. In a word, Hank Morgan will remake Camelot so that his mer-its, moral and intellectual, will be better appreciated. That, in itself, does not mean that Twain, through Hank, couldn't express his own deeply held convictions along the way. It does mean that the author's conception of human nature may cut across the grain or otherwise modify the Yankee's plans to improve the human condition. For Hank Morgan is at once a hardheaded New England man and an impractical knight-errant.

Hank prides himself on his Yankee origins, "practical; yes, and nearly barren of sentiment" (*CY*, 9). From time to time, however, he displays an almost tearful sense of what he owes himself. In chapter 26, for example, the monks examine one of Hank's innovations, the newspaper, with slack-jawed wonder. "These grouped bent heads, these charmed faces, these speaking eyes—how beautiful to me! For was not this [the newspaper] my darling, and was not all this mute wonder and interest and homage a most eloquent tribute and unforced compliment to it?" (CY, 262). Morgan seems to have forgotten that he did not really invent the newspaper, that it was the work of many centuries and many minds, even in the crude Alabama form of journalism Clarence produces; Hank inherited that form of literature and merely reintroduced it into an earlier era. Similarly, he did not prophesy the appearance of the eclipse, nor did he invent TNT. He merely remembered how to do these things. This is one of a great many ironies in the book. So far as we know, Morgan, despite his ability to "make anything" or to "invent" a new way to make a thing, can claim only one true invention, the miller-gun, and he is inordinately proud of that device. He does not really create the technological wonders that so amaze Arthurian England; he simply introduces them to an alien environment. Similarly, his democratic sympathies are sincere, but he did not invent republican institutions. He is genuine, too, in despising aristocratic pretension, but he is not exempt from wanting the fawning admiration of the multitude. In chapter 40, when he feels his bloodless revolution will soon effect a republic, Hank confesses a "base hankering to be its first president myself. Yes, there was more or less human nature in me; I found that out" (CY, 304).

If there is no inherent moral or mental difference between Hank Morgan and those creatures of sixth-century England whom he sometimes regards as brutes and beasts, then the meritocracy Hank envisions must be realized in two ways. He will have to try to retrain the average man and woman—to eliminate superstition and ignorance, to cultivate different kinds of habits, and to train them not merely to take up other sorts of occupations but to have different kinds of aspirations. But he will also have to restructure society as a whole—by providing greater opportunities for more people and by eradicating obstacles to genuine progress, but also by establishing some institutions and eliminating others. Even if Morgan were to accomplish these changes, however, his project is necessarily doomed. The reality of history demands that whatever portion of his dream Morgan achieves must be erased in some catastrophic way without leaving a trace (save a bullet hole in a breastplate of Sir Sagramor's chain mail) in order to put medieval England back on its sleepy, centuries-long path to political and industrial progress. If Hank Morgan (or Mark

Twain) has a creed, then, the narrative that expresses it is at best destined to become a legend, for all the improvements he works in the land will be blasted to smithereens.

We are principally interested in Mark Twain's preoccupation with human nature, and for that reason we need to be a bit careful here. The fundamental assumptions about human nature operating in *A Connecticut Yankee* do not differ materially from those he articulated in, say, *What Is Man?* There are, of course, differences in tone between those two texts—in the first there is a comic zest and fierce hopefulness; in the latter, at least in the utterances of the Old Man, there is a sometimes irritating and smug complacency—but in both the working parts of the human machine "automatically functioning" are pretty much interchangeable. In *A Connecticut Yankee*, though, the social and cultural environment permits the author to examine how an average human being will act under given circumstances and what altered forms of influence enhance or suppress, enlarge or distort, human beings as a mix of temperament, habit, training, and custom. In other words, from our limited perspective, Twain's social philosophy is something of a bank shot into his convictions about humanity at large.

It is frequently conceded that *A Connecticut Yankee* is a welter of inconsistencies and contradictions, and I don't mean to try to impose some improvised coherence upon the book. Nevertheless, it is perhaps worthwhile to describe the most salient terms of opposition. First, there are certain articles of faith, for Hank Morgan and presumably for Twain as well, that make the Yankee's utopian project something more than an exercise in self-aggrandizement. These may be expressed almost epigrammatically: "A man *is* a man at bottom," says Hank, and as a consequence at all times "there is plenty good enough material for a republic in the most degraded people that ever existed" (*CY*, 231). Twain reaffirmed this judgment in a July 17, 1899, letter to his wife: "the various merchants, military men, the various Tom-Dick & Harrys of *all* walks, whom I know—in this long list I find goodness the rule & ungoodness the exception. I should still find this the case among all tribes of savages in all parts of the earth & in all the centuries of history. I detest MAN, but nevertheless this is true of him" (*LLMT*, 253–54). The fundamental goodness of humankind acting in combination with enlightened self-interest makes universal suffrage a safe bet—"where every man in a State has a vote, brutal laws are impossible." And, Hank insists even more hopefully, in every nation in every time, "the bulk of its ability was in the long ranks of its nameless and its poor" (*CY*, 183). Clearly, these are more generous endorsements of democracy and the trustworthiness of the general populace than Twain was disposed to make in the 1870s.

On the other hand, there are pessimistic assumptions about the human condition at play in the novel as well. Twain divides his attention between individual possibilities and personal liberty and a reigning herd mentality. The serfs and slaves of Arthur's England may be an infuriatingly docile and all too tractable lot, but in many ways they do not differ from that mob that proposes to lynch Colonel Sherburn. In chapter 20, Hank has a "curious revelation" about the people he would make citizens: "Their entire being was reduced to a monotonous dead level of patience, resignation, dumb uncomplaining acceptance of whatever might befall them in this life. Their very imagination was dead. When you can say that of a man, he has struck bottom, I reckon" (*CY*, 134–35). In a similar vein, he notes that "chains cease to be needed when the spirit has gone out of the prisoner" (*CY*, 123). Hank sadly recognizes that such liberty as he means to bring to Camelot will involve an emancipation of the mind as well as of the body and that that will take a generation. As a notebook entry indicates, Twain himself thought problems basic to human nature might last a bit longer than that: "There are in Conn, at this moment & in all countries, children & disagreeable relatives chained in cellars, all sores, welts, worms & vermin. . . . This is to suggest that the thing in man which makes him cruel to a slave is in him permanently & will not be rooted out for a million years" (*N&J3*, 414).

That Twain should entertain these two distant positions regarding human nature is unremarkable. Vacillations of thought and feeling are on exhibit in most of his more interesting works. However, in *A Connecticut Yankee*, it appears that Twain was not merely yielding to certain mood swings so much as he was, at least at times, contemplating coexisting qualities in the human creature. Certainly that is the suggestion of his remark in this notebook entry: "Show me a lord, & I will show you a man who you couldn't tell from a journeyman shoemaker if he were stripped; & who, in all that is worth being, is the shoemaker's inferior: & in the shoemaker I will show you a <dumb> dull animal, a poor-spirited insect: for there is enough of him to rise & throw/chuck his lords & royalties into the sea where they belong, & he doesn't do it" (*N&J3*, 411). Hank Morgan and Mark Twain share a belief in the first half of this equation; they are passionately anti-aristocratic. Only gradually, however, does Hank Morgan come to realize what Twain assumed from the beginning—that the masses are enslaved by long-standing habits and customs, and these cannot be eradicated in short order. The up-to-date, quixotic reformer eventually discovers that it is he, not the knights-errant, who is tilting at windmills. The story of Hank Morgan's adventures in progress is, essentially, one of diminishing expectations and narrowing possibilities.

Abraham Lincoln had thought that the interests of the largely industrializing and republic-minded North and the slaveholding and largely agrarian and aristocratic South would one day be reconciled by the "better angels of our nature." Hank Morgan seems to believe that "Persimmons's Soap," "Peterson's Prophylactic Toothbrush," and "Noyoudont" mouthwash will do the trick; at the very least they will contribute to national hygiene if not the domestic welfare. "If I had the remaking of man, he wouldn't have any conscience," Hank declares. Conscience may do much good work in the world, but in the long run it doesn't pay: "it would be much better to have less good and more comfort" (CY, 121). Thus it is that he initially sets out to supply the kingdom (and himself) with conveniences. This impulse was perfectly in keeping with his original inspiration to "Have notions and habits of thought of the present day mixed with the necessities of that"; his book would be full of comic "contrasts" but not particularly satiric ones. Hank Morgan might sincerely prefer a chromo of "Washington Crossing the Delaware" to the Bayeux Tapestry, but that would have more to do with his orientation than with absolute judgments. There was, potentially, plenty of comedy to be had by casting Hank in the role of a latter-day Robinson Crusoe, cast ashore on a primitive island, in this case sixth-century England, and improvising such creature comforts as he might, but it was comedy with no special sting.

Likewise, his dealings with the "natives" might be made funnier still if Hank had merely pretended to go on adventures and had augmented his reputation through tall-tale bravado, as Twain had originally planned for him to do. This sort of joke is analogous to the one he used in *A Tramp Abroad* by proposing a pedestrian tour of Europe but hardly walking anywhere at all. Something of these qualities survives in *A Connecticut Yankee*. Even Robinson Crusoe, in his confrontations with the natives, was saved not by his superior weaponry but because, in their innocence, the warriors believed his musket was an "inexhaustible fund of death." In chapter 39, after he has dispatched Sir Sagramor with a shot from his revolver, and with greater calculation than Crusoe, Hank plays a "bluff" in his challenge of the remaining knights. He has eleven shots remaining in his pistols and five hundred mounted adversaries. The bluff works; the knights scatter after the ninth shot finds its mark, and Hank rakes in his chips and then some. He ups the ante by engraving a permanent challenge to the knights in brass and from time to time adds to its proportions. Eventually, his boast becomes that he will take fifty assistants and "stand up *against the massed chivalry of the whole earth and destroy it*" (*CY*, 443). For Twain's purposes, this gesture is preliminary to the Battle of the Sand Belt, but it comes out of the early conception of Hank Morgan as the theatrical teller of tall tales.

By half, Morgan's authority and power in Camelot derive from his nervy showmanship, not from his technological savvy. He amazes Marco, Dowley, and the rest by confidently telling them what wages will be a thousand years hence. He sees Merlin as the competition and triumphs over him not by exposing the fraud of his magic but by convincing the masses that his own is greater. Hank meets in the "rival magician" in chapter 24 someone equally adept at the hyperbolic bluff. This "celebrity from Asia" could confidently tell what the Sultan of Egypt was doing, but he couldn't discover how many fingers Hank held up behind his back. Nevertheless, the magician is a good showman and can weasel out of the discrepancy easily enough. With the aid of the telephone, Hank eventually prevails in this contest of wits, but the experience is an eye-opening one for him: "Observe how much a reputation was worth in such a country. These people had seen me do the very showiest bit of magic in history, . . . and yet here they were, ready to take up with an adventurer who could offer no evidence of his powers but his mere unproven word."[42] When dealing with the gullible multitudes, it becomes clear, "a man can keep his trade-mark current in such a country, but he can't sit around and do it; he has got to be on deck and attending to business, right along" (*CY*, 24). Evidently, Hank forgets this lesson. Otherwise, he would never have left for France and given the church the opportunity to reverse the course of his civilizing efforts.

When Twain decided to have Hank sally forth to face the ogre and save the damsels in distress, instead of sitting at the round table and pretending to conquests he never made, the author had further altered his conception of his title character and the direction his novel would take. As Howard Baetzhold observes, "Instead of dodging the quest for the captive princesses and lying about it, he would carry it through to reveal that the princesses (and by implication all royalty and nobility) were actually hogs. And instead of using his Gatling gun and electrified fence to defeat Arthur's enemies, he would turn them against the whole chivalry of En-

---

42. This, of course, is precisely what Twain had in mind for Hank Morgan to do in an earlier conception of the narrative.

gland and the values for which they stood." More and more, Baetzhold adds, Hank Morgan would become "the spokesman for Clemens's current opinions."[43] Thereafter, his novel acquired the sort of anger and focus associated with full-fledged satire. Baetzhold's observation is astute and unarguably true. Louis J. Budd, Henry Nash Smith, the editors of the Mark Twain Papers, Baetzhold himself, and many others have identified the sources for and the objects of Twain's satire,[44] and Twain himself had originally intended to include an appendix that would authenticate the historical accuracy of his damning account of medieval barbarism. Daniel Beard's illustrations, prompted by the insightful reading of an artist who had his own liberal social commitments, made some of the acerbic qualities as they applied to the modern day all the more obvious, even to Twain himself.

It would be futile, of course, for Twain to satirize in a novel published in 1889 such practices as *le droit de seigneur*, divine right of kings, feudalism and slavery, compulsory tithing, rank superstition, unthinking loyalty to nobility, and many other gross errors as they existed in sixth-century England. To the extent that *A Connecticut Yankee* is a satire at all, it is concerned with the survivals of such medieval practices in the nineteenth century, and particularly in a country, notably but not exclusively England, where an established Church and a curious allegiance to nobility still linger to the hurt of the people. As satirist, Twain himself could occupy the somewhat exalted role of the humorist as he had defined it in a letter printed in the *Hartford Courant* in 1888—someone devoted to "the deriding of shams, the exposure of pretentious falsities, the laughing of stupid superstitions out of existence." The humorist, he added, is "the natural enemy of royalties, nobilities, privileges, and all kindred swindles, and the natural friend of human rights and human liberties."[45] As a democrat and a world citizen, Twain could exult in the evidence he saw that the end of such privileges was at hand. He did this, for example, in an interview shortly after his novel was published: "I began to think some months ago that the time was ripe for this [novel]. And sure enough it is, for there is Brazil getting rid of its Emperor in twenty-four hours, there is talk of a republic in Portugal and federation in Australia" (*Interviews*, 104).

43. "Well, My Book Is Written—Let It Go," 50.
44. See, for example, Budd, *Mark Twain: Social Philosopher*, chap. 6; Smith, *Mark Twain's Fable of Progress: Political and Economic Ideas in "A Connecticut Yankee"* (New Brunswick: Rutgers University Press, 1964); Baetzhold, *Mark Twain and John Bull*, chaps. 6 and 7, and "'Well, My Book Is Written—Let It Go.'"
45. *Hartford Courant*, June, 22, 1888, p. 5, col. 1.

As a satiric device, then, Hank Morgan can speak Twain's own current convictions. He can act as the adversary of all things superstitious, cruel, aristocratic, and enslaving. And he can advocate measures that many a card-carrying Hartford Mugwump or Manchester Liberal might approve—free trade and anti-protectionism in general, universal suffrage, competitive examination, common education, disestablishment of the church, and so on. That said, however, there are fundamental and I think important differences between Twain and his created character, and these point us in the direction of another dimension of the novel that has a more direct bearing on Mark Twain's thinking about human nature.

Though he is contemptuous of Sir Dinadan, the Humorist, Hank Morgan is not much of a humorist himself. His quip about the "page" Clarence being not much more than a "paragraph" is pretty lame. He tells an undisclosed humorous story to several monks at the Valley of Holiness five times before he gets even so much as a chuckle out of them (though this may say more about English audiences than about the quality of his jest). Hank's appetite for theatrics and self-indulgent, essentially private, humor tends toward practical jokes, and Twain himself frowned upon the practical joker as an inferior humorist. Hank may think it clever to have Sandy spice up her discourse by throwing in an occasional "bejabers," but he is oblivious to the fact that he has begun using more "wit ye wells" than is perhaps good for him. He believes that by placing knights between sandwich boards advertising "Persimmons's Soap" he will make knighthood look ridiculous, but no one besides himself suspects there is anything absurd about it. He is intent on besting Merlin in one way or another, and that frequently involves rather gratuitously blowing something up. This sort of public demonstration, guaranteed to strike terror in the hearts of the people and raise his reputation still higher, may be superior to tying mugs to dogs' tails, though I'm not sure how. What is more, many of the funniest parts of the novel would have been lost on Hank. He thinks it makes efficient good sense to hitch a constantly bowing hermit to a system of cords connected to a sewing machine, and to run him along on Sundays, too. Hank's slang is delicious, but it is comic because it so clashes with the Maloryesque discourse that surrounds it. The funniest application of the Yankee's idiom does not come from Hank at all; it occurs when the literal-minded Sandy names their daughter "Hello Central."

Hank Morgan is also remarkable for his repeated miscalculations. He can "predict" an eclipse, but he is continually caught off guard by the behavior of the Britons and, occasionally, by his own. He is surprised by the docility of a people who casually accept their bitter portion according to unjust and irrational laws. He is outraged by the villainy of Morgan le Fay for killing a page until he recognizes that, from the peculiar orientation that has been trained into her, she has committed a great generosity in paying for the boy. When they arrive at the ogre's castle, Hank sees nothing but a pigsty and hogs. Sandy is stunned: "And how strange is this marvel, and how awful—that to the one perception it is enchanted and dight in a base and shameful aspect; yet to the perception of the other it is not enchanted, hath suffered no change, but stands firm and stately still, girt with its moat and waving its banners in the blue air from its towers" (*CY*, 136). From her point of view, Hank suffers from the enchantment and is thus deluded; Hank reckons the opposite. Nevertheless, he stumbles into a revelation: "My land, the power of training! Of influence! Of education! It can bring a body up to believe anything" (*CY*, 139).

For Hank, Sandy is a lunatic, but if he told her of some of the technological wonders he has seen she would write him off as another. Still later, Hank confesses that he has been unfair in his expectations of Sandy: "It was not fair to spring those nineteenth century technicalities upon the untutored infant of the sixth and then rail at her because she couldn't get their drift" (*CY*, 158). That recognition does not mollify his exasperation with Marco, Dowley, and company, however, when they can't understand that wages have value in proportion to what one can buy with them. Hank is surprised as well that Marco, who seemed to have the makings of a man in him, should so quickly turn upon his benefactor when it seemed expedient. For Twain, however, it was a familiar fact that a man has his private and his public views and generally keeps the first hidden; in an emergency most men take refuge in the camouflage of prevailing opinion. Hank recognizes the king's "blunted" perceptions and his "inbred custom of regarding himself as a superior being," but he is nevertheless stupefied with the ease with which Arthur endorses a supposed meritocracy based on the "four generation" rule for preferment. Hank is also taken up short by Arthur's reaction to being sold into slavery—the king is not disturbed by slavery itself but by the fact that he commanded a mere seven dollars in the open market. Hank is at times equally obtuse about himself—"I realized, then, what a creepy, dull, inanimate horror this land had been to me all these years" and had grown so used to it "almost beyond the power to notice it" (*CY*, 174). He has no doubts about the power of influence and training, but he forgets that influence flows both ways. Finally, in chapter 42, he is once again surprised that all those who fill his colleges, man factories, and schools will go over to the enemy in wartime. "Did you think you had educated the superstition out of those people?" asks Clarence. "I certainly did think it," says Hank. Clarence's reply is brief and to the point: "Well, then, you may unthink it" (CY, 320).

VI

I could give other examples of Hank's misguided judgments and miscalculations, but the real point is that, however able a social engineer the Yankee may be, his grand plans for republican reform founder on his optimism, misapprehension, or conceit. Hank is constantly coming up against the facts of human nature and coming up short. The mere fact that he thinks a whole country can be transformed virtually overnight makes him a quixotic dreamer. Practical dreamer that he is, though, Hank has to keep scaling back his plans—he anticipates a gradual movement from monarchy to universal suffrage that will take place first in a few years, then in a few more years, and then in a generation or two; the transformation will be effected by common schools or maybe in his "man factories" or, finally, with those fifty youngsters who have not been so thoroughly trained in subjugation and cruelty. (Twain even makes this last option problematic, since we learn peasant children sometimes practice hanging one another.) Hank may well be a humanitarian; he is certainly an idealist. And in that sense he is a Quixote figure.[46] The analogy goes only so far, and no farther. His betrothed, Puss Flanagan, back in Hartford, is not really his Dulcinea, and in any event has no important role in his quest. Sandy and later Arthur may play inverted Sancho Panza figures, identifying in one way or another the peculiar realities of medieval England for him, but neither one of them was actually invited to join in his adventures. The force of the analogy has to do with Hank Morgan's impossible dream of a freeze-dried republic that can be accomplished quickly and efficiently through his sometimes devious, sometimes open maneuvers. Mark Twain may share in Morgan's sentiments and altogether approve his proposed reforms and nevertheless find the Yankee both admirable and quaintly ridiculous.

In any event, Hank Morgan does have a step-by-step recipe for progressive reform, and much of it can be derived from what he says in chap-

---

46. There is nothing original in this claim. Some reviewers of the novel, including W. D. Howells and Hamlin Garland, compared Twain's novel to Don Quixote. See Reviews, 285, 287, 291, 294, and 303.

ter 10, "The Beginnings of Civilization." Twain wrote chapters 21 through 42 in the summer and fall of 1888, and it was during this period that he wrote and interpolated chapter 10. (He would finish the book by March 1889.) The immediate purpose of that chapter was to establish a four-year hiatus between the tournament of chapter 9 and the beginning of Hank Morgan's journey to the ogre's castle with Sandy and to account for some of the changes Hank had introduced during that period.[47] His steps toward a republic are rather systematic. Hank assembled the brightest and most promising in order to train a "crowd of experts" in every sort of "handiwork and scientific calling" (CY, 64). He established a teacher factory for the purpose of staffing graded schools. He created Sunday schools and, as a check on the Established Church, a variety of Protestant sects, but no religious instruction is permitted in his common schools. He put mining on a "scientific basis," and, rather more subversively, sent forth confidential agents to undermine knighthood and little by little "gnaw" at prevailing superstitions. He secretly created a military and a naval academy, a newspaper, and telegraph and telephone communications. Finally, Hank tinkered with the method of taxation in order to make it more equitable and to generate greater revenue.

We later learn that the Yankee has also established a "Man Factory" where he is "turning groping and grubbing automata into *men*" (CY, 117). Apart from teaching men and women to read, we know nothing of what goes on in this factory, but the first mention of it in chapter 13, "Freemen," is in the context of giving the people a "new deal" and promoting a certain kind of "disloyalty" in those he has decided have the makings of manhood. In his notebook, Twain made it clearer what his purposes were: "true loyalty should have been to themselves—in which case there would have ensued a rebellion & the throwing off of that deceptive yoke [loyalty]"; and then speaking in Hank's voice Twain adds, "The first thing I want to teach is *disloyalty* till they get used to disusing that word *loyalty* as representing a virtue. This will beget independence—which is loyalty to one's best self & principles, & this is often disloyalty to the general idols & fetishes" (N&J3, 414–15). Behind these changes is a firm belief in nineteenth-century liberalism and laissez-faire capitalism, but so far as we can discern Hank means to create participants in a democratic social or-

47. Actually, Hank's first step toward the civilization he imagines (mentioned in chapter 9) was to establish a patent office, but it is doubtful that Twain saw intellectual property rights as fundamental to democratic reform. This gesture probably had more to do with Twain's own annoyance with literary piracy and copyright infringement than with the emancipation of the Britons.

der, not entrepreneurs in a competitive marketplace. At all events, the cunning vengeance with which he deals with Dowley, the "self-made man," indicates Hank's contempt for those who espouse vulgar and disingenuous notions of equality.

The Yankee's logic and system here are impeccable, and his argument follows the contours of the progress of civilization, as it had been mapped by Henry Buckle and others, insofar as it is grounded in an unwavering belief in natural law quietly but inevitably shaping events to its own, surely divine, purposes. Whether the force that works for progress is known as the Great Architect (Buckle), the Unknowable (Spencer), the Invisible Hand (Adam Smith), the Supreme Author (Jefferson and Thomas Paine), or the L'Homme Moyen (Quetelet) doesn't really matter. This providential power requires no interference from church or state to help it along. Natural law has its own methods and design that human reason may discover but cannot improve; and it works through the masses of men and women, not through exceptional individuals. Protective tariffs, the four-generation rule for nobility, the divine right of kings, the interdict, all these and other acts of intervention subjugate the people at the same time that they abrogate the will of the Creator—somewhat ironically, of course, since these measures are usually enacted in God's name. Civilization arises out of skepticism of, or disloyalty to, superstitious belief, is fostered by education and the wide dissemination of knowledge among the people, and owes little or nothing to protectionist institutions. Hank Morgan is explicit on this point: a nation's "institutions are extraneous, they are its mere clothing, and clothing can wear out, become ragged. . . . To be loyal to rags, to shout for rags, to worship rags, to die for rags—that is loyalty of unreason" (CY, 88).[48]

In four years Hank has created an incipient civilization, though he seems to grope for the proper metaphor for the progress to follow. His factories are the "nuclei" for future factories, which in their turn will become "steel missionaries" for civilization; he thinks of his sites for training the best and the brightest of the people as "nurseries"; and his instructors, we are told, were produced in "teacher factories" (CY, 64–65). It is uncertain whether his civilization will be the result of natural growth, missionary zeal, parental care, or mechanical manufacture. It is equally uncertain

48. Twain is speaking for himself as well, for he bristled at the complaint by Republicans that the Mugwumps were being disloyal to the party and gave broad application to his indignation in a talk he delivered at the Monday Evening Club on December 2, 1887, and titled simply "Consistency."

what sort of power his secret improvements harbor. At one point, he describes his impending bloodless revolution as a serene volcano with "rising hell in its bowels"; at another it is a glaring light, which he means to turn on one candlepower at a time.

While Twain was making notes for how Hank Morgan would bring a republican democracy to Arthur's England, he was concurrently plotting the Yankee's ultimate failure. Mixed in with his commentary about doing away with fetishes and idols is this note: "I make a *peaceful* revolution & introduce advanced civilization. The Church overthrows it with a 6 year interdict. A revolution cannot be established under 30 years—the men of old ideas must die off" (*N&J3*, 415). These three successive statements have the feel of a syllogism, and at least a part of the ambivalence and incoherence some critics have detected in *A Connecticut Yankee* may derive from the contradictory requirements of the narrative as Twain had conceived it. It was decided early on that Hank Morgan should die yearning for his "lost land"; thus, Twain must introduce some attachment to a country Hank initially finds barbarous. That was provided easily enough, though not very convincingly, by his marriage to Sandy. Likewise, when Twain committed his title character to exposing the fraudulence of aristocratic privilege and to attempting to realize his liberating "dream," he also prepared in advance to undo all that had been accomplished without leaving evidence of its prior existence. These were not contradictory impulses in the author but coordinated ones that would necessarily result in a certain crosshatching many critics find very dark indeed, perhaps even nihilistic. Perceived inconsistencies do not seem to disturb common readers very much, however. *A Connecticut Yankee* remains a popular tale because it is, by turns, rollicking comedy, affective melodrama, stinging satire, and anachronistic history lesson.

What then remains after all this building up and tearing down? There are at least two important inferences we might draw. One consequence is articulated by Sherwood Cummings. Due in part to "authorial fatigue and impatience," the last third of the novel is marred by a certain "meanspirited" quality and sheer exasperation with the human race. *A Connecticut Yankee* did not turn out to be the author's "swan song" to literature as he once supposed it might be, but, according to Cummings, it did signify Twain's final abandonment of a "deistic" conception of the universe: "Instead of nature's being a benevolent system, it was an inane process; instead of its being a gift from above, it was an arena for an evolution . . . that, after a billion years, resulted in the unprofitable outcome called man."[49] Out of that mood arose such statements as Hank's frustrated announcement that "there are times when one would like to hang the whole human race and finish the farce" (*CY*, 348).

A second and rather different consequence is identified by Howard Baetzhold. Hank Morgan's delirious reaching out across the centuries for his beloved Sandy at the close of the novel reaffirms "Clemens's own conviction of the importance of love and family."[50] Somewhat ironically, Baetzhold observes, the terms of that reaffirmation recall an author Twain had often attacked—Matthew Arnold. Nevertheless, in "Dover Beach," Arnold spoke of a dreamlike world, "so various, so beautiful," that in fact "hath really neither joy, nor love, nor light, / Nor certitude, nor peace, nor help for pain." Set against all this is the anodyne but evidently sufficient plea to his love—"let us be true / To one another!" Almost without exception, Hank Morgan extols the virtues of moral heroism not on the basis of an assertion of manly independence but because certain individuals are capable of self-sacrifice made on behalf of familial love and duty. A man suffers at the rack to spare his family slow starvation; his wife pleads for him to confess his crime and would gladly endure her fate if only his suffering could be over. For twenty-two years a man sits in the queen's dungeon the subject of a cruel hoax; through an aperture in his cell he can see his home and is made to believe that five times death has come for one or another of his family. In a moment of genuine nobility, King Arthur assists in the relief of a family stricken with smallpox, and a tear of sympathy rolls down his dusty cheek.[51] Mad in her desperation, a young woman steals a piece of linen to feed her child and is hanged as a consequence. Hank laments this punishment executed to protect property rights, for the crime was committed more by the state than by the mother: "oh, my God, is there not property in ruined homes, and orphaned babes, and broken hearts that British law holds precious" (*CY*, 274).

Twain himself was subject to these somewhat discordant moods, and they may forecast such works as "The Great Dark" or "Was the World Made for Man?" on the one hand, and the diaries of Adam and Eve on the other. And though Twain may well have believed that the damned human race was past redemption, much of his finest and most furious polemical

---

49. *Mark Twain and Science: Adventures of a Mind* (Baton Rouge: Louisiana State University Press, 1988), 169.

50. Baetzhold, "'Well, My Book Is Written—Let It Go.'" 75.

51. Once again Twain adhered to a utilitarian ethics, for he indicated that Arthur was in part crying for himself because Guinevere's loving attention was often directed toward Lancelot.

writing, written on behalf of pitiful human beings, was yet to come. These several impulses in the author need not be regarded as wholly contradictory or confused. "An ethics," wrote Kenneth Burke, "involves one ultimately in a philosophy of *being*, as distinct from a philosophy of *becoming*, because it aims to consider the *generic* equipment of man, as a social and biologic organism." To involve oneself in this sort of inquiry "tends to be anhistoric in quite the same way that an account of digestion or metabolism would be" and in any event needs no special transcendental underpinning. In terms more appropriate to Twain, we might say that he could accept Darwinian evolution as a philosophy of becoming without abandoning his long-standing interest in the moral nature of mankind. And if Twain had become "resigned" to certain brute historical and biological facts, Burke reminds us that resignation may take many forms, and one of those is to "'resign' oneself to struggle." Finally, Burke notes that though we live in a world where both existence and nothingness are equally unthinkable, "Our speculations may run the whole qualitative gamut, from play, through reverence, even to an occasional shiver of cold metaphysical dread—for always the Eternal Enigma is there, right on the edges of our metropolitan bickerings, stretching outward to interstellar infinity and inward to the depth of the mind. And in this staggering disproportion between man and no-man, there is no place for purely human boasts of grandeur, or for forgetting that men build their cultures by huddling together, nervously loquacious, at the edge of an abyss."[52] It is that attitude, or something like it, Twain brought with him as he entered the 1890s.

52. *Permanence and Change: An Anatomy of Purpose*, rev. ed. (New York: Bobbs-Merrill Co., 1965), 271, 272.

Chapter Five

1890–1899

I

The passage from *A Connecticut Yankee* that is most often cited, typically as evidence of Twain's deterministic philosophy but sometimes also in support of an evident faith in a transcendent realm of being, is this one:

Training—training is everything; training is all there is *to* a person. We speak of nature; it is folly; there is no such thing as nature; what we call by that misleading name is merely heredity and training. We have no thoughts of our own, no opinions of our own: they are transmitted to us, trained into us. All that is original in us, and therefore fairly creditable or discreditable to us, can be covered up and hidden by the point of a cambric needle, all the rest being atoms contributed by, and inherited from, a procession of ancestors that stretches back a billion years to the Adam-clam or grasshopper or monkey from whom our race has been so tediously and ostentatiously and unprofitably developed. And as for me, all that I think about in this plodding sad pilgrimage, this pathetic drift between the eternities, is to look out and humbly live a pure and high and blameless life, and save that one microscopic atom in me that is truly *me:* the rest may land in Sheol and welcome for all I care. (*CY*, 208)

Sherwood Cummings notes that, after so many years of allowing deterministic ideas to ferment within him, here was a full-fledged declaration of his position—"a major precipitation of attitude." Even so, as Cummings also observes, there are certain "troublesome" elements in the passage that make it more than a bit problematic.[1] For one thing, Hank Morgan may or may not speak for Twain in this instance; in any event, Hank's motives and the author's attitudes are not identical here. In context, Morgan is exasperated by Morgan le Fay's self-righteousness in wanting full moral credit for paying for a boy she so wantonly killed. Hank acknowledges that that attitude has been trained into her and that she is not to blame for it; nonetheless, there is a frustrated despair in his voice that seems to apply to the whole human race. If Hank was doing something more than merely blowing off steam, if he had taken his own words as a guiding principle, he would have abandoned his dream of transforming the realm into a republic, and this he does not do. If, on the other hand, Twain is speaking his own convictions through Morgan, do his several statements fit together in some meaningful way? It is worthwhile to linger over this passage for two reasons. First, because we may regard it as a premonitory gesture toward the attitudes Twain was developing as he entered the 1890s, its significance will acquire a broader and, I hope, more useful application later on. And, second, because by attempting to show that such notions as habit, heredity, training, and the "me" may plausibly be interpreted as coordinate not antagonistic concepts, we will spare ourselves the trouble and confusion of taking them up piecemeal later on.

It is no doubt a mistake to demand precision and consistency from a man whose own imagination was often volatile, even eruptive. Moreover, it is unnecessary and probably futile to argue for a limpid clarity and logical rigor in Twain's thought, but it may be useful to show that his thinking was not necessarily so murky and confused as is sometimes supposed. One thing to note right away, though, is that it is not at all clear in the quoted passage whether Twain is speaking in the role of naturalist philosopher or social psychologist. Either way, there are several questions one may put to the passage above: What sort of "nature" is he describing as "folly"? In what fashion are our thoughts and opinions "transmitted" to us? If the human creature is wholly composed of "heredity" and "training," what

1. In nearly every particular, I differ from Cummings in my reading of this passage, but his own interpretation is thoughtful and clearly stated in *Mark Twain and Science: Adventures of a Mind* (Baton Rouge: Louisiana State University Press, 1988), 168–71.

exactly is he referring to as that precious atom of self, that thing that is "truly *me*"? There is little doubt that, by 1890, Twain became a card-carrying determinist, but what sort of determinism compelled his belief?

In chapter 8 of *Sister Carrie*, Theodore Dreiser proclaimed that our civilization is in a "middle stage" of development—"no longer wholly guided by instinct"; "not yet wholly guided by reason."[2] Nevertheless, Dreiser assures us, evolutionary forces are ineluctably shaping human lives to better ends. And in *McTeague*, Frank Norris had the instinctual beast within McTeague grapple with a better "second self"—"it was the old battle, old as the world, wide as the world."[3] This is a familiar contest: atavistic impulses pitted against the vaunted claims of reason and civilized life. From the naturalistic point of view, these oppositions are unexceptional; from the psychological point of view, however, the reasoning is not very sophisticated and, in fact, is somewhat crude.

Even though Twain does not use the word *instinct* in the passage quoted above, that seems to be what he has in mind when he speaks of "heredity" and the transmission of thoughts. In *What Is Man?* the Old Man objects to the word *instinct* as a confusing term because it typically applies to habits and impulses that have "a far off origin," but also can apply to unthinking habits (such as putting the left leg in first in getting on one's trousers). He also dismisses the term as "meaningless" because it merely indicates *"petrified thought,"* "sleep-walking" thought (*WIM*, 190). It so happens that William James and John Dewey were also a bit chary of the word *instinct*, preferring instead the term *impulse* and in part for the same reasons. Instinct is typically defined, according to James, as a faculty "acting in such a way as to produce certain ends, without foresight of the ends, and without previous education in the performance."[4] The problem with regarding instinct in this way is that it presupposes that an animal acts according to large abstractions that it could in no way fathom or frame. James prefers to interpret these impulses in a physiological way: *"The actions we call instinctive all conform to the general reflex type; they are called forth by determinate sensory stimuli in contact with the animal's body, or at a distance in his environment."*[5]

2. *Sister Carrie*, ed. Donald Pizer, 2d ed. (New York: W. W. Norton and Co., 1991), 56.

3. *McTeague: A Story of San Francisco*, ed. Donald Pizer (New York: W. W. Norton and Co., 1977), 18.

4. *Principles of Psychology*, 2 vols. (1890; rpt. New York: Dover Publications, 1950), 2:383; this chapter on "Instinct" was previously published in *Popular Science Monthly* in 1887.

5. *Principles of Psychology*, 2:384.

Because instinct is built into the structure of the nervous system, the transmission of native impulses can be explained without reference to some grand and divine plan that outfits every creature for its office. The lion does not act out of a sense of self-preservation. Instead, certain phenomena excite in its nervous system determinate impulses that may act in succession. Hunger awakens in the lion the impulse to *seek* its prey. (The example is James's.) Certain stimuli (odors, for example) cause it to *stalk*; at a certain distance, the visible presence of its prey causes the lion to *spring* upon it. The sensation of the animal's flesh in contact with its fangs causes it to *tear* and *devour*. The net effect of these successive instinctual acts may testify to the evolutionary law of the struggle for survival, but that law is enacted through separate physiological processes. With human beings the problem is more complicated not because man has been divested of the primacy of his original instincts, as Dreiser would have it, but because human beings have more, not fewer, impulses than other animals. In animals, as well as in man, various impulses contradict one another (bashfulness and vanity, for example), but it is typically the accumulated experience of the individual and the situation into which these impulses insert themselves that settle which impulse will prevail.

Reason cannot decide the issue, for reason "can inhibit no impulses." The only things that can neutralize an impulse are another impulse operating contrary to it, acquired habits acting in opposition to it, or (as, say, in the sucking instinct of infants) the fact that the body has simply outgrown that particular impulse. What reason can and does do is to draw inferences *"which will excite the imagination so as to set loose* the impulse the other way."[6] The function that instincts play in the psychological life of the human being is neither great nor urgent, says James, because it seems to be the case that *"most instincts are implanted for the sake of giving rise to habits, and that, this purpose once accomplished, the instincts themselves, as such, have no raison d'être in the psychical economy, and consequently fade away."*[7] John Dewey goes even farther in identifying the preemptive nature of habit over instinct. Though instinct is prior to habit temporally, habit is actually the more primary, at least so far as human conduct is concerned. An infant, alive with instinctual needs and drives, is born into a social context and attended to by adults who themselves have formed habits. The opportunities the infant has to give these "native" qualities ex-

---

6. Ibid., 2:393; italics his. Twain takes the same position regarding the nature of reason in *What Is Man?* (*WIM*, 190).
7. *Principles of Psychology*, 2:402; italics his.

pression invariably require interacting with a "matured social medium."[8] Whatever these aboriginal impulses may in fact "be," their "*meaning*" is social and therefore acquired. A child's anger is a "burst of wasteful energy" unless and until it interacts with the responsive behavior of others. (To a degree, this is the very process Twain is illustrating in the opening paragraphs of "My First Lie and How I Got Out of It" [1899]—the nine-day-old infant Clemens is stuck by a pin and cries; adults tend to his needs; he likes the attention, so he acquires the lying habit of crying without any assistance from the pin.)

The speculative account I have thus far given of Hank's outburst (half lament, half complaint) is founded on psychological, not metaphysical, assumptions. What has given most critics pause, however, is the "me," and that one syllable may well introduce puzzling discrepancies into Twain's system. We will have an opportunity to return to this knotty philosophical problem in the next chapter. For now, it is enough to say, with William James, that in psychological terms the "me" poses no special difficulties. One has a sense of a "me" by virtue of having a body and thoughts that, through their "warmth and intimacy" of relation, seem to belong to one's self. I have a "me" because certain kinds of experience are "mine." This intimacy of relation in bodily acts and individual thoughts comes about, largely through the auspices of memory, because the self that has them seems to be continuous with and to resemble the self that came before.[9] Moment to moment, day to day, there is a continuity and resemblance in my experience. Lo and behold, the self that went to sleep last night awakes as the same self this morning! The human being appears to have a me and to feel a certain responsibility to and for it.

It is true that in later writings Twain does contemplate a self or mind that may be something more than and apart from a machine automatically functioning. In *A Connecticut Yankee*, though, he is hedging his bets in much the same way William James did in his *Principles of Psychology*. James allowed for the possibility of a "self of selves," but its existence or nonexistence had no particular bearing on understanding the psychic

8. *Human Nature and Conduct: An Introduction to Social Psychology* (New York: H. Holt and Co., 1922), 90.

9. In this chapter, James is particularly concerned with repudiating the Kantian notion of a "transcendental ego." He maintains that Kant's "transcendental unity of apperception" means nothing more than getting all one's perceptions in the same corral. To oversimplify James's position: It is simply not true that one cannot have "experience" without some transempirical ground, or "I," to authorize it. Not things alone, but the relations between and among things, are given in perception, and sensations do not need some supernatural cowpoke to keep the herd in line.

lives of human beings. Whether that "me" be a compound of familiar elements or something more grand (a transcendental ego, a soul, a second self, or an infinite I AM), it remains sufficiently small to be covered up by the point of a cambric needle. Even in so brief a passage as the one we are considering, Twain conflates several antagonistic elements with evident indifference. It doesn't really matter whether human nature originated with Adam or the clam. Insofar as humans are implicated in the immense design of things, can they ever know whether they are embarked on a "sad pilgrimage" (presumably journeying toward some infinitely distant heavenly city) or a "pathetic drift" (navigated, if at all, by the evolutionary principles of natural selection)? How many "eternities" can there possibly be? The pendulum swing between "the everlasting" and "deep time" is a large one indeed, more than any one person can handle. To continue the essentially pragmatic tack I have been taking: is it worthwhile to ask questions that probably can't be answered, and even if they could, would not make any material difference to our lives? The pragmatist says no, and so, it seems, does Twain.

My point in this perhaps tedious contemplation of a single passage from *A Connecticut Yankee* is not to make Twain into a full-fledged philosopher. I merely want to suggest that this passage may be seen as something more than a congeries of confused ideas and that Twain may be regarded as something other than an intellectual chump. In his thinking, these notions may or may not be nicely adjusted to one another, but, together, they do sketch an essentially mechanistic worldview, and that mechanical world has come to displace one that had earlier claimed his loyalty. When Twain has Hank Morgan insist that it is "folly" to speak of "nature," that that is a "misleading name" for heredity and training, Sherwood Cummings argues he is discarding Thomas Paine's idea of "the creation" as a world superintended by a benevolent creator. However, Twain may be speaking of human nature instead and concluding that it is sheer vanity to maintain that the "human" is some transcendent, transhistorical, and otherwise privileged condition. In the long run, it probably doesn't matter much whether he is speaking of the creation or the human creature.

More basic to my theme is the attitude Twain adopted toward this new dispensation, and that attitude may be hinted at through an apt comparison. In 1897, Joseph Conrad described his own despair regarding the world as it was inferable from scientific materialism:

There is—let us say—a machine. It evolved itself (I am severely scientific) out of a chaos of scraps or iron and behold!—it knits. I am horrified at the horrible work and stand appalled. I feel it ought to embroider—but it goes on knitting. You come and say: "this is all right; it's only a question of the right kind of oil. Let us use this—for instance—celestial oil and the machine shall embroider a most beautiful design in purple and gold." Will it? Alas, no. You cannot by any special lubrication make embroidery with a knitting machine. And the most withering thought is that the infamous thing has made itself; made itself without thought, without conscience, without foresight, without eyes, without heart. It is a tragic accident—and it has happened. . . . It knits us in and it knits us out. It has knitted time, space, pain, death, corruption, despair and all the illusions— and nothing matters.[10]

Mark Twain may employ a more delicate metaphor for the process than Conrad—the cambric needle is used for very fine stitchery—but at least in terms of expressed reaction Twain seems to be made of sterner stuff. Joseph Conrad contemplates the tragic accident that is human life and stands aghast at the horror of it all. Twain, on the other hand, surely believed that his "gospel" would scandalize the world at large, but for his own part he seems merely to have declared a cosmic "Shucks!"

II

From here on out, I will need to be selective and careful. During the last two decades of his life, Twain was prolific, but he was not necessarily productive. In a 1906 dictation later published as "My Literary Shipyard" (1922), he confessed that nearly always a book got "tired" and then his imaginative interest in it necessarily flagged. When that happened he was disposed to pigeonhole the manuscript until his "tank" filled once again and he could return to it. If his books got tired, Twain didn't seem to; he merely directed his energies elsewhere. He piled up thousands of manuscript pages during this period, but he also abandoned several works, failed to round others off to satisfactory completion, and embarked on large, unwieldy projects (most notably, his "Autobiography") that almost by definition could never be finished. And the titles of other works—beginning as they sometimes do with such phrases as "Fragments of," "Chapters from," "Passages from," "Extracts from"—indicate their partial character. Other titles beginning with "Concerning," "As Regards,"

10. Quoted in Ian Watt, *Conrad in the Nineteenth Century* (Berkeley: University of California Press, 1979), 153.

"A Letter To," and so forth register the topicality or severely focused nature of the pieces.

On the other hand, there are many admirers, myself included, who wish Twain hadn't finished and published some of the works he did. *The American Claimant* (1892) and *Personal Recollections of Joan of Arc* (1896), particularly, have not yet attained the obscurity they deserve. The first is disjointed, fantastic, and improvised; the second saccharine, tedious, and repetitive. Still, on two points at least these texts are related to my subject. In *The American Claimant*, Berkeley, son of the Earl of Rossmore, travels to America to trade places with an American claimant, who morally if not legally is the rightful heir to the title, and to try his hand at becoming a self-made man. The conflict between moral and legal rights had interesting satirical potential, but when the American claimant became Colonel Sellers, the narrative too readily gave itself over to burlesque and side-gags.

At any rate, in naive and sentimental ways, Berkeley (aka Howard Tracy) revels in the prospect of making his own way in a true republic. When he hears a blacksmith lash out at the English aristocracy and its moral obligation to relinquish such unearned privileges, the words blister the young idealist's conscience. Berkeley's friend Barrow dismisses the speech as so much blather, and the Englishman is eager to know why. The blacksmith left out of his argument "the factor of human nature," says Barrow[11]— namely, that human beings of every stripe, including the blacksmith, act out of a native selfishness and would themselves jump at the chance to become an earl. No shame attaches to the aristocrat who enjoys his advantages, Barrow continues; only when the people themselves rise up and demolish a system that allows such distinctions will the wrong be righted. This was a lesson Hank Morgan learned the hard way, and Barrow is merely reaffirming conclusions Mark Twain had drawn years before.

The American Claimant was serialized in January through March 1892. In August of that year, Twain began writing *Personal Recollections of Joan of Arc* (1896). The story of a mere girl who mobilized an entire nation to overthrow the English oppressors surely appealed to Twain, but it was a matter of record that Joan had restored an unworthy monarch to the throne and ultimately reestablished the authority of the French aristocracy. One reviewer pointed out that the "story does not undertake to explain the psychological phenomena which Joan presented, but simply tells the tale" (*Reviews*, 396). Evidently Twain himself had too much reverence for

---

11. *The American Claimant* (New York: Oxford University Press, 1996), 147.

the girl to treat her as a case study. Another reviewer said that the historical circumstances would provide the "modern analyst" with "an amazing illustration for a book on the psychology of the crowd," particularly if it was studied "in connection with the mental 'environment'" of the day (*Reviews*, 400). Twain addresses this aspect of his tale, but Sieur Louis de Conte, the narrator, is himself too much a believing admirer and a man of his time to play the part of modern analyst.

What is more, the author curiously grounded his treatment of the young martyr in premises that were antithetical to his customary utilitarianism. In the "Translator's Preface" we are told that Joan of Arc was "perhaps the only entirely unselfish person whose name has a place in profane history" (*JA*, viii). If Twain meant to test his views of human nature in this novel with an apparently well-documented case of self-sacrifice, he didn't make his thinking sufficiently clear to modern readers to ward off the judgment of his putting on display a rather empty sentimentality. The work is anomalous in a number of other ways, as well. Joan is, from the viewpoint of the wholly admiring narrator de Conte, extraordinary but nothing of a curiosity. Her heroism is motivated by whatever those voices are telling her, and her life is an example of the sort of special providence Twain himself had, on general principles, ruled out of court. Joan is exceptional in other ways. It is not simply that she hears voices; anyone can do that. But she listens to them, takes comfort in their prophecies, and heeds their counsel, and she does their bidding in absolute contradiction to her circumstances and her training.

The book is anomalous, too, in its relatively soft treatment of the French, though Twain remained unforgiving of the French aristocracy. For Twain, France epitomized coarse immorality, and he made a mighty exception to his biases when he ranked Joan alongside Christ as someone who transcended base human nature. In 1887, he had written in his notebook: "Who could endure a French Christ?" (*N&J3*, 292), but we are undoubtedly meant not only to endure but to admire this girl who above all else "severed her country's bonds" and came to symbolize the Genius of Patriotism (*JA*, 461). Huck Finn had the sort of shrewdness that allowed him to get out of many scrapes, but Joan's natural guilelessness allows her to outfox her captious prosecutors, who are every bit as treacherous as the enemies she faced on the battlefield. The narrator de Conte registers for the reader and for the author the extent of her greatness:

> Yes, Joan of Arc was great always, great everywhere, but she was greatest in the Rouen trials. There she rose above the limitations and infirmities of our human nature, and accomplished under blighting and unnerving and hopeless condi-

tions all that her splendid equipment of moral and intellectual forces could have accomplished if they had been supplemented by the mighty helps of hope and cheer and light, the presence of friendly faces, and a fair and equal fight, with the great world looking on and wondering. (*JA*, 417)

Twain returned to the subject of the Maid of Orleans in the essay "Saint Joan of Arc" (1904) and made it abundantly clear that she was a mental and moral miracle.[12] Her case was a conundrum, and she was the "*Riddle of the Ages*" (*CTSS2*, 591). He made explicit wherein her mystery lay. It is easy enough to account for a Napoleon, a Shakespeare, or an Edison, he said. Their important genius was largely the result of outside influences, "the training which it received while it grew, the nurture it got from reading, study, example, the encouragement it gathered from self-recognition and recognition from the outside at each stage of its development." Genius is born blind, "and it is not itself that opens its eyes, but the subtle influences of a myriad of stimulating exterior circumstances" (*CTSS2*, 591–92). This is consistent with Twain's creed, but the laws of human development simply don't apply in Joan's case: "In the history of the human intellect, untrained, inexperienced, using only its birthright equipment of untried capacities, there is nothing which approaches this. Joan of Arc stands alone" (*CTSS2*, 593). If Joan is an enigmatic exception to his materialist creed, Twain himself is nevertheless not ready to repudiate his gospel of training and circumstance; he simply acknowledges that her case falls outside an understanding of "freckled Human Nature," to borrow a phrase from Emily Dickinson. Nor does he affirm that the girl's authority derives from another sort of gospel; he merely accepts that Joan herself "had a child-like faith in the heavenly origin of her apparitions and her Voices" (*CTSS2*, 594).

Whatever his motivations for writing *Personal Recollections of Joan of Arc*, and whatever the intentions that lay behind it (and many explanations have been advanced for both),[13] the novel minimally serves to challenge Twain's own vaunted materialistic determinism. Actually, though he stood squarely upon his belief that training is everything, Twain continually tested that conviction in his last years. His interest in "mental telegraphy" (Twain's phrase for extrasensory perception) potentially did so. Though he was not above sermonizing on a wide variety of subjects, he

12. Joan's "sainthood" is merely a prospect and a wish at this time; she would not be officially canonized until 1920.

13. Peter Stoneley, in *Mark Twain and the Feminine Aesthetic* (Cambridge: Cambridge University Press, 1992), gives a balanced synopsis of the critical assessments of the novel in his text (91–100) and the accompanying notes (184–86).

also remained curious and inquisitive to the last. William Dean Howells believed that this dogged curiosity was part of the essential "Mystery" of Mark Twain: "It is in vain that I try to give a notion of the intensity with which he pierced to the heart of life, and the breadth of vision with which he compassed the whole world, and tried for the reason of things, and then left trying" (*MMT*, 100). Many of his late writings, as we will see in the final chapter, expanded upon or scrutinized his views of human nature. He rendered his fascination with dreams and the dream life; he recorded his interest in the here and hereafter, the infinitely vast and the infinitely small, and man's puny place within the universe; he expressed himself on the social behavior of bees, ants, and other creatures and compared man's moral nature to the rat, wolf, and oyster, typically to the advantage of the latter; and he even gave fanciful depictions of extraterrestrials who deigned to give directions to a mere human being from an insignificant planet.

These were not solely flights of fancy. If human beings were essentially receptacles of outside influences, then how one got one's bearings in the world, how one navigated in environments (familiar or alien, friendly or unfriendly), had telling consequences for how we should understand the human creature. If only in the laboratory of his imagination, Twain subjected his conception of human nature to a wide variety of circumstances and occasions—to prelapsarian Eden, where prior experience and training were impossible; to an unimaginably large and diverse version of Heaven, where prior training was irrelevant; to a fantastic voyage in a drop of water or in the veins of a tramp; and many other extraordinary settings as well. Those who are not guided by voices and apparitions find their way by other means. In large measure, this was the concern of *Tom Sawyer Abroad* (1894).

Tom Sawyer Abroad evidently had its origins in another, unspecified novel Twain was working on in 1892. He wrote Fred J. Hall, the manager of his publishing house, that he had dropped that novel because he found a better, and somewhat more subtle, way to use his "main episode." He would start Huck, Tom, and Jim on a balloon voyage across the ocean and slip in that episode in an "effective" and "apparently unintentional" way (*MTLP*, 313–14). Louis J. Budd suggests that that unidentified episode probably had to do with his satire of protective tariffs, which occurs in chapter 11, and with Tom's plan to transport genuine Arabian sand to America and sell it in vials.[14] Huck is excited by the idea of becoming as

14. *Mark Twain: Social Philosopher* (Columbia: University of Missouri Press, 2001), 157.

rich as "Creeosote" (*TSA*, 323), but his prospects are dashed when Tom remembers all the duties that would have to be paid on the sand and says they will have to give up the plan. The protective tariff, so Twain believed, like tithing for the poor or aristocratic privilege in general, was an artificial measure installed to insure the unearned increment.

Despite its lively title, *Tom Sawyer Abroad* is long on talk and short on adventure. The three do come into the possession of a high-powered balloon, and predictably Tom becomes "Tom Sawyer, Erronort." They have a couple of scrapes with lions and tigers, sandstorms, and angry natives, but most of their time is spent arguing about time and eternity, form and principle, space and location, proportion and perspective. Twain boasted in a letter that he could manufacture incidents and extend the trio's adventures indefinitely by trotting them through England, Germany, and elsewhere as needed (*MTLP*, 315), but almost immediately he was drawn to vernacular differences of opinion, not exotic differences of locale. The subjects of those talks between and among Huck, Tom, and Jim have mostly to do with one sort of artifice or abstraction or another. Tom usually prevails in their animated debates, but when he doesn't he pouts his way to another topic.

Bernard DeVoto thought highly of *Tom Sawyer Abroad*, ranking it "among the very best" of Twain's work. He believed it was a "deliberate exploration of the provincial mind and its prejudices, ignorances, assumptions, wisdoms, cunning" and that it "differentiates three stages of the mind, by way of the familiar Tom, Huck, and Nigger Jim."[15] He did not specify what those three stages are, however, nor did he attach the differences to specified characters. Without trying to second-guess DeVoto, we could nonetheless sort the three into several possible categories—the literate, semiliterate, and illiterate; the intellectual or abstract, the pragmatic or existential, and the ignorant or superstitious; or the socially empowered, the socially marginal, and the socially disenfranchised. In any arrangement, however, there is no inviolate hierarchy of understanding distributed among them. Sometimes Tom is right, and sometimes he is wrong; besides, Tom's superior exasperation and dismissiveness are held in reserve as his trump suit anyway.

Even before it becomes apparent that Tom, Huck, and Jim are bound for the Middle East, Tom proposes that they go on a "Crusade," and the subsequent dispute is characteristic of the comic differences of understanding throughout the book. Huck asks Tom to explain a crusade:

---

15. *The Portable Mark Twain* (New York: Viking Press, 1946), 31–32.

"A crusade is a war to recover the Holy Land from the paynim."

"Which Holy Land?"

"Why, *the* Holy Land—there ain't but one."

"What do we want of it?"

"Why, can't you understand? It's in the hands of the paynim, and it's our duty to take it away from them."

"How did we come to let them git hold of it?"

"We didn't come to let them git hold of it. They always had it."

"Why, Tom, then it must belong to them, don't it?"

"Why of course it does. Who said it didn't?"

I studied over it, but couldn't seem to git at the rights of it, no way. I says—

"It's too many for me, Tom Sawyer. If I had a farm and it was mine, and another person wanted it, would it be right for him to—"

"Oh, shucks! you don't know enough to come in when it rains, Huck Finn. It ain't a farm, it's entirely different. You see, it's like this. They own the land, just the mere land, and that's all they do own; but it was our folks, our Jews and Christians, that made it holy, and so they haven't any business to be there defiling it. It's a shame, and we ought not to stand it a minute. We ought to march against them and take it away from them."

"Why, it does seem to me it's the most mixed-up thing I ever see! Now, if I had a farm and another person—"

"Don't I tell you it hasn't got anything to *do* with farming? Farming is business, just common low-down business: that's all it is, it's all you can say for it; but this is higher, this is religious, and totally different."

"Religious to go and take the land away from people that owns it?"

"Certainly; it's always been considered so." (*TSA*, 260–61)

At this point, Jim jumps into the conversation. It strikes him that killing strangers who have not done him any harm is not necessarily the most Christian thing to do. Tom wins by fiat: "'Oh, shut your head! you make me tired!' says Tom. 'I don't want to argue any more with people like you and Huck Finn, that's always wandering from the subject, and ain't got any more sense than to try to reason out a thing that's pure theology by the laws that protect real estate!'" The comedy here is delightful, and the satire is pointed. The idea of Tom Sawyer playing the role of the scholastic philosopher and distinguishing between accident and substance in order to mount a campaign to sneak over to Africa one night and kill the pagans in their sleep for the sake of holy land (without the sacred anointment of oil reserves, it should be added) is predictive of Twain's anti-imperialist satires in later years. But there is nothing particularly philosophical or political behind Tom's adventures; Huck notes that Tom got his notions out of Walter Scott.

Mark Twain's chief interest in the narrative appears to have been in the nearly infinite and always comic ways he could confuse the issue (almost any issue) by conjoining two incompatible frames of reference. At the outset of their journey, for example, Huck is perplexed because it seems as though they have been traveling a good while but, according to the color of the land, they are still over Illinois. "What's color got to do with it?" asks Tom (*TSA*, 270). Huck points out that, as anyone who has ever looked at a map knows, Illinois is green, and Indiana is pink. Tom is disgusted with his comrade and undertakes to explain that a map is not devised to tell "lies" (that no two adjoining states are the same color) but to "to keep you from deceiving yourself" (about regulated territorial boundaries). Huck and Jim remain unconvinced, and things get even messier when Tom introduces the notion of longitude.

Huck had not believed the widow when she told him that the earth was a giant ball and had gone to the top of a hill to see for himself. In fact, observation proved to Huck that the world was flat. But now, aloft in the balloon, Huck has to concede that the earth does seem to be round, except for St. Petersburg, which remains for him in the "shape of a plate" (*TSA*, 265). Tom goes the widow one better when he declares that time on this globe is measured by degrees of longitude and that there are different times in different locations. Jim is not only disbelieving; he is bereft:

> "Mars Tom, who put de people out yonder in St. Louis? De Lord done it. Who put de people here whah we is? De Lord done it. Ain' dey bofe his children? 'Cose dey is. *Well*, den! is He gwine to *scriminate* 'twix 'em?"
>
> "Scriminate! I never heard such ignorance. There ain't no discriminating about it. When he makes you and some more of His children black, and makes the rest of us white, what do you call that?"
>
> Jim see the p'int. He was stuck. He couldn't answer. Tom says—
>
> "He does discriminate, you see, when he wants to; but this case *here* ain't no discrimination of His, it's man's. The Lord made the day, and He made the night; but He didn't invent the hours, and he didn't distribute them around. Man did that." (*TSA*, 273)

Tom rests easy with the human contrivances of longitude, meridians (which Huck to his dismay discovers are not really "on" the earth's surface at all), an international dateline (which means there are always two days chasing around the globe at the same time), and the sacrosanct au-

thority of "Grinnage" time (*TSA*, 287), but Jim sees mighty and disturbing consequences in this arrangement:

> "Mars Tom talkin' sich talk as dat—Choosday in one place en Monday in
> t'other, bofe in the same day! . . . Two days in one day! How you gwyne to git
> two days inter one day—can't git two hours inter one hour, kin you? can't git
> two niggers inter one nigger-skin, kin you? can't git two gallons o' whisky in-
> ter a one-gallon jug, kin you? No, sir, 'twould strain de jug. . . . sposen de Choos-
> day was New Year's—*now* den! Is you gwyne to tell me it's dis year in one place
> en las' year in t'other, bofe in de identical same minute? It's de beatenest rub-
> bage! I can't stan' it—I can't stan' to hear tell 'bout it." Then he begun to shiver
> and turn gray, and Tom says:
> "*Now* what's the matter? What's the trouble?"
> Jim could hardly speak, but he says—
> "Mars Tom, you ain't jokin', en it's so?"
> "No, I'm not, and it is so."
> Jim shivered again, and says—
> "Den dat Monday could be de Las' Day, en dey wouldn't *be* no Las' Day in En-
> gland, en de dead wouldn't be called. We mustn't go over dah, Mars Tom."
> (*TSA*, 273–74)

Herman Melville, in *Pierre* (1852), got a lot more metaphysical mileage
out of the contrast between man's time and God's time (between what he
termed the "chronometricals" and "horologicals"), but Twain got more
comedy out of the same material. Jim fears that his soul might come in late
on Judgment Day and miss the train to "everlasting" salvation; Tom
wants to know how fast they are closing in on Europe. And of course this
whole debate is itself an anachronism. During the time *Tom Sawyer Abroad*
takes place, in the United States alone railroads had established more than
one hundred time zones. It was not until 1883 that England and the United States fixed their watches according to Greenwich Meridian Time and
not until after the International Meridian Conference held in Washington,
D.C., in 1884 that the already common practice in many countries was
made official. Twenty-six countries voted in favor of the resolution;
France abstained, and not until 1911 did it assent to "mean time" being
kept in Greenwich, even then preferring a verbal sleight of hand—the
French referred to Greenwich time as "Paris Mean Time retarded by nine
minutes twenty-one seconds."[16] And France was not being merely chau-

---

16. Dava Sobel, *Longitude: The True Story of a Lone Genius Who Solved the Greatest Scientific Problem of His Time* (New York: Penguin, 1995), 168.

vinistic; it had a point. After all, except for historical tradition and a certain technological advantage, there was no real reason the site of mean time should have been located at Greenwich, England, and not Paris, France, or Scranton, PA. The arrangement was cobbled together for the purposes of mutual convenience. Even so, Jim's fears about missing out on Judgment Day in England are groundless. At the International Conference, Greenwich was named as the "initial meridian," which meant that it was left to Fiji, Somoa, Tonga, and other heathen nations to deal with the messy, jagged, and somewhat negotiable international dateline in the Pacific.

What binds these several conversations together is Twain's interest in abstractions, in the humorous contest between the world as it perceived and the world as it is understood. Tom undertakes to explain to the other two what a metaphor is through an illustration: "Birds of a feather flock together." Jim has a rebuttal: "But dey *don't*, Mars Tom. . . . Dey ain't no feathers dat's more alike den a bluebird's en a jaybird's, but ef you waits tell you catches *dem* birds a-flockin' together, you'll—" (*TSA*, 282). Huck sides with Jim because no one knows more about birds than Jim, and Tom is put out. Later Tom identifies the flea as a bird because both fly, but Jim will have none of it. Nonetheless, Tom argues the merits of the flea: relative to its size, the flea can jump farther and go faster than any other creature; and it can learn most anything. Tom has an outsize admiration for the flea: "S'pose you could cultivate a flea up to the size of a man, and keep his natural smartness a-growing right along up. . . . That flea would be President of the United States, and you couldn't any more prevent it than you can prevent lightning" (*TSA*, 293).

Tom insists upon all sorts of cockamamy notions with belligerent authority—that deserts were not created but just happened; that "perspective brings out the correct proportions" of things, and by way of illustration he observes that "Julius Caesar's niggers didn't know how big he was, they was too close to him" (*TSA*, 330); that the balloon they are in and the flying horse in the Arabian Nights are the same thing under different names because "it ain't the mere *form* that's got anything to do with their being similar or unsimilar, it's the *principle* involved; and the principle is the same in both" (*TSA*, 333); and that popes in the middle ages were learned in "scientific" cursing, not the haphazard and raggedy sort Huck and Jim are acquainted with. When Huck or Jim repudiates or even doubts Tom's flimsy arguments, as they both often do, Tom is dismissive and one time claims he would just as soon "have intellectual intercourse with a catfish" (*TSA*, 311).

Tom Sawyer Abroad is a welter of contradictory and often quite wrong explanations of place and perception, a comic medley of verbal, topo-graphical, and perceptual confusion. A line of camels far below is mis-taken for ants; no matter how fast the three seem to be crossing the "mon-strous big ring" of the Atlantic Ocean, they always seem to remain in the center of the circle. Nor can they seem to gain on the lake they see in the desert. It turns out to be a mirage, of course, and Tom explains that what they see is actually an ocular deception compounded of "air and heat and thirstiness pasted together by a person's imagination" (*TSA*, 303).[17] Jim reckons it is a ghost and that the Great Desert is haunted. Tom has an im-perfect understanding about what a "welkin" or an "indemnity" is, but that does not prevent him from using the words with casual authority. Af-ter a storm, the balloon needs to be emptied of sand. Tom decides that Jim should do three-fifths of the work and Tom and Huck a fifth apiece. It is not clear whether or not Tom knows it, but this is not the first time a black man has been defined as three-fifths a person.[18] If Twain himself intend-ed such a satirical irony, he didn't elaborate on it other than to have Huck say, "He was only nigger outside; inside he was as white as you be" (*TSA*, 326).

Tom, Huck, and Jim, each after his own fashion, ponder how one might ever arrive at the solid ground of proof. Jim is fond of drawing inferences and making comparisons, but Huck regards this as mere "reckoning": "But *reckoning* don't settle nothing. You can reckon till the cows come home, but that don't fetch you no decision" (*TSA*, 308). Jim argues that the Great Sahara Desert was composed of the materials left over after God cre-ated the universe, but Tom says that argument is just a theory, and "theo-ries don't prove nothing, they only give you a place to rest on, a spell, when you are tuckered out butting around and around trying to find out something there ain't no way *to* find out" (*TSA*, 311). Huck compares the relative value of knowledge and instinct and decides in favor of the lat-ter: "for all the brag you hear about knowledge being such a wonderful thing, instink is worth forty of it for real unerringness. Jim says the same" (*TSA*, 337). *Tom Sawyer Abroad* is full of ad hominem arguments, specious analogies, casuistry and hairsplitting, category errors, appeals to author-ity, and the like. If Twain was inching toward some serious moral or so-cial issue, if he was seriously distinguishing between different forms of thinking or drawing some clear conclusion about human nature, he did

17. Twain did not explain Joan of Arc's visions in these terms, however.
18. Not so coincidentally for the purposes of taxation and congressional represen-tation, the Constitution of the United States, article 1, section 2, assigned slaves this fraction of humanity.

not make those purposes very clear. Instead, he seems to be enjoying the sheer fun of having Huck, Tom, and Jim splash around in a murky quagmire of thought and opinion. On the other hand, when he had Jim ask, you "can't git two niggers inter one nigger-skin, kin you?" or Huck acknowledge that Jim was only a "nigger" on the outside, Twain was, knowingly or unknowingly, commenting on the purely silly farce of "Those Extraordinary Twins" and ultimately on the extremely serious but still antic treatment of race in *Pudd'nhead Wilson*.

III

By December 1892, Mark Twain had a large pile of manuscript pages on hand that would eventually become two stories. By means of a "Caesarean section," he extracted from the narrative he was calling "Those Extraordinary Twins," for that was the "mother" that gave birth to the child, a novel he would name *Pudd'nhead Wilson*. It was published serially in the *Century* (December 1893–June 1894). The remainder, with the addition of some bracketed bridge passages and some light revision, would be published as "Those Extraordinary Twins," appearing as a companion piece in the book publication of *Pudd'nhead Wilson* (1894). Whatever else one might want to say about it, though, that long manuscript (containing in germ both the "tragedy" that became the novel and the "comedy" that became the farcical short story) participated in the same frolicking mood of confusing the issue that characterizes *Tom Sawyer Abroad*.

At the outset, the primary vehicle for the sorts of comic confusions Twain indulged in had to do with conjoined twins, Angelo and Luigi Cappello. Here, quite literally, were two people stuffed into one skin—Angelo a teetotaling Methodist, but ready to become a Baptist, and full of principle, Luigi a freethinking tippler; Angelo a fair-skinned blond with blue eyes, generous and timid, Luigi a swarthy brunette, mischief-making and hot-tempered.[19] In several ways they cooperate with one another, but

19. When Twain adapted the twins to the purposes of *Pudd'nhead Wilson*, he separated the two, giving each the regulation number of limbs, and made them more nearly identical, though Angelo remained somewhat fairer than Luigi. This surgical operation was a success, but in his haste Twain forgot to make certain adjustments in the novel. For example, when Tom refers to the two as a human "philopena," the joke is altogether mysterious. On the other hand, the report of Luigi's killing a thief with the Indian dagger to protect Angelo was in the earlier instance an act of self-defense. Although Luigi declines the honor of acting in a selfless way, it is nonetheless deemed by all a "noble" act. This adventitious change of meaning is another sort of anomaly

due to differences in temperament they also often act at cross-purposes. To disrupt Angelo's tuneful rendition of "Greenland's Icy Mountains," Luigi launches into the rackety "Old Bob Ridley." One drinks tea, the other coffee. If Angelo puts too much sugar in his tea, Luigi gets dyspeptic. Angelo wants to attend a temperance meeting; Luigi makes sure Angelo will be drunk by the time he gets there. Luigi agrees to a duel with Judge Driscoll, but Angelo fidgets too much for him to draw a proper bead on the old man. Luigi stands his ground until the stroke of midnight Saturday when the control of the legs is transferred to Angelo, and he (or they) takes flight.

The comedy Twain was able to get out of this arrangement would surely be grotesque were it not for the fact that the two do not think of themselves as freaks. To the contrary, though in a depressed mood Angelo might wish to be as other men, he soon enough abandons such "diseased imagining": "How awkward it would seem; how unendurable. What would he do with his hands, his arms? How would his legs feel? How odd, and strange, and grotesque every action, attitude, movement, gesture would be . . . how lonely, how unspeakably lonely" (*PWET,* 144). This is a "natural" attitude, the narrator assures us, as is the twin's inclination to think of other, so-called normal men as "monsters" and "deformities." However, even before David Wilson, Tom Driscoll, and Roxana began to upstage the prevailing burlesque concerning the twins, Twain was introducing serious questions into his fantastic narrative, though he was not disposed to treat them in a particularly sober way.

The "me" that claims Hank Morgan's allegiance in *A Connecticut Yankee* is something of a conundrum in the case of the Siamese twins. Both the narrator in his preface and several of the characters in the story itself do not quite know how to refer to the twins—are they two or one? a he or a they, or perhaps an it? The twins are (or is) unquestionably human—they stand on two feet, reason and feel, converse and deliberate. But do they qualify as a person? They make moral decisions, but depending on which twin has control of the legs that week, they are not necessarily able to act on those decisions. Angelo gets baptized; Luigi catches cold. Luigi takes a drink; Angelo gets drunk. Luigi gets elected alderman, but he cannot fulfill his public duty because he brings along with him to the meetings an unauthorized citizen. One falls in love; the other spoils the courtship. For all that, however, they are never "lonely," and in Twain's comedy it

---

because Twain typically avoided selfless acts as violating his theory of human behavior.

may be more just to think of the two as a community than as two individuals. In fact, at the trial to decide an assault case brought by Tom Driscoll, Judge Robinson decides to try the two as a "corporation" instead of as two individuals.

Since they cannot testify against themselves and will not disclose which twin had control of the legs at the time of kicking Tom Driscoll, Judge Robinson finds it impossible to assign guilt. Judge Driscoll, on the other hand, is intent on a duel to settle this private matter of family honor.[20] Tom mistakenly names Angelo as the one who kicked him, but Angelo refuses to duel. Ironically, Luigi serves as proxy for his brother, who had no part in delivering the insult in the first place.[21] None of this matters much anyway because the only ones who get hurt in the duel are innocent bystanders.

It is probably a mistake to think of all the layered and often ironic complexities of either tale as deliberate. Twain was playfully capitalizing on comic opportunities as they arose in dramatized situations or as they spontaneously occurred to him. Nevertheless, the joined twins pose an interesting complication to Mark Twain's beliefs about human nature. The brothers argue with one another; they filibuster, compromise, lobby, cooperate, and negotiate because their life is a joint venture. Robert Louis Stevenson had depicted an antagonistic twinned nature in *Dr. Jekyll and Mr. Hyde* in 1886, but Twain did not permit himself to probe subterranean impulses as his younger friend had done.[22] Instead, the differences between Luigi and Angelo are clearly visible and more a matter of temperament than anything else, and the motives for and consequences of

20. In "Those Extraordinary Twins," Tom Driscoll tells his uncle that Angelo kicked him, though in *Pudd'nhead Wilson* he claims it was Luigi. In the farce, Tom presumably names Angelo out of jealousy because they are rivals for Rowena's affection.

21. When the duel is represented in *Pudd'nhead Wilson*, Twain has already introduced the complication of the switched babies. Tom names Luigi as his assailant, and the Judge challenges him. But in this latter rendering, Tom has not yet become the changeling who is in fact Roxy's not Percy Driscoll's son. In this instance, the duel acquires what Hershel Parker would call an "adventitious" irony because the Judge has decided to avenge the insult "the blood of my race" has suffered. Neither his "blood" nor his "race" is in fact involved in the matter.

22. The comparison is not altogether gratuitous. One reviewer of *Pudd'nhead Wilson* made the comparison as well. What is more, Twain reread Stevenson's novel years later and arrived at the sort of conclusion about human duality he had avoided in writing his novel: *Dr. Jekyll and Mr. Hyde* "was an attempt to account for our seeming *duality*—the presence in us of another *person*; not a slave of ours, but . . . with a character distinctly its own" (quoted in Ron Powers, *Mark Twain: A Life* [New York: Free Press, 2005], 586).

their behavior are essentially social.[23] The "sinister" side of the Cappello brothers derives from popularly held attitudes toward race, not interior impulses. And those attitudes seem to have been the object of Twain's satire in this farce before he so radically revised it. Despite the burlesque treatment, "Those Extraordinary Twins" is a tale that might have had real bite in an era John Higham calls the "Nationalist Nineties,"[24] but when the story was eventually published it was presented as a narrative mistake that needed to be disentangled from the more serious story of the changelings. Still, the presence of the twins (joined or separated) had a purpose.

Angelo and Luigi introduce a foreign element into Dawson's Landing, and not merely due to their "freakish" appearance. They happen to be Italians. In March 1891, a New Orleans jury failed to convict a group of Italian immigrants accused of killing the police commissioner. Outraged citizens lynched eleven men—ten murdered in their cells, and one dragged outside, hanged, and shot. The national and international fallout was considerable. Italian Americans throughout the land protested; the Italian government was incensed. The American secretary of state treated the whole affair in a cavalier fashion; newspapers often approved the actions and argued that it was a well-known fact that Italy used America as a dumping ground for undesirables. A *New York Times* writer observed: "These sneaking and cowardly Sicilians, the descendants of bandits and assassins, who have transported to this country the lawless passions, the cutthroat passions and the oathbound societies of their native country, are to us a pest without mitigation. Lynch law was the only recourse open to the people of New Orleans."[25]

Things heated up. The Italian foreign minister was brought home, and

23. The notion of temperament accounts for individual differences between and among people. Among other things it accounts for the fact that two people may view the same object in different ways, and for reasons that have to do with physiology, heredity, or other factors. Differences in temperament do not necessarily indicate the existence of some intrinsic or immutable self. The person allergic to peanuts may not have the same pleasing associations with going to the circus as do many others; "rosy fingered dawn" may be a curious description for a native of Nome, Alaska.

24. See chapter 4 of *Strangers in the Land: Patterns of American Nativism, 1860–1925* (New York: Atheneum, 1963). Louis J. Budd and Eric Sundquist have noted the significance of the New Orleans lynchings to both "Those Extraordinary Twins" and *Pudd'nhead Wilson. See*, respectively, *Mark Twain: Social Philosopher*, 155–56, and "Mark Twain and Homer Plessy," in *Mark Twain's "Pudd'nhead Wilson": Race, Conflict, and Culture*, ed. Susan Gillman and Forrest G. Robinson (Durham: Duke University Press, 1990), 67–69.

25. *New York Times*, March 16–17, 1891.

Italy demanded indemnity for the families of the slain, which was eventually paid to the extent of some $25,000. There was saber rattling on both sides of the Atlantic; there was even talk of war. Apologists conceded that otherwise "good" Italians were bullied and coerced into their misdeeds by a "Capo Mafia" (words that gained sudden currency in the land).[26] As it happened, Clemens and his family were in Rome and Venice for several weeks in 1892 and in Florence later the same year. Twain must have heard something of the complaints about the event from the Italian point of view, and he was working on "Those Extraordinary Twins" at the time. In the manuscript, before it was separated into two stories, Twain had alluded to the principal features associated with the stereotypical dreaded Italian, though they were mostly to be found in the conduct and person of Luigi—a dark complexion and fiery temper, a spotty and violent past (though Tom Driscoll knows Luigi killed a man in self-defense he nevertheless calls Luigi an "assassin"), and ownership of the supposed Italian weapon of choice, a dagger, albeit a gem-studded Indian one, not a stiletto. Twain's satire, however, has more to do with the reactions of the people of Dawson's Landing than it does with the twins.

It is a volatile population. They are alternately dumbstruck by the brothers' appearance, infatuated by their rank and accomplishments, enamored of their attention and good breeding, admiring of Luigi's pluck and outraged by Angelo's cowardice. They are gullible—Luigi, for the fun of the "swindle," convinces Aunt Betsy and Aunt Patsy that he and his brother are not twins at all. They are whimsical—the town divides into the Luigi and Angelo factions over temperance and has the twins run against one another for alderman. And they are dangerous. Luigi spoils Angelo's teetotaler speech by getting him tipsy and is elected. But Angelo is not permitted to attend the town meetings, and Luigi can't attend without him. City government comes to a standstill until someone proposes a hanging:

> "That's the ticket."
> But others said—
> "No—Count Angelo is innocent; we mustn't hang him."
> "Who said anything about hanging him? We are only going to hang the other one." (*PWET*, 184)

---

26. When Twain named the twins "Cappello"—Italian for hat, but deriving from capo, or head—he may have been making some punning point about anti-Italian hysteria without insisting on it.

This is the same community that labeled David Wilson a "pudd'nhead" because he wanted to own half-interest in a noisy dog so that he could kill his half. As farcical as "Those Extraordinary Twins" is, it seems unlikely that Twain would have had his twins hanged (or rather one of them) as merely a convenient way to conclude his tale. Instead, the moral of his comedy seems clear. One cannot get rid of the supposed "bad" elements in a community without also eliminating the virtuous ones. The hysterical pro–Anglo Saxonism and anti-immigration feelings of the 1890s, so dramatically acted out in the New Orleans lynchings, promoted mob rule and unthinking passions and called forth an ugly chauvinism. What is more, those feelings were counterproductive and simply stupid. The story of the Siamese twins remains a comedy, however, because it wreaks havoc with conventional pieties and settled opinion in slapstick fashion. The "tragedy" that was pushing its way to the fore was literally and figuratively a different story.

IV

While Mark Twain was tinkering with his Extraordinary Twins manuscript, James W. Paige continued to tinker with the typesetting machine that promised to put the investor-writer on Easy Street. Though Twain hoped against reason for the machine's eventual success, it became clear to him that his investment was taking him down the road to financial ruin. In 1891, he stopped payments supporting the project and turned his attention to salvaging his undercapitalized publishing house. That same year, the Clemenses' Hartford house was closed down and the servants placed elsewhere; the family removed to Europe.

Paige was a perfectionist, which is another way of saying that his invention was doomed to failure from the beginning. Twain was not, which is another way of saying that eventually both "Those Extraordinary Twins" and *Pudd'nhead Wilson* would be published but deeply flawed as well. At the same time that Twain fretted over his indebtedness, he worried about his public image. *The Prince and the Pauper* did something to make him a more respectable eminence in the literary world, and his work in progress, *Personal Recollections of Joan of Arc*, might tilt the scales still further in his favor. At length, he might restore his fortunes and the reading public might come to see him as Howells and his own family saw him—a morally serious and deeply respectful man, not the American Vandal but an altogether proper American Victorian. For the moment, however, it graveled him that he was misperceived by the public at large, much as David Wilson had been when he stepped off the boat at Dawson's Landing. At least insofar as public estimation was concerned, neither Wilson, nor many other characters Twain created during this period, nor Twain himself, was "focused" right, and this was a vexing problem he might deal with in imaginative if not practical terms. At any rate, much of the short fiction Twain was writing at this time, along with *Pudd'nhead Wilson*, combined, at least thematically, the interrelated concerns of self-approval and public perception, social caste and personal merit, private selves and social vocations.[27]

Hershel Parker's systematic analysis of the existing manuscript and his speculative description of the genesis of *Pudd'nhead Wilson* calls into question many claims that have been made about the novel. For our purposes, among the most important points Parker makes are the following: In the beginning, there was no changeling plot and Tom Driscoll had not even a single drop of black blood in his veins. All of Tom's negative qualities—his cowardice, his gambling, his drinking, and his thievery—were a part of his nature before Twain came up with the swapped-babies wrinkle in his haphazardly plotted narrative. What is more, the invention of Roxy herself evidently came out of the blue. The first mention of Roxana in the manuscript occurs, without explanation, when Tom Driscoll is trying to guess at Pudd'nhead Wilson's scheme to catch the thief who has been raiding the town and who presumably has the twins' Indian dagger. Tom is stumped and decides to "give Roxana's smarter head a chance at it."[28] When Roxy does come on stage it is not her intelligence that is emphasized, however, but her decisive fury; she smashes Tom's whiskey bottle and insists that her "son" must toe the line, for to do otherwise is to risk being disinherited by Judge Driscoll. Twain later introduced the switched-babies incident to account for the change of Tom's situation and along the way created in his mother one of Twain's most memorable characters.

---

27. The short stories "Luck" (1891), "The Esquimau Maiden's Romance," "The £1,000,000 Bank Note," and "Is He Living or Is He Dead?" treat with remarkable variety characters who are not "focused" right. One blunderer has the world's esteem, another man is in possession of a million-pound note he cannot possibly cash but is otherwise penniless and lives on credit, a painter stages his own death in order to boost the value of his work, and the Eskimo maiden curses her wealth (twenty-two iron fishhooks) because it caused her to suspect the motives of the one man she loved. I have dealt with these stories in greater detail in *Mark Twain: A Study of the Short Fiction* (New York: Twayne Publishers, 1997), 89–101.

28. Quoted in Parker, *Flawed Texts and Verbal Icons* (Evanston: Northwestern University Press, 1984), 125.

Only after writing to the end did Twain go back and write the early history of the new main characters. In other words, their beginnings were an afterthought written to account for their already realized condition. He had already dramatized Roxy's offering herself to Tom to be sold as a slave and Tom's subsequent betrayal by selling her down the river. He had also introduced Pudd'nhead Wilson's hobby of fingerprinting before, but, without the changeling element in the plot, it might have served merely to solve the crime of the theft without also serving as a natal autograph that discloses Tom Driscoll's "true" identity as Valet de Chambre. Twain then turned his attention to the back-and-fill job of establishing the history of these events and characters.

Apparently, Mark Twain "created" these characters (or at least rounded them out) by reasoning backward from who they "were" to how they came to be that way. His understanding of human nature of course figured into his thinking, and he applied in the process those chief instruments of his creed—the external influences of training, heredity, and habit—as explanatory principles.[29] In the case of Tom Driscoll, that should not have been a difficult task. Tom (Chambers) became a "bad baby" very soon after his mother effected the "usurpation" of the real Tom's position. The occasion for it was the irritation of teething, but the solicitude of Roxy fostered a demanding and greedy temper in the boy. His physical frailty and fearfulness derive, in part, from the servile attention he receives from his servant, who also happens to be his mother. His self-indulgent cruelty was helped along by Chambers (Tom Driscoll) who serves as both whipping boy and bodyguard. Tom's overbearing manner was consistent with his social status as a Driscoll. Tom Driscoll acquired his appetite for gambling and drink at Yale.[30] Finally, the total package, the "self" that goes by the name of Thomas à Becket Driscoll, was the product of a slaveholding culture.

Even Tom, amid the dizzying complexities of his newfound identity,

29. David Wilson is more a presence in the novel than a developed character, and Twain himself admitted that he thought of Pudd'nhead as a "piece of machinery," not a character (*LLMT*, 291). Wilson's Calendar, along with whatever witticisms he gets off at the Freethinker Society meetings, reveals him to be clever and sardonic. But when an ironist decides to forgo any sense of self-respect and to linger for two decades in a town whose mental vision is not "focused" for irony, a reader might reasonably expect to know why. Twain merely says Wilson's Scottish "patience and pluck" decided him on this course.

30. Given his southern aristocratic upbringing, his taste for spirits might have already been developed. Huck and Buck Grangerford, it will be recalled, join in the toast to the Colonel with a small tumbler of sugar and brandy.

imperfectly recognizes the significance of slavery to his situation when he asks himself in a passage later removed from the novel, "Why was he a coward?" At first he decides his cowardice comes from his "nigger *blood*." This may be so in the sense that generations of "insult and outrage" constitute the "circumstances" in which meekness and cowardice have displaced an original courage and vitality. But Twain, as opposed to Tom, would characterize this "instinct" as a product of training or "petrified habit" and not an absolute condition founded on racial difference. Likewise, Tom believes his baseness comes from his white blood: "Whence came that in him which was high, and whence that which was base? That which was high came from either blood, and was the monopoly of neither color; but that which was base was the *white* blood in him debased by the brutalizing effects of a long-drawn heredity of slave-owning, with the habit of abuse which the possession of irresponsible power always creates and perpetuates, by a law of human nature. So he argued" (*PWET,* 211).

Had Twain pressed harder in Tom's self-interrogation, he might have created a character fully as interesting as his mother, Roxy. Several excised passages indicate the author pondered Tom Driscoll's epiphany and the psychological consequences that might flow from it. Tom's loathing of the Negro suddenly becomes self-loathing, though, true to the force of habit, his self-identification with the slave is only temporary and intermittent. His status in Dawson's Landing as the son of Percy Driscoll and the ward of York Driscoll, the wealthiest, most important, and self-important, man in town, is abruptly translated into that of a white man's "bastard." Tom, once the motherless but free and white child, now stands abased before a mother whose very presence he finds odious. Tom, the haughty and arrogant slaveholder and heir apparent to his supposed uncle's estate, discovers himself a commodity that that same uncle could sell at will.

Tom's unwanted revelations typically give way to established habits. Still, in another excised passage Twain acknowledges that one of the few "changes" in Tom that became permanent had to do with a desire for vengeance: "He hated the whites, he would steal from them without shame, and even with a vengeful exultation; he loathed the 'nigger' in him, but got pleasure out of bringing this secret 'filth,' as he called it, into familiar and constant contact with the sacred whites; he privately despised and hated his uncle and all his aristocratic pretensions" (*PWET,* 202). Mark Twain was not the sort of writer to develop a character along the lines suggested in this passage; William Faulkner's Joe Christmas or Richard Wright's Bigger Thomas is a better candidate for that kind of character. But the central insight is Twain's, and had he emphasized rather than downplayed the element of miscegenation in the narrative, he might have created a more compelling and disturbing narrative. Twain might have developed, for example, the romantic interest between Tom and Rowena, conceived before Tom had any black blood in him. Instead of love, however, Tom might have become motivated by the perverse but understandable desire to secretly contaminate white society in every quarter, including the bedroom. Instead the author pretty much eliminated the Tom-Rowena dimension from the novel altogether, in deference to a reader's sensitivities to interracial romantic interests, perhaps, but also due to a certain fastidiousness in Twain himself.

Nonetheless, Tom Driscoll remains an interesting creation. The closing sentence in the passage quoted above ("So he argued") makes it an even question whether Tom's reasoning is itself more the product of a habit of mind than of any true insight he has into the question of race or his own, newly discovered identity.[31] He is "arguing" with himself, but according to premises and a vocabulary that have been trained into him. After all, neither "white blood" nor "black blood" has much at all to do with the qualities he is describing. Following his line of reasoning, presumably non-slaveholding whites (Swedes or Finns, for example) are exempt from the "brutalizing effects" of abusive power. Likewise, Africans who have never been slaves possess the original and undiminished courage of a proud and uncompromised people. In other words, neither blackness nor whiteness, and certainly not "blood," has anything to do with the questions he is trying to answer. An inherited social fabric of mastery and subjugation, founded on the "legal fiction" of race and trained into a people who fall one side or the other of an altogether specious color line, promotes a certain set of qualities, perhaps even a temperament, but not much more. In this sense, too, the term *nigger* does not necessarily designate a racial category so much as it describes a hurtful and degrading social condition.[32] Twain may have had this distinction in mind when he

31. In another excised passage, Twain notes that Tom was unaccustomed to thinking at all, and his newfound condition had caused a "whirlwind" of confusion to his thoughts (*PWET*, 201).

32. Just as Hank Morgan discovers that most of the serfs in Arthur's England have had the "manhood" ground out of them, in *Pudd'nhead Wilson* Twain seems to be assigning to the same sort of phenomenon the term *nigger*, without specific attachment to the concept of race. More to the point, Mark Twain had known for some time one of the few things that Quentin Compson learned during his abbreviated stint at Harvard: "a nigger is not a person so much as a form of behavior; a sort of obverse reflection of the white people he lives among" (William Faulkner, *The Sound and the Fury*, ed. David Mintner [New York; W. W. Norton, 1994], 55).

wrote Fred J. Hall about the revisions he had made in the novel and declared that now three people "stand up high, from beginning to end, and
only three—Pudd'nhead, 'Tom' Driscoll and his nigger mother Roxana"
(*MTLP*, 354). Why, except for differences in training, should Roxana be a
"nigger," but not Tom?

Mark Twain's reasoning backward from the sudden appearance of
Roxy in his story to the sort of three-dimensional character she became
would have been less intricate but no less substantial. Her abrupt appearance in the novel indicates that from the beginning she was conceived
to be intelligent and iron-willed. How, though, given the sort of reasoning Tom engages in (that the institution of slavery makes the slave meek
and cowardly) could Roxy have evaded the common fate? The answer
seems quite simple. The impulses toward docility that have been trained
into Roxy are overruled by another, stronger impulse that had the allure
of holy sanction in Victorian America—the maternal instinct. In her desperation to prevent her baby from ever being sold down the river, she at
first decides to drown herself and the child and thus take them to the other side, where the Lord and Master doesn't sell his children. Then she concludes that the baby at least might make a more immediate crossing by
transferring her child to the cradle of the master's son. In abiding by her
maternal instinct, however, she is forced to give up its natural corollary—
motherhood; the choice is unnatural, but this is a slaveholding society in
which every human relation is skewed. Roxana may well be an American
Medea, as Sherley Anne Williams argues, derived not from ancient jeal-
ousies but "from the grotesque fact of black enslavement" itself.[33] Roxana's vengeful defiance, though, avoids public assault and instead is full
of conniving and deception. Among those deceptions is the self-deception
brought about by playing the role of ministering and obsequious servant
to her child, and this "exercise soon concreted itself into a habit; it became
automatic and unconscious; then a natural result followed: deceptions intended solely for others gradually grew practically into self-deceptions as
well" (*PWET*, 20).

These cultivated habits do not lessen the sting of the abuses heaped
upon her by her son, before he knows that he is her son. But Roxy is a
proud woman, and, ironically, she sometimes draws upon the same
sources of self-esteem that Judge Driscoll does—her lineage. In chapter

---

33. "Introduction" to *The Tragedy of Pudd'nhead Wilson and the Comedy of Those Extraordinary Twins*, ed. Shelley Fisher Fishkin (New York: Oxford University Press,
1996), xxxix.

14, she curses Tom Driscoll's cowardice and says he has disgraced his birth: "What ever has 'come o' yo' Essex blood? . . . En it ain't only jist Essex blood dat's in you, not by a long sight—'deed it ain't! My great-great-great-gran'father en yo' great-great-great-great-gran'father was ole Cap'n John Smith, de highes' blood dat Ole Virginny ever turned out; en *his* great-great-gran'mother or somers along back dah, was Pocahontas de Injun queen, en her husbun' was a nigger king outen Africa—en yet here you is, a slinkin' outen a duel disgracin' our whole line like a ornery low-down hound! Yes, it's de nigger in you!" (*PWET*, 75–76). This snarled genealogy could only be plotted on the multiple trunks of a banyan tree. Nevertheless, Roxy's proud attachment to her antecedents (what Judge Driscoll calls his "race") is as fierce as that of any other member of the First Families of Virginia. Sometimes Roxy's pride and her maternal instincts act at cross-purposes, but occasionally they are fused in a way that is to her liking. In one of the early passages, though written after the final chapters were completed, we are told that Roxy "saw herself sink from the sublime height of motherhood to the sombre deeps of unmodified slavery. The abyss of separation between her and her boy was complete. She was merely his chattel now . . . the humble and unresisting victim of [Tom's] capricious temper and vicious nature" (*PWET*, 23–24). At times she plots revenge upon him; at other times, though, she is proud of him, "for this was her son, her nigger son lording it among the whites and securely avenging their crimes against her race" (*PWET*, 24). In the submerged duel between Roxy and slaveholders, Tom all unknowingly acts as her proxy, allowing his "secret filth" to contaminate southern purity.

Robert Regan once described *Pudd'nhead Wilson* as a "*mélange des gènres*,"[34] and among the several genres Twain drew upon (burlesque, melodrama, plantation narratives, and detective fiction among them) the slave narrative and novels of "passing" figure importantly. *Pudd'nhead Wilson* is no conventional passing novel, however. Tom doesn't "pass" for white any more than Chambers passes for black; they are both white and simply placed on opposite sides of a color line. The only "black" character in the novel with a speaking role is Jasper, and his role was reduced to a walk-on part. If anything, Twain meant to show just how absurd and porous such racial demarcations are. Tom, in his raids on the town, deliberately disguises himself as a black woman by darkening his skin with burnt cork. Thus "black" Valet de Chambre becomes "white" Tom Dris-

---

34. *Unpromising Heroes: Mark Twain and His Characters* (Berkeley: University of California Press, 1966), 208.

coll who, in order to pass for a slave, must put on blackface. Likewise, Roxy, once slave but now legally free, offers herself to be sold as a commodity. She will allow herself to be sold in order to satisfy Tom's creditors; she thereby makes the ultimate maternal sacrifice. Tom, by selling her down the river, commits the ultimate filial betrayal. After two months of hell, Roxy escapes and returns to Tom's room in St. Louis, disguised as a man and also in blackface. Thus the "black slave" Roxy becomes a freedwoman who pretends to be a slave and then escapes from bondage and masquerades as a black man. Surely, this sort of maneuvering on Twain's part came out of a desire to confuse the issue and render the absurdities of conventional assumptions about race, gender, class, and many other things.

The history of the composition of the novel ought to, but probably won't, put to rest some portion of the interpretive disputes among critics—specifically, that Tom's selfish and conniving nature in any way derives from questions of race. Mark Twain had had Hank Morgan angrily declare, "Training is everything." He reaffirmed this creed in more jocular terms through one of David Wilson's maxims: "Training is everything. The peach was once a bitter almond; cauliflower is nothing but cabbage with a college education" (*PWET*, 23). In the ongoing debate between naturalists and environmentalists during this era, Twain was on the side of the environmentalists, lopsidedly so perhaps. A nervous Anglo-Saxon nationalistic sense of superiority combined with a somewhat managed view of Darwinian theory characterized the sort of racial thinking that eventuated in a full-fledged racism. John Higham puts it this way: "Thus the evolutionary theory, when fully adopted by race-thinkers, not only impelled them to anchor their national claims to a biological basis; it also provoked anxiety by denying assurance that the basis would endure."[35]

Fortuitously perhaps, by so concentrating on environmental factors Mark Twain had inoculated himself against some of the more virulent strains of fin-de-siècle racism. In fact, *Pudd'nhead Wilson* is not, in any conventional sense, about race as a biological category but about the "legal fiction" that goes by that name and purports to explain but actually enforces a certain human condition. To say, as we are apt to say these days, that race is a "socially constructed" concept is perhaps to give too benign a flavor to the notion. The fiction of race, particularly in antebellum America, may have been a construction, but it was also backed up by superstition, statute, tradition, economic interests, guns, whips, chains, and ropes.

---

35. *Strangers in the Land*, 135.

In any event, what makes Roxy "black" is not complexion but conditioning; before readers ever see the woman they have concluded that she is Negro due to her dialect. She is a proud, "sassy" woman around her "caste" and meek and deferential around white folk. In the early years, she abases herself to Tom, the son whom she has exalted to the role of her master. In one of the many paradoxical moves of the narrative, however, after she discloses their relationship, Roxy still cannot warm to her offspring. Roxy couldn't yet "love" Tom because there "'warn't nothing *to* him,' as she expressed it, but her nature needed something or somebody to rule over, and he was better than nothing" (*PWET*, 50). If Twain is indicating here that proud natures require mastery over other human beings, then he may also be saying something about an indwelling slaveholding mentality that derives from neither race nor gender but from class interests, however humble, and the fundamental need for self-approval.

More broadly, though, *Pudd'nhead Wilson* is about identity, and here too Twain plays fast and loose with conventional assumptions. Social roles, as Erving Goffman points out, provide the basis for a self-image because they carry with them a set of protocols that govern behavior. "A self, then, virtually awaits the individual entering a position; he need only conform to the pressures on him and he will find a *me* ready-made for him."[36] But in the topsy-turvy world that is Dawson's Landing, things don't work quite that way. David Wilson is a lawyer without a practice; Tom is a slave without a master. Roxy is a mother without a child or, perhaps worse, a mother with the wrong child, whom she describes as an "imitation nigger" (*PWET*, 39). Judge Driscoll is far more impetuous than judicious. David Wilson has every right to sneer at the community that labeled him a "pudd'nhead." However, when he is approached by a committee from the Democratic Party to run for mayor, or any other office he might name, he is overcome. In a passage Twain deleted from the novel we have Wilson's reaction: "He had never dreamed of a fairy land of that amazing sort before, asleep or awake. He was in such a whirl of happiness and emotion that he could not trust his voice, but had to do his thanks with fervent hand-grasps and the deep eloquence of watery eyes" (*PWET*, 212). If that isn't the reaction of an out-and-out pudd'nhead, I don't know what is.

And what absurd wreckage is left behind. Twain seized upon Francis Galton's book *Finger-Prints* (1892) for the assistance it would give him in wrapping up the several plot lines in courtroom fashion and not for any

36. *Encounters: Two Studies in the Sociology of Interaction* (Indianapolis: Bobbs-Merrill, 1961), 87–88.

scientific or ideological perspectives that were behind Galton's systematic inquiries.[37] Wilson dramatically reveals the true identities of Thomas à Becket Driscoll and Valet de Chambre in the courtroom and thus, to the satisfaction of the community and apparently himself, restores the social order. And what senseless and irreparable consequences follow. David Wilson has the fawning admiration of the community; every utterance he makes now, no matter how insipid, is "golden." The twins have had enough of their "Western adventure" and return to Europe. As for Roxy "the spirit in her eye was quenched, her martial bearing departed with it, and the voice of her laughter ceased in the land"; the church is her only comfort. Chambers is now Tom Driscoll and the last of that noble F.F.V. line; he is established as lord and master of the House of Driscoll. But his "manners were the manners of a slave," and he blankly sits in the kitchen because he is terrified of the parlor. Tom Driscoll is now Chambers and sentenced to life imprisonment for murdering the Judge, but Percy Driscoll's creditors come forward and claim him as their property. He is sold down the river, the same fate his mother had tried to spare him. There is a Greek-like symmetry to Tom's end, but Twain's earlier plan might have been even more effective; at least it would have been more American. He had Tom hang himself in order to avoid being sold. If Twain had concluded his story this way, it would have been an even question whether Tom committed suicide or, to rid himself of that drop of black blood, he conducted a lynching instead.

What makes *Pudd'nhead Wilson* interesting and innovative is that Mark Twain wrote a probing psychological novel that is wholly preoccupied with questions of social station and conduct. He inspects the interior lives of his characters, but the fact of slavery, as opposed to the fiction of race, makes for troubling conclusions about not only the body politic but a resulting anguished social psychology as well. And flickering in the background of this novel like heat lightning are references to money and the fickle sport it plays with human lives. David Wilson draws on his trifling savings to open a law practice but soon thereafter takes in his shingle and picks up a living as an accountant straightening out other people's books. Reminiscent of the curse of the Tennessee acreage, Percy Driscoll loses his fortune in land speculation down south. Roxy's bank fails, as many busi-

---

37. Francis Galton was the father of "eugenics," and he began his investigations of fingerprints with the hope that he could discern categorical racial differences in the whorls and ridges of the fingertips. In fact, he could not and considered the subject useful for forensic purposes but a dead end insofar as evolutionary theory was concerned.

nesses and banks were to do in the 1893 financial panic. Sam Clemens could identify with any of these characters, for his own financial distress was bothering him a great deal while he was writing this novel, but the character whose financial situation most resembles his own is Tom Driscoll's. Tom's fluctuating fortunes parallel Twain's own in the financial roller-coaster ride that was his investment in the Paige typesetting machine. Tom can't quite break his gambling habit and, like Twain, is plagued by creditors; at the same time Judge Driscoll repeatedly tears up and then redrafts the will naming Tom his heir. Then there is the loot Tom picks up in periodic raids upon the town. The most valuable prize he acquires is the Indian knife that, he learns, is studded with gems. But Pudd'nhead Wilson's scheme to catch the thief puts that treasure out of reach. The knife is "a bag of gold that has turned to dirt and ashes in my hands. It could save me, and save me so easily, and yet I've got to go to ruin. It's like drowning with a life-preserver in my reach" (*PWET*, 74). Such seemed to be the failed promise of the Paige typesetter, as well.

Whatever bitterness and distress Clemens was feeling during these years (and both must have been considerable at times), he mustered the imaginative vitality to create in *Pudd'nhead Wilson* a memorable though somewhat reckless book. In the early years, Clemens absorbed the tales and legends he had heard and conveyed to his readers in the voice of Mark Twain some portion of authentic sympathy for the figures who told them. In a word, he used his persona to make other people's lives vivid and colorful. By the 1890s, if not before, however, the imaginative process often worked the other way round. Mark Twain projected a portion of himself into his creations and inhabited their circumstances while at the same time scrutinizing and commenting, sometimes unsparingly, on their, and by extension his own, situation. The basis for Twain's probably uneasy identification with Tom Driscoll can be suggested, perhaps, by two anecdotes. After his bankruptcy in 1894, Clemens took measures to repair his reputation and his fortunes. He embarked on a round-the-world lecture tour to make money. He later referred to this tour as his "lecturing raid" and noted that he "lectured and robbed and raided for thirteen months" to pay off his creditors (*AMT*, 287). Tom Driscoll had raided and robbed the community of Dawson's Landing for similar reasons. Another anecdote is more telling. When, in December 1894, Clemens received word that the Paige machine had failed its latest and most important test, it hit him like a "thunder-clap" and "knocked every rag of sense out of my head." He should have seen it coming. Nonetheless, his surprised reaction to financial ruin imposed upon him an unwanted recognition—"how little we know ourselves and how easily we can deceive ourselves" (*MTB*, 2:993). The next night he went to a masked ball with his daughter Clara. He dressed in blackface as Uncle Remus. The gesture speaks, albeit ambiguously, for itself.

V

Mark Twain published two other significant works during the 1890s— *Following the Equator* (1897) and "The Man That Corrupted Hadleyburg" (1899). The first is sprawling, sometimes antic and discursive, but on the whole stately and highly focused. *Following the Equator* is a plainspoken compound of sarcasm and invective, intermittently mingled with trenchant humor and anecdote; it is satirical only for the morally hard of hearing. The second, by contrast, is a carefully circumscribed and modulated tale, but at bottom it is ambiguous, even formally incoherent, a steady satire apparently fixed upon no clearly defined satirical object. Twain's travel narrative takes him round the world and is a broad survey of social customs, political arrangements, and simple curiosities in several lands; his short story, by contrast, is firmly anchored in a single place, though Hadleyburg is so representative a village that it might be almost anywhere. On the face of it, then, these two works seem to have little in common. However, they do share one concern. Both dramatize from widely different positions the oftentimes ironic effects of training and in that sense test, expand, and ultimately reaffirm Twain's conception of human nature.

Whether the ironic consequences of social engineering or moral instruction come from without in the form of colonial expansion or from within in the form of self-imposed moral restraint, the net effect is to install in communities and individuals alike what we may call "trained incapacity." Kenneth Burke defines the phrase as "that state of affairs whereby one's very abilities can function as blindnesses. If we had conditioned chickens to interpret the sound of a bell as a food signal, and if we now rang the bell to assemble them for punishment, their training would work against them."[38] I defer any discussion of "Hadleyburg" for the moment except to say that the town's revised motto signals a belated

---

38. Burke uses the phrase in *Permanence and Change: An Anatomy of Purpose*, rev. ed. (New York: Bobbs-Merrill Co, 1965), 7, and attributes it to Thorstein Veblen. However no one, not even Burke himself when pressed, could locate the term in Veblen, and he conceded it might have been a phrase he had read in Randolph Bourne.

recognition that the prior training of its citizens, contrary to expressed intent, had incapacitated them, had made them vulnerable, even ridiculous: LEAD US NOT INTO TEMPTATION is emended to read LEAD US INTO TEMPTATION.[39]

The tenor and movement of *Following the Equator* are not so neatly encapsulated, though they are perhaps suggested sardonically by the author's prefatory remark attributed to Pudd'nhead Wilson: "To be good is noble; but to show others how to be good is nobler and no trouble." Among many other things *Following the Equator* is the record of Twain's observations on the effects of colonial encroachment upon the so-called savage way of life. The Western world means to show others how to be good without giving much thought to its own compromised moral authority; it will import to and impose upon the as yet to be civilized tribes and nations Christian gospel, capitalistic enterprise, and social progress. It promises salvation, opportunity, and enlightenment, but it delivers something else. This colonizing effort may be accomplished by means of coercion, temptation, conniving, even kidnapping, but in all of its available forms some amount of training is in order.

Following the Equator belongs in the company of Twain's other travel narratives, *The Innocents Abroad* and *A Tramp Abroad,* but because it records the circumnavigation of the globe it is more spacious and exotic. It is also, as some reviewers noted, a more mature work. Albert Bigelow Paine nicely characterizes the differences in mood between *Following the Equator* and the earlier travel books: "It was the thoughtful, contemplative observation and philosophizing of the soul-weary, world-weary pilgrim who has by no means lost interest, but only his eager, first enthusiasm" (*MTB,* 2:1054). Samuel Clemens had good reasons to be weary. By the time he began writing this book, he had lost his fortune and declared bankruptcy; he had embarked on a worldwide lecture tour to pay his creditors in full; and not long after completing the voyage, while still in England, he got word that his daughter Susy had died in Hartford of meningitis.

Part of that soul-weary interest, however, had to do with his impatience with the bland complacency of the colonizers and missionaries. He was exasperated by their utter inability to reflect upon the nature and conse-

---

39. The fact that Hadleyburg takes its motto from the Lord's Prayer makes an ironic commentary on the hypocrisy of the villagers, since, as Matthew says with contempt, there are those who pray "in the corners of the streets that they may be seen of men" (Matthew 6:5). But it may also make reference to Twain's own recent situation; certainly the petition to "forgive us our debts, as we forgive our debtors" touched a spot still tender from his recent bankruptcy.

quences of their benefactions. "There are many humorous things in the world," Twain observes, "among them the white man's notion that he is less savage than the other savages" (*FE*, 213). This frequently quoted passage is conclusion, not preamble. For such humor as it invites has already been recorded in a summary of the effectiveness of the "appliances" of civilization in exterminating native populations. The anonymous Australian squatter who, in a preemptive strike against the nearby aborigines, serves them up at Christmastime a delicious pudding laced with arsenic is not to be condemned for his inhumanity, Twain insists. The slow starvation that other civilizing gestures have accomplished is not so kind as the quick and tasty fatality dreamed up by this squatter. His sin, if sin there was, Twain sardonically remarks, has to do with his "departure from custom"; his spirit participated in the same spirit "the civilized white has always exhibited toward the savage" (*FE*, 211).[40]

There are, then, several concerns in *Following the Equator* that bear directly on our subject. Most obviously, there is the critique of the colonizing and Christianizing efforts throughout the world, a critique that was setting the stage for Mark Twain's full-scale assault on imperialism in his last decade. For, among other things, imperialist expansion is a campaign against human nature itself. Apart from the inhumane, venal, and self-righteous conduct of the colonizers, there is the near total obliviousness to the fact that the white man is, for the savage, not a savior but a circumstance, a new alien factor in the native's environment. Western civilizing efforts were cast in the co-optative mood, without regard for people, place, or sustaining traditions; in short, they display a complete disregard for the mainsprings of human nature. Put another way, under the cloak of Christian civilization, Americans and Western Europeans were attempting to reshape individual lives and whole tribes and communities in the interests of the gospel of wealth and the "good news" of the one true book. Twain does not tire of reminding his readers of the cultural myopia of Westerners: If the white man had "any wisdom he would know that his own civilization is a hell to a savage," but he doesn't (*FE*, 267). The missionary may honestly feel for the condition of the "repentant recruit" (a delicate phrase for the impressed slave), but "he would be surprised to see how differently the thing looked from the new point of view; however, it is not our custom to put ourselves in the other person's place" (*FE*, 87).

40. In a note to the quoted passage, Twain directs the reader's attention to chapter 27, which describes those civilizers with the "best intentions" whose actions nevertheless resulted in the absolute extinction of a Tasmanian tribe.

As a matter of education, however, the results were not simply to render prior training and custom inoperable, even sinful, but also to install habits that did not derive from accumulated experience in a specific environment. Without question, Twain found some native practices reprehensible, as is the case with the Indian band of murderers, the Thugee. Killing is the Thug's occupation and delight, and Twain commends the British for having eradicated the practice. Nevertheless, the Thug is not so very different from anyone else: "The joy of killing! the joy of seeing killing done—these are traits of the human race at large. We white people are merely modified Thugs; Thugs fretting under the restraints of a not very thick skin of civilization" (*FE*, 437). The sport of the Roman arena, the tortures of the Inquisition, the "delights of the bull-ring" or killing a rabbit in season are survivals of the same impulse. "Still," Twain concedes, "we have made some progress—microscopic, and in truth scarcely worth mentioning, and certainly nothing to be proud of. . . . We have reached a little altitude where we may look down on the Indian Thugs with a complacent shudder; and we may even hope for a day, many centuries hence, when our posterity will look down upon us in the same way" (*FE*, 437).

The progress of civilization is essentially insignificant and, in any event, is a very long time in coming. More to the point, Twain insinuates that the wholesale depredation of cultures may be sly commerce, but it is certainly doubtful Christianity. The habits of the savage were arrived at over many generations and fit the customs of the place—its weather, resources, and animating spirit. In the interests of gold, diamonds, timber, or other commodities, but under the banner of Progress, Westerners have undertaken to deracinate native peoples. Such deracination can be accomplished the old-fashioned way, by removing the natives from their land (as with the Tasmanians); but it can also be achieved by inculcating habits that ultimately transform one's familiar environment into alien territory. The resulting incongruities can sometimes make for bittersweet comedy. The Kanaka goes away to acquire "*civilization*" and returns transformed—once "he was unenlightened, now he has a Waterbury watch" (*FE*, 85). Among Europeans, the aborigines of Australia have the reputation for an inferior intellect, but Twain insists that that estimation must be due to a certain "race-aversion" (*FE*, 207). If the aborigine did not master agriculture, construct permanent dwellings, invent a written language, or concoct a counting system that reached above five, it was not due to incapacity. "Within certain limits," Twain concludes, "this savage's intellect is the alertest and the brightest known to history" (*FE*, 215).

For Twain, the interest of the aborigine has as much to do with the cultural homeostasis the tribe has attained as it does with the native's extraordinary physical agility, apparent indifference to pain, or mastery of the boomerang. Until the appearance of the white man, the aborigine sustained a viable population of around a hundred thousand people. Under the auspices of civilizing benefactors, the population abruptly declined by 80 percent, and Twain seems to be predicting that, like the Tasmanians, the aborigines will be altogether extinct soon enough. Even with the best of intentions, the whites continually fail to recognize that their "civilization is a hell to a savage" (*FE*, 267). The Tasmanian died from a broken heart for the loss of his homeland, but the white man reasoned otherwise: "*It is from the wrath of God, which is revealed from heaven against all ungodliness and unrighteousness of men*" (*FE*, 267). Thanks to Cecile Rhodes and other "convulsions of nature" (*FE*, 699) South African natives are robbed of their land, forced into labor, and, when too old to be useful, abandoned to starve. One does not have to be a Marxist to see that these are examples of an unhappy consciousness, though with a difference. Colonized peoples are alienated not merely from their labor but from their habitat, which is often sacred and sustaining to them.[41]

A more benign but no less insidious form of cultural reeducation occurs in the Calcutta school system. Attracted by the possibility of a government clerical post, Indian students enroll in the country's colleges and learn to despise the trades and handicrafts of their fathers. Their education supplies another example of trained incapacity, because there are a mere fraction of positions available relative to the numbers that aspire to them. By disdaining the useful trades of their ancestors they have consigned themselves at once to a certain haughty poverty and an obsequious reliance upon the favors of Englishmen. As for the evils of education itself, Twain has great fun in quoting from the Calcutta school examination: "Q. *Who was Cardinal Wolsey?*" A. "As Bishop of York but died in disentry [*sic*] in a church on his way to be blockheaded" (*FE*, 604). Q. "*What is the meaning of Ich Dien?*" A. "An honor conferred on the first or eldest sons of English Sovereigns. It is nothing more than some feathers" (*FE*, 604). Once again, Twain insists this bit of humorous anecdote does not furnish evidence of the limitations of the Indian student. To the contrary, these students had the handicap of thinking in one language and expressing themselves in

41. Twain makes his attitude particularly clear in chapter 53 when he gives a withering comment on English nobility who conduct a picnic in an Indian sepulcher. The Pudd'nhead Wilson maxim that introduces this chapter is: "True irreverence is disrespect for another man's god."

another. Not so with the Brooklyn students Twain also quotes: "Edgar A. Poe was a very curdling writer." "Ben Johnson survived Shakespeare in some respects." "Chaucer was the father of English pottery" (*FE*, 607).

Twain's obvious point is that training is everything, and education is a form of training. The fault lies with the manner of education inflicted upon the youth of Calcutta and Brooklyn. The schoolboy has learned "*things* not the meaning of them; he is fed upon the husks, not the corn" (*FE*, 603). The education of Helen Keller offers a counterexample. She recently passed the Harvard exam in Latin, German, French, history, and belles lettres "and brilliantly, too, not in a commonplace fashion. She doesn't know merely *things,* she is splendidly familiar with the *meanings* of them" (*FE*, 605). Anne Sullivan measured Helen Keller's capacities and adjusted her instruction accordingly, but in the public schools the teacher asks the student one minute to spell *cat* and the next to calculate an eclipse. The result of these bold leaps in instruction is not progress; it is instead "irrational caprice" and it lands the child in "vacancy" (*FE*, 597). Whatever else that vacancy may be, it is a radical disconnection between the individual and his or her world.

Insofar as *Following the Equator* at times is a meditation on human nature according to those outside influences Twain had already specified—training, heredity, temperament, environment, circumstance—the author is reaffirming his "gospel." But he is also testing and expanding his determinist philosophy. Some things remain a mystery to him: the Thug's anxious plea for a mother's forgiveness (*FE*, 444); the enigmatic appeal of life as a Trappist monk, demanding as it does a "sweeping suppression of human instincts" (*FE*, 648); and perhaps most mysteriously, the persistence of the suttee, wherein the widowed woman follows her husband in death. Of this last practice, Twain says that it is easy enough to "see how the custom, once started, could continue," but he cannot understand "how the first widows came to take to it" (*FE*, 456). Twain's systematic views on human nature can explain only a part of the peculiarities of human conduct, and he freely admits that one may build a theory out of the "*facts* of a custom" but that theory never quite explains the thing to one's satisfaction (*FE*, 452).

This confession testifies to Twain's ranging and unappeasable curiosity about his fellow human beings, and the general tenor of *Following the Equator,* as I have already said, serves as prologue to the author's antiimperialist writings of his last years. However, in its own way, the book also predicts Twain's imaginative fascination with inhabiting an incomprehensible, disorienting, even nightmarish world. Twain's confabulations in this vein (including "Which Was the Dream?"—begun only days after he completed *Following the Equator*) are sometimes seen as a dramatic departure from his special brand of philosophical determinism. After all, the solipsistic dream world depicted in the "Mysterious Stranger" manuscripts, for example, is fundamentally incompatible with the materialistic determinism he sets forth in *What Is Man?* and elsewhere. But Twain did not form his philosophy according to the requirements of the logician. In the context I have been describing, those dream fantasies are more a continuation of than a rupture with his prevailing view of human nature. If "savages" are deprived of familiar customs and time-honored habits and supplied, in their stead, with the knowledge of "things" but not their "meaning," they live in a world of husks but not of corn. They have landed in a "vacancy," without map or exit strategy. The sort of world that does not ratify the claims an individual may justifiably have upon it is, essentially, a world of dream. I am using the word *dream* here in its everyday meaning; it requires no Freudian seasoning. However, I am reminded of the observation of a former philosophy teacher: "The *only* difference between the waking world and the dreaming world is that in the waking world you make plans." "If physicists took this distinction to heart," he went on to say somewhat mysteriously, "our picture of reality would be quite different." Often, in his letters, notebooks, and fables, Twain, too, seems to have recognized this singular difference, as we will see in the final chapter.[42]

In any event, the sort of tack I am taking here may help to explain the otherwise odd and intrusive references to unbidden memories and perplexing dreams that occur in *Following the Equator*. More than once, Twain notes the resemblance between memory and dream, or rather he blurs the distinction between them. In chapter 2, passengers abruptly turn from the topic of dreams to discussing unusual feats of memory. One traveler reads from his notebook of the remarkable Brahmin who was a "memory expert" (*FE*, 36), and he adds that he wrote down the details because they were so improbable that he might come to believe he had dreamed them. Twain himself recalls the man who as a child spoke Kanaka until English altogether displaced that language; in a fit of delirium, though, the man reverted to an earlier life and spoke only Kanaka. In a later chapter, Twain

42. I cannot share Henry Nash Smith's conviction that Twain's interest in dreams represented a literary turn "from the outer world to the inner," for dreams and memory ultimately have their origin from without, or at least are not spontaneously generated out of nothing. See *How True Are Dreams?: The Theme of Fantasy in Mark Twain's Later Work* (Elmira, N.Y.: Elmira College Center for Mark Twain Studies, 1989), 20.

anxiously awaits his return to Hawaii—"memories of my former visit to the islands came up in my mind while we lay at anchor in front of Honolulu that night. And pictures—pictures—pictures—an enchanting procession of them" (*FE*, 57). When a cholera epidemic prevents them from disembarking, he sees his "dream of twenty-nine years go to ruin" (*FE*, 58).

The most noteworthy remark on memory as a potent ingredient in the mental economy occurs when he sees a "burly German" strike a servant: "It carried me back to my boyhood, and flashed upon me the forgotten fact that this was the *usual* way of explaining one's desires to a slave. I was able to remember that the method seemed right and natural to me in those days, I being bred to it and unaware that elsewhere there were other methods; but I was also able to remember that those unresented cuffings made me sorry for the victim and ashamed for the punisher" (*FE*, 351). This sudden memory, as Susan Gillman observes, "forges a final, important relationship between Twain's antebellum past and the imperial present."[43] Quite apart from the content of the memory, however, is the mere fact of it as a powerful element in one's social psychology:

> It is curious—the space-annihilating power of thought. For just one second, all that goes to make the *me* in me was in a Missourian village, on the other side of the globe, vividly seeing again these forgotten pictures of fifty years ago, and wholly unconscious of all things but just those; and in the next second I was back in Bombay, and that kneeling native's smitten cheek was not done tingling yet! Back to boyhood—fifty years; back to age again, another fifty; and a flight equal to the circumference of the globe—all in two seconds by the watch! (*FE*, 352)

Clemens's boyhood memory may serve as commentary on the cruelty of colonial occupation, but in this instance his memory drives out present perception, if only for a moment. This fact of mental life introduces an interesting variable into Twain's system. Man may well be an automaton, automatically functioning and wholly conditioned by outside influences. Still, some of those influences may be unconsciously stored as memories and suddenly, under given circumstance, emerge as vivid realities. If this is so, then the comprehensible antecedent conditions that may explain human conduct are supplemented, from time to time, by antecedents that cannot be anticipated, calculated, or even discerned. This enlargement of

43. "Mark Twain's Travels in the Racial Occult," in *Cambridge Companion to Mark Twain*, ed. Forrest Robinson (Cambridge: Cambridge University Press, 1995), 205.

Twain's view of human nature is one he would dramatize in a dozen different ways and in many, mostly uncompleted, manuscripts. The atom of self, the *"me,"* Hank Morgan prized is in this instance the disturbing inheritance of the boy Sam Clemens, neither outgrown nor discarded. Twain's announced revulsion at the cruelty in Bombay combines with his recollected acceptance of the practice fifty years earlier, for both are part of him. Twain may rationally condemn the cuffing of slaves, but he knows that what was trained into him once has not been, perhaps cannot be, altogether eradicated. This recognition of a latent callousness trained into him provides telling commentary on the blessings of civilization abroad in the world.

On balance, Twain's round-the-world trip was not a happy one. He recalled that the only really pleasant parts of the trip were the days at sea and his visit to India. Yet, in *Following the Equator,* these experiences are the very ones that seem to slip beyond his grasp. "When I think of Bombay now," he writes, "at this distance of time, I seem to have a kaleidoscope at my eye; and I hear the clash of the glass bits as the splendid figures change, and fall apart, and flash into new forms, figure after figure." These "remembered pictures float past me . . . always whirling by and disappearing with the swiftness of a dream leaving me with the sense that the actuality was the experience of an hour, at most, whereas it really covered days, I think" (*FE,* 358). Likewise, at sea, with "no newspapers to excite you; no telegrams to fret you or fright you—the world is far, far away; it has ceased to exist for you—seems a fading dream. . . . This sort of sea life is charged with an indestructible charm. . . . If I had my way I would sail on for ever and never go to live on the solid ground again" (*FE,* 616–17).[44]

Palpable realities can be transformed into dreamlike memories, but the process, it seems, can work the other way round as well. Twain has a dream that probably supplied him with the germ for the later tale "Three Thousand Years Among the Microbes": "I dreamed that the visible universe is the physical person of God; that the vast worlds that we see twinkling millions of miles apart in the fields of space are the blood corpuscles in His veins; and that we and the other creatures are the microbes that charge with multitudinous life the corpuscles" (*FE,* 132). More interesting than the dream itself is the commentary of "Mr. X," a missionary from In-

---

44. When he came to write "The Great Dark," a fantasy tale about a vast and indefinite voyage in a drop of water, the author's attitude changed from deep contentment to resigned acceptance.

dia: Twain's dream "is not surpassable for magnitude . . . and it seems to me that it almost accounts for a thing which is otherwise nearly unaccountable—the origin of the sacred legends of the Hindoos. Perhaps they dream them and then honestly believe them to be divine revelations of fact. It looks like that, for the legends are built on so vast a scale that it does not seem reasonable that plodding priests would happen upon such colossal fancies when awake" (FE, 132). Christian or Hindu, man is a weak creature, Mr. X continues, and requires the help of a strong God. If the feats of the Hindu god Hanuman are larger than those of Samson, why should Christianity make any inroads in India?

The upshot of my inquiry here is that, far from forsaking his conviction that man is merely a machine automatically functioning, Twain was ferreting out the possible consequences and implications of that view. In a word, I cannot agree with Sherwood Cummings that a part of Twain "loathed his own Gospel" as it was expressed in *What Is Man?* and elsewhere.[45] This statement presupposes that what Twain said he believed and what he wanted to believe were irreconcilably opposed. In point of fact, Twain boasted about his determinist gospel in letters and took some satisfaction in believing it to be scandalous, even though it might make his wife "shudder." At all events, there was an easier way for Twain to escape the disturbing significance of his gospel—he could simply change his mind.

Indeed, it is because human beings are buffeted about by external influences that they can become so lost in their own world. Habits and customs, centuries old, are rooted out of native peoples and replaced with Western, progressive ones, and the result is disorienting, even grotesque. The familiar becomes unfamiliar. Vivid memories of lived facts take on the quality of dreams. Dreams are taken for revelations. Facts become fancies, and fancies become facts. "I dreamed I was born, & grew up, & was a pilot on the Mississippi," Twain wrote Susan Crane on March 19, 1893, "& a miner & journalist in Nevada, & a pilgrim in the Quaker City, & had a wife & children & went to live in a Villa out of Florence—& this dream goes on and *on* & sometimes seems *so* real that I almost believe it *is* real. I wonder if it is? But there is no way to tell, for if one applied tests, *they* would be part of the dream, too, & so would simply aid the deceit. I wish I knew whether it is a dream or real."[46]

But that is the problem. One cannot always distinguish dream from reality. Hank Morgan suspects that he may be dreaming he is in Camelot

---

45. See *Mark Twain and Science*, 213.
46. See *The Portable Mark Twain*, ed. Tom Quirk (New York: Penguin, 2004), 573.

and is about to be burned alive, but he also knows from past experience "of the life-like intensity of dreams, that to be burned to death, even in a dream, would be very far from being a jest" (*CY*, 37). In "The $30,000 Bequest" (1904) Saladin and Electra Foster are under the mistaken impression that they will inherit $30,000; as a consequence, they acquire the "day-dreaming habit" and let everyday responsibilities go: "how soon and how easily our dream-life and our material life become so intermingled and so fused together that we can't quite tell which is which any more" (*CTSS2*, 608). The special character of the dream is that one cannot make plans that realize an intended result. What is more, though it may be true that the dream is an entirely subjective state, that fact does not foreclose on the sort of determinism Twain espoused.[47] To the contrary, everyone, man and mollusk alike, is caught up in the universal law of evolution, which operates according to no plan. "Evolution is a blind giant who rolls a snowball down a hill," Twain wrote in "The Secret History of Eddypus" (1902). "The ball is made of flakes—*circumstances*. They contribute to the mass without knowing it. They adhere without intention, and without foreseeing the result" (*Fables*, 378). "Individuals do not make events." He continues, "it is massed *circumstances* that make them. Men cannot order circumstances, men cannot foresee the form their accumulation will take nor forecast its magnitude and force" (*Fables*, 379). Insofar as one feels adrift in a world of unrealizable intentions colliding with unanticipated events, one is not so very far from living in a dream world. Whatever else "The Man That Corrupted Hadleyburg" discloses (and judging by the rich and vigorous variety of critical interpretation, it must do many things besides),[48] this powerful fable illustrates just this point—that the best-laid plans of men, if not mice, may wreak unintended havoc and despair.

47. We need not automatically assume that the world of mind and the world of matter are irreconcilably opposed. In 1904, William James published the essay "Does Consciousness Exist?" His answer was no. He argued that the mental and physical stand in relation to entities that are neither mental nor physical. This philosophical position later became known as "neutral monism"; the theory was monistic in the sense that it posited a single, ultimate reality, but it was pluralistic also, in the sense that there was a multiplicity of independent reals. Twain did not know the essay, of course, and would not have had the patience to read it if he had. My only point in identifying this middle position is to suggest that we do not have to conclude that Twain was off his rocker in holding these two realms in imaginative solution, or at least no more off his rocker than was William James.

48. James Wilson surveys a representative range of critical opinion in *A Reader's Guide to the Short Stories of Mark Twain* (Boston: G. K. Hall, 1987), 199–215. I have offered an analysis of my own in *Mark Twain: A Study of the Short Fiction*, 103–9. Here I emphasize elements in the story that seem to advance Twain's thinking on human nature and to propel him into the assorted subjects of his last decade.

"The Man That Corrupted Hadleyburg" has the feel of a plot-driven tale and in fact is permeated with wry and ironic twists of incident that wend their way to what appears a calculated conclusion. But the données of the story are implausible to say the least. For one thing, the mysterious stranger who signs his letters "Howard L. Stephenson" has apparently received an injury at the hands of one or another citizen of the village, and he means to exact his revenge. We never learn what that injury was; nor do we know how a whole town could have committed it. We do know that he wants to make the entire town suffer and contrives a masterful plan that will do just that. Without explanation, however, he soon enough settles on the "nineteen principals," presumably the best-heeled men of the town. But that doesn't hold up either, because Edward Richards, the lighted figure in the story, is a bank cashier, ground down by overwork and poverty. Stephenson knows how to hit the town where it hurts, by exposing its inveterate righteousness as altogether factitious. Nevertheless, Reverend Burgess is for some reason exempted from the stranger's wrath. Perhaps he knows that Burgess was ill-used by the town. The citizens mean to ride Burgess out of town on a rail for some unspecified offense he did not commit, but Stephenson's knowledge of this seems unlikely as well, because only Edward Richards knows that Burgess was innocent, and he did not even tell his wife. We as readers know that Richards privately warned Burgess of the town's plan, but only because he felt guilty for not publicly declaring the reverend's innocence.[49]

At the town hall meeting to disclose the virtuous villager who is entitled to the bag of gold, the gathering turns into a melodramatic travesty set to a tune from the *Mikado*. Someone asks how many claimants have delivered letters to Burgess, and he tells them "nineteen" (*CTSS2*, 422); a few minutes later, the town is cheering and jeering the "eighteen immortal representatives" (*CTSS2*, 425) of Hadleyburg virtue, apparently untroubled by the missing letter. All of these events have consequences as the story unfolds, but not one of them is believable. What is more, the mysterious stranger's test of Hadleyburg virtue is deviously designed, but there seems to be no really proper way to respond to the temptation. Edward Richards's moral superiority is mistakenly established by his apparent indifference to wealth, by the belief that he did nothing at all to pursue the bag of gold. My point is to identify not Twain's carelessness

49. It is perhaps convenient to assign some supernatural (perhaps satanic) powers to the mysterious stranger. That might explain how he knows Burgess is innocent, but it would not explain why he doesn't know that Richards is guilty.

but instead his indifference to such matters. He appears more interested in two other dimensions of his tale, and both bear upon his views of human nature and the human condition.

First, all the characters act in strict accordance with Twain's "gospel." The townsfolk insure their well-known and long-standing moral rectitude by teaching "the principles of honest dealing to . . . babies in the cradle" (*CTSS2*, 390). Training soon enough "hardens and solidifies" into established and unthinking habit. Artificial honesty becomes "second nature" in Hadleyburg (*CTSS2*, 400); even so, public opinion, more than a trained conscience, acts as the guardian of this well-advertised moral asset. Pecksniffian virtue, located in one's neighbors, rides roughshod over all the citizens but three. Jack Halliday, the "no account," is immune, but he lost his self-respect long ago. Reverend Burgess seems genuine, but he lives under the cloud of some imagined offense. And Barclay Goodson, though jaundiced, was probably a good man, but he is dead. The rest are products of habits and training and are motivated by the desire for self-approval, which, as Twain stressed in "Corn-Pone Opinions" (1901), can only be had by receiving the approval of other people. It simply does not matter that Hadleyburg is a "mean town, a hard, stingy town, and hasn't a virtue in the world" apart from the honesty it is so conceited about (*CTSS2*, 400). Every person inside the city limits requires the approval of all the others, and the begrudging respect they receive from the nearby town of Brixton fortifies the arrangement.

Second, the several plans of individuals go horribly awry due to a dizzying array of circumstances, but those circumstances are, in fact, what make the events. Twain had long ago registered his objection to the "great man" theory of history and seems to be recurring to that theme in his story. The motto "Lead Us Not into Temptation" is something of a protective tariff against moral dissolution and thereby inhibits moral and intellectual progress. Whether the town's experience with temptation leads to a "fall" (fortunate or otherwise) is a different kind of question. In any event, the story as a whole is the record of events that cut across the grain of individual purposes. After brief deliberation, Richards, like a "somnambulist" who was having a "bad dream," arrives at a "definite purpose" and goes off to publish the stranger's letter in the local paper. Almost instantly, he and the editor, Cox, repent of their good deed and rush back to the newspaper offices to stop the publication—too late, because Brixton and towns beyond have just that day changed their timetable, requiring the mail be sent twenty minutes early. That unforeseeable circumstance advertises Hadleyburg's exceptional virtue throughout the land, which in turn attracts many special correspondents and distinguished strangers to the town hall meeting, which, so it happens, supplies a chorus of scoffers to sing out their gleeful contempt: "Corruptibles far from Hadleyburg are—But the Symbols are here, you bet!" In greedy expectation, Deacon Billson, Lawyer Wilson, Gregory Yates, Nicholas Whitworth, and the rest of the nineteen secretly practice their "little impromptu speeches of thankfulness" (*CTSS2*, 412) for the moment when each will be recognized as the sole beneficiary of the stranger's largesse. Each family spends in the imagination some portion of the anticipated wealth; some even take out real loans to accomplish their dreamy aspirations.

Stephenson's plot "fails," to the degree that he believes Richards has resisted his manufactured temptation. Burgess did not read Richards's letter to the assembly, but that is because Burgess is repaying a debt he believes he owes to Richards. Stephenson tries to repair the damage he believes he has caused by contriving another plot that will get up a substantial reward for Edward Richards's good character, but Richards takes it for another trap and eventually burns the checks. For their part, after church Edward and Mary Richards nod at Burgess in appreciation; but Burgess pays no attention to the gesture because he has not seen it. In consequence, the Richardses think Burgess has snubbed them and begin to suspect all sorts of dreadful things. They conclude that Burgess's sincere note of gratitude was a sarcasm. Each of these misapprehended events pushes the couple further into a mad delirium and hastens their deaths. Perhaps the only good thing that comes of the whole sorry episode in the history of Hadleyburg is that Harkness defeats Pinkerton in the local election, but that is an unintended byproduct of events. Besides, we have no reason to think Harkness is a better man than Pinkerton. If Twain's story is a ringing indictment of untested virtue, the mayhem, disappointment, even madness the tale describes seem in excess of any moral lesson to be learned.[50] Mary Richards may conclude that everything is "ordered" by some inscrutable, superintending Providence, but Mark Twain seems to be suggesting that the whole spectacle of human life is ultimately a crapshoot. It is determined in the sense that human conduct is regulated by outside influences and training, but insofar as human beings are implicated in large natural movements that work through natural selection,

50. Susan K. Harris astutely observes that Twain "hid his deterministic tale under a moralistic one that was both accessible and palatable to a readership accustomed to sentimental short stories which consistently implied not only that moral regeneration was possible, but that it was easy." *Mark Twain's Humor: Critical Essays*, ed. David E. E. Sloane (New York: Garland Publishing, 1993), 471.

there is no particular destination or plan to which the determined lives of men and women are tending.

In May 1899, Twain confided to Howells that what he had wanted for a long time was to write a book "without reserves . . . a book which should say my say, right out of my heart, in the plainest language & without a limitation of any sort." "I believe I can make it tell what I think of Man, & how he is constructed, & what a shabby poor ridiculous thing he is, & how mistaken he is in his estimate of his character & powers & qualities & his place among the animals" (*MTHL*, 698–99). Twain was probably referring to a version of *The Mysterious Stranger* he was working on at the time. No matter. He was entering the twentieth century and the last decade of his life armed with a snarling contempt for his species, full confidence that he knew how man was "constructed," and an informed vision of the mind-boggling vastness of the stage upon which puny human dramas were enacted. Even so, the writings of Mark Twain's last years were not uniformly cynical or despairing. At times he displayed an angry sympathy with his kind; at others, he revealed political commitments that might damage his reputation, just as they might advance the cause of social justice for some portion of his fellow creatures. He could indulge in fond memory one day and concoct futuristic fantasies the next. By 1900, Twain may have had a bellyful of the "damned human race," but he still might caution humankind to be on the lookout for the untoward event or encourage them to hang tight and muddle through. Twain's diverse moods, convictions, and talents took him in several directions at once; humor remained his wayward traveling companion to the last.

Chapter Six

I

There is no reason to dispute Hamlin Hill's well-documented assertion in *Mark Twain: God's Fool* that the last decade of Clemens's life was a kind of "hell," much of it of his own making.[1] The story of the seemingly gratuitous depredations upon his security and happiness is a familiar one— the deaths of family members and friends, illness and pain, public humiliation and financial despair; likewise the adjectives (none of them pretty) to describe Twain's moods—cynical, bitter, angry, suspicious, irrational, depressed, alienated, lonely, petty and trivial, hurt and hurtful. Hill was able to find a way to chart the contours of Twain's last ten years and to organize the immense corpus of written materials he produced during that time according to certain watershed moments: the beginning of the new century until Olivia's death in 1904, his "Indian Summer"; Twain's compromised life from that period until he reached the high-water mark of public acclaim in receiving an honorary degree from Oxford in 1907, his "Götterdämmerung"; and his final three years when he tended to withdraw from the limelight and preferred to drift along in the role of "The Derelict."

1. *Mark Twain: God's Fool* (New York: Harper and Row, 1973), xvii.

The task of organization for our purposes is somewhat different, for we are concerned with the diverse written record left behind and its relation to his preoccupation with human nature. And it is diverse—fables, philosophical dialogues, soliloquies, autobiographical dictations, tales, sketches, polemical essays, speeches, fantasies, and the like. Some of them were published, some not; some of them were meant for publication at some distant future date when they would not give offense; some were published anonymously (*What Is Man?* for example); some were so formless as to refuse publication except as fragments, extracts, or specimens; many were left uncompleted at the time of his death (most notably, *The Mysterious Stranger* manuscripts). The enormous bulk of texts (thousands upon thousands of pages) owes something to the fact that Twain found solace in his work; for it lifted his spirits and was an engrossing activity he was able to love without stint.

Thanks to the negotiations of Henry H. Rogers, Mark Twain arrived at a lucrative agreement with Harper and Brothers. He could milk that cash cow any time he wanted, but, perhaps to his credit, much of what he wrote was not meant for publication. Without the regulatory checks and balances that help one chart literary production (the demands of publishers, the judgment of critics, the appetites of readers, as well as clear indications of the author's professional ambition), the pattern one may impose on the materials threatens to become arbitrary. It is clear, at any rate, that Twain's interests as they are reflected in his writings developed, more or less, as a sheaf—some stalks growing tall and sending off shoots of their own, others languishing in the shade of predominating interests, still others barely germinating at all. One might choose to chop up the whole and bale it as a single, symmetrical, and unified point of view; certainly that is a tidier way than the one I propose: namely, to follow certain individual strands of Twain's thought and show such affiliations one with the other as seems justified.

Broadly speaking, there are three kinds of writing during this period that deserve some extended attention. First, there are the polemical writings. These include but are not restricted to Twain's anti-imperialist essays; his philosophical dialogue *What Is Man?* belongs; so, perhaps, does his diatribe against Mary Baker Eddy and Christian Science or "A Dog's Tale" (1903) (which was reprinted as a pamphlet by the National Anti-Vivisection Society in London), but they don't contribute very much to our understanding of Twain's theory of human nature. The polemical writings at least participate in the same sort of argumentative mood that prompted such essays as "To the Person Sitting in Darkness" or "King

Leopold's Soliloquy." Second, there are those fantasies that draw upon Twain's readings in science and generally concern the immensity of the universe and mankind's insignificant place in the scheme of things. "Extract from Captain Stormfield's Visit to Heaven," "The Great Dark," "Three Thousand Years among the Microbes," and other odd feats of the imagination belong in this group. As opposed to contemplating life in established and familiar political and social communities, these works dramatize the vastness of time and space and depict the human creature in a kind of cosmic free fall, disoriented, perplexed, lost. Finally, there are the works preoccupied with isolation, loss, and loneliness. For our purposes, two key texts are sufficiently representative. *No. 44, The Mysterious Stranger* was written in the summer of 1904 and is notable for its emphasis on dream and for the starkness of its conclusion. "Eve's Diary" was written one year later and is remarkable for its comic tenderness and pathos. These three groups are not generic. Instead, they represent kinds of interest in the author that motivated their creation. One pervasive theme saturates most of them, however; they counsel humility at the same time that they excoriate moral cowardice. In any event, this arrangement leaves out much, and there is considerable overlap and considerable slippage here, but it does cut a sufficiently wide swath through the richly various writings to map the contours of Mark Twain's thought in his final years.

What gives a rough-and-ready unity to this grouping, of course, is the creative and comic intelligence behind the work. Ever true to his gospel, Twain assigned his ability to rebound and to indulge in his capacity for mirth-making to his temperament. After his daughter Susy's death Twain wrote Howells in February 1897 of his continuing grief:

> This mood will pass, some day—there is history for it. . . . Indeed I am a mud image, & it puzzles me to know what it is in me that writes, & that has comedy-fancies & finds pleasure in phrasing them. It is a law of our nature, of course, or it wouldn't happen; the thing in me forgets the presence of the mud image & goes its own way wholly unconscious of it & apparently of no kinship with it. (*MTHL*, 2:664)

After his daughter Jean's death on December 24, 1909, he wrote a moving essay, "The Death of Jean," and omitted this passage from the piece:

> Shall I ever be cheerful again? Yes. And soon. For I know my temperament. And I know that the temperament is *master of the man*, and that he is its fettered and

helpless slave and must in all things do as it commands. A man's temperament is born in him, and no circumstances can ever change it.

My temperament has never allowed my spirits to remain depressed long at a time. (*MTB*, 4:1552)

If Twain's temperament pushed him to write, the deep satisfaction of the work kept him interested. He once confessed to Howells that he felt an "intellectual drunk" when writing without the harassing obligation to publish the result. In addition to the tonic relief, even exhilaration, that work provided him, there was in the man a relentless curiosity as well. As William R. Macnaughton nicely observes, much of Twain's late writing is "the work of an author whose fascination with the present is made more meaningful by his knowledge and love of the past and whose concern for individuals is strongly influenced by a relatively coherent theory about men in general."[2]

"Life had always interested him," wrote Howells in *My Mark Twain*, "and in the resurgence of its interests after his sorrow had ebbed away he was again deeply interested in the world and in the human race, which though damned, abounded in subjects of curious inquiry" (*MMT*, 91). Twain himself testified to this sort of satisfaction in the voice of Satan in *Letters from the Earth*. Satan stands stupefied and perplexed by the idea of heaven that human beings have imagined for themselves. They have eliminated from eternal paradise "the one ecstasy that stands first and foremost in the heart of every individual of his race—and of ours—sexual intercourse!" (*CTSS2*, 885). After that satisfaction, Satan continues, is the thrill of exercising one's intellect; every human being "takes a keen pleasure in testing it, proving it, perfecting it. . . . Not one of them could be happy if his talent were put under an interdict" (*CTSS2*, 886). But that is precisely what humans have done, for there is not a "rag" of intellectuality in their concocted heaven. Sexual gratification has a limited shelf-life, at least for the male—"After 50 his performance is of poor quality, the intervals between are wide, and its satisfactions of no great value to either party" (*CTSS2*, 915)—but the gratification of one's intellectual curiosity has staying power. Since Clemens turned fifty in 1885, we may assume that in his last decade he sought out second-order thrills.

Twain's last years may have been hellish, but there remained available to him some avenues to temporary happiness, and one of them was to

2. *Mark Twain's Last Years As a Writer* (Columbia: University of Missouri Press, 1979), 203.

ponder the nature of his fellow human beings and to test and perfect his gospel. We may be disappointed in the diminished quality of most, but by no means all, of his literary productions during these years, but, for that, Twain does not require our pity. In matters of curiosity, he remained energetically alive, and, I suspect, from time to time he must have been as happy as a clam.

What Is Man? was begun in 1898, when Mark Twain was in Vienna and dramaturgy was much on his mind. The inquiry is cast in the form of a Socratic dialogue between the seasoned and content Old Man and the naive and idealistic Young Man, but its method is more in line with a dramatic dialogue in which two differing personalities come into collision as they contemplate the fundamental nature of humankind. One might almost say the work is a dramatic monologue, because the Young Man hardly has any meaningful say in the exchange; he essentially plays the part of a chorus in a Greek play, there to ask the right sort of question at the right time and to register his, and by imaginative extension the community's, troubled reaction to the patient outlay of the suppressed or discounted facts of life as we know it. The Young Man's idealism founders on the cheerless rocks of the Old Man's broad experience, his supposedly impeccable logic, and the demonstration of his self-assurance.

As a piece of writing and as an artifact of Twain's convictions, *What Is Man?* is unremarkable. There is nothing there that he hadn't decided upon and, often enough, dramatized to much better effect years before. Twain may have derived some pleasure from refining and "perfecting" his doctrine; the text was augmented and substantially revised over a several-year period, before it was published anonymously in a limited edition in 1906. However, he did little to "test" his system; he merely recapitulated and formalized preexisting attitudes. The familiar concepts and terms are all there—the emphatic conclusion that man is an automaton whose fundamental desires are selfish; that all ideas come from the outside and that the master impulse, or conscience, is nothing more than a "hunger for self-approval" (*WIM*, 206); that man is a "chameleon" and either through training or cowardice takes on the moral coloring of prevailing opinion. It is probably a mistake to conclude that *What Is Man?* is dreary reading simply because the thought itself is cynical and despairing. As we have already seen in works such as *A Connecticut Yankee* or *Pudd'nhead Wilson*, when Twain attempted to deepen his understanding of created characters or to explain otherwise mysterious social institutions or self-destructive behavior according to his creed, he could be startlingly original and provocative. When his gospel was an instrument of inquiry into human nature it could become an invigorating and clarifying agent. But when Twain turns his searchlight onto the system itself the whole thing appears rather stale and lifeless.

Twain thought his tract might scandalize many readers; he certainly did not think it would bore them. He was naturally disappointed with the lack of critical response it received, not so much because he believed himself to be an original philosopher or even a committed iconoclast declaring war on religion but because, as Paul Baender has shown (*WIM*, 16), he wanted to make converts. Twain boasted that if he could read the piece aloud to even the most resistant auditors, he could convert them. If this is so, then *What Is Man?* is more of a script to be performed or a sermon to be delivered than anything else; the published argument rarely created the desired effect, at any rate. This is a curious fact. If Twain thought that in his representation of the Old Man he had depicted an enviably serene and enlightened figure, he failed. Far from being aglow with his earned wisdom, the Old Man more often seems annoyingly self-satisfied. Mark Twain's sincere defense of his gospel in letters to W. D. Howells and Joseph Twichell is far more fiery and eager.

On the other hand, Twain was not equipped to play the role of evangelical nihilist, as Flannery O'Connor has Hazel Motes do in *Wise Blood:* "I preach the Church Without Christ. I'm member and preacher to that church where the blind don't see and the lame don't walk and what's dead stays that way." In her introduction to the novel, O'Connor says that *Wise Blood* is "a comic novel about a Christian *malgré lui*."[3] Some critics have been disposed to paint Mark Twain in this way and have argued that his determinism was merely an insincere dodge to alleviate a constitutional and largely Puritanical conscience. If human beings are the product of outside influences, so the argument goes, they are not responsible for the things they do and therefore ought not feel the pangs of guilt. The argument is not convincing. If I back my car over the family cat and then protest "It's not my fault!" I don't feel any better, and it's not likely to improve the disposition of the cat either. Eventually, Twain would blame the Creator for supplying human beings with a moral sense but without also giving them the wherewithal to conduct a moral life. Twain's venting his anger in a quarrel with God is not apt to erase those guilty feelings. Nevertheless, this line of argument is appealing to some because it dislodges Twain from conscious belief and authority over his stated convictions and allows the critic to replace the writer with a creative consciousness more

3. *Three by Flannery O'Connor* (New York: Signet, 1962), 60, 8.

to one's liking. It is a little late in the day for me to proclaim that Twain secretly believed what he openly denied, for throughout I have tried to hold fast to Twain's stated intentions and to ponder how they might be rendered intelligible. He did, though, augment and somewhat modify his gospel nonetheless. At any rate, Twain was too cheerful by disposition to serve, as did Hazel Motes, as martyr to his anti-Christian creed.

II

The interest (for us) in Twain's philosophy resides in the fact that (for him) his gospel had explanatory power. As we have already seen in the figure of Tom Driscoll, the author could fashion an incisive portrait of the interior life of a man bedeviled by the wholly socially constructed notion of race; or in Huck Finn record the affective drama of a boy's bout with his conscience that had little or nothing to do with innate moral impulses. The same system permitted Twain to lambaste certain customs or institutions that he had held in contempt long before he had formulated his creed—his disgust with aristocratic false privilege, for example, or with the timid acquiescence of the masses to cultural and political practices that were contrary to their own best interests. His commitment to democratic institutions and political liberty in no way required the writer to embrace the idea of individual human freedom as well, but it did argue powerfully against any form of intellectual or social protective tariff that limited the dissemination of knowledge and as a consequence encouraged pernicious superstition and mindless tradition. His doctrine also provided him with a platform from which to launch satirical attacks upon American and European imperialists, Christian missionaries, political machines, brutal tyrants, and bloodthirsty lynch mobs. At the same time, however, Twain's own intellectual curiosity urged him to test and to examine the sufficiency of his deterministic outlook. More and more he came to believe that the human race was incapable of acting according to rational self-interest and damned due to its own timid desire for self-approval. But he was committed to his democratic impulses and sought in his darkening conception of human nature some reason to hope for a better future and a social arrangement that fostered the best that was in at least a few of us.

When he contemplated political and social concerns, Twain must have recognized that the increasing complexity of global politics, colonial expansion, political corruption, and industrial and commercial greed presented problems that called for economic or legislative solution. But he remained a believer in progress so long as laissez-faire capitalism, technological innovation, and a principled and informed electorate held sway in our national life. He was more sensitive to and better acquainted than most with the fact that the new century introduced a nest of issues and difficulties along with shameful opportunities for exploitation, but he continued to frame the questions and to seek the answers in personal and moral, not economic or political, terms. However astute or insipid his opinions about corporate trusts, the Boxer Rebellion, war in the Philippines, the silver standard, Christian Science, and a host of other subjects upon which he had a ready opinion, our interest here is how he sized up the problems and sought answers that were consistent with his still evolving theory of human nature. From our vantage point in the twenty-first century, Twain's social and political attitudes may appear quaint, but his moral indignation at the failures he discerned in himself and his kind remains fresh and instructive to us even now. Perhaps, as a matter of temperament, Twain was inclined to pit an indignant conscience against vast forces beyond the reckoning of even the most informed and intelligent citizen. He was bound for disappointment, and as Louis J. Budd has remarked, there were times when "Twain was finally betrayed into despair by some of his richest habits of mind."[4]

In 1902, Twain wrote to one of his "angelfish" and expressed his agreement with her assessment of him: "Yes, you are right—I am a moralist in disguise; it gets me into heaps of trouble when I go thrashing around in political questions" (*Letters*, 2:719). "To the Person Sitting in Darkness" (1901) is the work of an unreconstructed moralist, and it sets the tone for most of Twain's polemical writings. A compound of sarcasm, vitriol, and outrage, the essay pretends to offer advice about how the Blessings-of-Civilization Trust can better disguise from the affected heathen its treachery and hypocrisy. The strategy of the satire is to expose America's double-dealing and thereby humiliate the populace into adopting a more honorable course, such as the one Twain supposed we had pursued in Cuba, at least at the beginning. The adventure in the Philippines is a disgrace, and "we have debauched America's honor and blackened her face before the world" (*CTSS2*, 471). "To the Person Sitting in Darkness" is too pointed and focused to lead readers to think of its author as "thrashing around" in political questions; and it served well enough as a piece of propaganda for the Anti-Imperialist League to distribute it as a pamphlet in an edition of over 125,000 copies. On the other

---

4. *Mark Twain: Social Philosopher* (Columbia: University of Missouri Press, 2001), 205.

hand, Twain's attack is grounded in two assumptions: that moral character should dictate national policy; and that humiliation strikes at the very heart of man's desire to think well of himself.

Mark Twain was ready and willing to play the part of the nation's conscience, but his tactics to excite the moral feelings of fellow citizens seem strangely antique in a world governed by the realpolitik maneuvering of, say, a Bismarck, the shaping of public opinion by William Randolph Hearst, or the manipulation of the marketplace by Jay Gould or J. P. Morgan. In a speech to the Acorn Club in 1901, Twain saw fit to import the language of Edmund Burke spoken against the perfidious "moral personality" of William Hastings and the English East India Company and adapt it to the conniving of Richard Croker and Tammany Hall. As a matter of course, he was also importing an eighteenth-century worldview as equal to the difficulties of the twentieth. By contrast, in "The United States of Lyncherdom" (1923), also written in 1901 but not published during the author's lifetime, he would apply his conclusions about individuals to whole communities—both are by nature imitators. Twain's satire here is not only more aggressive than in the speech, its argument seems to draw upon contemporary sociological studies of group psychology.

The recent increase in lynching is due to "the inborn instinct to imitate—that and man's commonest weakness, his aversion to being unpleasantly conspicuous, pointed at, shunned, as being on the unpopular side. Its other name is Moral Cowardice" (CTSS2, 481). There is but one morally brave man born in every 10,000; the remaining 9,999 are plagued by the Moral Sense, which "teaches us what is right, and how to avoid it—when unpopular" (CTSS2, 482). The solution to the lynching problem, Twain sardonically observes, is to advertise for a few brave sheriffs to stand up to mob violence; the human tendency to imitate will soon enough produce many more like them. He concludes his essay with a statement that is more reminiscent of the idealism of the Young Man in *What Is Man?* than it is of the worldly-wise philosopher: in the 75 million people of the United States there must be other brave men to set the proper moral example, "and it is the law of our make that each example shall wake up drowsing chevaliers of the same great knighthood and bring them to the front" (CTSS2, 486).

One book in particular may have had some influence on Twain's thinking on this score, and even if it did not, it sheds some light on the sort of thought he was engaging in in his last decade—Gabriel Tarde's *Les lois de l'imitation* (1890; English translation *The Laws of Imitation*, 1903). In this sense, the argument of Twain's anti-lynching essay, unlike the somewhat anachronistic "Edmund Burke on Croker and Tammany," is fashionably up-to-date.

Gabriel Tarde's *Laws of Imitation* is scientific in the sense that it tries to account for social facts according to certain natural laws. Instead of concentrating on statistical analyses of communal behavior, Tarde placed the emphasis on interpersonal relations. Each individual is a distinctive entity, yet it is a fact that human communities do somehow manage to harmonize their wants and interests. That process belonged to what was then known as "imitation theory," and Tarde was in most particulars its founder. Socially, writes Tarde, "everything is either invention or imitation." From molecules to the movements of armies, it is obvious that repetition is fundamental, and repetition is both the messenger for change and the cause for resemblance. If one drops a stone in a pond (Tarde's example) the vibrations radiate outward in mathematically measurable ways from the center; brain cells replicate the activities of neighboring cells in much the same way. Heredity, training, and habit are merely the agents of different kinds of repetition. In the social realm, imitation is the agent of change, and society is defined "as a group of beings who are apt to imitate one another, or who, without actual imitation, are alike in their possession of common traits which are ancient copies of the same model."[5]

The process is comprehensive. "All resemblances of *social origin* in society are the direct or indirect fruit of the various forms of imitation,—custom-imitation or fashion-imitation, sympathy-imitation or obedience-imitation, precept-imitation or education-imitation; naïve imitation, deliberate imitation, etc." Social cohesion is established by means of imitation; innovation, on the other hand, whether it be a political idea, a scientific discovery, a technological improvement, or a work of art, seems to benefit from a "supersocial" attitude in which the individual invents rather than copies, though each innovation is itself the beneficiary of previous ones. Sometimes the process of imitation is deliberate, as in learning to play a musical instrument. More often, the process is unconscious—full of resentment, the conquered nevertheless takes on the habits of the conqueror; all unknowingly, the lord acquires the accents of the serf. The movement may be conservative; aristocracies tend to feed and thrive on the "imitation of custom." Or it may be liberal; democratic societies are given to the "imitation of fashion." In either case, in the beginning of every society some display of authority must have been exercised by certain

5. *The Laws of Imitation* (New York: Henry Holt and Co., 1903), 3, 68.

strong individuals, but they did not rule exclusively through terror or deception. Instead, they ruled "through *prestige*. The example of the magnetizer [hypnotizer] alone can make us realize the profound meaning of this word. . . . He has prestige—that tells the story. . . . We have prestige in the eyes of anyone in so far as we answer his need of affirming or of willing some given thing. Nor is it necessary for the magnetizer to speak in order to be believed and obeyed. He need only act; an almost imperceptible gesture is sufficient."[6] (Certainly, this is consistent with Mark Twain's insistence upon the individual's desire for self-approval; even a nod from a person of prestige may validate our desire for self-worth and belonging.)

According to discoverable laws of imitation, social change can be traced and even measured statistically.[7] Once started, imitations spread in a geometrical progression, and the process is accelerated and broadened with improved means of communication.[8] The effects of one innovation may be checked or modified by another, and the appropriation of innovations may be "accumulated" or "substituted." In either case, because as a rule imitation travels downward from social superior to social inferior due to the hypnotizing effects of prestige, some degree of evolutionary progress is inevitable.[9] Tarde was at all events sanguine about democratic societies and noted that the development of virtually instantaneous means of communication in the United States (telephones, telegraph, and newspapers) hastened a process whereby the concept of Union takes precedence over the states. Likewise, in democratic societies the force of public opinion and majority rule acquires the allure of prestige, but, Tarde cautions, one should not forget that nine hundred ninety-nine votes out of a thousand are but "echoes" of the first. (One recalls Twain's exasperation in "Corn-Pone Opinions" with voters who sheepishly vote their party without considered regard for the political questions involved, and Twain sardonically notes that some regard Public Opinion as the Voice of God.)

Perhaps the most interesting remark in *Laws of Imitation*, at least as it

6. Ibid., 14, 78.

7. Tarde was building on the work of Quetelet and his followers, but he argued that the "plateaux" of statistical study disclose "uniform reproduction" and are not so important as the "ascending" lines that indicate the spread of some kind of imitation (ibid., 114).

8. Ibid., 115.

9. In a 1900 review-essay, the American sociologist Lester Ward gave a comprehensive summary of Tarde's philosophy and suggested that it was sufficiently Darwinian that the word *imitation* could be replaced with the word *adaptation* without any damage to the argument ("Social Laws: An Outline of Sociology," *Science*, February 16, 1900, pp. 260–63).

bears on Twain's thinking about human nature, is this one: "*Society is imitation and imitation is a kind of somnambulism.*" Every act of perception to some degree is an act of memory and as such implies a kind of habit. This, according to Tarde, is a psychological fact. If what is remembered has its origin in socialized life, however (in reading or conversation or in recalling similar acts by others), it is also a social fact. And the social, Tarde insists, "like the hypnotic state, is only a form of dream, a dream of command and a dream of action. Both the somnambulist and the social man are possessed by the illusion that their ideas, all of which have been suggested to them, are spontaneous."[10] Social man is largely in a hypnotic trance, and whether he stand in thrall before fashion or custom, prestige exerts its persuasive fascination, and imitation is the result. We do not need to summarize any more of this elaborately argued book to begin to see its relevance. Tarde's influence upon Twain's thinking, whether much or little or none at all, is not to the purpose here. Instead, the Frenchman's system offers a lens through which to view a shifting emphasis, at least occasionally, in Twain's outlook and perhaps to explain it. Most immediately, far-fetched as it may seem, Twain's determinism, framed by these sorts of considerations, does not necessarily stand in firm opposition to his interest in dreams as is often assumed. With or without an acquaintance with Gabriel Tarde, anyone who insisted, as did Twain, that man is a machine automatically functioning would soon enough conclude that life itself is a form of sleepwalking. As Tarde put it, social life itself is a kind of dream. That is a subject we will return to later on, but there are other, more obvious correspondences between Tarde's theories of imitation and Twain's thoughts on human nature.

First, neither the word nor the concept of imitation enters into the philosophical dialogue *What Is Man?* in any important way, but it does elsewhere. In "The United States of Lyncherdom," for example, Twain writes: "The child should also know that by a law of our make, communities, as well as individuals, are imitators; and that a much-talked-of lynching will infallibly produce other lynchings here and there and yonder."[11] The increase in lynchings in the United States "comes of the inborn human in-

10. *Laws of Imitation*, 87, 77.

11. Albert Bigelow Paine tampered with Twain's essay in ways that make it seem as though the imitative crime he is worried about is the one committed by a Negro in Missouri, when in fact he is concerned with the crime of lynching. See Terry Oggel's "Speaking Out About Race: 'The United States of Lyncherdom' Clemens Really Wrote," in *Prospects: An Annual of American Cultural Studies 25*, ed. Jack Salzman (New York and Cambridge: Cambridge University Press, 2000), 115–58.

stinct to imitate—that and man's commonest weakness, his aversion to being unpleasantly conspicuous" (*CTSS2*, 481). Tarde himself had written in *La criminalité comparée* (1890) and *La philosophie pénale* (1890) on the ways crime proliferates and challenged Cesare Lombroso's idea of the criminal as an evolutionary throwback. But in *Laws of Imitation* he does not confine himself to the criminal mind. On the other hand, neither does Twain. For the satirist instances the human instinct to imitate as a potential cure to the criminal problem of lynching; if one or two good sheriffs subdue the mob, he proposes, many other like-minded sheriffs will rise up in imitation of them. Twain describes the same phenomenon in jocular terms in "Corn-Pone Opinions." The flaring hoop skirt appears and everyone laughs; six months later is it admired. "Why? Was the resentment reasoned out? Was the acceptance reasoned out? No. The instinct that moves to conformity did the work. It is our nature to conform." By and by everyone yields to that "vague something recognized as authority" (*CTSS2*, 508).

It is the herd instinct that encourages people to commit what Twain called the "lie of silent assertion." The common desire for self-approval permits whole nations to blink irrational or unacceptable practices and thereby quietly acquiesce in the persecution of Dreyfus, Chamberlain's manufactured war in South Africa, or the institution of chattel slavery in the United States. Hank Morgan discovered that the realization of his republic would have to wait for a mighty long time, for old habits and superstitions die hard. And Twain himself lamented that civilization makes but small advances in a hundred years. However, Twain was beginning to believe that human beings were far more tractable than he once suspected. In "As Regards Patriotism" (1901–1902), an essay he decided not to publish, Twain was contemptuous of the "newspaper-and-politician-manufactured" patriotism he saw abroad in the land (*Weapons*, 117). This national feeling has been trained into the people and is simply Moral Cowardice wrapped in the flag. "There is nothing training cannot do," he claimed. "Nothing is above its reach or below it. It can turn bad morals to good, good morals to bad; it can destroy principles, it can re-create them; it can debase angels to men and lift men to angelship. And it can do any one of these miracles in a year—even in six months" (*Weapons*, 118).

Surely Twain is using the word *training* a bit more loosely than he had in the past. He does not seem to mean patient apprenticeship or rote instruction or even whatever they were doing in Hank Morgan's man factories. At any rate, the remark is at once hopeful and despairing. In *Following the Equator*, Twain commented on the "microscopic" moral advance civilization had made over several centuries. In this, he was following the Spencerian argument.[12] Only a few years later, however, Twain seemed to believe human conduct and human habits might be remade relatively quickly. Instead of the steady, ineluctable law of progress, human conduct can be made and remade in a few months. That is not necessarily good news; the sources of outside influences that shape an individual and construct his attitudes are often located in a "windy and incoherent six-dollar sub-editor of his village newspaper" (*Weapons*, 117), and the vicissitudes of public opinion are tyrannical in their own way. This stands in stark contrast to his attitude in *Life on the Mississippi*, where he praised the northern river towns for their independence of mind, due in part to the number of newspapers they could claim. By 1900, Twain ought to have felt personally the full force of manipulating public opinion and the leverage that prestige can confer. Among many other helpful gestures, Henry Huttleston Rogers had made a concentrated effort to improve Samuel Clemens's financial situation and to restore "Mark Twain's" reputation. Rogers used the resources of Standard Oil (including corporate lawyers and publicity agents) to publicize and to a degree manufacture Twain's reinvigorated good character. The ploy worked, and Mark Twain probably enjoyed greater popularity and influence after than he had before his bankruptcy.[13] Twain used his acquired moral authority to address the nation in unmistakably serious terms.

He could explain the despot and the villain easily enough according to the familiar tenets of his gospel of human nature. "The Czar's Soliloquy" (1905) and "King Leopold's Soliloquy" (1905) are cases in point. For Czar Nicholas II, standing naked before his mirror, it is obvious that clothes and a title constitute his only prestige, and in the wake of his more recent "deeds of violence" that authority is fast fading. King Leopold II is a more interesting study in tyranny and evil. He is like any other man; he desires self-approval. But he too knows, from the press clippings he perversely keeps by him and reads aloud that, due to meddling missionaries, senti-

12. In a letter in 1890, Spencer, having reached his seventieth year, lamented: "Sanguine of human progress as I used to be in earlier days, I am now more and more persuaded that it cannot take place faster than human nature is itself modified; and the modification is a slow process, to be reached only through many, many generations" (*Herbert Spencer on Social Evolution*, ed. J. D. Y. Peel [Chicago: University of Chicago Press, 1972], 258). At least in this particular, Clemens, even as he approached his own seventieth birthday, found in this conception of human nature as an imitating organism some slight reason to hope for speedier progress.

13. See Greg Zacharias, "Henry Rogers, Public Relations, and the Recovery of Mark Twain's Character," *Mark Twain Journal* 31, no. 1 (1993): 2–17.

mental journalists, and the damnable "kodak" that documents the cruel amputations of Congolese slave-workers, his bloody reign is jeopardized. Leopold is a "monster" whose equal cannot be found in human history. Nevertheless, as Twain depicts him, Leopold's evil nature is as "banal" as Hannah Arendt found Adolph Eichmann's to be. Leopold disdains the masses but is superstitiously obsequious to God, whose favor he doubts to the extent that he nervously keeps kissing his crucifix. The masses may indeed rise up against these men. Nicholas perhaps overplayed his hand in St. Petersburg with the bloody massacre of peaceful petitioners for reform, and Leopold's efforts to buy up and suppress news of his latest infamy may not continue to be successful. On the other hand, the haughtiness of tyrants and the timid servility of the populace are the products of training generations old, and habits of custom are not easily overcome. Leopold, at least, banks on the "ancient and inherited instinct" that shames ordinary men and women to see a king degraded; that is his "protection" (*CTSS2*, 685).

Czars and kings are bred to cruelty and contempt, the products of circumstance and training, but Twain had more difficulty explaining the selfless nature. As we have already noted in the previous chapter, he published the essay "Saint Joan of Arc" in 1904 and puzzled over how such a girl, without the benefit of training, experience, or privilege, could rise to lead her people. Joan is a "Riddle" that cannot be solved. Emilio Aguinaldo is another. This poor and largely uneducated young man triumphantly led the Philippine revolution against Spain but was subsequently betrayed by an imperialist United States that promised freedom but desired conquest. The only way to fathom the magnitude of the young man's achievement, Twain wrote in an unpublished review of Edwin Wildman's biography *Aguinaldo* (1901), is to think of him as a "negro in a Gulf State, where his race is despised, detested, and kept down with a master-hand" (*Weapons,* 89). Yet the fact remains that he rose in the world by the consent of those who would despise him: "Joan of Arc and Aguinaldo were peasant-born and poor; uneducated, and obscure; without friends, and without influence, in the beginning. They were sincere, honorable, just; both wrought for the same great ideal, both earned the trust of their peoples, both had it to the full—even to worship—and kept it to the end. For the cause, the one suffered death, the other a harder fate—life, with captivity" (*Weapons,* 100).

Twain was typically insistent that an individual genius can be "explained" by its social environment and antecedent conditions, but in Joan and Aguinaldo he found perplexing exceptions. A Napoleon, an Edison, a Raphael, a Wagner, or a Shakespeare[14] is the product of training, encouragement, study, and example; they were all fostered by the "atmosphere in which the talent was cradled" (*CTSS2*, 591). Perhaps without knowing it, Twain was drifting toward a reconsideration of what was once known as the "great man theory of history." If so, his philosophy of human nature and human society might require some revision, and his thinking may have been helped along by his reading in William James. He might have read James's "Great Men and Their Environment" when it appeared in the *Atlantic Monthly* in October 1880, or he might have come across it in *The Will to Believe and Other Essays in Popular Philosophy* (1897).[15] In any case, he would have found in James a cogent challenge to social determinism of character. Once again, I am not positing an influence. The relations between Mark Twain and William James have been thoughtfully traced by Jason Gary Horn, and he focuses on what he calls Twain's "religious psychology of the divided self."[16] My interest is primarily in Twain's social psychology, and James's essay is particularly useful in defining a difficulty Twain might have faced in refining his gospel.

James begins with the question, "What are the causes that make communities change from generation to generation?" These changes, simply put, are

> due to the accumulated influences of individuals, of their examples, their initiatives, and their decisions. The Spencerian school replies, The changes are irrespective of persons, and independent of individual control. They are due to the environment, to the circumstances, the physical geography, the ancestral conditions, the increasing experience of outer relations; to everything, in fact, except the Grants and the Bismarcks, the Joneses and the Smiths.[17]

By asserting that social change comes about through individual initiatives, James nevertheless claims to be well within the realm of determin-

14. In *Is Shakespeare Dead?* Twain decides that Shakespeare could not have written his plays because his own training, particularly in law, was insufficient to account for the dramatized familiarity with practices outside his experience. His treatment of the subject is so playful, however, that one may conclude along with some reviewers that *Is Shakespeare Dead?* is something of a hoax.

15. We know, at any rate, that Twain took an interest in James. He had acquired *Principles of Psychology* (1890) around 1892 and *The Varieties of Religious Experience* (1902) in 1903.

16. *Mark Twain and William James: Crafting a Free Self* (Columbia: University of Missouri Press, 1996), 2.

17. *The Will to Believe and Other Essays in Popular Philosophy* and *Human Immortality* (New York: Dover Publications, 1956), 218.

ism but not to have given himself over to "fatalism." He also claims to be closer to Darwinian principles of natural selection and evolutionary process than are the Spencerians. Any peculiarities in animals or humans that distinguish them from their kind may be seen as "variations"; these are adaptive changes produced by molecular accidents about which we know next to nothing, and the function of the environment is to *"preserve or destroy"* these variations but not to cause them. James continues, "The relation of the visible environment to the great man is in the main exactly what it is to the 'variation' in the Darwinian philosophy. It chiefly adopts or rejects, preserves or destroys, in short *selects* him."[18] When the environment accepts the great man, the environment itself changes, but social evolution is the result of the interplay between two factors—the individual "bearing all the power of initiative and origination in his hands"; and the social environment wielding the "power of adopting or rejecting both him and his gifts." James understood that "great men" (by which he means exceptional persons who may or may not be recognized or exalted) require their occasions. Many rare individuals, Darwin included, were they born in another epoch or another place "might have died 'with their music in them,' known only to their friends as persons of strong and original character and judgment."[19] Twain reckoned likewise: Edison's surroundings and atmosphere "have the largest share in discovering him to himself and to the world; and we should expect him to live and die undiscovered in a land where an inventor could find no comradeship, no sympathy, no ambition-rousing atmosphere of recognition and applause—Dahomey, for instance" (*CTSS2*, 592).

James went further in his analysis, expressing his disdain for the "science of history" and singling out Taine and Buckle as the perpetrators of this folly. Similarly, in the essay "The Importance of Individuals," reprinted in *The Will to Believe* as the "natural supplement" to his essay on great men, James declared his opposition to the sociologist's "average man" arrived at statistically. As we have seen, Twain had entertained and been responsive to the ideas advanced by the scientific historian and the social statistician, in part, probably, because the utilitarian position seemed to be a fundamentally democratic one, committed to progress and the general welfare. But be that as it may, William James, too, occupies an essentially democratic point of view. He thought that by "picking out from history our heroes, and communing with their kindred spirits,—in imagining as

18. Ibid., 223, 226.
19. Ibid., 232, 242.

strongly as possible what differences their individualities brought about in this world, while its surface was still plastic in their hands, and what whilom feasibilities they made impossible,—each one of us may best fortify and inspire what creative energy may lie in his own soul." These are Emersonian sentiments. However, William James knew as well as Mark Twain that even if you write a better book, preach a better sermon, or build a better mousetrap, the world may or may not beat a path to your door. Innovators often enough have their influence through sometimes unacknowledged imitation. In fact, James glossed the passage quoted above with this note: "M. G. Tarde's book (itself a work of genius), Les Lois de l'Imitation, Études Sociologique, . . . is the best possible commentary on this [James's] text,—'invention' on the one hand, and 'imitation' on the other, being for this author the two sole factors of social change."[20]

We must conclude that, on balance, Twain clung to the chief tenets of his gospel, but he had always had a sympathy and respect for the common man and woman whose quiet decencies, native intelligence, and cheerful endurance go unrecognized and unrewarded. In a sketch probably written in 1894, he claimed to appreciate the curious intelligence of a man he met in a Cincinnati boardinghouse in the 1850s, a Scotchman named Macfarlane; and he was struck by the folk wisdom of a slave named Jerry he had known as a child and worked it up into the essay "Corn-Pone Opinions." However, both men may have been inventions. Saint Joan and Aguinaldo were real enough, but they were betrayed and ended badly. Hank Morgan was a great innovator, though most of his inventions were merely imports from the future, but he was as anxious about preserving some precious "me" as about his reputation as the "Boss." Sometimes public opinion errs in the other direction. In 1891, Twain published a story called "Luck," presumably based on a real man Joseph Twichell had told him about. It was the story of a man he named Scoresby, a blunderer and an ass whose several stupidities were taken by the public for heroic achievements, and he rose in the world as a consequence. Often enough, those of genuine merit were recognized for their qualities. The recuperation of Twain's own public reputation was a case in point, though in "The Turning Point of My Life" (1910) he modestly attributed his literary fortunes to a measles epidemic in Hannibal when he was a child. Nevertheless, Twain duly admired Ulysses S. Grant, Henry H. Rogers, Thomas Edison, and others and pretty much accepted the public estimation of them. But if Twain was looking for some place where

20. Ibid., 261.

every individual of virtue and talent were recognized and rewarded, he would have to go searching beyond the world as we know it. That is exactly what he did in writing "Extract of Captain Stormfield's Visit to Heaven," published in two installments in *Harper's Monthly* (1907–1908).

This story began forming in his mind some forty years before it was eventually published. In 1868, Captain Ned Wakeman told Twain about a dream he had had about a visit to heaven. Twain made notes at the time and worked on the story intermittently thereafter. "Extract from Captain Stormfield's Visit to Heaven" does many things: it ridicules human notions about what heaven is and is all about; it comically exhibits the unfathomable vastness of the universe, in which people, nations, and the planet itself are triflingly insignificant; and it celebrates those individuals who at long last are recognized for their gifts. Heaven is no democracy; God reigns with untroubled and indifferent authority. But "When the Deity builds a heaven, it is built right and on a liberal plan" (*CTSS2*, 848). There are Eskimos there, and Tartars, Negroes, and Chinamen, "people from everywhere." Each person brings along established traditions, customs, and languages, and every individual is a collection of habits and desires that will find satisfaction in heaven. This much is built according to the familiar utilitarian plan, but "heavenly justice" has less to do with seeking public approval than it does with rewarding intrinsic merits that never got their opportunities and went unrealized in life. Good people, says the character Sandy, suffered unjustly in life and "warn't rewarded according to their deserts, on earth, but here they get their rightful rank" (*CTSS2*, 852). Thus it is that Caesar and Napoleon must walk behind a horse doctor from Afghanistan, a knife grinder from ancient Egypt, and a bricklayer from Boston. Not one of them ever saw combat, but they had military greatness in them. Edward Billings, a tailor from Tennessee, wrote poetry "Homer and Shakespeare couldn't begin to come up to; but nobody would print it, nobody read it but his neighbors, an ignorant lot, and they laughed at it" (*CTSS2*, 852). In heaven, though, "Shakespeare walked backward before that tailor from Tennessee, and scattered flowers for him to walk on, and Homer stood behind his chair and waited on him at the banquet" (*CTSS2*, 855).

None of this is exculpatory of the Creator, however. After all, he could have provided the opportunity for the individual to exercise his or her greatness; he could have given that knife grinder from Egypt a war to cut his teeth on, for example. Nor was Twain violating his own principles of determinism. In a portion of the manuscript he chose not to publish in *Harper's*, Twain made it clear that at the moment of creation, every indi-

vidual was a mixture of varying amounts of twenty-eight "Moral Qualities." The person with a "dipperful of Honesty and a spoonful of Dis-
honesty" or the one made up of a "dipperful of Moral Courage and a
spoonful of Moral Cowardice" produced the "splendid man, ready to
stand up for an unpopular cause and stake his life on it" (*BMT*, 187–88).
This procedure introduced "variety" into the human race, but it also
turned out to be "the worst mixed-up mess of good and bad dispositions
and half-good and half-bad ones a body could imagine . . . a tagrag-and-
bobtail Mob of nondescripts, and not worth propagating; but what could
the Authorities *do*? Not a thing. It was too late" (*BMT,* 188). But we have
already drifted away from the polemical and into the fantastical, and that
is the subject for the next section.

III

Mark Twain and his creations are always getting lost. They lose their
identities; they lose their fortunes; they lose their minds. They get lost in
caves, in the fog, in snowstorms, even in the darkened room of a German
inn. They get lost on the river and on the ocean; they get lost in time and
in space. They get lost on rafts, on mules, on foot, on icebergs set adrift in
the sea; they get lost beneath the surface of the earth and above it in a hot-
air balloon. There is nothing very original in this. Thoreau observed that
if you turn around once you are lost, which ironically is a step in the right
direction. Ishmael, in a drowse at the tiller, turns his back on the prow and
compass and is lost metaphysically. The experience prompts him to ad-
vise: "Look not too long in the face of the fire, O man! Never dream with
thy hand on the helm! Turn not thy back to the compass."[21] But Twain
seems to get lost not so much in moral or spiritual terms as just plain lost.
And a compass, or a map, does not seem to do much good.

In *Tom Sawyer Abroad,* Tom insists that the purpose of a map "ain't to
deceive you, it's to keep you from deceiving yourself." Huck and Jim remain unconvinced, and so should we. Given Twain's preposterous "Map
of Paris" or Colonel Sellers's improvised map of the Pacific Railroad or
the less than reliable maps in "The Private History of a Campaign That
Failed," maps appear rather to be invitations to self-deception than otherwise. Besides, Twain evidently liked the prospect of getting lost because

21. Melville, *Moby-Dick; or, The Whale,* ed. Harrison Hayford et al. (Evanston and
Chicago: Northwestern University Press and the Newberry Library, 1988), 424.

it afforded him ample comic and dramatic opportunities—as for example in the high resolutions and teary forgiveness of the miners lost in a snow-storm in *Roughing It,* who wake up to find themselves fifteen yards from a comfortable inn but annoyingly saddled with their good intentions. In a rather different way, as we have already observed, Twain found himself lost when memory drove out present perception. This happened in 1896 in Bombay when he witnessed the German strike a servant and vivid memories of his boyhood rushed in upon him. It also happened in 1882 when he returned as an adult to his hometown, Hannibal, Missouri, and recalled "a time when the happenings of life were not the natural and log-ical results of great general laws, but of special orders and were freighted with very precise and distinct purposes—partly punitive in intent, part-ly admonitory; and usually local in application" (*LOM,* 375). But those great "general laws" (particularly the laws of astronomy and geology) were disorienting in their own way, and one might say that a whole gen-eration, afflicted by the findings of nineteenth-century science, was lost in the cosmos. At any rate, in his last decade Twain spent a good deal of imaginative energy domesticating imponderables and humanizing the incomprehensible.

In April 1896, Twain recorded in his notebook, "All world distances have shrunk to nothing. . . . The mysterious and the fabulous can get no fine effects without the help of remoteness; and there are no remoteness-es any more" (*WWD,* 87). Only a few years later, Twain understood that remoteness was near at hand and that he could get lost in his easy chair, assisted only by a basic sort of arithmetic and a couple of mind-boggling facts. Sometime in 1909, for example, he sat down to compute in miles the actual length of a light-year. Albert Bigelow Paine recalls coming in one morning to find Twain sitting before several sheets of paper with "Inter-minable rows of ciphers" on them and his face aglow with self-satisfaction. According to Paine, the "unthinkable distances of space" (and one might add the great reaches of what we now call "deep time" as well) threw Twain into a sort of "ecstasy" (*MTB,* 4:1509–10). He did not, at any rate, appear to share in the modern dread that the vastness of space is terrify-ing and that one cowers, rather insignificantly, on the abyss of the un-fathomable. Instead, he delighted in trying to make the unthinkable vivid, even palpable. Insofar as human nature is concerned, to know who we are depends in part on knowing where we are.

Twain indulged himself in the sort of imagining I am describing in the sardonic little essay "Was the World Made for Man?" (1903). His an-nounced answer to the question he posed there was yes, but his comic explanations imply an emphatic no. It takes time for God to prepare the world for man, he argues, for he has to do some experimentation meantime. The Creator must first prepare the world for the oyster, because man will want to eat oysters when he arrives upon the scene. And it will take nineteen million years to get things set up for that tasty morsel:

> You must make a vast variety of invertebrates, to start with—belemnites, trilobites, jebusites, amalekites, and that sort of fry, and put them to soak in a primary sea, and wait and see what will happen. Some will be a disappointment . . . but all is not lost, for the amalekites will fetch the home-stake; they will develop gradually into encrinites, and stalactites, and blatherskites . . . and at last the first grand stage in the preparation of the world for man stands completed, the Oyster is done. (*CTSS2*, 573)

However, the oyster, vain little bivalve that he is, is apt to mistake that the long background to his debut signifies that the world was made for the oyster. And so it goes through the ages—the pterodactyl, thirty million years in the making, likewise thought the world was made for him, as did all the other saurians. But look about you, and you will see that the only saurian to survive in our time is the lonely Arkansawrian. Twain concludes the essay with a figure that makes the hundred-million-year preparation of the world for man both comprehensible and absurd: "If the Eiffel tower were now representing the world's age, the skin of the paint on the pinnacle-knob at its summit would represent man's share of that age; and anybody would perceive that that skin was what the tower was built for. I reckon they would, I dunno" (*CTSS2*, 576).

Twain was as fascinated with space as he was with time. In "Extract from Captain Stormfield's Visit to Heaven," he played with the same sort of comparisons that amused him in idle hours. When the story opens, Captain Eli Stormfield has been sailing his vessel through space for some thirty years and at a considerable clip. We are not told how fast he is going, but we know he likes to race comets traveling two hundred thousand miles a minute. There is really no contest, however: "it was as if the comet was a gravel train and I was a telegraph despatch." But then he comes across a real comet so big that when his ship approaches he feels like a "gnat closing up on the continent of America." This comet, it so happens, is tearing through space in order to deposit its cargo of lost souls in hell. When Stormfield thumbs his nose at the captain, he realizes he has waked up a pretty ugly customer. The captain of the comet gives the command to jettison his entire cargo—"Eighteen hundred thousand billion quintillions of kazarks." A "kazark," we learn, is exactly the *"bulk of a hundred and sixty nine worlds like ours!"* (*CTSS2*, 831)—and he leaves Stormfield in his dust.

Twain goes on in this vein. Stormfield's ship arrives at one of the many thousand gates of heaven, though he rather suspected he was bound for the other place. The gate he arrives at is the wrong one, however, and he has to identify his point of origin: "Why the world of course." "*The* world," replies the clerk. "H'm! there's billions of them! . . . Next!" (*CTSS2*, 831). Eventually, they pull out a map the size of Rhode Island and locate the earth, a fly speck locally known as "the Wart." One is tempted to describe Twain's fanciful rendering of the sheer magnitude as hyperbolic, except that the distances that astronomers invite us to contemplate are no less fantastic.

If Twain delighted in conveying a sense of infinite space, it seems that he was even better at rendering a sense of eternity. Stormfield checks out a harp and a pair of wings and heads for the nearest cloud. He sits beside a kind old gentleman and launches into a tune. After about sixteen or seventeen hours, his neighbor asks:

> "Don't you know any tune but the one you've been pegging at all day?"
> "Not another blessed one," says I.
> "Don't you reckon you could learn another one?" says he.
> "Never," says I; "I've tried to, but I couldn't manage it."
> "It's a long time to hang to the one—eternity, you know." (*CTSS2*, 837)

I suspect that not even Thomas Aquinas himself could have given a more eloquent accounting of eternity, but those who doubt it are invited to sing a few choruses of ninety-nine billion bottles of beer on the wall.

There is another sort of infinity, however—the infinitesimal. Here, too, Twain tried his hand at comprehending the incomprehensible, notably in "The Great Dark" (1898) and in "Three Thousand Years among the Microbes" (1905). From a philosophical and mathematical point of view, the infinitesimal is a much more significant problem than the infinite. This problem is not exclusively tied to how small a unit of matter may be without being susceptible to further subdivision. More important, from a philosophical point of view, is whether space might be infinitely subdivided. Space is that arena where the molecule, the atom, the quark, or some yet to be discovered subatomic particle is allowed to move and thus to permit change—and change is the chief instrument of time. In the nineteenth century, German and French mathematicians introduced highly complicated notions of limits that effectively exiled the infinitesimal from scientific and philosophical thinking. Without some notion of the infinitesimal, however, the world lacks continuity; it does not hang together in any rational way. Philosophers such as Charles Sanders Peirce and Henri Bergson clung fast to notions of the infinitesimal, for without it neither temporal change nor even the concept of the "now" was possible. William James, too, held to such a worldview, though in rather different terms, terms that, because they were less intricate, were perhaps closer to the ways Twain thought about the subject. James could unhappily imagine a discontinuous universe, nonetheless: "The world is One just so far as its parts hang together by any definite connexion. It is many just so far as any definite connexion fails to obtain." Pragmatism, as it does with most oppositional arrangements, stands squarely between absolute postulates of the One or the Many. Of all the possible universes, however, "The lowest grade of universe would be a world of mere 'withness,' strung together by the conjunction 'and.'"[22]

I do not for a moment mean to suggest that these heady intellectual and scientific difficulties occurred to Mark Twain, at least not in the fashion I have been describing them. Nor was he likely to have been aware of the enormous implications that might be heaped on the back of such a tiny and unpretentious Atlas. Nevertheless, it is interesting to note, and curious too, that, by whatever means, Twain was often able to arrive at conclusions that were congruent with contemporary scientific fact and philosophical understanding. In 1913, Paul Carus, the editor of the respected philosophical journal *Monist*, observed that Twain's "philosophy" was in essential agreement with the facts of science and psychology and that his argument was a sound one.[23] That said, I do not insist that Mark Twain the philosopher should ever preempt Mark Twain the humorist. His thinking, taken as a whole, is frequently contradictory; humor is not logical rigor, and flights of fancy are no substitute for controlled experiment and scientific observation. Instead, it is enough to observe that contemplation of the infinitely small should not be dismissed as trivial, and the ruminations of an infinite jester, however accidentally, may dramatize potent human and humanizing truths.

As Don Florence observes, Twain "implies a sense of fixity or the eternal in his discussions of human nature."[24] This is certainly true in his antic comparisons between the past and the present, as in *The Innocents*

22. James, *Pragmatism and Four Essays from the "Meaning of Truth"* (Cleveland and New York: Meridian Books, 1955), 105.
23. "Mark Twain's Philosophy," *Monist* 23 (April 1913): 181–223.
24. *Persona and Humor in Mark Twain's Early Writings* (Columbia: University of Missouri Press, 1995), 82.

Abroad; but he also playfully dramatizes a continuity of human conduct whether observed through a microscope or a telescope. During the last decade of his life, there were personal reasons Twain might have wanted the world to hang together as well, so broken and fragmentary was his own life. His philosophical vision is unmistakably expressive of his own despair and bitterness, but it may have been therapeutic as well, restoring to him a certain perspective. In point of fact, at least part of Twain's intent in both "The Great Dark" and "Three Thousand Years among the Microbes" is moral not philosophical—to install within his readers (and perhaps within himself as well) some accurate and respectful sense of the nevertheless absurd proportions of things and the modest position human beings occupy in the world. William R. Macnaughton has argued that the primary purpose of the determinism of *What Is Man?* (more obvious in an earlier version, "What Is the Real Character of Conscience?") was "to make human pride look ridiculous."[25] And in *Letters from the Earth,* Satan is dumbfounded by human vanity in claiming to be God's noblest work. Surely, Twain's fantastic journeys into the universe have a similar function. Whether it is a conversation in the next cubicle or a comet in the next galaxy, human wisdom and Nature herself counsel the same axiomatic conclusion: "It's not about you."

In "The Great Dark," Mr. Henry Edwards and his family, through the mysterious intervention of the Superintendent of Dreams, find themselves aboard a ship that is lost in a drop of water beneath a microscope. The captain of the ship, though he is loath to admit it, is helplessly lost— Greenland is not where it is supposed to be; there is no Gulf Stream; the ship is pursued by some monstrous spider squid; and the sky is in perpetual semidarkness. Edwards is confounded: "Were all the laws of Nature suspended?" he asks himself (*WWD,* 111). Those laws are intact, but the conditions of his natural environment have changed enormously.

Edwards is no longer certain whether his present situation is dream or reality. He takes stock of this new understanding of the human condition: "[W]e see that intellectually we are really no great thing; that we seldom really know the thing we think we know; that our best built certainties are but sand-houses and subject to damage from any wind of doubt that blows" (*WWD,* 125). A character from Tom Stoppard's *Arcadia* makes a similar observation but with greater satisfaction:

It makes me so happy. To be at the beginning again, knowing almost nothing. Relativity and quantum looked as if they were going to clean out the whole

25. *Mark Twain's Last Years As a Writer,* 84.

problem between them. A theory of everything. . . . [However,] we're better at predicting events at the edge of the galaxy or inside the nucleus of an atom than whether it will rain on auntie's party three Sundays from now. . . . It's the best possible time to be alive, when almost everything you thought you knew is wrong.[26]

Stoppard ends his philosophical drama by having two characters respond to the chaotic uncertainty of things in most human terms; they begin to waltz, and the curtain closes. Twain's lost sea captain concludes "The Great Dark" a bit differently: "I don't know where this ship is. . . . If it is God's will that we pull though, we pull through—otherwise not. We haven't had an observation for four months, but we are going ahead, and do our best to fetch up somewhere" (*WWD*, 150).

"Three Thousand Years among the Microbes" is more rambling than "The Great Dark," but it is more incisive, too. After a failed biological experiment, the narrator finds himself transformed into a cholera germ and in the blood of a tramp named Blitzowski. This fanciful point of view permitted Twain to make comments on the relativity of beauty, time, class, currency, and many other things. The narrator, who later dubs himself Huck, sees with a microbe eye and now knows for a certainty that "Nothing is ever at rest—wood, iron, water, everything is alive. . . . [T]here is no such thing as death, everything is full of bristling life. . . . Heaven was not created for man alone, and oblivion and neglect reserved for the rest of His creatures. Man—always vain, windy, conceited—thinks he will be the majority there. He will be disappointed. Let him humble himself" (*WWD*, 447). The vision of the world Twain articulates here is known as hylozoism (a two-dollar word for an indiscriminate pantheism), but he has added his humorous touches to the picture. His moral purpose is to deride human vanity and expose the human tendency to look down on lower life forms. "Well, it's a picture of life," he says. "The king looks down upon the noble, the noble looks down on the commoner," and so on all the way to the bottom, "the burglar looking down on the house-renting landlord, and the landlord looking down upon his oily brown-wigged pal the real estate agent—which is the bottom, so far as ascertained" (*WWD*, 528).

Huck knows that Blitzowski is merely a tramp, but for the microbes he is the entire and sacred universe. A sleeping sickness germ called the "duke" knows something Huck does not know, however, for he has a microbe microscope. Within the blood of microbes known as "Sooflasky" are other microbes, known as "Swinks":

26. *Arcadia* (London: Faber and Faber, 1993), 47–48.

Then the inexorable logic of the situation arrived and announced itself. . . . there being a Man, with a Microbe to infest him, and for him to be indifferent about; and there being a Sooflasky, with a Swink to infest him and for the said Sooflasky to be indifferent about . . . and it also follows, of a certainty, that below that infester there is yet another infester that infests him—and so on down and down and down till you strike the bottomest bottom of created life—if there is one, which is extremely doubtful. (*WWD*, 527)

So what, if anything, are we to make of Twain's playful contemplation of the infinite and the infinitesimal? For one thing, Twain extended the reach of his fundamentally democratic imagination outward to the fringes of the universe and inward to the single-celled world teeming with class-conscious life's anxious desire for acceptance. Twain the determinist might conceive of a microbial world regulated by a desire for self-approval, but Twain the democrat railed against self-satisfaction and smugness in the human animal. Clive James once remarked that Twain was "democratic all the way down to his metabolism," but perhaps that is something of an understatement.[27] He seems to have been democratic all the way down to his subatomic particles. For another thing, the world Mark Twain imagines hangs together; it has a fine sense of connectedness. Every particle of atomic dust participates on equal terms with the angels in some as yet undetermined purpose. Everything has a "mission," he declares, and our duty is clear: "let him do the service he was made for, and keep quiet." Huck the microbe perceives the folly of human ways and the value of an inquisitive mind: "We live to learn," he says, "and fortunate are we when we are wise enough to profit by it" (*WWD*, 448). Finally, the universe itself teaches us to be humble in our station and not to indulge in feelings of superiority, not to lord it over any living creature . . . except, perhaps, the real estate agent.

IV

We conclude with works that, if they don't exactly contradict Twain's theories of human nature, nevertheless do explore precincts of human experience that appear to be exempt from the customary mechanisms that make the human machine go. The first is *No. 44, The Mysterious Stranger,* a dream fable with, at least for some, a perplexing and provocative conclusion that seems to represent a departure, even an escape from deter-

27. "The Voice of America," *New Yorker*, June 14, 1993, p. 81.

minism. *No. 44* has the feel of bewildering finality. The "Diaries" of Adam and Eve, by contrast, dramatize first things. In prelapsarian Eden, human nature is not yet damned by a Moral Sense and not yet enlightened by human history. Nor is it the product of prior training and acquired habit. Adam and Eve have to invent their own humanity.

Mark Twain had been preoccupied with the subject of dreams most of his life, but in his last years the subject became an important literary interest for him. Dreams do not figure in any important way in his conception of human nature as a form of social psychology. Dreams may be related to oneself and others the morning after, but otherwise they are not shared experience. Nor do dreams pose any real counterargument to a materialistic determinism of the sort Twain had been espousing for some time; after all, a dream may be brought about as much by a bad taco as by childhood trauma. However, if dreamland threatens to displace or subsume the material world, one is left with a philosophical idealism or, perhaps worse, an appalling solipsism that tends to subvert Twain's philosophical announcements in *What Is Man?* and elsewhere. By examining Twain's interest in dreams, then, and specifically how that interest is dramatized in the concluding chapter of *No. 44, The Mysterious Stranger*, we may perhaps measure the degree of his commitment to his "gospel."

In and of itself, the dream is not an impediment to addressing the very real dilemmas of the waking world. Twain could, and did, register his opinions about the Boer War, the Boxer Rebellion, and many other things in fictions that were disclosed in dreams. Nevertheless, it is unavoidably true that the subject of dreams so saturates the late writings that it seems to be more than a literary device and more than a motif. It may well be an obsession of the sort Bernard DeVoto said it was—the repeated and nearly insane desire to say again and again, until at last the author himself might come to believe it, "It was not my fault." The most familiar, even notorious, statement about the truth and weird efficacy of dreams comes at the end of *No. 44, The Mysterious Stranger*. According to DeVoto the resolution to Twain's anxious brooding over a guilty conscience appears in these paragraphs spoken by No. 44, a nephew of Satan:

> "You perceive, *now*, that these things are all impossible, except in a dream. You perceive that they are pure and puerile insanities, the silly creations of an imagination that is not conscious of its freaks—in a word, that they are a dream, and you the maker of it. The dream-marks are all present—you should have recognized them earlier. . . .
>
> "It is true, what I have revealed to you: there is no God, no universe, no hu-

man race, no earthly life, no heaven, no hell. It is all a Dream, a grotesque and foolish dream. Nothing exists but You. And You are but a *Thought*—a vagrant Thought, a useless Thought, a homeless Thought, wandering forlorn among the empty eternities!"

He vanished, and left me appalled; for I knew, and realized, that all he said was true. (*MS*, 187)

The significance of this passage for critics varies enormously; for many of them it is a powerful statement of something. In a way, the disclosure that life is a dream provides the critical opportunity to make of Mark Twain, the announced determinist, an advocate of . . . what?—many things perhaps, but surely not of a human automaton who receives all its ideas from the outside. Thus, for the biographer or critic, Twain becomes a Wrong Way Corrigan, the pilot who in 1938 set out for California and wound up in Ireland. Mark Twain, too, was apparently flying in the direction of a mechanistic social psychology but in fact traveling in opposition to his official flight plans. So it is that Sherwood Cummings can say that at the end of *No. 44* Twain was "turning away from his determinism" because "a part of Mark Twain loathed his own gospel." Henry Nash Smith is more measured but emphatic: "At the end of Mark Twain's career he was on the verge of finding release from the determinism that haunted him." Finally, according to Smith, Twain did not solve the "paradox" that bothered him because he believed that dreams "are both true and false."[28] William Gibson observes that the conclusion to *The Mysterious Stranger* "argues the extreme Platonic view that the final and only reality resides in the individual soul, all else being illusion" (*MTMS*, 28). Gibson acknowledges that 44's "parting speech is credible insofar as one accepts his authority as a character and his premises in the argument," but in a nonexistent universe it is difficult, to say the least, to assign authority to any character—to a hostile God, an impish demon, a kind counselor, or to anyone else. And so, for Gibson, the problem remains (*MTMS*, 33). For Bernard DeVoto (whose interpretation was based on the flawed Paine-Duneka text published in 1916), Twain's creation and manipulation of his "symbols of despair" in *The Mysterious Stranger* struggle toward some truce with God and the world and with the terms of his own abiding feelings of guilt. DeVoto is so eloquent and passionately insistent on the point

---

28. Cummings, *Mark Twain and Science: Adventures of a Mind* (Baton Rouge: Louisiana State University Press, 1988), 213; Smith, *How True Are Dreams? The Theme of Fantasy in Mark Twain's Later Work* (Elmira, N.Y.: Elmira College Center for Mark Twain Studies, 1989), 20.

that we are apt to believe him. One certainly would like to believe, at any rate, that if Twain had indeed approached the abyss of madness, he had nonetheless "come back from the edge of insanity" and had achieved "as much peace as any man may find in his last years."[29]

On the face of it, then, the final statement of No. 44 poses textual, biographical, and philosophical difficulties. However, the interpretive situation, complicated as it is, is even more complex because there is deep uncertainty about what kind of statement it is. For William Gibson, the conclusion is a "key" to understanding—a key that "fits nothing in the plot of the 'Schoolhouse Hill'" fragment of the Mysterious Stranger Manuscripts; a key that fits "much of the action and imagery" in "The Chronicle of Young Satan" manuscript; and a key that "fits nearly everything in the second half of 'No. 44,'" the manuscript which it was written to conclude" (MTMS, 28). Henry Nash Smith, by contrast, finds the passage memorable, "but it can hardly be regarded as part of a work of fiction; it is a direct communication from the author to the reader. Its force is ideological, not imaginative."[30] John Tuckey believes those last moments dramatize a "psychic wholeness," "a full assimilation" of the unconscious into the conscious; the "illusion of separateness" dissolves at the moment "44 vanishes in the act of completing August's enlightenment" (MS, 195). Coleman Parsons, on the other hand, traces a rich literary and intellectual tradition Twain might have drawn upon in creating his "didactic romance" and points out that "Determinism and solipsism are autobiographical-experiential projections on a narrative canvas, human and emotional to their very roots, not intellectual." What commends 44's final speech is not its logic but its "truth of feeling and beauty of phrasing."[31]

I do not want to dispute any of these positions. My concern here is with the possible implication that Twain's theory of human nature, his insistence on training, temperament, heredity, and the like, a theory developed over several decades, was something he held lightly and, in a pinch, might casually abandon. What I do want to do, however, is to give both the concluding chapter to No. 44 and the conclusions of its commentators a little less heft and authority. The perplexing final chapter is not necessarily an effort to escape the implications of determinism, still less is it the articu-

29. Mark Twain at Work (Cambridge: Harvard University Press, 1942), portions reprinted in Mark Twain's "The Mysterious Stranger" and the Critics (Belmont, Calif.: Wadsworth Publishing, 1968), 108.

30. How True Are Dreams? 17.

31. "The Background of The Mysterious Stranger," American Literature 32 (March 1960): 55–74, rpt. in Mark Twain's "The Mysterious Stranger" and the Critics, 126.

lation of some well-reasoned metaphysical conclusion about the nature of reality. It may well be the statement of a man who is world-weary and more than a little bit sad, but that does not mean he was standing on the verge of insanity. We may establish a less severe perspective by succinctly rehearsing the compositional history of *The Mysterious Stranger* and placing the creation of that troublesome last chapter in the context of some of Twain's other writings during his last decade.

Often enough, Twain used dreams or dreamlike situations as narrative devices that enabled him to get at those "remotenesses" that he believed were necessary for fabulous and mysterious effects. Captain Stormfield's visit to heaven is really a dream journey, and Henry Edwards is conducted into the world of "The Great Dark" by the Superintendent of Dreams. At times, the dream figures as a constrictive and oppressive condition. In fact, an earlier intention for "The Great Dark" was to lay a "tragedy-trap" for the reader (*MTHL*, 2:676), one in which the early going was comic but was also paving the way for a despairing and unsettling conclusion. Perhaps to his credit, Twain decided against the sort of lonely and confused despair suggested by an excised episode about a "mad passenger" from another planet who was separated from his family and traveled widely in "Dreamland." Instead he ended on a note of affirmation—the stalwart captain announcing his resolution to keep on keeping on.

As John S. Tuckey observes, while Twain was in Vienna in 1898 he took a serious interest in the substance of dreams and was reading in William James's *Principles of Psychology*, Sir John Adams's *Herbartian Psychology*,[32] and Georg Christoph Lichtenberg's *A Doctrine of Scattered Occasions*. Lichtenberg, in particular, may have had some influence on the making of "The Great Dark," for this eighteenth-century German philosopher had suggested that a dream may also be a "life and a world."[33] Twain had con-

---

32. Adams sent Clemens a copy of the book in 1898. In 1900, Adams, along with James Mark Baldwin, visited Clemens in London. Baldwin gave Clemens a copy of his own textbook in psychology, *The Story of the Mind* (1899). Clemens apparently misread Adams's book, assuming that he would agree that the human mind is a "mere machine," something Adams decidedly did not believe; and he dismissed Baldwin's statement in *The Story of the Mind* that the human mind "is not a mere machine doing what the laws of its action prescribe" by simply writing "it *is*" (see Gribben, *Mark Twain's Library: A Reconstruction*, 2 vols. [Boston: G. K. Hall, 1980], 1:9, 41–42). Clemens's reactions to both books demonstrate how tenaciously he clung to his "gospel" even in his last decade. His longstanding insistence that the human mind is a machine automatically functioning and that it receives all its ideas from the outside should serve as a cautionary gesture for those who assert the author might casually abandon his own theory of the mind for some sort of bland idealism or bitter solipsism.

33. *Lichtenberg: A Doctrine of Scattered Occasions*, ed. P. P. Stern (Bloomington: Indiana University Press, 1959), 58.

sidered having the narrator quote Lichtenberg on the possibility of confusing the waking world with the dreaming world, and, as Tuckey indicates, Lichtenberg's remark that "a man can really never know whether he isn't sitting in a madhouse" may have had a formative influence on the mad passenger episode (*WWD*, 17).

Twain would not have learned a great deal about dreams from James's *Principles of Psychology*. Somewhat surprisingly perhaps, James has little to say about the subject, but what he does say is suggestive:

> The world of dreams is our real world whilst we are sleeping, because our attention then lapses from the sensible world. Conversely, when we wake the attention usually lapses from the dream-world and that becomes unreal. But if a dream haunts us and compels our attention during the day it is very apt to remain figuring in our consciousness as a sort of sub-universe alongside of the waking world. Most people have probably had dreams which it is hard to imagine not to have been glimpses into an actually existing region of being, perhaps a corner of the "spiritual world." . . . The "larger universe," here, which helps us to believe both in the dream and in the waking reality which is its immediate reductive, is the total universe, of Nature plus the Supernatural. The dream holds true, namely, in one half of that universe; the waking perceptions in the other half. Even to-day dream-objects figure among the realities in which some "psychic-researchers" are seeking to rouse our belief. All our theories, not only those about the supernatural, but our philosophic and scientific theories as well, are like our dreams in rousing such different degrees of belief in different minds.[34]

Both James and Twain shared an interest in psychical research, in mental telepathy in particular, and in the mind cure. James's statement, though, provides an entering wedge into the sort of fantastic drama of "duplicates," of waking selves and dreaming selves, that Twain got into *No. 44, The Mysterious Stranger*. In addition to these two selves Twain posits an immortal spirit, or soul, that is not "functioned by" brain and nerves, or rather he has August learn from 44 that there is this third "entity" (*MS*, 124). Twain seems to be implying that the dream self is as much a physiological phenomenon as is the waking self; both are "brothers" born of the same womb and destined to live and die together. This may help to explain why August Feldner's duplicate, the dream sprite Emil Schwarz, is so anxious to put off the "bonds of flesh" (*MS*, 151) and to achieve some vague form of immortality.

34. *Principles of Psychology*, 2 vols. (1890; rpt. New York: Dover Publications, 1950), 2:294n.

There are several reasons Licthenberg might have appealed to Twain. Licthenberg had, for example, a sardonic sense of humor, which, like Twain, he sometimes expressed in aphorisms. But there was also a certain system to the German philosopher's thinking that Twain might have also found attractive. Lichtenberg, too, believed man to be a "machine" and that an individual acts "in all things from self-interest." Essentially, the human being exists in three states—"Man as a product of Nature; as a product of his species (society); as a product of his self: cultivated, knowing man." Lichtenberg was principally interested in the last category, the self in isolation, whose nature is enigmatic and constituted of innumerable layers of responses, from material instincts to pure reason. As J. P. Stern, his editor, comments, for Lichtenberg our motives and the origins of our ideas "lie far below the clear regions of reason. Reality resides in instincts, emotions, appetites, and vital fears . . . , reason is merely derivative in the sense of imposing order and coherence where there would be living chaos."[35]

Whether or not Twain shared an interest in this sort of overarching reality, he certainly could respond to curious feelings of isolation and could associate them with dreams. For many years, Twain had thought of the subtractions from his life as something of a "bad dream" from which he might one day awake. And in the brief essay "Old Age" (1905) he traced the contours of a man's life, from infancy to youth and manhood to that final destination, "Old Age, white-headed, the temple empty, the idols broken, the worshippers in their graves, nothing left but You, a remnant, a tradition, belated fag-end of a foolish dream" (*Fables*, 442). During his wife's prolonged illness, his daughter Jean's bouts with epileptic seizures, and Clara's nervous breakdown after her mother's death, Mark Twain must surely have recognized that he was expendable and oftentimes in the way. His mirth-making temperament was not so tonic to others, evidently, as it was to himself. After the death of his wife, Twain himself had become one of those derelicts he was writing about in 1905–1906, drifting about in "a starless gloom, rudderless" (*Fables*, 243). On the night of Olivia's death, Twain expressed himself quite clearly to Howells: "I am tired & old; I wish I were with Livy" (*MTB*, 4:1219). The disputed conclusion to *No. 44* may speak to the fated ontological condition of human beings; in terms of the author's state of mind, however, it seems to say something rather more simple, but no less affecting: "I'm lonely." It is certain, however, that to embrace solipsism as an article of belief would not get

35. *Lichtenberg*, 321, 227, 228.

him any closer, even in prospect, to his beloved Livy; it would merely confirm his sense of complete isolation.

More immediately, though, Lichtenberg's remarks on dreams may have had some generative effect on the creation of *No. 44, The Mysterious Stranger*. Twain's text grew out of an attempt to revise an earlier version, "The Chronicle of Young Satan," in 1902; soon enough the so-called Print Shop version of his story had acquired an interest of its own.[36] He worked on the story off and on for six years before he abandoned it for good. In the spring of 1904, though, not long before Olivia Clemens died in June, Twain began to write, or at least had firmly in mind, the "Conclusion" to *No. 44;* he finished it in the summer Olivia died (*MS*, 28–29). When he returned to the work in 1905, Twain apparently destroyed many manuscript pages amounting to some thirty thousand words and wrote chapters 26 through 32. In 1908, Twain wrote chapter 33 (the "Assembly of the Dead") as something of a bridge to the conclusion he had fashioned four years earlier. The perplexing "Conclusion," then, was preserved and prepared for, and Twain's maneuvering toward that preconcerted end may have been another attempt to spring a "tragedy trap" on his reader at the end of his narrative. In any event, these passages from Lichtenberg may have some bearing on the conception of Twain's tale, and they may serve to clarify some of the mysteries of the text:

> An odd thing about dreams is this: if I dream that I am being taught something, [the content of that teaching in the dream] cannot possibly consist of anything more than the ideas lying about in my mind, which I now recollect and combine; and a person is called into being to go with them. . . .
>
> When I dispute with someone in a dream and he refutes and instructs me, it is I myself who am instructing myself, in other words, reflecting. This reflecting then is envisaged as conversation.[37]

The sum and substance of these remarks and others like them have a bearing on how we might take *No. 44*. Twain may not have intended the figure of No. 44 to be understood as anything other than an invented person called into service on behalf of the dreamer and who, in turn, leads the dreamer to a certain kind of self-knowledge. In other words, this narrative may be just what 44 implies it is—a dream fable.

36. The composition of this text is discussed in John Tuckey, *Mark Twain and Little Satan, the Writing of The Mysterious Stranger* (West Lafayette: Purdue University Press, 1963), and by William Gibson, "Introduction" to *MTMS*, 1–34.

37. *Lichtenberg*, 321.

When we take the work in this literal-minded way, several of the problems of understanding it disappear. No. 44 is not a supernatural being with special knowledge and powers; he is a voice that delivers (in unusual combinations to be sure and uncorrected by reason and unaffected by that damnable Moral Sense) ideas already available to the dreamer. No. 44 says as much when he reveals that he is August's "poor servant" who has "revealed you to yourself" (*MS*, 186). Moreover, when we understand the work in this way, even though the setting of the dream narrative may be Austria in 1490 and August Feldner may serve as the narrator, the actual dream is located in the mind of someone (probably Mark Twain) who will eventually awake safely abed in New York around 1905. The waking world and the dreaming world have cross-pollinating effects and, together, constitute the "total universe" to use James's phrase, but one does not subsume the other. And 44's advice to Feldner to "Dream other dreams, and better!" is more practical than mysterious, for there will be other perhaps less despairing dreams on other occasions. Likewise, apparent anachronisms can be accounted for in this way. No. 44 may fetch from one end of the prehistorical spectrum a brontosaurus and the Missing Link and from the other end of the spectrum a telegram written by Mary Baker Eddy and published in a Boston newspaper on June 27, 1905. There is no mystery in this because they are equally part of the mental lumber lying around in the dreamer's mind.

Twain does get some good humorous effects out of his dream drama: He speaks of a time when "dream-transportation" had ceased and Western Union hadn't yet come into being, and 44 reports on the Roman's stopgap measure of reading chicken entrails to get a hold on future events. He has 44 transform Marget's maid into a cat and then has her awkwardly try to learn her trade by curiously inspecting August's room; she fearfully jumps up on a chair when she sees a mouse. Twain peppers the dialogue with slang expressions ("side-track," "jag," "cake-walk") and refers to devices (the phonograph, the camera, and so forth) that are strange to August but not to his reader. And he has No. 44 put together some exotic meals—corn pone from Arkansas, coffee from Vienna, whale from the Pleistocene era, and canned manna from Moses's day. Even before the appearance of 44, there is the comedy of the argot of the print shop, and on balance August speaks a modern vernacular slang that he could not have picked up in an Austrian castle in 1490. In fact, Twain makes no attempt, as he did in *The Prince and the Pauper,* to replicate the discourse of the day, and this seems to be one of the earliest clues to the reader that this is a dream tale after all.

No. 44, The Mysterious Stranger could not have been very difficult to write. It is largely improvised and unchecked by the requirements of space, time, dramatic occasion, or probability. Twain's inventions, such as they are, are often reminiscent of earlier work. The fierce dignity of the cook Katrina is evocative of Aunt Rachel in "A True Story"; the fearless Doangivadam is a composite of Miles Hendon of *The Prince and the Pauper* and that anonymous sheriff who reportedly held off an unruly lynch mob. Doangivadam is a "man" and he bravely defies the striking print-shop workers, whom Twain identifies as a "herd." The Duplicates recall Colonel Sellers's plan to materialize the dead as a free labor force in *Colonel Sellers as a Scientist,* and the impossible love rectangle between and among August/Emil and Marget/Lisbet is pure burlesque, as unresolvable as some of Twain's early hoax tales. No. 44, like Tom Sawyer, loves "shows and spectacles, and stunning dramatics," "to astonish people, and show off, and be and do all the gaudy things a boy loves to be and do" (*MS,* 168). As often, though, he plays the role of the Old Man in *What Is Man?*—a wise sage who will instruct August in the nature of human existence, even if it means destroying the boy's faith and idealism. And in this role his preachments are familiar—that man is a machine who has no original ideas; that he is a moral coward (as August more than once proves by his own conduct); that to be a human being is nothing to be proud of; that God is indifferent to pitiful humankind; that the history of the world is a history of famine, disease, war, betrayal, greed, and death; that all actions and events are determined and not chosen.

In a word, there is not much new here except perhaps that the whole is conceived as a dream vision. Even the spontaneous quality (shifting from topic to topic, from present to past, and the like, suggestive of a dream-like state) was something Twain had been practicing right along in his autobiographical dictations. By 1904, Twain had discovered the "right way" to write his autobiography: "talk only about the thing which interests you for the moment; drop it the moment its interest threatens to pale, and turn your talk upon the new and more interesting thing that has intruded itself into your mind meantime."[38] This is not very different from the way Emil Schwarz, the dream sprite, speaks of his life, "in a skipping and disconnected fashion proper to his species. He would sidetrack a subject right in the middle of a sentence if another subject attracted him, and he did this without apology or explanation—well, just as a dream would, you know" (*MS,* 158). And 44, too, seems to suffer from attention deficit

38. Quoted in Ron Powers, *Mark Twain: A Life* (New York: Free Press, 2005), 621.

disorder: "He would contrive the most elaborate projects, and put his whole mind and heart into them, then he would suddenly drop them, in the midst of their fulfillment, and start something fresh" (*MS*, 182). The same might be said for Twain himself in these years, a writer who began any number of literary projects, including *The Mysterious Stranger* manuscripts, but had difficulty seeing them through to completion.

Perhaps because *No. 44, The Mysterious Stranger* does have a "Conclusion" of sorts, this text has received greater critical attention than many other works of Twain's last years. Certainly this last chapter fulfills the purpose of springing a "tragedy-trap," if that was Twain's intention, and it does have the feeling of an overwhelming and appalling finality. But beyond that, it is difficult to see what, if anything, it is supposed to mean. To insist, on the one hand, that the mind always works with "*materials from the outside*" (*MS*, 115) and, on the other, that "*Nothing exists save empty space—and you!*" (*MS*, 186) is to adopt an untenable, if not absurd, position. This paradox is the concoction of a metaphysically challenged mind. Even the solipsist keeps his or her "experiences" as companion.[39] How on earth, or elsewhere, are we to imagine thought without content, consciousness without an object of which it is conscious? And Twain further invites us to imagine this imperishable thought (surely not a self and probably not even an entity) lost in space, with neither hope, memory, or regret, without direction, purpose, or destination. If Twain's extreme brand of solipsism expressed in this chapter conveys anything, it is the intense kind of loneliness he often felt, particularly after his wife died. *The Mysterious Stranger* is a drama not of thought but of feeling; it is really a tall tale of loneliness. Little by little, Twain raises the stakes of this cosmological poker game until even God and Creation have to fold. Finally, the author's intermittent feelings of estrangement and alienation are imaginatively transformed into an absolute condition. August is left "alone in shoreless space, to wander its limitless solitudes without friend or comrade forever" (*MS*, 186).

---

39. F. C. S. Schiller defined solipsism this way: "It may best be defined perhaps as the doctrine that all existence is experience and that there is only one experient. The Solipsist thinks *he is the one*" (*Mind*, April 1909, p. 171). Twain goes well beyond this conception of solipsism. No. 44's announces that life is a dream and 44 is himself the creation of August's imagination. The moment August realizes the truth of this remark he will banish No. 44 (and presumably all other creatures of his freakish imagination) and everything will "dissolve into nothingness" (*MS*, 186).

V

Mark Twain had concluded his essay "Old Age" on a similar note of dreary isolation. At the end of one's life there is "nothing left but You, centre of a snowy desolation, perched on the ice-summit, gazing out over the stages of that long *trek* and asking Yourself 'would you do it again if you had the chance?'" (*Fables*, 442). Despite Twain's autobiographical dictations that allowed him to recover in memory what he had lost in fact, it seems there was little he would have cared to repeat if he had had the chance. There was not much of the Emersonian "up again old heart" left to Mark Twain in his final years. If we may judge from the diaries of Adam and Eve, however, he felt differently about his life with Livy, for it is generally conceded that these works deal humorously and tenderly with his abiding love and memory of his wife. That was the eventual effect of the pieces, but that is not how they began.

Extracts from Adam's Diary (1893) and *Eve's Diary* (1905) are companion pieces, but they were not conceived in that way.[40] "Extracts from Adam's Diary" was first published in 1893 and belongs to a cluster of stories composed that year which deal, albeit in a humorous way, with financial worries or the painful separation from a loved one.[41] Olivia Clemens's health had always been frail, and the family was especially concerned about her in 1891–1892 until they learned from doctors that her heart condition was not as serious as they had thought. It is a sense of relief mixed with the recollection of recent anxiety that informs the tone of *Extracts from Adam's Diary*, and to a degree *Eve's Diary* is the beneficiary of a certain lightness of touch that probably does not disclose the depth of Twain's depressed loneliness after Olivia's death. *Eve's Diary* was written in Dublin, New Hampshire, in July 1905, and it too has a background that would have in-

40. The texts published in *The Bible according to Mark Twain* more reliably represent Twain's original intentions, and those are the texts referenced here. The rather complicated compositional histories of the diaries of Adam and Eve and of "Autobiography of Eve" are summarized in *BMT*, xvi–xix, 3–7, 17–19, and 35–41.

41. Those other stories are "The Californian's Tale," "The Esquimau Maiden's Romance," "The £1,000,000 Bank Note," and "Is He Living or Is He Dead?" "The Californian's Tale" is the most sentimental of the lot, but it best illustrates Clemens's fear of what life would be like without Livy, for it depicts a lonely California miner who had lost his wife nineteen years earlier and on the anniversary of her death goes slightly mad. He had become one of those "living dead men" Twain had seen in the West, men whose thoughts were made up of "regrets and longings—regrets for their wasted lives, and longing to be out of the struggle and done with it all" (*Collected Short Stories of Mark Twain*, ed. Charles Neider [New York: Doubleday and Co., 1957], 267).

fluenced the tone of that piece. Sometime in 1901 or 1902 (that is, at a time when his wife was ill but there was still hope for her recovery) Twain tried his hand at the "Autobiography of Eve" and had Eve begin her life story with a few selections from her diary. It soon becomes clear to the reader that those excerpts from her first years in Paradise are in fact a thousand years old and that Eve is now "bent, broken, withered, widowed, my head is white with unnumbered sorrows" (*BMT*, 49). She has lost Adam, and her world is at once empty and overcrowded with the offspring of her offspring.

It well may be that in the "Autobiography of Eve" Twain was beginning to write yet another "tragedy trap," though of a Malthusian sort. Unlike *No. 44, The Mysterious Stranger*, which ultimately arrives at a final and complete loneliness, the "Autobiography of Eve" begins in loneliness but was meant to end with the world so thick with six billion people that death (whether in the form of pestilence, war, famine, or an impending flood) is considered a "benefaction" (*BMT*, 264). Eve's autobiography, then, is an apocalyptic work. Obedience to the divine injunction to be fruitful and multiply and to subdue the earth has careened out of control, and the earth no longer possesses the means of subsistence for the multitudes. But Eve's autobiography is also a lamentation. Eve has learned the lesson of disappointment every mother learns—that her children are grown and gone from her, "to return no more but in visions" (*BMT*, 49). And in a continuation of Eve's story, Twain has Eve lose her daughter Gladys to that curious invention, death. (Such expressions of personal grief as Twain got into this work, then, had reference to the death of his daughter Susy, not that of Olivia Clemens.) The text works at cross-purposes, though. Death is the great benefactor to the race, but it also is the hurtful author of loss and grief.

Soon enough, this autobiography got diffuse. Twain had difficulty keeping Eve as the focal point of his narrative and introduced other characters and narrators. He created Reginald Selkirk, the "Mad Philosopher," for example, and through him introduced such Twainian notions as the "Laws of Intellectual Averages" and the "Law of Periodical Repetition."[42]

---

42. Neither of these ideas was particularly novel. The first is merely an extension of Quetelet's idea of *l'homme moyen;* the second derived from the premises of classical nineteenth-century physics—that is, if the universe is composed of a definite amount of matter and energy, in the wide expanse of eternity events were destined to repeat themselves. What is important, though, is that Twain in citing these so-called laws was taking his leave of any hopeful faith in progress, either in the human race or in human history.

Selkirk is a statistician who uses "the facts of the past to forecast the probabilities of the future. It is merely applied science" (*BMT*, 267). His dire predictions about the fate of an overpopulated world are not prophecy but science. In a word, Twain was losing track of the most original and affecting part of his story: how the first parents invented human nature. He expressed the important interest of the tale in a passage spoken by an aged and somewhat nostalgic Eve, a passage he later excised from the manuscript: "Ah, well, in that old simple, ignorant time it never entered our unthinking heads that we, humble, unknown and inconsequential little people, were cradling, nursing and watching over the most conspicuous and stupendous event which would happen in the universe for a thousand years—the founding of the human race" (*BMT*, 263).

Some of the comedy and pathos of inventing the human got into Eve's autobiography, but it was not until Twain returned to the project a year after Olivia's death, in the summer of 1905, that he was content to tell his story in a more spare and direct and tenderly affectionate way. The interest of *Eve's Diary* will always remain in the somewhat remarkable fashion Twain was able to write a deeply felt but also comically amusing eulogy to his wife told mostly from Eve's own point of view. Nevertheless, both Eve's "Autobiography" and *Eve's Diary* contribute to our understanding of Twain's view of human nature. Most important, in his inquiry into the founding of the human race, the author deprived himself of most of the basic principles of his gospel. In the beginning, there was no social milieu to be born into, no inherited traditions or shared institutions, no trained habits or strong instincts to determine their lives. Still, Twain did not relinquish his conviction that man originates no ideas from within. Adam and Eve have a user's manual for the Garden of Even, so to speak, in God's injunction that they shall not eat the fruit of the tree of the knowledge of good and evil; otherwise they will die. Necessarily, this edict gets their curiosity up. Eve asks Adam what evil is. Adam answers, "I suppose it is the name of something, but I do not know what." Eve persists. What is death? "I have no idea . . . it is impossible for me to make even a plausible *guess* concerning a matter about which I am absolutely ignorant. A person can't *think*, when he has no material to think *with*. Isn't that true?" (*BMT*, 58). Eve concedes the point.

This was Twain's way of affirming that human beings are machines automatically functioning but also of indicating just how vulnerable these two were in the Garden. Adam and Eve are true innocents; they are ignorant, but they are not stupid. Both recognize that they are in some way "experiments" in something. And by temperament they are both "scientists," as well. Adam discovers the first natural law in the Garden, the "Law of Fluidic Precipitation," the law that states water runs downhill. For her part (while Adam is trying to invent the multiplication table but can't get past 6 times 9 is 27) Eve tackles a more difficult question: how does milk get inside the cow. She had already discovered that air contained water in "invisible suspension" in the atmosphere. Then it hit her: *"the milk was not taken in by the mouth, it was condensed from the atmosphere through the cow's hair"* (*BMT*, 56). Of course the revelation called for a revision of her formula for water from H2O to H2O,M, with M standing for milk. The motivation for these discoveries has less to do with an inborn curiosity in Adam and Eve than it does with each wanting to gain the approbation of the other. For this comedy of first things, Twain brought into conjunction two distinct and largely incompatible frames of reference, the scientific and the scriptural, but the actors themselves were actuated by the familiar social psychology Twain had articulated in *What Is Man?* as well as in "Corn Pone Opinions" and elsewhere.

Twain was even more ingenious in the way he dramatized Eve's desire for a mate without recurring to some innate, biological instinct as explanation for it. In the opening pages of her autobiography, Eve describes her first days in Eden. She is lonely, and she almost instantly becomes aware of a certain "lack" (*BMT*, 42). The other creatures have mates, but she has none. She is humiliated before the other animals and feels a need for their regard. Thus it is that Twain replaces a "maternal instinct" (something he had earlier assumed as an article of faith) with the need to think well of oneself and to envy the other animals who in only a matter of a few months have begun to establish families. And thus, in order to find out who and what she is, Eve sets out to find her mate.

After Olivia's death, Twain returned to the idea of Eve's story and in many ways reconceived the project. He was content to eliminate Eve's autobiography and instead to have excerpts from her diary along with an occasional reference to Adam's diary tell the tale of their life together. Eve would not become a widow; instead Adam would survive her. This was in keeping with the piece refashioned as a eulogy to his wife. Twain eliminated all reference to the disastrous effects of overpopulation and the correctives of war and famine, and except by implication he did not indicate that Adam and Eve grew old and infirm. He did not insist that all thoughts come from without; this too was implicit. At the conclusion of *Extracts from Adam's Diary*, written in 1893, Adam comes to the belated conclusion that "it is better to live outside the Garden with [Eve] than inside it without her. At first, I thought she talked too much; but now I should be sorry to have that voice fall silent and pass out of my life" (*BMT,* 16). By 1905, Olivia's voice had fallen silent, and a different sort of conclusion was in order. After the fall, presumably many hundreds of years, Eve utters a prayer that she and Adam will "pass from life together," but if that cannot be, then she prays that she shall be the first to die—"life without him would not be life; how could I endure it?" (*BMT,* 33). Her prayer is answered. Adam stands at Eve's grave. The last lines of "Eve's Diary" are not hers but Adam's: "Wheresoever she was, *there* was Eden" (*BMT,* 33).

As effective as these words are to serve as terse eulogy to Olivia, they also serve as Adam's epitaph. For without the other, Adam is not Adam, and Eve is not Eve. This is not mere sentiment; it is a fact of human nature, and one that Twain sought to dramatize in these paired diaries. Susan K. Harris has observed that Eve coaxes Adam out of himself, causes him to forgo his reticence, his aloof self-absorption, his irascible complacency. It is Eve who teaches Adam that mysterious word "we," Harris points out.[43] But we might go further and say that, without Eve, Adam has no self. Two passages, one from George Herbert Mead and another from Isaiah Berlin, define human nature in a way that comports well enough with Mark Twain's final thoughts on the matter and in any event clarify one of the purposes of the diaries. In *Movements of Thought in the Nineteenth Century,* Mead insists that "the human self arises through its ability to take the attitude of the group to which he belongs—because he can talk to himself in terms of the community to which he belongs and lay upon himself the responsibilities that belong to the community. . . . The structure of society lies in these social habits, and only in so far as we can take these social habits into ourselves can we become selves." In characterizing John Stuart Mill's conception of human nature, Berlin writes, "Man is incapable of self-completion, and therefore never wholly predictable; fallible, a complex combination of opposites, some reconcilable, others incapable of being resolved or harmonised; unable to cease from his search for truth, happiness, novelty, freedom, but with no guarantee . . . of being able to attain them."[44] Both of these statements, in different fashion, emphasize that the human is unavoidably social; without a sense of the communal there is a felt lack, an incompleteness that can only be realized in communion with other selves. And in Eden, a world popu-

43. See *Mark Twain's Escape from Time: A Study of Patterns and Images* (Columbia: University of Missouri Press, 1982), 126–27.

44. *Movements of Thought in the Nineteenth Century,* ed. Merritt H. Moore (Chicago: University of Chicago Press, 1936), 375; Berlin, quoted in John Gray, "The Case for Decency," *New York Review of Books,* July 13, 2006, p. 21.

lated by two, one's self is located in that one other. It is that fact that gives *Eve's Diary* a buoyancy where otherwise one ought to find only sorrow and regret.

With an amusing artlessness, Eve gets her bearings in the world. She discovers time and space. She remembers yesterday but not the day before. It could have happened, she admits, when she was not watching, but from now on she will keep a sharp lookout for any other "day-before-yesterdays" and make a note of it. She wears herself out trying to clod the stars out of the sky and then tries to travel to the world's rim where they are close to the ground, but with no success. Distances are deceiving, she concludes. In this rough-and-ready way Eve gets to know the world by trial and error. She knows she is an experiment but not the whole of it. "I am the main part of it, but I think the rest of it has its share in the matter" (*BMT,* 20). Eve loves the moon and is sad when it slides down out of the sky, and in her sadness realizes "that the core and centre of my nature is love of the beautiful" (*BMT,* 21). She wants to wear the stars in her hair and dress herself in flowers, and she delights in the hum of bees and the song of birds. Mistaking her own image in a pond for her "sister" she is enamored of the "lovely white body painted there in the pool" (*BMT,* 25). She brings something new into the world—fire—and believes that is beautiful as well and even suspects it might be useful some day. The inadvertent by-product of her invention is the first cooked food, a baked apple, though she also burns down half the Garden along the way to this discovery.

All in all, then, apart from her felt lack of a mate, Twain portrays in Eve a certain self-sufficiency. She is resourceful, curious, intelligent, appreciative, and all the rest. She loves the animals, but she is lonely for her own kind. Given Eve's love of beauty, though, it is comically interesting that the object of her heart's desire is Adam. This other experiment may be a man but is probably a reptile. "It has no hips; it tapers like a carrot; when it stands, it spreads itself apart like a derrick; so I think it is a reptile, though it may be architecture" (*BMT,* 22). If this reptile turns out to be a man, however, it will not be an *it* but a *he,* and she decides to call it "he" "until it turns out to be something else" (*BMT,* 23). Nonetheless, Eve desires Adam's esteem and wishes to please him, and she is willing to overlook or forgive his obvious deficiencies. In both *Extracts from Adam's Diary* and "The Autobiography of Eve," Adam is something of a buffoon, but those qualities are toned down in "Eve's Diary." Eve herself does not know exactly why she loves this creature: "The Garden is lost, but I have found *him,* and am content. . . . If I ask myself why I love him, I find that I do not know, and do not really care to know" (*BMT,* 31). Adam's qualities are doubtful. He has low tastes and is not kind; he does not care for flowers but prefers thumping the melons and squeezing the fruit to see how "those properties are coming along" (*BMT,* 26). His singing sours the milk; he is self-educated and therefore knows a great many things that are not so; he is neither gracious, considerate, nor chivalrous. Eve knows that Adam is industrious, but she worries because he conceals the fact so regularly that she wonders why he keeps that single secret from her. At length Eve concludes that she loves him "merely because he is *mine* and is *masculine.* There is no other reason, I suppose" (*BMT,* 32).

Eve's Diary makes it clear that, even under the simplest and most primitive circumstance, human beings are entangled in a web of social relations. One's "self" is distributed among the several social relations it has. So constituted, each self seeks the approval and ratification that only other selves may provide. In those rare and valuable relations, such as that enjoyed by Adam and Eve, one is pleased by the other's happiness, fearful for his or her well-being, distressed by the other's displeasure. Twain was content to identify this relation in properly Victorian terms as "love," but he located its force and origin in human selfishness and analyzed it with a deterministic logic that Livy herself found odious. And around those emotional interests, habits form, relations solidify, commitments become precious. The picture of Adam at Eve's grave has a pathos about it, and, to the extent that Twain identified himself with the figure, he dramatized his loss of Olivia alongside his deep gratitude for the memory of her.

But, unlike Adam, Mark Twain had other associations in the world, not so intimate as the one with his wife to be sure, but real enough. After Olivia's death he turned to them with a will and a purpose. He did not tire of pointing out that, willy-nilly, human beings are implicated in one another's lives. God may have turned his back on that long-ago experiment in Eden as insignificant and of no consequence and thus rendered the human race a tribe of orphans. Nonetheless, a human family survives, and its members have social and moral duties to one another. Twain lashed out against King Leopold in an interview, for example, as if it were a personal matter because it was. Modern means of transportation and communication have made "the whole world one neighborhood . . . [Leopold's] crimes are the concern of every one of us, of every man who feels that it is his duty as a man to prevent murder, no matter who is the murderer or how far away he seeks to commit his sordid crime" (*Interviews,* 523). In other and presumably more agreeable ways Twain committed himself to the human family. He played a grandfatherly role to his angelfish; he kept up his friendships and his writing as best he could given his limited energies and dwindling interest; he deplored American imperialist adventurism and scolded his countrymen for cultivating in their children patriotism in the place of citizenship. He advised that Americans look to a children's theater in the East Side of New York where immigrant children were not merely assimilating the nation's values, he believed, but drinking from the source of those values and not the contemporary brew of blind loyalty, sloth, and corruption that was passed off as a suitable substitute.

For Twain, the human world was trivial in the scheme of things; it was a world that would not be redeemed and probably could not be repaired. The human race was in all likelihood damned, but the instruments of its annihilation were as yet undetermined. Cholera germs or Gatling guns might do the trick, so might overpopulation or simple greed, moral cowardice or moral complacency. In any case, the prospects did not look good. In *Letters from the Earth,* God confides that human beings are an "experiment in Morals and Conduct" and that "Time will show whether they were worth the trouble" (*CTSS2,* 882–83). If we may judge from the tone of his late writings, God was more sanguine about the outcome than was Sam Clemens. But through it all Mark Twain played the role of humorist as well as moralist. Humor was his profession, but it was also his medicine and it seemed to be good for what ailed him. When asked by an interviewer around Thanksgiving Day 1905, "What is it that strikes a spark of humor from a man?" Twain responded: "It is the effort to throw off, to fight back the burden of grief that is laid on each one of us. In youth we don't feel it, but as we grow to manhood we find the burden on our shoulders. Humor? It is nature's effort to harmonize conditions. The further the pendulum swings out over woe the further it is bound to swing back over mirth" (*Interviews,* 522–23). Twain confronted the incompleteness of human nature in himself and others and relied on humor to harmonize those conflicting interests that abound in a world where all-too-human selves contend with one another. A hundred years after his death, we may not have advanced very far beyond Mark Twain's low estimate of us. At any rate, it is tempting to dismiss his assessment as mere calumny. Nevertheless, if Mark Twain's satire and his sympathies still matter, it may be because he so acutely traced the lineaments of human character. His writings remain powerful, in part, because human nature has not changed very much. It just may be that Twain knew us better than we are disposed to admit. Time will tell.

Index